Federal Tax Policy

Studies of Government Finance: Second Series

TITLES PUBLISHED

Federal Tax Policy

JOSEPH A. PECHMAN

FOURTH EDITION

Studies of Government Finance

THE BROOKINGS INSTITUTION

WASHINGTON, D.C.

Copyright © 1983 by
THE BROOKINGS INSTITUTION
1775 Massachusetts Avenue, N.W., Washington, D.C. 20036

Library of Congress Cataloging in Publication data:
Pechman, Joseph A., 1918–
  Federal tax policy.
  (Studies of government finance. Second series)
  Includes bibliographical references and index.
    1. Fiscal policy—United States.   2. Taxation—
United States.   I. Title.   II. Series.
HJ257.2.P4   1983   336.2′00973   83-23126
ISBN 0-8157-6964-4
ISBN 0-8157-6963-6 (pbk.)

9 8 7 6 5 4 3 2 1

THE BROOKINGS INSTITUTION is an independent organization devoted to nonpartisan research, education, and publication in economics, government, foreign policy, and the social sciences generally. Its principal purposes are to aid in the development of sound public policies and to promote public understanding of issues of national importance.

The Institution was founded on December 8, 1927, to merge the activities of the Institute for Government Research, founded in 1916, the Institute of Economics, founded in 1922, and the Robert Brookings Graduate School of Economics and Government, founded in 1924.

The Board of Trustees is responsible for the general administration of the Institution, while the immediate direction of the policies, program, and staff is vested in the President, assisted by an advisory committee of the officers and staff. The by-laws of the Institution state: "It is the function of the Trustees to make possible the conduct of scientific research, and publication, under the most favorable conditions, and to safeguard the independence of the research staff in the pursuit of their studies and in the publication of the results of such studies. It is not a part of their function to determine, control, or influence the conduct of particular investigations or the conclusions reached."

The President bears final responsibility for the decision to publish a manuscript as a Brookings book. In reaching his judgment on the competence, accuracy, and objectivity of each study, the President is advised by the director of the appropriate research program and weighs the views of a panel of expert outside readers who report to him in confidence on the quality of the work. Publication of a work signifies that it is deemed a competent treatment worthy of public consideration but does not imply endorsement of conclusions or recommendations.

The Institution maintains its position of neutrality on issues of public policy in order to safeguard the intellectual freedom of the staff. Hence interpretations or conclusions in Brookings publications should be understood to be solely those of the authors and should not be attributed to the Institution, to its trustees, officers, or other staff members, or to the organizations that support its research.

Foreword

FEDERAL TAX POLICY has been a pervading economic and political issue in recent years. Some have blamed tax policy for the poor performance of the economy during the 1970s. The rise in tax rates resulting from the taxation of nominal incomes during periods of rapid inflation fostered resentment and dissatisfaction. Reduction of marginal tax rates was a principal theme of the 1980 election campaign. As a result of these and other developments, in the nine years between 1974 and 1983 Congress enacted eight major tax laws, which reduced marginal tax rates, liberalized depreciation allowances, introduced new savings incentives, and increased excise taxes on oil and tobacco. All these changes were controversial, and many believe that the federal tax system remains in need of substantial simplification and reform.

This fourth edition, like its predecessors, is intended to explain the intricacies of the tax system so that the interested citizen may better understand and contribute to public discussion and resolution of the main issues. It reflects tax developments between 1977 and 1983, and it emphasizes the newer issues: the effects of taxation on economic incentives; inflation adjustments for income tax purposes; comprehensive income taxation; the relative merits of graduated income taxes and expenditure taxes; tax limitations by state governments; and changes in the fiscal relations between the federal and the state and local governments. In the interest of brevity, the discussion sometimes omits details that others might regard as important. For further information and different points of view, the reader should refer to the extensive literature cited in the bibliographical notes.

Joseph A. Pechman, former director of Economic Studies and now senior fellow at the Brookings Institution, has had long experience in tax research and in the making of tax policy. He acknowledges once again his gratitude for editorial assistance on the earlier editions from Charles B. Saunders, Jr., Virginia C. Haaga, and Elizabeth H. Cross and for research assistance from Andrew T. Williams, John Yinger, and Evelyn P. Fisher. He also acknowledges with gratitude the constructive review and comments on the earlier editions by Henry J. Aaron, Boris I. Bittker, Richard Goode, Arnold C. Harberger, and Stanley S. Surrey.

In preparing this edition, the author received valuable suggestions and assistance from Benjamin Bridges, Susannah Calkins, Albert J. Davis, Harvey Galper, Harry L. Gutman, Frederick C. Ribe, Milton Russell, Walter S. Salant, Karen R. Silver, C. Eugene Steuerle, Lawrence H. Thompson, Eric J. Toder, James M. Verdier, and James W. Wetzler. Gail C. Morton and John Karl Scholz programmed the calculations of the effects of the income taxes presented in chapters 4 and 5.

The author is particularly grateful to Nancy D. Davidson who, in her role as editor of this edition, greatly improved the readability, accuracy, and consistency of the manuscript and also supervised the preparation of the manuscript for publication. Sallyjune A. Fusci and Lydia Weber prepared the figures. Judith Cameron assisted in the preparation of the extensive appendix tables, Harold Appelman and Barbara Behringer provided research assistance, Penelope Harpold reviewed the tables for accuracy, and Nancy Snyder performed an outstanding job of proofreading. Evelyn M. E. Taylor had the major responsibility for preparing the typescript on the word processor; she was assisted by Valerie J. Harris, Kirk W. Kimmell, Charlotte Kaiser, Jacquelyn G. Sanks, and Susan F. Woollen. Vickie L. Corey and Dorothy M. Poole adapted the word processor output for computer-assisted typesetting.

This volume is the eighteenth publication in the Brookings Studies of Government Finance second series, which is devoted to examining issues in taxation and public expenditure policy. Research on the revenue and distributional implications of the structural features of the income taxes was supported initially by the Ford Foundation and later by the National Science Foundation.

The author's views are his own, and should not be ascribed to the Ford Foundation, to the National Science Foundation, or to the officers, trustees, or other staff members of the Brookings Institution.

December 1983   BRUCE K. MACLAURY
Washington, D.C.   *President*

To Sylvia, Ellen, and Jane

Contents

9. State and Local Taxes   247

Appendixes

Index   403

Text Tables

Appendix Tables

Figures

CHAPTER ONE

Introduction

FEDERAL, state, and local government receipts now amount to almost one-third of the gross national product. They come from a variety of taxes, as well as from fees, charges, and other miscellaneous sources. The taxes cover almost the entire spectrum: income taxes, general and selective consumption taxes, payroll taxes, estate and gift taxes, and property taxes.

Despite the large amount of money collected—$928 billion in 1982—U.S. taxes are by no means the heaviest in the world. Most advanced European countries impose relatively higher taxes. In 1981, for example, taxes ranged between 37 and 51 percent of the gross domestic product in Austria, Denmark, France, Germany, the Netherlands, Norway, and Sweden, but were 31 percent in the United States (appendix table D-5). Japan, with taxes of 27 percent of GDP, has the lowest tax burden among advanced industrial countries.

Features of the U.S. Tax System

The most distinctive feature of the U.S. tax system is that it places great weight on individual and corporation income taxes. These account for 44 percent of the total revenues (including receipts from social insurance taxes) of all levels of government. At the federal level they account for 57 percent (table 1-1).

A second feature is the growth in importance of payroll taxes, which were introduced in the 1930s when the social insurance programs were enacted. These taxes now produce over a third of federal revenues and over a fifth of total government revenues in the United States.

A third feature is the federal nature of the revenue system (figure 1-1): the national and state governments have independent taxing pow-

1

Table 1-1. *Federal and State and Local Taxes and Other Revenues,*
by Major Source, 1982

	Revenues[a]	
Major source	Amount (billions of dollars)	Percentage of total
Federal		
Individual income	296.7	49.1
Corporation income	46.5	7.7
Excises	32.4	5.4
Estate and gift	7.6	1.3
Payroll	204.5	33.9
Other	16.2	2.7
Total	603.9	100.0
State and local		
Individual income	51.8	16.0
Corporation income	12.7	3.9
Sales	95.5	29.5
Estate and gift	2.6	0.8
Payroll	4.0	1.2
Property	86.5	26.7
Other	71.0	21.9
Total	324.1	100.0
All levels		
Individual income	348.5	37.6
Corporation income	59.2	6.4
Sales and excises	127.9	13.8
Estate and gift	10.2	1.1
Payroll	208.4	22.5
Property	86.5	9.3
Other	87.3	9.4
Total	928.0	100.0

Source: *Survey of Current Business,* vol. 63 (July 1983), tables 3.2, 3.3, 3.4, 3.6. Figures are rounded.
a. Revenues are defined as receipts in the national income accounts less contributions for social insurance other than payroll taxes. Federal grants-in-aid are not included in state and local receipts.

ers, and the local governments derive their taxing powers from the state
governments. There is duplication among the tax sources of the three
governmental levels, especially between the federal government and
state governments, but the tax structures differ markedly. The federal
government relies primarily on income taxes, the states on consumption
taxes, and the localities on real property taxes.

Two-thirds of all government receipts go to the federal government,
but state and local receipts have been rising rapidly during the past three

Figure 1-1. *Receipts of Federal and State and Local Governments, 1955–82*

Billions of dollars (ratio scale)

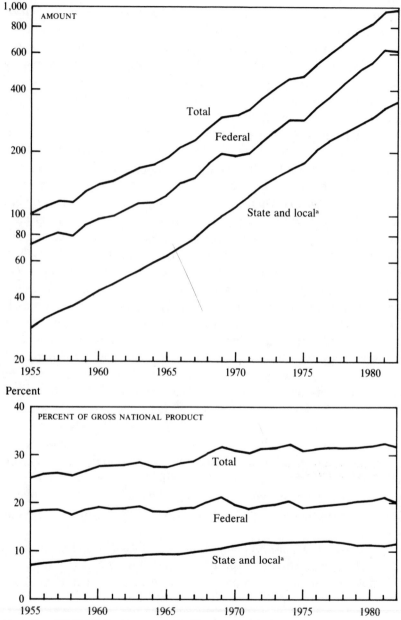

Source: Appendix table D-3. Receipts are on a national income accounts basis.
a. State and local receipts have been adjusted to exclude federal grants-in-aid.

decades because of the growth in demand for the public services that are operated and administered primarily by state and local governments. Although all governments finance most of their revenue needs from their own sources, there is a well-developed system of intergovernmental assistance that transfers funds from higher to lower levels of government. Federal grants have been declining in recent years, and at least part of these revenues are being replaced by state and local sources.

The broad outlines of the tax system have remained about the same since World War II, when the federal government greatly expanded the coverage of the individual income tax and substantially increased corporation tax rates. Nevertheless, the structure has not been static— during the past twenty-five years great changes have occurred at all levels of government. Federal income tax rates have been reduced substantially; increases in the personal exemption and the adoption of a standard deduction have eliminated from the income tax rolls most individuals and families officially classified as poor; the exemptions, standard deduction, and individual income tax rate brackets are scheduled to be indexed for inflation beginning in 1985; depreciation allowances have been liberalized, and an investment credit has been in effect since 1962, except for five months in 1966–67 and twenty-eight months in 1969–71 when it was suspended for stabilization reasons; practically all selective excise taxes other than the taxes on liquor and tobacco and the highway and airway user taxes have been reduced or eliminated; payroll taxes have been raised substantially to finance large increases in social security benefits; and numerous revisions have been made in the income tax bases. At the state and local levels, tax rates have risen steadily. Traditional opposition to state income and sales taxes has broken down; three-quarters of the states now have both. To alleviate the burden of property taxes, relief is provided for low-income families or the aged in thirty-two states through income tax credits or rebates. State and local governments have also been improving administration of the property tax, which continues to be the major revenue source for local governments.

These developments foreshadow continued change and evolution in the years ahead. Tax rates will be raised or lowered as domestic and international circumstances require. Reforms in the federal individual and corporation income taxes will continue to be made. Consideration is being given to methods of simplifying the income tax by broadening the tax base and lowering the tax rates. The idea of substituting a graduated consumption expenditure tax for part or all of the individual income tax is being debated. Experts agree that it will be necessary to perfect the 1976 and 1982 revisions of the federal estate and gift taxes. State and local finance and intergovernmental fiscal relations will continue to be a major concern to policymakers at all levels of government.

This book explains these and other issues in federal taxation and discusses alternative solutions. Chapter 2 examines the relation of taxation to economic growth and stability and of tax policy to overall economic policy. Chapter 3 describes the tax legislative process, discusses its weaknesses, and suggests ways to improve it. Chapters 4 through 8 are devoted to the major federal tax categories: the individual income tax, the corporation income tax, consumption taxes, payroll taxes, and estate and gift taxes. Each chapter describes the basic features of the tax under review, recent changes in the law, and the problems yet unsolved. Chapter 9 analyzes the issues in state and local taxation that are relevant to federal policy.

Goals of Taxation

Taxation is a major instrument of social and economic policy. It has three goals: to transfer resources from the private to the public sector; to distribute the cost of government fairly by income classes (vertical equity) and among people in approximately the same economic circumstances (horizontal equity); and to promote economic growth, stability, and efficiency. From these standpoints, the U.S. tax system is both a source of satisfaction and an object of criticism. Recent tax cuts and increases in defense spending have generated large federal deficits, which will be difficult to remove. The federal part of the tax system is progressive, thus placing a proportionately heavier burden on those who have greater ability to pay. But the federal income tax structure is widely acknowledged to be seriously defective and to distort economic activity. Federal tax receipts are responsive to changes in business activity and therefore automatically cushion the effect on spending of changes in private incomes. The state and local part of the system is not progressive and is less responsive to changes in income; as a result, fiscal crises recur at the state and local levels during periods of economic contraction or slow growth.

The U.S. tax system as a whole is either proportional to income or

Figure 1-2. *Effective Rates of Federal, State, and Local Taxes under the Most Progressive and Least Progressive Sets of Incidence Assumptions, by Population Percentile, 1975*[a]

Effective rate (percent)

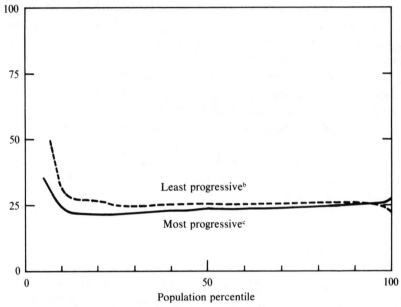

Population percentile

Source: Brookings 1975 MERGE data file.
a. Population percentiles are ranked in order of comprehensive income, from low to high.
b. Assumes that one-quarter of the corporation income tax is borne by consumers, one-quarter by wage earners, and one-half by shareholders.
c. Assumes that half the corporation income tax is borne by shareholders and half by owners of capital in general.

slightly progressive, depending on who bears the burden of the major taxes (figure 1-2). Some say the system is not progressive enough; others believe that the burdens at the top of the income scale, which are mainly due to the taxes on property incomes, are too heavy. But there is a consensus in favor of at least *some* progression in the overall tax burden. Some believe that special provisions go too far in attempting to promote economic incentives; others believe they do not go far enough. Nonetheless, tax policy is generally regarded as a legitimate device for promoting economic growth and stability, provided the particular measures chosen are effective in accomplishing their objectives. Within these broad areas of agreement, there is considerable controversy about the relative emphasis that should be placed on equity and economic objectives.

These issues involve difficult, technical questions of law, accounting, and economics. They are often obscured by misunderstanding, lack of information, and even misrepresentation. Yet they have important implications for the welfare of every citizen and for the vitality of the economy. This volume attempts to provide factual and analytical information that will help readers make up their own minds. It was prepared in the belief that tax policy is too important to be left solely to the experts, and that taxation can and should be understood by the interested citizen.

CHAPTER TWO

Taxes and Economic Policy

DURING most of the nation's history, federal budget policy was based on the rule that tax receipts should be roughly equal to annual government expenditures. Declining receipts during a business contraction called for an increase in taxes or a reduction in expenditures, while surpluses that developed during periods of prosperity called for lowered tax rates or increased expenditures. This policy reduced private incomes when they were falling and raised them when they were rising. By aggravating fluctuations in purchasing power, the policy of annually balanced budgets accentuated economic instability.

In the 1930s new concepts of budget policy emerged that emphasized the relation of the federal budget to the performance of the economy. It is now understood that higher taxes and lower government expenditures help fight inflation by restraining private demand; lower taxes and higher expenditures help fight recession by stimulating private demand. Budget surpluses restrain private spending during prosperity; deficits stimulate spending during recessions.

More recently, monetary policy has demonstrated the immense influence it has on economic activity. Private expenditures can be stimulated or restrained by increasing or reducing the growth of money and credit. Consequently, monetary policy must be coordinated with fiscal policy to achieve stable growth.

This chapter explains how the fiscal and monetary actions of the government affect economic activity and the rate of economic growth. Taxes will be emphasized because the focus of this volume is on taxation. But changes in government spending cannot be ignored, as the rapid increase in expenditures for the Vietnam War clearly showed in the latter part of the 1960s. That experience and the vicissitudes of the 1970s and the early 1980s also demonstrated that the growth and stability of the economy depend not only on fiscal decisions, but also on many other government decisions, particularly those concerning monetary policy.

Fiscal economics is based on national income analysis as it has developed over the past fifty years. The essence of this analysis is that total output or gross national product equals the total spending of consumers, business, and government. At any given time, there is a level of output that is consistent with high employment of the nation's supply of labor and with nonaccelerating inflation. This level is called *potential* or *high-employment GNP* (figure 2-1). The major objectives of economic policy are to stabilize the economy at high employment, maintain price stability, and promote economic growth and efficiency.

Stabilization Policy

The federal government exerts great influence on total spending, and hence on output, through its fiscal and monetary policies. In this section, the mechanics of fiscal policy are described first. Then, the mechanics of monetary policy and how monetary policy can modify the impact of fiscal policy are explained. The section ends with a brief discussion of the impact of expectations on the effectiveness of fiscal and monetary policies.

Fiscal Policy

The government alters total spending in the private economy directly by varying its own spending or indirectly by raising or lowering taxes. If expenditures are increased or if taxes are lowered, the increased spending of households and businesses requires additional output. The production and sale of this output in turn generates still more income and spending; and the cycle repeats itself, although in diminishing magnitudes. The cumulative increase in GNP is therefore a multiple of the initial increase in government expenditures or reduction in taxes. Correspondingly, reductions in expenditures or increases in taxes reduce GNP by a multiple of the initial action.

The process of income and output creation through fiscal policy may be illustrated by the following hypothetical examples. Assume that out of each dollar of GNP twenty-five cents is taken in federal taxes and the remaining seventy-five cents goes to consumers and business, and that consumers and business together spend 80 percent of any additional income they receive after taxes. For the moment, assume also that

Figure 2-1. *Gross National Product, Actual and Potential, and Unemployment Rate, 1955–82*

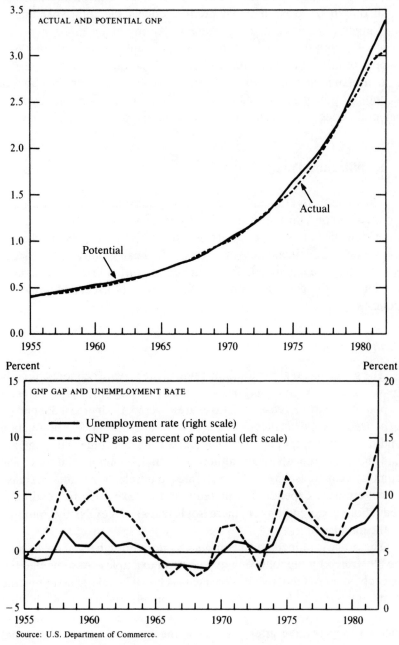

Source: U.S. Department of Commerce.

monetary policy "accommodates" a change in fiscal policy; that is to say, the supply of money and credit is expanded just enough to avoid any increase in interest rates. (The effect of relaxing this assumption is explained later.)

If the government increased its purchases of goods and services by $10 billion, private income before tax would initially rise by the same amount. Tax revenues would be $2.5 billion higher, and private disposable income would rise $7.5 billion, of which consumers and business would spend $6 billion. This additional spending would generate another increase in income, with $1.5 billion going to taxes and the remaining $4.5 billion to consumers and business. Of the latter amount, consumers and business would spend $3.6 billion, which would generate still another round of rising income and spending, and so on. The total increase in GNP (including the initial $10 billion of government purchases) would amount to $25 billion (10 + 6 + 3.6 + · · ·). This is a multiplier of 2.5 times the original increase in spending.

Consider what would happen if, instead of increasing its purchases, the government reduced tax rates by the equivalent of $10 billion. Consumers and business would again spend 80 percent of the higher after-tax incomes, or $8 billion. This would generate the same amount of additional private income, of which consumers and business would receive $6 billion and spend $4.8 billion, and so on. The total increase in GNP would be $20 billion (8 + 4.8 + · · ·), or two times the original tax cut. The difference between the multipliers in the two illustrations reflects the differences in first-round effects of the expenditure and tax changes: in this round output is raised by the entire amount of an increase in purchases but by only 80 percent of a tax reduction. (The first-round effects of an increase in transfer payments—say for social security, unemployment compensation, or welfare—is similar to that of a tax cut. Hence, the multiplier for transfer payments is more nearly like that of a tax cut than of an increase in government purchases.)

If purchases and taxes were increased simultaneously by the same amount, the effects of the two actions would not cancel one another because, dollar for dollar, purchases have a more potent effect on the economy than tax changes. For example, under the assumptions in the previous illustrations, if a tax increase of $10 billion were enacted together with a $10 billion increase in government purchases, the former would reduce GNP by $20 billion and the latter would stimulate a $25 billion increase, leaving a net increase of $5 billion. In other words, an increase in purchases that is fully financed by an increase in taxes will on balance increase the GNP. (This illustration assumes that the change in spending resulting from an increase or decrease in private disposable income will be the same regardless of the source of the income change and that investment and other economic behavior will not be influenced by the government's actions. In reality, the responses of the various sectors to changes in taxes and spending are far more complex, and estimates of the multipliers vary greatly.)

The effect of changes in government purchases and taxes on the government's deficit depends on the increase in GNP generated by the fiscal stimulus and on tax rates. In the previous examples, federal tax revenues were assumed to rise by 25 percent of any increment to GNP. Thus the $25 billion increase in GNP resulting from an increase in purchases of $10 billion would raise tax receipts by $6.25 billion (0.25 × $25 billion), partially offsetting the increase in the deficit caused by the spending increase; the net impact would be an increased deficit (or a reduced surplus) of $3.75 billion. If taxes were reduced by $10 billion at the initial level of income, the $20 billion increase in GNP would raise tax receipts by $5 billion (0.25 × $20 billion), partially offsetting the revenue effect of the tax cut and resulting in a $5 billion net increase in the deficit. Thus, the indirect effects of a tax cut are not strong enough to offset the direct revenue loss entirely and convert the tax cut to a net revenue gainer, as some have argued. On the other hand, if purchases and taxes were raised simultaneously by $10 billion, the $5 billion increase in GNP would raise tax receipts by a further $1.25 billion (0.25 × $5 billion) and *reduce* the deficit (or increase the surplus) by that amount.

Built-in Stabilizers

In addition to discretionary changes in taxes and expenditures (that is, deliberate government actions to vary taxes or the rate of expenditures), the fiscal system itself contributes to stabilization by generating automatic tax and expenditure adjustments that cushion the effect of changes in GNP. These *built-in stabilizers* moderate the fall in private income and spending when GNP declines and restrain the increase in private income and spending when GNP rises. They are automatic in the sense that they respond to changes in GNP without any action on the part of the government.

The two major groups of built-in fiscal stabilizers are taxes, in particular income taxes, and transfers, such as unemployment compensation and welfare payments.

The federal individual income tax is the leading tax stabilizer. When incomes fall, many people who were formerly taxable drop below the taxable level; others are pushed down into lower tax brackets. Conversely, when incomes rise, people who were formerly not taxed become taxable, and others are pushed into higher tax brackets. Under the rates in effect in 1981, federal individual income tax receipts automatically increased or decreased by over 15 percent for every 10 percent increase or decrease in real personal income (see appendix table D-14). Since consumption depends on disposable personal income, automatic changes in receipts from the individual income tax keep consumption more stable than it otherwise would be.

Variations in receipts from the corporation income tax are proportionately larger than variations in individual income tax receipts because profits fluctuate more widely than individual incomes over business cycles. The variation in corporate profits is a major nonfiscal stabilizer in the economic system. When economic activity slows down, profits fall both in absolute terms and as a percentage of GNP. Since profits fall disproportionately, other income components such as wage and salary incomes of consumers are partially protected from the downturn: they fall less than in proportion to the decline in GNP. Consumer spending therefore falls by less than it might if corporate profits were less volatile. (Another component of personal income, dividends, is relatively unaffected by short-term swings in profits because corporate managers try to keep dividends in line with long-term earnings.) Swings in before-tax profits could still be destabilizing if investment spending by corporations fluctuated in proportion to changes in profits. There is little firm evidence, however, that investment is sensitive to that extent to profit swings. In any case, the corporation income tax helps forestall possible swings in investment by absorbing much of the volatility in before-tax profits.

The yields of a general consumption tax (such as a general sales tax) or a proportional payroll tax respond about in proportion to changes in income. However, these taxes are less effective as automatic stabilizers than the individual income tax, which responds more than in proportion to income. The federal government relies on specific excise taxes, which are even less effective automatic stabilizers than a general consumption tax, because they are levied on the number of units (for example, cents

Figure 2-2. *Effect of Level of Activity on Federal Surplus or Deficit*

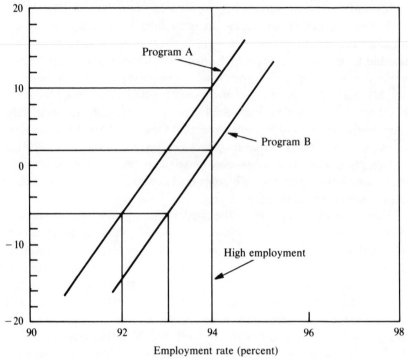

Surplus or deficit (billions of dollars)

Employment rate (percent)

per gallon) rather than as a percentage of the value of purchases and thus do not increase as prices increase.

The major built-in stabilizer on the expenditure side of the budget is unemployment compensation. In the United States, insured workers who become unemployed are entitled to benefits for up to twenty-six weeks in most states. During recessions, eligibility for benefits has been extended for periods of up to sixty-five weeks. These payments help maintain consumption as output and employment fall. As incomes go up and employment increases, unemployment compensation declines. Other transfer payments (for example, social security and food stamps) also tend to increase more rapidly during recessions, but their cyclical fluctuations are much smaller than the fluctuations of unemployment benefits.

The effect of built-in stabilizers on the federal surplus, as distinct from the discretionary actions of the government, can be calculated.

Because of the built-in stabilizers, the actual surplus or deficit reflects the prevailing levels of income and employment, as well as the government's fiscal policy. Figure 2-2 shows how the effect of the built-in stabilizers may be separated from the discretionary changes.

Each line in the figure shows the surplus or deficit that would be realized at various levels of employment under two different budget programs, A and B. For simplicity, it is assumed that the tax system is the same, but that expenditures are $8 billion higher under program B. (The surplus is therefore $8 billion lower or the deficit $8 billion higher.) The lines slope upward, indicating that as employment and income increase tax revenues increase and the deficits become smaller or the surpluses larger. The effect of the built-in stabilizers is given by the slope of each line: the greater the slope, the larger the impact of the built-in stabilizers on the surplus or deficit. In figure 2-2, both programs have the same built-in stability features because the tax systems are identical. However, an actual deficit of $6 billion is realized when employment is at 92 percent of the labor force under program A and at 93 percent under program B. Clearly, program B is more expansionary than program A. Differences between programs will also be due in practice to differences in tax rates; in such cases, the lines would not be parallel, but the slope of each line would still measure the built-in flexibility of each program.

The High-Employment Surplus or Deficit

Most people look to the actual surplus or deficit as a guide to whether fiscal policy is restrictive or expansionary. Figure 2-2 shows, however, that actual surpluses or deficits can be misleading. Business contractions or expansions cause changes in the deficit or surplus even when fiscal policy variables do not change. Consequently, the effects of two fiscal programs on demand may be compared only by examining the surplus or deficit at a given level of employment. By convention, the comparison is made at a high level of employment (originally 96 percent of the labor force, currently 94 percent). Defined in this way, in figure 2-2 the "high-employment surplus" is $10 billion under program A and $2 billion under program B. The difference of $8 billion reflects the assumed difference in expenditures. In practice, differences in the effects of alternative fiscal programs are due to differences in tax rates as well as expenditures.

There are two types of budget statements in current use—the official *unified budget* and the *national income accounts budget*. The unified budget is the official accounting statement of the federal government, whereas in the national income accounts the budget was designed to measure the influence of the government's fiscal activities on the economy (see figure 2-3). Consequently, the high-employment surplus or deficit is usually computed on a national income accounts basis, but it can be adjusted to the definitions in the unified budget.

The budget program that is appropriate at a given time depends on the strength of private demand for consumption and investment goods. When private demand is high, a large high-employment surplus is called for; when private demand is weak, the high-employment budget should shift toward a deficit. Efforts to achieve a larger surplus or a lower deficit than is consistent with high employment would depress employment and incomes. If the budget called for too small a high-employment surplus, total demand would be too high and prices would rise.

An important characteristic of the actual and high-employment budgets is the tendency of revenues to increase as the economy grows and individual and business incomes increase. Inflation raises receipts even more as money incomes are adjusted to compensate for the rise in prices. At 1984 income levels and tax rates and on the assumption of 94 percent employment and inflation of 5 percent, federal receipts increase by about $65 billion a year, or 1.7 percent of potential GNP. Other things being equal, therefore, the high-employment surplus would rise by about $65 billion, less the automatic increases in expenditures resulting from normal increases in the number of beneficiaries of government programs, cost-of-living adjustments, and so on. With 10 percent inflation the rise in federal receipts would be close to $105 billion a year, or 2.6 percent of potential GNP. Indexing of the individual income tax rate brackets and exemptions, which is scheduled to be introduced in 1985, would reduce the automatic growth in receipts to $55 billion in the case of 5 percent inflation and $85 billion in the case of 10 percent inflation.

This upward creep in high-employment revenues has been called the *fiscal dividend*. It measures the leeway that is, so to speak, automatically available in the federal budget to finance higher federal expenditures without raising tax rates. During the early 1960s the fiscal dividend was used to finance tax rate reductions as well as expenditure increases. More recently, sharply accelerating commitments for defense, large cuts in tax rates, and the introduction of indexing have more than exhausted the fiscal dividend and led to high and rising deficits even at high employment. These deficits, called *structural* deficits to distinguish them

The Two Budgets

The official budget statement of the federal government is the *unified budget,* which is an instrument of management and control of federal activities financed with federally owned funds. This budget includes cash flows to and from the public resulting from all federal fiscal activity, including the trust funds, and the net lending of government-owned enterprises. Thus the unified budget provides a comprehensive picture of the financial impact of federal programs, but it does not measure their contribution to the current income and output of the nation. For this purpose, economists make use of the statement of receipts and expenditures in the official national income accounts, often called the *national income accounts budget.*

Like the unified budget, the national income accounts budget includes the activities of trust funds and excludes purely intragovernmental transactions (for example, interest on federal bonds owned by federal agencies) that do not affect the general public. But there are significant differences between the two in timing and coverage. The national income accounts budget includes receipts and expenditures when they affect private incomes, which is not necessarily when the federal government receives cash or pays it out. This adjustment involves putting receipts (except those from personal taxes) on an accrual basis and counting expenditures when goods are delivered rather than when payment is made. The adjustment for coverage excludes purely financial transactions because these represent an exchange of assets or claims and not a direct addition to income or production.

There are some differences in the size of surpluses or deficits between the two accounts, and even in their movements (figure 2-3).

Figure 2-3. *Federal Surpluses and Deficits, Two Budget Concepts, Fiscal Years 1955–82*

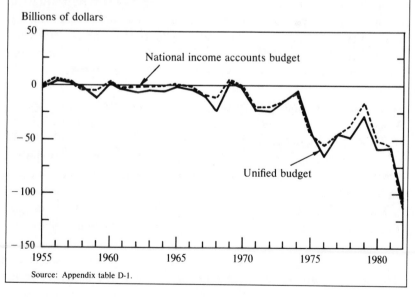

Source: Appendix table D-1.

from the *cyclical* variations in the budget balance during recession and recovery, will plague fiscal planners for years to come.

The automatic increase in federal receipts that accompanies the increase in incomes resulting from real growth or inflation is also called the *fiscal drag* because it retards the economy unless it is offset by rising expenditures or tax reductions. This terminology becomes fashionable— in periods such as the early 1960s and the mid-1970s—when government expenditures do not rise fast enough to absorb the automatic growth in tax receipts.

According to current estimates, except for the years 1965–68, when Vietnam War expenditures grew rapidly, and 1971–72 and 1975, when antirecession tax cuts were made, the federal budget would have been in surplus or close to balance in nearly every quarter between 1955 and 1975 had high employment been maintained (figure 2-4). However, the actual budget showed a deficit during most of the period because of the disappointing performance of the economy. In 1964, 1971, and 1975, the high-employment surplus was sharply decreased by tax reductions to stimulate the economy. In each instance, employment began to climb as soon as, or shortly after, the tax cuts went into effect, and the budget deficits declined. These experiences illustrate the principle that in slack periods temporarily enlarged deficits ultimately help improve both the condition of the economy and the federal budget.

On the other hand, planning for a larger surplus without regard to the strength of private demand may produce unsatisfactory rates of employment and output and also create budget deficits. The sharp increases in the high-employment surplus in 1959–60, 1969, and 1974 clearly helped bring about the recessions of 1960–61, 1970–71, and 1974–75.

Fiscal policy has erred at times on the side of excessive ease as well as restraint. The rapid buildup of military expenditures for the Vietnam War wiped out the high-employment surplus beginning in mid-1965. The high-employment deficit averaged 0.3 percent of potential GNP in 1966, 1.2 percent in 1967, and 0.4 percent in 1968. Monetary policy did not offset this fiscal stimulus and an inflation that lasted well over a decade was generated.

The 1981 tax legislation, which cut individual income tax rates by 25 percent over three years and also made large reductions in other taxes, was another policy error that had serious economic consequences. Supporters of the tax cuts claimed not only that the cuts would improve economic incentives, but that the improvement would be large enough

Figure 2-4. *High-Employment Surplus as a Percentage of Potential Gross National Product, National Income Accounts Basis, 1955–82*

Percent

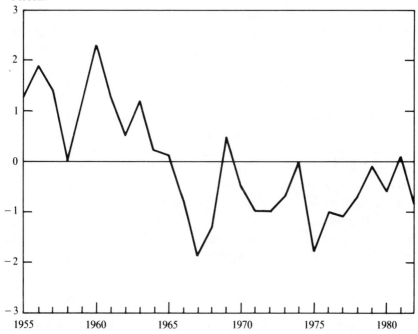

Source: Appendix table D-2. Assumes high-employment unemployment rate increased from 4 percent in 1955 to 5.1 percent in 1975.

to increase total output sufficiently to offset the loss in tax revenues. However, a tight monetary policy and expectations of a severe and permanent imbalance between spending and receipts pushed interest rates up sharply, more than offsetting the stimulating effect of the tax cuts. The economy was prevented from growing, and deficits increased (figure 2-4). This episode demonstrates the need for restraint in cutting taxes in the face of rising expenditures and for coordination of fiscal with monetary policies.

Although it is the most convenient single measure of the fiscal stimulus, the high-employment budget must be used with considerable care. In the first place, the degree of fiscal restraint needed at any given time depends on the strength of private demand. The high-employment surplus appropriate for one period may not be appropriate for another. Second, differences in the composition of expenditures and taxes have an important bearing on the significance of the high-employment surplus. For example, an increase in the high-employment surplus resulting from a reduction in government expenditures on goods and services would be more restrictive than that resulting from a reduction in transfer payments of the same amount. Third, the restrictiveness of a given *amount* of surplus, say, $50 billion, would be much greater in a $2,000 billion economy than in a $4,000 billion economy. In making comparisons over time, the high-employment surplus should be expressed as a percentage of potential GNP (see figure 2-4). Finally, there is no simple way to adjust the high-employment surplus for the effect of price increases. Most calculations of the high-employment surplus remove the effect of the built-in response of the federal budget to a business recession but do not remove the built-in response of the budget to inflation. For these reasons, the meaning of the high-employment surplus is likely to be unambiguous only during relatively short periods when changes in expenditures and taxes and in the rate of growth of prices are relatively small. Analysis of the fiscal impact of the budget over long periods requires more detailed information than the high-employment surplus provides by itself.

Expenditure versus Tax Adjustments to Promote Stability

Changes in both expenditures and tax rates can be used for stabilization purposes. Although expenditure changes have somewhat larger multiplier effects, they are not necessarily preferable to changes in tax rates. In the first place, government expenditures should be determined by long-run national needs and not by short-run cyclical considerations. The controlling principle is that government outlays should not exceed, or fall short of, the level at which the benefit to the nation's citizens of an additional dollar of expenditures would be the same in public and private use. This level is unlikely to rise or fall sharply during such short periods as a business contraction or expansion. Second, considerations of economic efficiency argue against large short-run variations in expenditures. For example, it would be wasteful to slow down construction of a road or hydroelectric plant, once construction had begun, in the interest of reducing aggregate spending. Third, there might be a long delay between a decision to undertake an expenditure and its effect on output and employment. When recessions are relatively brief—as they have been since the end of World War II—the impact of a decision to change an expenditure is often not felt until recovery is well under way.

But during periods of rapidly rising defense expenditures, such as occurred during the Korean and Vietnam wars, a slowing down or deferment of some government programs usually becomes necessary to keep total demand from outstripping the productive potential of the economy. The increase in defense spending in the 1980s is not expected to strain industrial capacity, but it has led to reductions in nondefense spending in the attempt to restrain the growth of total federal spending.

Of the various taxes, the individual income tax is the most suitable for stabilization purposes. Under the withholding system for wages and salaries, changes in tax rates can be made effective in a matter of days and can also be terminated quickly. In most cases, the effect of a tax change on a worker's take-home pay is indistinguishable from the effect of a change in the gross weekly wage. Corporation income tax rate changes are not likely to have significant effects on investment if it is known or expected that the changes will be of short duration. Moreover, expected changes in investment incentives may have a perverse effect in the short run; the expectation of a reduction may accelerate business spending, and the expectation of an increase may delay spending. Consumption tax changes could also have a perverse effect for the same reason. Nevertheless, once they become effective, investment tax incentives or consumption tax changes can be as powerful as individual income tax changes in stimulating or restraining demand. To avoid the short-run perverse effects, changes in investment incentives and in consumption taxes are usually implemented quickly, or, in the case of investment incentives, even retroactively to the beginning of the year or the date the legislation was proposed.

Most economists believe consumption depends on income expected to be received regularly and is not much affected by temporary changes in income. According to this hypothesis, an income tax that is expected to be temporary would have some effect on consumer spending, but it would be less powerful than one that is expected to be permanent. Income tax changes also operate with a lag, because consumers do not alter their spending immediately in response to changes in disposable income.

Tax changes are often assumed to have the greatest effect on consumption if they are concentrated in the lower income classes. This view presupposes that the poor spend proportionately more out of any additional dollars they receive than the rich. The empirical evidence, however, supports the view that the effect of a tax change on private spending is more or less independent of its distribution among income classes. Thus, if the distribution of the tax burden is considered equitable, tax rates could be moved up or down uniformly for stabilization purposes under a simple formula, such as an equal percentage-point change in the rates for all brackets. If the existing tax is *not* considered equitable, tax rates can be modified to achieve both the stabilization and distributional objectives.

Tax rate changes are sometimes criticized on the ground that they are too small to exert a measurable economic effect. With 80 million taxpayers, a $40 billion individual income tax cut would be equivalent to an average increase in take-home pay of less than $10 a week per taxpayer, a negligible amount in comparison with a total GNP of $4,000 billion. The comparison is erroneous, however, because it compares weekly and annual income flows. A $40 billion annual tax cut would amount to 1 percent of the GNP, whether expressed on a weekly, monthly, or annual basis. Because tax changes have a multiplier effect, a tax cut of this magnitude would give a substantial stimulus to the economy. The *deviation* from high-employment GNP that tax cuts are intended to narrow is usually less than 10 percent, so a tax cut equivalent to 1 percent of the GNP, with its multiplier effect, would have a significant impact on demand.

Tax adjustments can be used to restrain as well as to stimulate demand and are therefore important instruments for counteracting inflation. It may be impractical, if not impossible, to cut back government expenditures when inflation threatens. About 75 percent of federal expenditures are for defense, social security, unemployment compensation, other income security programs, and interest on the national debt, which should not or cannot be altered for short-run reasons. If the inflationary pressure is the direct result of an increase in government spending for defense or war purposes, tax increases must be used to withdraw excess purchasing power from the income stream.

The time required to complete the legislative process is an obstacle to the prompt use of tax changes for stabilization purposes. Congressional consideration of major tax legislation may take eighteen months or more. Proposals have been made to give the president authority to make temporary changes in individual income tax rates or to speed up congressional procedures for action on presidential recommendations. However, recent changes in congressional budget procedures require consideration of overall fiscal policies, and the need for giving the president authority to vary tax rates temporarily is no longer urgent (see chapter 3).

Automatic Budget Rules

It is now widely understood that following a policy of annually balanced budgets would accentuate business fluctuations. But many people continue to believe it unwise to rely exclusively on discretion to guide budget decisions. Discretionary policy depends heavily on forecasting techniques that are still subject to error. In addition, delays and uncertainties in congressional action make it difficult to adjust fiscal policy promptly and by economically appropriate amounts. Many people also fear that removing budgetary restraint would lead to excessive federal expenditures. To avoid these pitfalls, attempts have been made to formulate rules that would reduce the element of judgment in budget decisions without impairing economic growth and stability.

A well-known plan is the *stabilizing budget policy* of the Committee for Economic Development, a nonprofit organization of influential businessmen and educators. Under this policy, tax rates would be set to balance the budget or yield a small surplus at high employment. The rates would remain unchanged until there was a major change in the level of expenditures. Reliance would be placed on the built-in stabilizers to moderate fluctuations in private demand.

The drawback of the CED plan is that it may not always be possible to achieve high employment with a balance or a small surplus in the federal budget, so that it may be desirable to have a high-employment deficit at times. Nor does it offer a systematic method for raising additional revenues should federal expenditures rise by more than the amount of the automatic growth in tax receipts, or for lowering taxes should federal expenditures rise by less than the amount of the automatic growth in tax receipts. When federal expenditures rise rapidly, it would be both hazardous and unwise to keep tax rates unchanged for long periods.

A second approach would be to enact a formula that would trigger increases or decreases in tax rates when certain predetermined economic indexes were reached. For example, legislation might provide for a 1-percentage-point reduction in income tax rates for every increase of 0.5 percent in unemployment above 6 percent of the labor force, or an increase of 1 percentage point for every rise of 2 points in a general price index such as the consumer or the wholesale price index. While this type of formula would add to the effectiveness of the built-in stabilizers if the changes were correctly timed, no one index or set of indexes could be used with confidence to signal an economic movement justifying tax action.

A third approach is to introduce an amendment into the Constitution requiring a balanced budget. Such an amendment would eliminate discretionary fiscal policy and induce excessive reliance on other aggregate control measures (for example, regulation of credit activities) for stabilization purposes. It would also be virtually impossible to enforce a balanced budget once a fiscal year began. The loss of fiscal flexibility and the encouragement of subterfuge to avoid the balanced-budget constraint argue strongly against the balanced-budget amendment.

Clearly, budget policy cannot be based on a rigid set of rules. Nevertheless, the search for budget rules has improved public understanding of the elements of fiscal policy. Emphasis is placed on the automatic stabilizers for their cushioning effect on private disposable incomes and spending. Recognition of the capacity of the federal tax system to generate rising revenues has alerted policymakers to the need for making positive decisions about the relative social priorities of public and private expenditures, so that the appropriate amounts can be allocated to tax reduction and to higher government expenditures.

Monetary Policy

Monetary policy is concerned with the amount of money people and businesses have in their pockets and in accounts at depository institutions (banks, saving and loan associations, and other financial institutions, such as credit unions), and the terms on which money can be borrowed (interest rates and repayment requirements). Spending is likely to be higher the larger the stock of money and the easier the terms on which money can be borrowed. The Federal Reserve, the central bank of the United States, regulates the stock of money by increasing or decreasing either the reserves that depository institutions hold or the fraction of those reserves that must be held against their deposits. It has three methods of changing financial conditions.

1. The Federal Reserve can buy federal government securities from private brokers and dealers or sell securities to them. When it buys securities, its payment to the seller increases the amount of reserves

held by depository institutions. This occurs directly if the seller is a bank or other depository institution; if the seller is a business or an individual, reserves increase when the seller deposits the Federal Reserve's payment. When depository institutions find themselves with more reserves than they need, they lend more (although not necessarily to the maximum permissible limit) or buy securities themselves. The greater supply of loan funds puts downward pressure on interest rates, and, because loans show up as increased deposits of the borrowers (and later as deposits of others with whom the borrowers have business transactions), increases the money supply. If the depository institutions use the additional reserves to increase their security holdings, prices of securities may increase, interest rates will be under downward pressure, and there will again be a tendency for the money stock to increase. Easier financial conditions in turn stimulate spending. To reduce borrowing and spending, the Federal Reserve can sell government securities, thus initiating in reverse the chain reaction just described. Purchases and sales of securities by the Federal Reserve are commonly referred to as "open-market operations."

2. The Federal Reserve can add to reserves by lending the depository institutions money for short periods (up to fifteen days on a renewable basis). It encourages or discourages bank borrowing by lowering or raising the "discount rate," which is the rate of interest charged on such loans. Changes in the discount rate are not very important for their quantitative effect on reserves, but they may have an important psychological effect on credit markets by signaling the direction monetary policy is taking.

3. The Federal Reserve can regulate the amount of reserves a depositing institution must hold by raising or lowering the reserve-requirement ratios (the fraction of a deposit that must be held in a non-interest-earning account at the Federal Reserve). It uses this power infrequently.

Unlike the fiscal authorities, who ordinarily determine fiscal policy for a period of a year (except during emergencies), the Federal Reserve engages in open-market operations almost daily. This gives monetary policy a degree of flexibility that fiscal policy cannot have. However, reliance is not placed exclusively on monetary policy for short-run stabilization purposes, because the results of monetary action may have unbalanced effects on the economy. For example, tight money is particularly burdensome on small businesses, on those who must secure mortgages to purchase homes, and on state and local governments, which must continue to borrow to construct essential facilities. To combat inflation it may be more appropriate to reduce consumer and business spending across the board, and this may be accomplished more effectively by a general income tax increase. In practice, fiscal and monetary policies both have significant effects on the economy. Notwithstanding their different degrees of flexibility in the short run, they should be used together for stabilization purposes.

As fiscal and monetary policies are used to promote stable growth at high employment, care must be taken that the effect of one will not inadvertently cancel the other. For example, suppose the economy were in recession and the federal government increased expenditures or reduced taxes in an effort to accelerate business activity. As private expenditures increased, individuals and business firms would need more money and credit to conduct their business affairs. If the supplies of money and credit failed to increase, the greater demands for them would drive interest rates up. Higher interest rates would tend to reduce business spending and home construction, thus offsetting some of the effect of the initial spending increase. Fiscal policy thus requires an accommodating monetary policy if it is to have its strongest impact on output and inflation. The combination of monetary and fiscal measures most appropriate for obtaining any desired output and inflation response cannot be formulated as a single rule appropriate to all situations.

Rational Expectations

The failure of monetary and fiscal policies to maintain price stability and economic growth in recent years has led to the development of a new theory regarding the impact of macroeconomic policies on economic behavior. The most extreme version of this theory assumes that markets efficiently provide information about demand and supply conditions for goods and assets, and that individuals and firms make efficient use of all the information available to them. It also assumes that people do not make systematic mistakes in their expectations about future economic events, including government policy. This theory, if correct, would revolutionize economic policy. For example, all unemployment would be regarded as voluntary because individuals could always find work by accepting wages below their customary wage. In this theory, output varies because people make mistakes about the current economic situation, but these mistakes are quickly rectified. Thus, cyclical unemployment should decline and the economy should return to its track of normal growth without extraordinary countercyclical policies.

The implications of rational expectations for fiscal and monetary policies are particularly significant. Since households and businesses are assumed to be aware of what government usually does during periods of economic instability, they are already using this information in making their economic decisions, and, it is assumed, possession of this information causes them to act in the same way that the expected policy would induce them to act when it is put into effect. Therefore, putting it into effect accomplishes nothing. It is argued, therefore, that anticipated countercyclical fiscal and monetary policies have very little effect on work, saving, and investment decisions.

The policy prescription of the rational expectations school of economists is basically that the government can help stabilize the economy only by persuading economic agents that it will conduct itself in a predictable and credible fashion. *Unexpected* changes in macroeconomic policies, it is conceded, do affect economic behavior. But it is difficult, if not impossible, for the government to conduct a systematic policy that will remain unexpected for long. Furthermore, changes in policies that were unsystematic or purely random would be more likely to harm than help the economy.

The strongest variants of the rational expectations models are based on assumptions that many regard as unrealistic. The theory assumes that fluctuations in economic activity recur because buyers and sellers have imperfect information about future economic developments. However, this explanation of the business cycle fails to explain long periods of slack and boom in the modern economy. It is undeniable that expectations affect economic behavior, but it is still too early in the development of the theory of expectations to abandon the more traditional views about the impact of fiscal and monetary policies.

Policies to Promote Economic Growth

Fiscal and monetary policies are useful in promoting long-run economic growth as well as short-run stability. The objective of growth policy is to provide relatively high employment for the labor force and industrial capacity at stable prices. Growth may be disappointing for two reasons: the resources of the economy may not be fully employed because the economy is in recession, or the rate of growth of potential output at high employment may be too low. The policies required under these circumstances differ, although they are often confused.

Achieving Full Employment and Stable Prices

Fiscal and monetary policies can contribute to economic growth by keeping total demand roughly in line with the productive potential of the economy. An economy operating at less than high employment is, by definition, one in which potential GNP is larger than the total of actual spending by consumers, business, and government. The remedy is to increase private or public spending through fiscal and monetary stimulation. Conversely, when total demand exceeds the capacity of the economy to produce goods and services without inflation, the remedy is to curtail private or public spending through fiscal and monetary restraint.

Although the broad principles of stabilization policy are clear, they are difficult to apply. Failure to spend the normal increase in revenues, or to reduce tax rates by that amount, will produce successively larger high-employment surpluses, which may hold actual output below the economic potential of the economy. The high unemployment and the large gap between potential and actual GNP in 1958–61, 1970–71, and 1974–75 (see figure 2-1) were caused largely by excessively restrictive fiscal policies that arose in this way and were not offset by monetary policy. On the other hand, too large a growth in government expenditures relative to normal revenue growth may produce excess demand, which in turn leads to rising prices. The inflation that began in mid-1965 was triggered by the jump in Vietnam War expenditures, which were superimposed on an economy already operating at close to full employment. A temporary 10 percent surtax on individual and corporation income taxes was enacted in the summer of 1968, but this was about three years after the decision to escalate the war had been made.

It now seems clear that it will always be difficult to maintain high employment in a modern industrial economy and simultaneously keep price increases within acceptable limits. Since the end of World War II, prices have shown a tendency to rise in the United States and other industrial countries, even when total spending has been below potential GNP. Many economists believe this can be resolved only by supplementing fiscal and monetary policies with some form of wage-price or "incomes" policy to keep wage increases roughly in line with the average growth in productivity of the economy as a whole and to inhibit price increases not justified by cost increases. Under such a policy, prices would decline in industries with above-average productivity increases and rise in industries with below-average productivity increases, but the average of all prices would be stable. These principles were established by the Council of Economic Advisers in 1962 as voluntary "guideposts" for wage and price behavior.

The guideposts had the strong backing of Presidents John F. Kennedy and Lyndon B. Johnson and appeared to have had a modest effect in restraining wage and price increases (a judgment that some professional economists dispute) until mid-1965, when the rapid buildup of military expenditures for the Vietnam War upset the balance between supply and demand. Mandatory price and wage controls were imposed by President Richard M. Nixon in August 1971 and remained in effect until April 1974. These controls seemed to moderate the rise in prices, but they were allowed to lapse after food and fuel price increases generated a double-digit inflation that could not be contained by controls. President Jimmy Carter also established price and wage norms in 1978–80, but these were ineffective in containing the inflation generated by the oil price increase in 1979 and the resulting worldwide inflation.

Despite the many failures of incomes policies in the United States and other countries, the search for a workable incomes policy continues. Some economists have recently suggested that appropriate wage and price behavior can be encouraged by tax incentives or penalties. Such tax-based incomes policies seem attractive in theory, but would be difficult to implement.

Experience has shown that the major effect of inflation on growth is felt when the attempt is made to restore balance in the economy after inflation has become unacceptably high. Inflation distorts the distribution of the national income among different groups. Each group tries to protect itself against erosion of its share through wage or price increases or increases in government transfer payments. Such pressures continue to be felt long after excess demand has been removed by fiscal and monetary restraint, and they tend to prolong the inflationary episode. Thus, without an effective incomes policy, it has been possible to halt inflation only at the cost of high unemployment and slow growth for relatively long periods. It is, of course, much less costly and disruptive in social and economic terms to avoid inflation in the first place.

Raising the Growth Rate

If full employment is maintained, the rate of economic growth depends on the growth of potential output. The factors affecting potential output are the size of the labor force, the length of the average workweek and workyear, and productivity (output per man-hour). Productivity depends on the size of the capital stock, the quality of human resources, the attitudes and skills of management, the efficiency of resource use, and technological progress. These factors are influenced to some extent by government fiscal and monetary policies. These policies' most direct and quantitatively most important influence, however, is on the rate of national investment in both physical and human resources.

To increase the rate of growth, the rate of national investment must be raised to a higher level and held there for a long time. The federal government can contribute to increasing the investment rate through fiscal and monetary policies in three ways: it can adopt a policy of budget surpluses and low interest rates when the economy is operating at high employment; it can increase investment in physical and human capital directly through its own expenditures; and it can adopt tax measures that provide incentives for private saving and investment.

SAVING THROUGH BUDGET SURPLUSES. The key to understanding growth policy is the relation between saving and investment. Measured statistically, national saving during a period is the difference between national output produced in that period and the amounts currently spent by consumers and by government; private investment is also that part of the national product not currently consumed or used for government purposes. Thus national saving is equal to private investment. In effect, through saving, the nation sets aside resources for private investment purposes. (International transactions are ignored in this simplified description.)

When the federal government runs a budget surplus, it adds its own saving to that generated by the private economy. When the budget is in deficit, national saving is reduced, unless offsetting changes in private saving occur. Since increased saving and investment raise the growth rate, the federal government can stimulate growth by increasing its budget surpluses at high employment.

This growth strategy can be implemented only if there is a sufficient increase in investment in the private economy to use up the additional saving generated in the federal budget. Otherwise, the federal surplus will lead to a reduction in total demand and higher unemployment rather than more growth. In other words, the high-employment surplus must be just large enough to offset any expected deficiency in private saving. If there is more than enough private saving for the existing investment demand, the budget should be in deficit even at high employment.

An important ingredient of any strategy to increase private investment is monetary policy and, more broadly, the mix of fiscal and monetary policies. Ready access to credit and low real interest rates that hold down the cost of borrowing will stimulate investment. Stringent financial conditions restrain the growth of credit and raise interest rates. Therefore, the best combination of fiscal and monetary policies for promoting private investment would be a budget surplus with relatively easy financial conditions. In implementing such a combination of policies, it is important to avoid taxes that impair investment and saving incentives.

In practice, the extent of financial ease that a nation can afford is limited by balance-of-payments considerations. If interest rates are low and access to credit is easy relative to financial conditions in the rest of the world, firms, individuals, and private financial institutions will want to move funds out of the United States to take advantage of higher interest rates abroad. Under the system of floating exchange rates now in effect for the world's major currency blocs, such an outflow of funds will reduce the value of the dollar relative to other currencies. This change in exchange rates works to narrow the differences in financial conditions between the United States and the rest of the world. Because of the financial interdependence of national economies, the United States can thus be inhibited from going too far with a policy of financial ease. If interest rates must be kept higher than otherwise desired for balance-of-payments reasons, fiscal policy may have to be easier (that is, the surplus may have to be lower or the deficit higher) to maintain demand and employment on their desired paths.

INCREASING INVESTMENT DIRECTLY. It is not generally realized that investment is undertaken by government as well as by private firms. Outlays on education, training of manpower, health, research and development, roads, and other public facilities are essential elements of national investment. Such outlays are not substitutable for private investment, or vice versa. Education and research expenditures are among the most important components of national investment, yet most of these expenditures are paid for by government (primarily state and local in the case of education, and primarily federal in the case of research). There is no basis for judging how total investment should be distributed between the public and private sectors, and it is important to avoid doctrinaire positions about one or the other. Both types of investment contribute to the nation's economic growth.

Public investment is financed directly by government through taxes or borrowing. If private demand is strong, the appropriate policy for growth would be to raise enough tax revenues to pay for needed government investment as well as to leave an additional margin of saving for private investment.

INCREASING SAVING AND INVESTMENT INCENTIVES. Given the aggregate level of taxation, the tax structure can be an important independent factor in determining the growth potential of the economy. The tax structure may encourage consumption or saving, help raise or lower private investment in general or in particular industries, stimulate or restrain investment by Americans in foreign countries and by foreigners in the United States, and subsidize or discourage particular expenditures by individuals and business firms. Most tax systems, including that of the United States, have numerous features that affect saving and investment. For example, the federal income taxes provide liberal depreciation allowances, an investment credit, offsets for business losses against other income over a period of nineteen years, averaging of individual income for tax purposes over a period of five years, and preferential treatment of capital gains and of income from mining. These and other provisions will be discussed in later chapters.

The "Debt Burden"

Effective use of fiscal and monetary policies to promote high employment and growth objectives is hindered by excessive growth of the national debt. A long succession of annual deficits and the resulting rise in the national debt could impose dangerously heavy burdens on future generations. The current economic burden of the taxes needed to pay interest on a rising national debt is also not inconsequential. Furthermore, as a practical matter, large deficits make it extremely difficult to pursue a monetary policy appropriate for promoting economic growth.

Growth of the national debt imposes a burden on future generations if it crowds out private capital formation. In this respect, there is a difference between debt created under conditions of excessive unemployment and debt created under conditions of full employment.

In a situation of substantial unemployment, an increase in the public debt finances deficits that government uses to purchase goods and services directly or to make transfer payments. Since there are unemployed resources, the goods and services acquired by government or by the recipients of transfer payments do not take the place of goods and services that might otherwise have been produced. If accompanied by an appropriate monetary policy, the debt increase can be absorbed without impeding the flow of funds into private capital formation. In fact, the higher level of economic activity will stimulate private investment. The community will be better off today because the expenditures have been made; and future generations will also benefit to the extent that the expenditures increase private and public investment in human or physical capital that will yield future services.

The situation is altogether different if the economy is already fully utilizing its resources. Then an increase in government expenditures that leads to a deficit (or reduces a surplus) in the federal budget cannot increase total output. In the absence of offsetting policies, prices will rise at an accelerating rate. Offsetting tax increases or monetary restraint will be required to avoid an increase in inflation; that restraint, moreover, must reduce private consumption or investment. If the impact is on consumption, taxpayers will have in effect exchanged a collective good or service for current consumption. If the impact is on private or public investment, later generations will be worse off to the extent that the rate of growth of productive capacity has been reduced.

Usually, when the federal government ran high-employment surpluses (see figure 2-4), the debt added in peacetime was not burdensome in an economic sense. Deficits were incurred to restore or maintain high employment; these deficits raised output and employment and actually increased the resources available to current and later generations. But the situation has been drastically changed since 1981, when large three-year tax cuts were enacted and defense spending was increased sharply. Unless reversed, the large structural deficits generated by this policy will raise interest rates, crowd out investment, and slow the growth of the economy.

The existence of the national debt means that interest must be paid to holders of the debt, and tax rates are therefore higher than they would be without the debt. The transfer of interest from general taxpayers to bondholders is a burden on the economy if the taxes levied to pay interest on the debt reduce saving or lower economic efficiency. (If the government debt could be paid back by a per capita tax—which would have no

Figure 2-5. *Relation of Net Federal Debt and Net Interest on Debt to the Gross National Product, Fiscal Years 1947–82*[a]

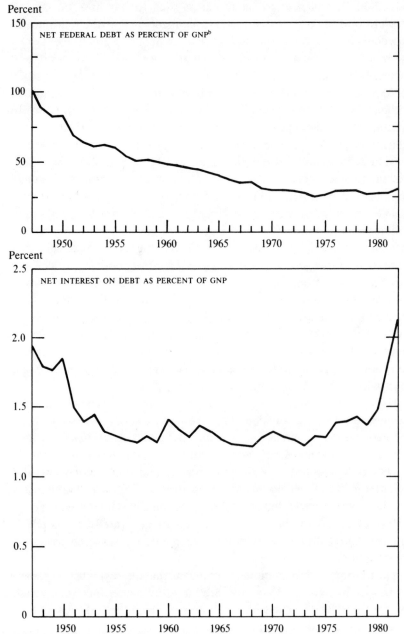

Percent

NET FEDERAL DEBT AS PERCENT OF GNP[b]

Percent

NET INTEREST ON DEBT AS PERCENT OF GNP

Sources: Office of Management and Budget and U.S. Department of Commerce.
a. Net federal debt is debt held outside U.S. government accounts and Federal Reserve banks. Interest on net federal debt is total interest payments to the public less interest earned by Federal Reserve banks.
b. Net federal debt at the end of calendar years as percent of fiscal year GNP.

effect on economic incentives—and the market for bonds were competitive, the debt would be exactly equivalent to the tax receipts and therefore would not burden future generations.) Until recently, the debt burden in the United States represented a small fraction of federal expenditures (less than 10 percent before 1981), but the percentage has been rising since then. The ratio of net federal debt to the gross national product declined between the end of World War II and 1974 (figure 2-5), and net interest payments, which fell markedly in the early postwar years, amounted to only slightly more than 1 percent of GNP between the mid-1950s and the mid-1970s. The growth of the economy over this period kept the burden of the debt in relation to total production from rising, even though the interest rates paid on the debt increased. Since the mid-1970s, however, the ratio of the debt to GNP has been roughly stable and the ratio of interest payments to GNP has been increasing.

Large, continuous deficits at high employment will culminate in one of two scenarios, either of which would retard economic growth. If the monetary authorities accommodated the large deficits by a policy of monetary ease, the rise in aggregate demand would soon generate accelerating inflation, which could be brought under control only by bringing the economic expansion to a halt. If the monetary authorities restrained growth of money and credit, interest rates would rise and the economy would grow slowly, if at all. Thus, a growth-promoting monetary policy can be pursued only if the budget at high employment is at or close to balance.

Summary

The strength of the economy depends heavily on the fiscal policies pursued by the federal government. These policies involve the use of tax and expenditure changes to promote high employment, economic growth, and price stability. The fiscal system itself generates automatic tax and expenditure changes that help dampen fluctuations in private disposable income and spending. Although they are extremely important, the built-in stabilizers can only moderate downward and upward movements in business activity. To halt and reverse such movements, the built-in stabilizers must be supplemented by discretionary changes in government expenditures or tax rates.

There is no reason why tax changes are inherently superior to expenditure changes as fiscal instruments for influencing aggregate demand, or vice versa. At any given level of government expenditures, the level of economic activity depends on the ratio of tax receipts to expenditures. When private demand is low and the economy is operating below capacity, taxes are too high relative to expenditures. In these circumstances, the ratio should be reduced—by cutting taxes, by raising expenditures, or both. Conversely, when demand is too high, taxes should be raised or expenditures reduced, or both. The appropriate action at any particular time depends on the relative need for private and for public expenditures.

It is impossible to formulate a general rule regarding the budget surpluses or deficits required for stabilization purposes. If private demand is weak, full employment may not be possible without federal deficits. If private demand is strong, surpluses will be needed to prevent prices from rising. On the basis of the past record, there is little reason to believe that the U.S. economy needs the stimulus of sustained deficits to remain at high employment. Indeed, large structural deficits are likely to lead to economic instability and slow growth.

The first step toward a policy to promote economic growth is to maintain high employment of resources. This requires avoidance of both rapid inflation and deep recessions. Once started at a rapid rate, inflation cannot be halted without interrupting the growth of the economy, sometimes for long periods. Recession not only wastes human and physical resources but also leaves a legacy of inadequate investment, which retards the growth of productivity.

After high employment has been achieved, the growth rate can be increased only by raising the rate of growth of potential output. This will require more saving and more investment. The best strategy for increasing saving and investment is to combine a large budget surplus with a relatively easy money policy. The surplus would increase national saving; easy money would increase private investment by making credit more readily available and by reducing interest rates. Saving and investment incentives may also be improved through higher depreciation allowances, investment credits, and other structural tax provisions.

CHAPTER THREE

The Tax Legislative Process

THE PROCESS of decisionmaking in tax policy is one of the most interesting, puzzling, and controversial features of the federal legislative process. It can be speedy and effective or slow and ponderous. A small army of people participate, but only a few key figures are familiar to the public. The process has been criticized by many, but attempts to alter it have been unavailing.

Basic to an understanding of how the process works is the stipulation in Article I, Section 8, of the Constitution that "Congress shall have power to lay and collect taxes." Congress has always guarded its taxing power jealously. Presidents can recommend changes, but only Congress has the power to translate these recommendations into law. Practically every major presidential tax proposal is thoroughly revised by Congress, and not a few are either ignored or rejected outright.

A tax law is always a compromise among the views of powerful individuals and groups. The president, the secretary of the treasury, and members of the two congressional tax committees—the House Committee on Ways and Means and the Senate Committee on Finance—are subject to great pressure from the numerous political, economic, and social groups affected by the bill or attempting to have it changed to their advantage. Substantial delays in enactment of tax legislation occur when the participants have difficulty finding a formula to reconcile major opposing interests.

The tax legislative machinery is backed by competent staffs of experts in both the legislative and executive branches of the federal government. Taxation is one of two major policy areas to which a joint congressional committee is assigned (the other is economic policy). Established in 1926, the ten-member Joint Committee on Taxation (formerly the Joint Committee on Internal Revenue Taxation) consists of five senior members each from the House Ways and Means Committee and the Senate Finance Committee. The five members from each house include three from the majority party and two from the minority party. Its official functions are to review large refunds proposed by the commissioner of internal revenue and to make studies for the two tax committees. The Joint Committee itself does not participate in the legislative process. In practice, it provides a technical staff of about forty lawyers and economists to prepare and advise on tax legislation for the committees. Additional staff help is furnished to the majority and minority members by the committees themselves and by the legislative counsels of the House and Senate, who do the actual drafting. In recent years, the tax staff of the Congressional Budget Office, consisting of about a dozen economists, has prepared analyses of tax issues for use by the committees and members of Congress. Treasury experts are also available for assistance during the legislative process. Through long and intimate association, the committees have learned to rely on the various staffs for background information needed to help formulate a consensus and to assist in translating committee decisions into legislative language.

The present tax structure is an outgrowth of legislation dating back to the beginning of the republic. The laws were first assembled and codified in the Internal Revenue Code of 1939, which was completely revised and superseded by the Internal Revenue Code of 1954. Changes in the tax laws have since been enacted as amendments to the 1954 code.

The code is a technical and complex legal document. Many of its sections reflect years of study and analysis by government and nongovernment tax experts. Few people have mastered its technicalities and nuances. Nevertheless, it is the vehicle through which the federal government now collects over $700 billion of internal revenues annually. It is also the basis on which each year over 170 million tax returns are filed, 75 million refunds are paid, 3 million delinquency notices are served to taxpayers, and more than 1,500 people are convicted of tax crimes.

Between 1948 and 1982 Congress enacted twenty-two major tax bills and dozens of lesser bills. Most bills required months of preparation before the president made his recommendation, and from one to forty-four months before it was passed by Congress. (In a few cases, notably in 1954, 1976, and 1982, the bills originated in Congress and did not follow from presidential recommendations.) The two tax committees listened to hundreds of witnesses present thousands of pages of testimony. The final bills ranged in size from a few pages to a peak of 984 pages in 1954, when the code was recodified. Nine of the major bills increased taxes on balance, twelve reduced them, and in one tax liabilities remained unchanged; the amounts involved ranged from increases of $10.2 billion in 1968 and $27.0 billion in 1982 to a reduction of $162.1 billion in 1981 (table 3-1).

The tax system cannot be understood without an appreciation of the personalities, pressures, forces, and conflicts that come into play in making the many difficult decisions that shape a tax bill. This chapter describes the manner in which Congress considers and enacts tax legislation and also describes some of the key actors in the process. It is concerned only with tax legislation; tax administration and enforcement, which play an extremely important role in the taxpayer's dealings with the tax system, fall outside the scope of this book.

Executive Preparation of a Tax Bill

The Treasury Department has primary responsibility for the vast amount of work that goes into preparation of the president's tax recommendations. The work is supervised by the assistant secretary for tax policy. He has at his disposal three staffs: an Office of Tax Analysis, consisting of about thirty-five economists and statisticians who provide economic analyses of domestic and foreign tax issues, estimates of the revenue effects of tax changes, and revenue projections for the budget; an Office of the Tax Legislative Counsel, consisting of about twenty tax attorneys and an expert in accounting who are responsible for legal and accounting analyses of tax problems, drafting of tax legislation, and review and approval of tax regulations; and an Office of International Tax Counsel, consisting of six attorneys who are responsible for negotiating tax treaties and for legal analysis of tax issues and legislation concerning foreign-source income and foreign citizens. The assistant secretary calls on the technical, legal, and statistical facilities of the Internal Revenue Service for assistance as needed. He may also seek advice or assistance from consultants in academic, business, and professional fields or in other government agencies.

It is difficult to pinpoint how and when the decision is made to study a particular tax or set of taxes. The impetus often comes from outside groups and experts after considerable public discussion, agitation, and pressure, or from staff recommendations based on their analysis of the issues and discussions with business and academic groups. Occasionally the congressional committees request assurances that certain matters

Table 3-1. Legislative History of Major Federal Tax Bills Enacted, and Revenue Gain or Loss, 1948–82

Title of act	Date of president's message	Date of House passage	Date of Senate passage	Date of enactment	Time between initiation and enactment (months)	Full-year revenue gain (+) or loss (−) (billions of dollars)
Revenue Act of 1948	a	2/2/48	3/22/48	4/2/48[b]	3[c]	−5.0
Revenue Act of 1950	1/23/50	6/29/50	9/1/50	9/23/50	8	+4.6
Excess Profits Tax Act of 1950	d	12/5/50	12/20/50	1/3/51	3	+3.3
Revenue Act of 1951	2/2/51	6/22/51	9/28/51	10/20/51	8	+5.7
Internal Revenue Code of 1954	1/21/54[e]	3/18/54	7/2/54	8/16/54	7	−1.4
Excise Tax Reduction Act of 1954	a	3/10/54	3/25/54	3/31/54	2[c]	−1.0
Federal-Aid Highway Act of 1956	2/22/55	4/27/56	5/29/56	6/29/56	16	+2.5
Revenue Act of 1962	4/20/61[f]	3/29/62	9/6/62	10/16/62	18	−0.2[g]
Revenue Act of 1964	1/24/63	9/25/63	2/7/64	2/26/64	13	−11.4
Excise Tax Reduction Act of 1965	5/17/65[f]	6/2/65	6/15/65	6/21/65	1	−4.7
Tax Adjustment Act of 1966	1/24/66[e]	2/23/66	3/9/66	3/15/66	2	h
Revenue and Expenditure Control Act of 1968	8/3/67	2/29/68	4/2/68	6/28/68	11	+10.2
Tax Reform Act of 1969	4/21/69	8/7/69	12/11/69	12/30/69	8	−2.5
Revenue Act of 1971	8/15/71	10/6/71	11/22/71	12/10/71	4	−8.0
Tax Reduction Act of 1975	1/15/75	2/27/75	3/22/75	3/29/75	2	−22.8[i]
Tax Reform Act of 1976	a	12/4/75	8/6/76	10/4/76	44[c]	+1.6[j]
Tax Reduction and Simplification Act of 1977	2/22/77[e]	3/8/77	4/29/77	5/23/77	3	−8.6[k]
Revenue Act of 1978	1/30/78	8/10/78	10/10/78	11/6/78	9	−18.9[k]
Crude Oil Windfall Profit Tax Act of 1980	4/26/79	5/28/79	11/17/79	4/2/80	11	+12.2
Economic Recovery Tax Act of 1981	2/18/81[e]	7/29/81	7/31/81	8/13/81	6	−162.1[l]
Tax Equity and Fiscal Responsibility Act of 1982	a	12/15/81	7/23/82	9/3/82	11[c]	+27.0
Highway Revenue Act of 1982	11/30/82	12/7/82	12/21/82	1/5/83	1	+3.7

Sources: *Congressional Record, Congressional Quarterly, Annual Reports of the Secretary of the Treasury,* and *General Explanations* of revenue acts by the Joint Taxation Committee.

a. Not recommended by the president.

b. Passed by Congress over the president's veto.

c. Time elapsed from date of first consideration by House Ways and Means Committee.

d. Revenue Act of 1950 directed the House and Senate tax committees to report to their respective houses on excess profits tax bill retroactive to July 1 or October 1, 1950. No special message by the president.

e. Recommended by the president in his budget message.

f. Recommended initially in the budget message transmitted in January of the year indicated.

g. Net after offsetting revenue increases of about $800 million.

h. Bill introduced graduated withholding for individual income tax purposes and accelerated corporation income tax payments, but did not alter tax liabilities.

will be taken up in the next tax bill. Or the president, after formal or informal consultation with his advisers, may signal a new departure in tax policy in a speech or news conference. For example, the first official word that President John F. Kennedy was considering a large tax reduction came in a news conference on June 7, 1962; and President Ronald Reagan proposed the three-year tax cut enacted by Congress in 1981 during his campaign for election.

Studies of possible tax legislation are constantly in progress at the Treasury, the Joint Taxation Committee, and the Congressional Budget Office. Intensive work on a particular measure in the executive branch may begin after a decision is made by the president on the advice of responsible officials in his administration. The Council of Economic Advisers and the Office of Management and Budget are equal partners in making decisions on fiscal policy, and they participate in decisions on major features of the tax bill. Decisions on technical tax questions in proposed legislation are usually made within the Treasury (subject, of course, to the approval of the president).

Materials prepared by the Treasury on the various aspects of the tax program include economic, legal, and accounting memorandums discussing each problem from almost every angle. The analysis reviews the history of the problem, evaluates its impact on particular groups and industries and on the economy as a whole, and presents the equity, economic, revenue, and administrative arguments for and against various solutions. Lawyers, accountants, economists, and statisticians participate in this evaluation. Task forces, committees, or informal working groups consisting of representatives of the Treasury, other federal agencies, and congressional staffs may be organized to consider alternative solutions. At one time, most of the work was done within the executive branch, but in recent years members of the staffs of the tax-writing committees and of the Joint Taxation Committee have played crucial roles in formulating ideas for new tax legislation. Discussions are held by executive and congressional personnel with industry and labor representatives, officials of business corporations, professional groups, the academic community, and other knowledgeable people. The extent of outside participation varies from pro forma consultation to actual

i. Includes $8.1 billion rebate on 1974 individual income taxes.

j. Does not include the effect of estate and gift tax revisions, which reduced revenues by $728 million in fiscal 1978 and by increasing amounts to $1.4 billion in fiscal 1981.

k. Excludes revenue effect of extending temporary tax provisions or making them permanent.

l. Revenue effect in 1984 when second- and third-year tax cuts are fully effective.

development and drafting of specific legislative proposals. (For example, the 1981 depreciation provisions were drafted by outside experts who assisted President Reagan in the development of his tax program.)

Work on a major tax bill begins months before the administration's recommendations are transmitted to the Congress; in some cases, the lead time may be as much as a year or longer. (There is a separate track for "technical" bills, miscellaneous tax legislation, and special interest bills, which are managed primarily by the congressional staffs and are fed into the legislative calendar when time permits or when an influential committee member can persuade the chairman to take up the bill.) The information amassed during these months of research and analysis is funneled through the assistant secretary for tax policy. He may initiate new studies, suggest other approaches, and ask for still more information. He also consults the various experts individually or in groups to narrow the range of alternatives. The secretary of the treasury keeps in touch with the work at all stages and makes the final decision on the program that is submitted to the president, after consulting other government officials and members of the White House staff.

In a typical year the main features of the administration's tax proposals are completed by mid-December. At this time, the president reviews the proposals and approves or modifies them. Final revenue figures are estimated by the Treasury on the basis of an economic projection prepared by the Council of Economic Advisers in consultation with other federal agencies. Drafts of sections to be included in the budget message and the economic report are prepared, and a start is made on the materials to be submitted for congressional consideration.

The president sometimes mentions the broad outlines of his tax program in the State of the Union message. Further elaboration is given in the budget message, which must be transmitted fifteen days after Congress convenes, and the broad economic justification is presented in the economic report, which is due on or before January 20. (In practice, there is some slippage, and with the consent of Congress the messages may be transmitted one or two weeks after they are legally due.) When the program covers a broad field or is particularly complicated, or when the president wishes to emphasize the importance of his recommendations, he transmits a special tax message to Congress, usually at the end of January or in February; occasionally, when circumstances require new tax legislation, a special tax message is transmitted later in the year.

Disclosure of a major tax program signals the beginning of public debate. Representatives of business, farm, labor, and other groups begin to make pronouncements about the wisdom of the program. National organizations like the U.S. Chamber of Commerce, the National Association of Manufacturers, the AFL-CIO, the major labor unions, trade associations, and citizens' committees scrutinize the program carefully from the standpoint of their own interests and what they regard as the public interest. Major aspects of the program are discussed in newspapers and periodicals and on radio and television.

By the time the House Ways and Means Committee opens public hearings on the bill (usually in February or March), the lines of support and opposition are drawn. At this point Congress takes over.

The Bill in Congress

Article I, Section 7, of the Constitution states: "All bills for raising revenue shall originate in the House of Representatives." Accordingly, a tax bill technically begins its legislative history in the House and is transmitted to the Senate after the House has completed action. In every other way the Senate is an equal partner in the tax legislative process and frequently makes extensive and fundamental changes in the House version. In recent years, the Senate has proceeded on its own and attached major provisions or major new tax legislation onto minor bills sent over by the House.

The Ways and Means Committee

The tax legislative process begins in the Committee on Ways and Means of the House of Representatives. The committee consists of thirty-five members divided between majority and minority parties in approximate proportion to their representation in the House. It has responsibility for revenue, debt, customs, foreign trade, health, welfare, and social security legislation—which makes it the most powerful committee in the House.

The committee begins its study by scheduling public hearings for persons who request an opportunity to testify. The Ways and Means Committee room, which seats 250 people, is usually filled to capacity for the first witness, the secretary of the treasury. His testimony typically begins with a long statement prepared by the office of the assistant secretary for tax policy, which gives the full rationale for the administration's position. For example, Secretary W. Michael Blumenthal's presentation on the 1978 bill in January 1978 lasted two days and totaled 525 closely printed pages, including a main oral statement of 54 pages and 471 pages of supplementary tables, technical explanations, and memorandums of analysis.

The secretary ordinarily reads his statement without interruption. The chairman then opens the interrogation and turns the questioning over to each member of the committee, alternating between majority and minority party members in order of seniority. Committee members may take this opportunity to make a public record of the positions they expect to take. Sympathetic members ask questions to buttress the administration's position or to help prepare the way for suitable compromises on difficult issues; those who are opposed attempt to trap the secretary into making untenable, erroneous, and inconsistent statements so as to discredit the tax proposals. The secretary, in turn, is usually well briefed and handles most of the questions himself, turning to an associate for assistance only in connection with technical matters. Occasionally, he handles a question by promising a written reply to be included in the printed record.

After the secretary's testimony, the committee may hear witnesses from other executive agencies. Frequently, the director of the Office of Management and Budget and the chairmen of the Council of Economic Advisers and the Federal Reserve Board are asked to appear before the committee. Testimony is then heard from bankers, businessmen, lawyers, economists, and others representing the interests of private groups (and sometimes of individual clients). Except when the administration's witnesses testify, the broader "public interest" is not usually well represented. In recent years, representatives of public interest organizations have begun to appear, and in a few instances the committee has invited professional economists and tax lawyers to testify as experts, but the preponderance of the testimony is from special interest groups.

Meanwhile, the committee members are besieged in private by large numbers of people seeking changes in the bill. Through these contacts, the committee evaluates the strength of the forces aligned for and against each provision of the bill.

The hearings continue until all interested parties have testified. The length of the hearings depends on the importance of the bill, the controversy it has aroused, and the positions of the committee chairman and ranking members. If there is considerable opposition, the hearings may continue for months. Thus, fifteen days of hearings were held in 1981 by the Ways and Means Committee on what eventually became the

Economic Recovery Tax Act of 1981, but the 1973 hearings on the bill that ultimately became the Tax Reform Act of 1976 lasted about three months.

After concluding the hearings, the committee goes into a markup session in which draft legislation is prepared for presentation to the House. Formerly held as closed-door executive sessions, these meetings have been open to the public since 1974. This change has generated considerable controversy, with proponents claiming that such "sunshine" procedures are necessary to bring congressional decisionmaking into the open and opponents claiming that decisions made in full view of the lobbyists will be more favorable to the special interests. Although the House rules specify that the full committee must vote in open session, the committee may vote to hold a closed session; moreover, members of each party caucus separately to consider their positions on proposed legislation. As a result, there are numerous important negotiations on a tax bill that are not observed by the public.

The markup sessions are conducted in an informal, seminar type of atmosphere. Members of the committee discuss the bill freely, calling mostly on the congressional staffs and sometimes on the Treasury and the Internal Revenue Service for information and assistance. Each proposal is carefully explained by staff members, and the relevant information and opinions assembled during the hearings are summarized. Votes are taken only after members are satisfied that they have all the information needed to make up their minds.

Several people play a major role in the process of negotiation and compromise that takes place in a markup session. The most important is the chairman of the Ways and Means Committee, who is not only the presiding officer but also the chief moderator. The ranking spokesman for the minority exercises substantial influence, particularly if he can persuade a few members of the majority to side with him. The partisan professional staffs also influence the decisions of their superiors on tax matters. The chief of staff of the Joint Taxation Committee supervises the large secretariat that assists the Ways and Means Committee in its deliberations. He attends all sessions, joins in negotiations on the bill, and helps shape compromises proposed by the chairman and other committee members. The assistant secretary of the treasury acts as chief negotiator for the administration (under instructions from the president and the secretary of the treasury).

As tentative decisions are reached, they are translated into legislative language. Preparation of the legislative draft is the responsibility of the legislative counsel of the House of Representatives, but the staffs of the Ways and Means Committee, the Joint Taxation Committee, and the Treasury are regularly called on for assistance. The drafting process is painstaking, as the draft must make the intent of the committee as explicit and the provisions of the bill as unambiguous as possible. At the same time, crucial technical details must be resolved in order to make complicated provisions workable and administrable. Considering the complexity of the material and the time pressures on those who are responsible for the drafting, relatively few errors are made in the process, which is usually completed shortly after the last tentative decision has been made by the committee.

At this time, work begins on the committee's report under the direction of the chief of staff of the Joint Taxation Committee. The report, frequently several hundred pages in length, contains a detailed statement of the committee's rationale for recommending the bill, estimates of its effect on revenues, and a section-by-section analysis of its provisions. It also contains the minority views of committee members who disapprove of the bill. As the only written record of the reasons for the committee's actions, the report serves to inform members of the House and provides a basis for later interpretation of the legislation by the Internal Revenue Service and the courts.

When the report is completed, the chairman of the Ways and Means Committee sends the bill to the House.

House Approval

According to the rules of the House of Representatives, revenue legislation is "privileged" business, which is given priority consideration on the floor. In practice, however, the approval of the Rules Committee is sought before the bill is placed on the calendar for floor action. This is done so that the tax bill can be debated under a "modified closed rule," which requires the House to accept or reject the entire bill except for a limited set of amendments approved for a floor vote by the Ways and Means Committee.

Because it is conducted under a modified closed rule, debate on the tax bill in the House is brief, usually lasting only two or three days. The Ways and Means Committee chairman acts as floor manager and chief proponent. Other members of the majority are assigned to defend particular aspects of the bill. The opposition, led by the ranking minority member of the committee, may attack the bill with vigor and predict great harm to the nation if it is enacted. But the chairman and ranking minority member of the committee often work closely together on a tax bill and occasionally join forces to push a tax bill through the House.

At the end of the debate, a motion is presented to recommit the bill to the Ways and Means Committee, sometimes with instructions to report it back with one or more specified amendments. This motion enables opponents of the bill to obtain a vote on a modified version without having to reject the bill altogether. Then there is a final vote on the bill itself. Only on rare occasions has a major tax bill reported by the Ways and Means Committee been rejected by the House.

The Senate Finance Committee

After House passage, the bill is sent to the Senate, where it is immediately referred to the Committee on Finance. This committee of twenty influential senators has jurisdiction over taxation, foreign trade, health, social security, revenue sharing, veterans' affairs, and other financial matters. Its organization and operations are similar to those of the Ways and Means Committee.

The Finance Committee begins by holding public hearings (sometimes while similar hearings are taking place in the House), and the secretary of the treasury is again the principal witness. His appearance here is no less an ordeal than his appearance before the Ways and Means Committee. He may largely repeat his arguments, though focusing his testimony on the House version of the bill. He may ask the committee to modify or reject certain provisions that are unacceptable to the administration; or he may accept the House modifications with only a slight demurrer. The secretary is followed by much the same parade of witnesses that appeared before the Ways and Means Committee, in many instances repeating their earlier statements, but often focusing on their objections to particular provisions of the House bill.

In the markup sessions, most of the cast of characters that assisted on the House side now appears on the Senate side. The administration and the representatives of private groups lobby vigorously for their views while these sessions are in progress.

The Finance Committee considers amendments to the bill proposed by its members, frequently in response to the proposals of special interest groups. On rare occasions the committee approves a substantially unamended version of the bill, but typically the bill is changed significantly before it is reported to the Senate. For example, the Senate Finance Committee report on the 1976 tax bill listed over sixty major amendments to the House bill and converted the revenue gained from tax reform to a large revenue loss. The entire 1982 tax reform bill was tacked on by the Finance Committee to a House bill consisting of five miscellaneous tax provisions, because the House did not have a major tax bill of its own.

When the Finance Committee has agreed on a bill, the staff prepares the committee report, which covers the same ground as the Ways and Means Committee report (often in identical language) and explains the reasons for the Finance Committee amendments.

The Senate Debate

Unlike the House, the Senate places no limit on debate or amendments to a tax bill (although debate on budget reconciliation bills, which often include tax legislation, is limited to twenty hours). Many amendments are offered on the floor. Some are intended to change the entire character of the bill, and some are completely unrelated to its subject matter. Administration officials are usually very active at this stage. The president's aides and Senate leaders of his party work together to defeat amendments that are unacceptable to the administration or to restore provisions deleted by the Finance Committee.

Senate discussion of a tax bill is longer and more colorful than that in the House. Individual senators take the occasion not only to go on record but also to try to persuade their colleagues. The debate usually concerns features of the bill that directly affect the pocketbooks of particular groups and individuals and is often highly technical. The debates on many of the tax bills (for example, on the 1951, 1962, 1964, 1969, and 1976 acts) are among the most informed discussions held on the Senate floor.

Most of the amendments proposed on the floor are opposed by the administration or the Finance Committee and are rejected; but the Senate has been known to act against the wishes of both the administration and the committee majority. On the other hand, the Senate debate is another stage in the entire legislative process when the administration may successfully exercise pressure (including the threat of a presidential veto) against the wishes of the powerful committee chairman and ranking committee members. Such pressure is used sparingly and only when needed on a major issue.

After the bill has been debated and amended to the satisfaction of the Senate, it is brought to a vote. If it fails to pass, the bill will normally be sent back to the committee, but sometimes the legislation is abandoned. If the Senate passes the House bill without amendments, it is sent directly to the president. If the Senate amends the bill—and this is the rule rather than the exception—further congressional action is necessary. (During the twenty-five days of Senate debate on the Tax Reform Act of 1976, 209 amendments were proposed, of which 143 were accepted and made part of the Senate version of the bill.) The House generally adopts a motion to disagree with the Senate amendments, thus calling for appointment of a conference committee to adjust the differences between the two versions.

The Bill in Conference

The conference committee is appointed by the speaker of the House and the president of the Senate. Each usually appoints four or five from the majority and three or four from the minority. On occasion, there is a difference in the number of conferees from the two chambers, but this has no bearing on the final decision reached by the committee, since each chamber votes as a unit with a majority controlling each group. The members of the committee are normally the senior members of the two tax committees, unless they elect not to serve.

Conferees are usually presented large "blue books" detailing issue by issue the provisions of the House and Senate bills and the differences between them. Technically, the conferees are charged only with eliminating differences, but in practice they may go beyond their mandate. For example, in 1982 the conferees lowered the thresholds at which unemployment insurance would be taxed, even though neither the House nor the Senate bill had dealt with the issue. However, the change was needed to accommodate an increase in unemployment benefits without raising the cost of the bill.

The conferees, including even the minority members, are usually committed to arriving at a compromise. Special interest groups are often excluded from observing this final process, in part because some of the provisions they seek must be dropped in order to reach an explicit or implicit revenue target. When the conferees are close to a decision, they may meet in a small room in the Capitol, effectively excluding special interest groups altogether or limiting the number of staff participants.

Conferences may last from a day or two to a week or more, depending on the number of amendments, differences between the two versions, and the complexity of the bill under consideration. Congressional and Treasury staff members are called upon to explain the issues, evaluate the feasibility of suggested compromises, and provide revenue estimates. It is common for the members from each house to meet separately and in private, using staff members as go-betweens to arrive at compromises. The formal sessions of the conference committee are open to the public, but they are used merely to announce the decisions made in private. The bill remains in conference until all differences between the House and Senate versions have been reconciled. High officials of the administration, including the secretary of the treasury and the president, follow the deliberations of the committee carefully and may intervene (directly or through subordinates) with individual conferees to obtain support for the administration's position.

The conference report lists the amendments accepted by each house and gives a highly technical explanation of the changes. Floor statements explaining how the two bills were reconciled provide the essential information necessary for interpreting the legislation.

After approval of the conference report by both houses, the bill is sent to the White House.

Presidential Action

As is the case in all legislation, the president has ten days to consider the bill. During this period, the various government departments analyze the bill and submit their views in the form of written memorandums to the Office of Management and Budget. The major issues are then summarized by the OMB, and the president makes his final decision, often after hours of consultation and soul-searching with key officials and White House staff members.

By the time the bill reaches the president's desk, administration forces in Congress have tried every legislative device to modify it to meet his requirements. For this reason, the president rarely vetoes a tax bill, even though few of them satisfy him in every detail. In the past thirty-five years, only four important tax bills have been vetoed: the Revenue Act of 1943, by President Franklin D. Roosevelt; the Revenue Act of 1948, on three occasions in 1947 and 1948 by President Harry S. Truman; the Revenue Adjustment Act of 1975, by President Gerald R. Ford; and the congressional rollback of an oil import fee, which he had originally imposed, by President Jimmy Carter in 1980. Congress passed the 1943 and 1948 tax bills and the 1980 rollback of the oil import fee over the presidents' vetoes by the necessary two-thirds majority. (The 1943 veto led to the temporary resignation of Senator Alben Barkley from his position as majority leader.) The Tax Reduction Act of 1975, which extended the 1975 tax cuts to 1976, was signed by the president after Congress revised the original bill to include compromise language expressing the intention of Congress to combine further tax reductions with expenditure reductions.

The president usually issues a statement when he has acted on the bill. If he has approved it, the statement is brief and expresses pleasure at its enactment. Occasionally he takes exception to some of its provisions, even though he has signed it, or claims credit for tax reductions he did not propose. If he has vetoed the bill, he issues a longer statement or message explaining why it is unacceptable.

A tax bill may stipulate that the rates take effect within a few days after its final approval. For example, the lower withholding rates provided by the 1964 act became effective eight days after the president signed it. Some of the excise tax reductions of 1965 were put into effect the day following enactment. The 1982 act was approved by the president on August 13, 1981, and the first of three personal income tax cuts became effective through withholding on October 1, 1981. Some tax bills have been retroactive, reducing or increasing tax liabilities from the beginning of the calendar year, fiscal year, or quarter in which the bill was finally approved. Others have taken effect at the end of the year.

After the president has signed the bill, the Internal Revenue Service prepares to administer the new law by issuing new tax forms, advice to taxpayers, revised instructions to withholding agents, and so on, and new regulations are prepared by the Treasury. The issuance of regulations may be a lengthy process, sometimes requiring several years if the legislation is particularly complex. Long before these tasks have been completed, a new tax bill may be under way, and the same harassed officials who are responsible for implementing the old law begin the new tax legislative cycle.

Improving the Process

The tax legislative process has been examined by numerous congressional committees, political scientists, students of taxation, citizen and professional committees, and other groups. Opinion is generally critical: tax laws are unnecessarily detailed and complicated and divert attention from the major policy issues; the committees and other members of Congress are said to be unnecessarily influenced by special interest groups who do not speak in the national interest; and there is no systematic way to consider revisions of the structure of the tax system. However, revised procedures were enacted in 1974 for congressional consideration of the budget. The process has been effective in coordinating overall tax and expenditure policies, and it has had considerable effect on tax legislation.

Simplifying the Tax Law

Almost every bill dealing with the structural provisions of the tax system contains a mass of detailed amendments to the Internal Revenue Code that deal with complicated, sometimes esoteric matters and are written in language that few people can understand. The committee reports on such bills, which are intended primarily to provide a legislative history and to explain the intent of Congress to the Internal Revenue Service and the courts, are also lengthy and difficult to understand. For example, the report of the Senate Finance Committee on the 1982 tax reform bill consisted of 465 closely packed pages of technical language. For anyone but the expert it is virtually impossible to distinguish the major issues from the minor in such a report, let alone to decide how they should be resolved.

When tax bills are finally brought to the floor of the House or Senate, few representatives or senators are familiar enough with the fine points to understand the implications of the legislation and to debate them with the committee chairmen, who have expert staff assistance to help them cope with the technicalities. Fewer still have the necessary skill and experience to introduce amendments on their own and to persuade the House or the Senate to overrule their tax committees. The emphasis on detail obscures the major policy issues, conceals large tax benefits that may be introduced by influential committee members on behalf of special interest groups, and slows down the pace of congressional action on tax reform.

The practice of legislating every detail of the tax structure arose partly because Congress has not been willing to leave the details of the tax law to the interpretation of tax administrators and partly because the courts have not consistently construed the code on the basis of underlying theme and congressional purpose. To break this practice, Congress would have to declare its intention to make general tax policy and leave the details to be worked out by the Treasury Department through its regulations. The specific language of the regulations might be subject to review and comments by the staff of the Joint Taxation Committee. When there are differences of opinion, the issues might be brought to the attention of the joint committee itself, which could consider remedial legislation if it concluded that the proposed regulations would not carry out the congressional intent. Many tax experts believe that the tax legislative and administrative process would be much more effective and less vulnerable to the influence of lobbyists under such a procedure, but the likelihood of its being adopted is admittedly small.

Representation of the Public Interest

Individuals who appear before the two tax committees hardly represent a cross section of opinion on tax matters. The committees generally permit representatives of organized groups to testify and even allow individuals to testify on behalf of their own views; expert testimony comes only from administration officials and, on occasion, a few invited economists and tax lawyers. The result is that, day after day, the committees are subject to a drumfire of complaints against the tax system, arguments against the elimination of special tax advantages, and reasons for additional preferences.

In such an atmosphere, the secretary of the treasury and, to a lesser extent, the chairmen of the tax committees assume the role of defenders of the national interest. They spend much of their time fighting off new tax advantages and are only moderately successful in eliminating old ones. Whether taxes are to be raised or lowered, most of the witnesses find good reasons for favoring the groups or individuals they represent. The secretary and the chairmen take a broader, national view and try to strike a balance among competing claims. Since the stakes are high and there are no generally accepted criteria for evaluating questions of tax policy, their decisions may be regarded as arbitrary or contrary to the public interest by some groups and vigorously opposed in open hearings or in behind-the-scenes lobbying. Occasionally, they are supported by some of the national citizens' organizations, but testimony from them— although more frequent in recent years—is still the exception rather than the rule.

Fortunately, the committee members are not neophytes in the legislative process. Most of them have the capacity to detect a self-serving witness. Furthermore, they have an excellent opportunity to check the merits of the public testimony in markup sessions or in private with the staffs of the Joint Taxation Committee, the Congressional Budget Office, and the Treasury and outside experts. When the issues are particularly significant and complicated, the staffs prepare summaries of the pros and cons of the various positions. (In 1975 twenty-seven pamphlets on specific tax reform issues were prepared for the Ways and Means Committee.) Through such methods, individual committee members familiarize themselves with the major issues and evaluate the mass of information hurled at them.

It would nevertheless be helpful to give the public, committee members, and other congressmen easier access to impartial analysis and expert opinion on tax matters. Two things can be done to improve consideration of tax legislation, particularly matters relating to tax structure.

First, the Joint Taxation Committee or the two separate committees might provide background material before a tax issue is put on the legislative calendar. It should be possible to divide the entire field of taxation into several categories and to hold periodic hearings on each category to keep the subject continually under review and to solicit new ideas. The procedures might follow the pattern set by the hearings on the Ways and Means Committee's famous 1959 *Tax Revision Compendium*, a three-volume collection of articles by leading tax experts, which has influenced professional and legislative views on tax policy for many years.

Second, the joint committee might organize expert commissions or task forces once every five years to review the major problems in taxation and to make recommendations for legislative action. This type of advisory council was set up to consider social security matters once every four years by the Social Security Act, and a special commission was appointed in 1981 to deal with the growing imbalance of social security benefits and receipts. These advisory groups have had a significant impact on the development of the social security system, particularly the 1981 commission, whose proposals, transmitted in January 1983, were enacted by the Congress and approved by the president virtually intact in April of the same year.

But procedural changes by themselves will not greatly improve the results of the tax legislative process. Powerful forces are arrayed against major changes in the tax structure, while there is no effective lobby for the general public. The key may be to reform the campaign financing laws so that congressmen will not be dependent on the financial support of powerful lobbies for their election. Until the people elect representatives and senators who are able to resist pressure from special interest groups, progress in reforming the tax system will continue to be slow.

Reforming the Tax Structure

A serious drawback of the tax legislative process is that revisions to modify the structure of the tax system (as distinct from changes in exemptions or tax rates) are difficult to make. Once a particular provision has been added to the internal revenue code, it usually remains there long after the reasons that led to its enactment cease to apply. Tax preferences are hard to dislodge, unless a president goes after them or the need for revenue is so urgent that the tax-writing committees are willing to entertain revisions to broaden the tax base.

Many tax experts and national citizens' organizations have recommended that the major tax provisions should automatically expire, say, once every five years. Such "sunset" provisions could force the administration and Congress to consider the pros and cons of every tax provision on a fixed time schedule and in a systematic way. The sunset dates could be staggered to ease the legislative burdens; for example, personal deductions could be considered one year, capital gains provisions a second year, capital-consumption allowances a third year, and so on. Similar sunset provisions now apply to a number of expenditure programs and to over twenty-five tax provisions (including such provisions as the residential energy tax credits, the tax exemption for small issues of industrial development bonds, and the charitable deduction for nonitemizers).

Sunset legislation for the internal revenue code has been introduced in Congress on a number of occasions. Although this approach merits consideration, Congress has shown little interest in implementing it. At a minimum, expiration dates should be attached to future tax expenditures and a schedule should be adopted by the tax-writing committees to review existing tax expenditures.

Consideration of Overall Fiscal Policies

Legislative control over the fiscal policies of the federal government was at one time divided between the appropriations committees and the tax committees. The appropriations committees, which act through a large number of subcommittees working on individual agency appropriations, view their role as primarily that of watchdog over the efficiency of government operations rather than of general policymaker; the tax committees tend to be conservative about changing the level of taxes, particularly in the upward direction.

Fiscal policy planning and guidance by the president are undertaken primarily through his annual budget messages and economic reports. These are reviewed and considered by the Joint Economic Committee, which was created by the Employment Act of 1946. Its hearings, which are usually brief but structured to bring out opposing views, and its report on the president's economic report have improved public and congressional understanding of economic policy problems. However, the Joint Economic Committee does not have authority to propose or initiate legislation.

A major impetus to reforming the congressional budget process was provided by President Nixon, who in 1973 attempted to impound appropriations previously approved by Congress and the president. Congress realized that it had no mechanism to prevent such action or even to consider it in relation to the budget as a whole. To establish an orderly process for budget planning, the Congressional Budget and Impoundment Control Act of 1974 was enacted. This act set up new procedures to prevent a president from impounding previously approved appropriations without congressional approval and also to reform the congressional budget process.

The legislation requires the president to notify Congress when he intends to impound any appropriations. The impoundments are allowed to take effect unless they are disapproved by both houses of Congress within forty-five days after the president's notification. During fiscal

1982 the president proposed the impoundment of appropriations of $7.7 billion, of which Congress approved $4.1 billion.

The Congressional Budget Act also set up new procedures for considering the president's budget and for making decisions on overall fiscal policy. The act requires Congress to approve two concurrent resolutions that will provide the basis for congressional consideration of taxes in relation to expenditures. The first resolution, which must be enacted by both houses by May 15 of each year, specifies levels of budget outlays and budget authority for the next fiscal year (which begins on October 1), the recommended level of taxation, the surplus or deficit that is "appropriate in the light of economic conditions," and the appropriate statutory debt limit. This resolution is intended to provide guidance to the committees that are responsible for decisions on appropriations and taxes. Reconciliation of actual legislation with the targets in the first budget resolution has been a major element in the tax legislative process in recent years. A second concurrent resolution reaffirming or revising the level of expenditures, appropriations, and receipts and the debt limit of the first resolution must be passed by September 15. (In some instances, the first resolution has stipulated that it will become the second if a second resolution has not passed by October 1.) Any differences between the amounts specified in the second resolution and the actions of the appropriations and tax committees must be reconciled by September 25, although this date is difficult to meet and has slipped badly on occasion. The resolutions are not subject to approval by the president, but Congress cannot adjourn for the year until the appropriations and taxes are reconciled with the budget resolution.

The legislation set up the Congressional Budget Office to provide expert staff support for Congress in evaluating the budget. The office, which is the congressional counterpart of the Office of Management and Budget in the executive branch, prepares a report on the choices in the president's budget within two weeks after the budget is submitted, makes budget projections for each of the next five fiscal years, estimates five-year costs of all bills reported out by congressional committees, and projects the revenue losses from tax expenditures (see appendix C). It also issues useful reports on specific budget issues, the state of the economy, and the relation between the budget and economic developments. The budget committees in both houses also have professional staffs to help them evaluate budget policies and to decide on the appropriate level of expenditures and revenues in the concurrent resolutions.

Congress has generally followed the new procedures. The resolutions are seriously debated in the committees and on the floor of each house. After enactment, Congress has usually lived up to the guidelines laid down in the resolutions; in several instances, the budget committee chairmen have succeeded in cutting appropriations that threatened to raise expenditures for particular categories above the limits set. Tax changes that would otherwise have taken a long time to implement are now legislated as part of the annual budget reconciliation process, either in a separate tax bill or in the final budget reconciliation bill. In 1981 President Reagan used the new congressional budget procedures to put his tax and expenditure program through Congress almost intact. In 1982 Congress enacted a tax increase over the initial objections of the president in order to reduce prospective deficits. Congress may have difficulty agreeing on a budget resolution, but this reflects the difficulty of the issues rather than an inadequacy of the procedures. While procedures alone cannot ensure good fiscal policies, Congress has taken the legislation seriously, and decisions on the budget are being made more often on the basis of overall economic and budgetary needs.

Summary

The tax legislative process begins in the Treasury and other federal agencies, where tax problems are analyzed and solutions are proposed for the president's consideration. The president transmits his recommendations to Congress, where they are carefully reviewed by the two powerful tax committees, revised to compromise the conflicts of major opposing interests, and sent in turn to the House and Senate floors for approval. Differences between the two bills are settled by a conference committee, the revised version is returned to both houses for approval, and the bill becomes law when the president signs it or when Congress passes it over his veto.

The tax legislative process is unique in several respects. The work concerns a highly complex set of laws, yet all the decisions are made (as they should be) through the political process. Leading roles are played by the president, the secretary of the treasury and his assistant secretary for tax policy, the chairmen of the two tax committees, and the chief of staff of the Joint Taxation Committee. Behind the scenes, competent staffs in both the executive and legislative branches help move the tax bill through its various stages. For all these people, passing a tax bill is a grueling experience, demanding physical stamina as well as analytical and political acumen.

Greater attention is being given in Congress to overall fiscal policies since the enactment of new congressional budget procedures in 1974 and the establishment of the Congressional Budget Office. However, reform of the tax process is still needed: first, to permit Congress to concentrate on major policy issues rather than on details of the tax law; second, to give better representation to the public interest in the deliberations of the Ways and Means Committee and the Finance Committee; and third, to create the conditions under which structural reform of the tax system is considered by Congress in a systematic way.

Some believe that the federal tax legislative process impedes progress toward a better tax system, but this is an unfair assessment of the work of the congressional tax committees and an unrealistic appraisal of the balance of forces for and against tax reform. Many questionable provisions have crept into the U.S. tax laws as a result of the influence of special interest groups. But the tax expenditure budget continues to call attention to the major tax preferences, and new proposals are being made to broaden the tax base and simplify the internal revenue code. The 1982 tax bill was a positive step toward tax reform. Moreover, the overall distribution of federal taxes continues to be progressive despite the strong interests arrayed against progressive and equitable taxation. More progress will be made along these lines only when sufficient political power is mobilized to persuade the tax committees, and Congress as a whole, that tax reform has widespread and determined popular support.

CHAPTER FOUR

The Individual Income Tax

ANY SURVEY of tax sources should begin with the nation's most productive source of revenue, the individual income tax. All advanced industrial countries levy a direct tax on individual incomes, but nowhere is this tax as important as in the United States. In recent years, 45 percent of federal budget receipts have come from this source.

The individual income tax is uniquely suited to raising revenue in a democratic country, where the distribution of income, and thus of ability to pay, is unequal. Theoreticians may disagree about the meaning of the term "ability to pay," but the close association between a person's income and his or her taxpaying ability is commonly accepted.

The individual income tax has still another attractive feature. Income alone does not determine a person's ability to pay; family responsibilities are also important. A single person may be able to get along on an income of $10,000 a year, but a married man with two children would have great difficulty in making ends meet on that income. The individual income tax takes such differences into account by allowing personal exemptions and deductions, which are subtracted from an individual's total income to arrive at the income subject to tax.

For almost thirty years after its adoption in 1913, the individual income tax applied mainly to a small number of high-income people. Exemptions were high by today's standards, and few incomes were large enough to be subject to tax at the lowest rate, let alone the higher graduated rates. In the national effort to raise needed revenue during World War II, exemptions were drastically reduced. They have been raised several times since then, but remain low by pre-1940 standards. Tax rates were also raised in World War II and have remained much higher than in earlier years. At the same time, personal incomes have continued to increase with the growth of the economy and with inflation. The combination of lower exemptions, higher rates, and higher incomes has increased the yield of the individual income tax manyfold. In 1939 tax liabilities were about $1 billion or almost 1 percent of personal income; in 1984 they will reach $330 billion, more than 12 percent of personal income.

This tremendous expansion would not have been possible without both ready compliance with income tax laws and effective administration. In many countries where compliance is poor and administration is weak, there is great reluctance to rely heavily on the income tax. In this country, the record of compliance is good—although it could still be improved—and practical methods have been developed for administering a mass income tax at a cost of only about 0.5 percent of the tax collected. In the early 1940s many people—even highly placed officials of the Internal Revenue Service—doubted that an income tax covering almost everyone could be administered effectively. Although some problems remain, in an advanced country the administrative feasibility of an individual income tax of almost universal coverage is no longer questioned.

There are good economic and social reasons for using the income tax as a major source of revenue. The automatic flexibility of the tax promotes economic stability, and the progressive rates reduce the concentration of economic power and control. Some believe that the income tax impairs work and saving incentives and thereby reduces the nation's economic growth. These are difficult questions, which will be discussed later. Nonetheless, it is correct to say that the modern individual income tax, if carefully designed and well administered, is a powerful and essential economic instrument for a modern industrial economy.

The Structure of the Federal Income Tax

The basic structure of the federal income tax is simple. Taxpayers add up their income from all taxable sources, subtract certain allowable deductions and exemptions for themselves, their spouses, their children, and other dependents, and then apply the tax rates to the remainder. But this procedure has many pitfalls for the taxpayer, and difficult questions of tax policy arise at almost every stage. It is therefore important to understand the main features of the income tax structure.

Adjusted Gross Income and Taxable Income

The two major concepts of income that appear on the tax return are adjusted gross income and taxable income.

Adjusted gross income is the closest approach in the tax law to what an economist might call "total income." But it departs from an economic definition of income in important respects. It is the total income from all taxable sources, less moving expenses and certain other expenses incurred by employees in earning that income, payments into self-employment or individual retirement accounts, a special deduction for two-earner couples, and alimony. In general, only *money* income is treated as taxable, but many items of money income are excluded. These include 60 percent of realized capital gains on assets held for more than one year, interest on state and local government bonds, certain transfer payments (for example, unemployment compensation and social security benefits of most workers, welfare payments, food stamps, and veterans' benefits), fringe benefits received by employees from their employers (the most important of these are contributions to pension and health plans), and income on savings through life insurance. The emphasis on money income means that unrealized capital gains, in-kind fringe benefits for employees, and such imputed incomes as the rental value of owner-occupied homes are automatically excluded.

Taxable income is computed by making two sets of deductions from adjusted gross income. The first are those personal expenditures that are allowed as deductions by law—charitable contributions; interest paid; state and local income, general sales, and property taxes; medical and dental expenses above 5 percent of adjusted gross income; and losses from casualty or theft above 10 percent of adjusted gross income. In lieu of these deductions, the taxpayer may use the *standard deduction*, which was 10 percent of adjusted gross income (up to a maximum of $1,000) for the period 1944–69 and was gradually increased to a flat $2,300 for single persons and $3,400 for married couples in 1979. Once converted to flat amounts, it was possible to incorporate the standard deduction in the rate schedules as a zero bracket and it is now called the *zero-bracket amount*.

When the standard deduction was first adopted in 1944, it was used by over 80 percent of those filing returns. As incomes have risen and deductible expenditures have increased, the percentage using the standard deduction has declined. In 1981 the standard deduction was still used on 63.8 million returns, or two-thirds of the 95.4 million filed (appendix table D-6). But the amount of the standard deduction was smaller than the itemized deductions, which have increased with the growth of homeownership, consumer credit, state and local taxes, and

Figure 4-1. *Ratio of Taxable Individual Income to Personal Income,*
1947–81[a]

Percent

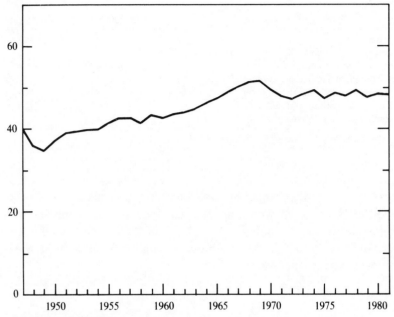

Source: Appendix table B-5.
a. Taxable income beginning in 1977 excludes zero-bracket amount.

higher interest rates as well as the normal increase in expenditures that
occurs as incomes rise. Total deductions reported on all 1981 returns
were $401 billion; of this amount, $145 billion were standard deductions
and $256 billion were itemized deductions.

The second set of deductions provides allowances for personal
exemptions. The exemptions for the taxpayer, his spouse, and other
dependents are $1,000 per person. The law also gives one additional
exemption each to the husband and wife if they are over sixty-five years
of age and still another exemption to the blind.

Figure 4-1 traces the changes in the tax base (that is, taxable income)
since World War II. In 1947 only about 40 percent of personal income
was subject to tax; this rose to 52 percent in 1969 and remained just
under 50 percent between 1970 and 1981. The increase was caused by
the upward shift in incomes during the postwar period. In 1981, 48.0
percent of personal income went into the tax base, 19.8 percent repre-

Table 4-1. *Derivation of the Federal Individual Income Tax Base from Personal Income, 1981*

Derivation of the tax base	Amount (billions of dollars)	Percentage distribution
Personal income	2,435	100.0
Conceptual differences between adjusted gross income and personal income[a]	482	19.8
Adjusted gross income not reported on tax returns or reported by individuals who were not taxable	232	9.5
Personal exemptions and deductions	551	22.6
Taxable income (tax base)	1,170	48.0

Source: Appendix tables B-2 and B-4. Figures are rounded.
a. For details, see appendix table B-1.

sented differences in definition between personal income and adjusted gross income, 9.5 percent either was not reported on tax returns or was reported by persons who were not taxable, and 22.6 percent was accounted for by exemptions and deductions (table 4-1). Stated somewhat differently, almost $5 billion out of every $10 billion of personal income went into the tax base.

Tax Rates

The tax rates are graduated by a bracket system (table 4-2). Under this system, the income scale is divided into segments, or brackets, and graduated rates are applied to the income in each bracket. Rates increase by no more than 6 percentage points from one bracket to the next to avoid large and abrupt increases in tax rates as incomes rise. People with taxable incomes of $50,000 or less read their tax liabilities directly from a tax table. Those with incomes above $50,000 calculate their tax liabilities from tax rate schedules.

There are now four rate schedules for different categories of taxpayers. The basic rates, which apply to married taxpayers filing separate returns, range from 11 percent in the first taxable income bracket above the zero-bracket amount to 50 percent in the top bracket. For married couples filing joint returns, the tax rates are applied to half the taxable income of the couple, and the result is multiplied by two. As table 4-2 shows, this income-splitting feature doubles the width of the rate brackets for married couples. Single persons have a special rate schedule that ensures that their tax is never more than 120 percent of the tax imposed on joint

Table 4-2. *Federal Individual Income Tax Rates, 1984*

Income in dollars; tax rates in percent

Married persons filing joint returns		Married persons filing separate returns		Single persons		Heads of households	
Taxable income	Tax rates	Taxable income	Tax rates	Taxable income	Tax rates	Taxable income	Tax rates
0–3,400	0	0–1,700	0	0–2,300	0	0–2,300	0
3,400–5,500	11	1,700–2,750	11	2,300–3,400	11	2,300–4,400	11
5,500–7,600	12	2,750–3,800	12	3,400–4,400	12	4,400–6,500	12
7,600–11,900	14	3,800–5,950	14	4,400–6,500	14	6,500–8,700	14
11,900–16,000	16	5,950–8,000	16	6,500–8,500	15	8,700–11,800	17
16,000–20,200	18	8,000–10,100	18	8,500–10,800	16	11,800–15,000	18
20,200–24,600	22	10,100–12,300	22	10,800–12,900	18	15,000–18,200	20
24,600–29,900	25	12,300–14,950	25	12,900–15,000	20	18,200–23,500	24
29,900–35,200	28	14,950–17,600	28	15,000–18,200	23	23,500–28,800	28
35,200–45,800	33	17,600–22,900	33	18,200–23,500	26	28,800–34,100	32
45,800–60,000	38	22,900–30,000	38	23,500–28,800	30	34,100–44,700	35
60,000–85,600	42	30,000–42,800	42	28,800–34,100	34	44,700–60,600	42
85,600–109,400	45	42,800–54,700	45	34,100–41,500	38	60,600–81,800	45
109,400–162,400	49	54,700–81,200	49	41,500–55,300	42	81,800–108,300	48
162,400 and over	50	81,200 and over	50	55,300–81,800	48	108,300 and over	50
				81,800 and over	50		

Source: Internal Revenue Code.

returns with the same total taxable income. Single persons who are heads of households also use a special rate schedule, with rates that are about halfway between the rates for single persons and the rates for joint returns.

Although the tax rates are graduated, much of the tax base is concentrated in the lowest brackets. In 1980, when the rate rose to a maximum of 70 percent (before credits), 55 percent of taxable income was subject to rates of less than 20 percent, and less than 4.4 percent was taxed at rates of more than 50 percent (appendix table B-6).

For taxpayers with certain tax preferences, the law requires payment of an *alternative minimum tax* to ensure that the tax is at least a minimum percentage of a broad measure of income. The tax base for the alternative minimum tax is adjusted gross income plus selected tax preferences less certain itemized deductions. The preferences are the 60 percent exclusion for long-term capital gains, accelerated depreciation, percentage depletion for oil and gas, intangible drilling and development expenses in excess of costs for oil and gas drilling, and the dividend exclusion. The itemized deductions include the deductions for casualty losses, charitable contributions, housing interest, and other interest up to the amount of property income reported on the returns. An exemption of

$30,000 ($40,000 for married couples) is allowed and the tax rate is 20 percent of alternative minimum taxable income.

Reporting Requirements

Tax returns must be filed by single persons with income above $3,300 and married couples filing joint returns with income above $5,400. These income limits are raised by $1,000 for persons who are over sixty-five years of age. Married persons filing separate returns and dependents with unearned income must file if their income is above $1,000.

Taxpayers may choose one of three forms for filing their final tax return. Form 1040 is the standard form, which is used by people with substantial incomes from nonwithheld sources and those who have itemized deductions. Form 1040A is a simpler form that can be used by persons with taxable income of less than $50,000 and with wages and salaries, unemployment compensation, and interest and dividends. Form 1040EZ is a still simpler form and may be used by persons with wages and salaries, no more than $400 of interest income, and taxable income of less than $50,000. In 1980, 57.1 million persons filed Form 1040 and the remaining 36.8 million filed Form 1040A. (Form 1040EZ was introduced in 1982.)

Methods of Tax Payment

Between 1913 and 1942 federal income taxes were paid in quarterly installments during the year following receipt of income. When the coverage of the income tax was extended to the majority of income recipients during World War II, it was realized that the old system could not operate successfully. People with low and middle incomes tend to use their income as it becomes available. Their future incomes are uncertain, and it is difficult to budget for taxes that do not become due until some time after the income is received. If income stops because of unemployment or sickness, an income tax debt accrued in the prior year may become a serious burden. Even high-income taxpayers find it easier to meet tax payments currently than a year later, particularly when incomes fluctuate. Synchronization of tax payments with receipt of income is also economically desirable to maximize the stabilizing effect of the income tax.

The current payment system, introduced in 1943, is based on the principle that taxes become due when incomes are earned, rather than in the following year when tax returns are filed. In practice, the system remains fully current for most wage and salary earners because their taxes are withheld by their employers. People who receive other types of income estimate their tax and pay it in quarterly installments during the year in which it is received.

WITHHOLDING. Withholding for income tax purposes applies at progressive rates (ranging from 12 percent to 37 percent in 1984) to the earnings of all employees except farm labor, domestic servants, and casual workers. Employees with additional income that is not subject to withholding may elect to have an extra amount withheld from their wages or salaries in order to reduce or avoid the quarterly installment payments. Withholding is also available for pensions and annuities at the request of the recipient.

The amounts withheld by the employer are remitted to the government quarterly if they total less than $200 a month. Employers withholding between $200 and $2,000 are required to deposit the tax withheld in an authorized bank within fifteen days after the end of the first two months of a quarter and by the last day of the month following the final month of a quarter. Employers withholding more than $2,000 a month are required to make deposits of the amounts withheld four times each month.

The withholding system is the backbone of the individual income tax. In 1981, the latest year for which data are available, the total tax liability amounted to $291.1 billion. Withholding brought in $261.0 billion; payments of estimated tax and tax credits, $50.6 billion; and final payments on April 15 of the following year, $34.9 billion. These payments exceeded the total tax due by $55.4 billion, which was refunded to the taxpayers or credited against next year's tax (appendix table D-7).

DECLARATION OF ESTIMATED TAX. Since withholding applies only to wages and salaries and the rate cuts off at 37 percent rather than 50 percent, millions of taxpayers do not have their taxes fully withheld; and no tax at all has to be withheld from nonwage sources. The declaration system was devised to take up the slack.

A declaration is required of all persons whose income is expected to exceed $20,000 ($10,000 for married persons if both spouses receive wages) or if the estimated tax exceeds the amount withheld by more than $400 in 1984 and $500 in 1985 and later years. Declarations are filed on or before April 15, and the estimated tax not withheld is payable in installments on April 15, June 15, and September 15 of the current year and January 15 of the following year (January 31 if paid with a final tax return). These requirements were set so that taxes will be paid currently by people whose income is not subject to withholding—farmers, businessmen, and recipients of property income—and people whose tax would be underwithheld because the withholding rates do not reach as high as the final tax rates. Farmers and fishermen may file their declarations on January 15 of the following year or omit them entirely if they file their final returns by March 1.

Taxpayers who do not pay as much as 80 percent of their final tax through withholding and declarations (66⅔ percent in the case of farmers and fishermen) pay an interest charge for the amount falling short of 80 percent. However, no interest is charged for any installment if the tax paid by the date of the installment is based on (a) the previous year's tax; (b) the previous year's income with the current year's rates and exemptions; or (c) 90 percent of the tax on the actual income received before the installment date.

As a result of the progressive withholding rates and the liberal requirements for declaration payments, the sums collected through declarations of estimated tax have been relatively small. Taxes withheld increased from $9.6 billion to $261.0 billion between 1944 and 1981, while declaration payments increased from $5.5 billion to $50.6 billion during the same period (appendix table D-7).

Final Tax Reconciliation

The reconciliation between final tax liability and prepayments is made on the final tax return, which is filed not later than April 15 (although an extension of two months can be automatically obtained by request). A taxpayer who owes more tax sends the Internal Revenue Service a check for the balance due along with the return; if too much tax has been withheld or paid as estimated tax, the excess is refunded or credited to the next year's tax if the taxpayer so requests.

Few returns have identical prepayments and final liabilities. In 1981 only 2.4 million out of a total of 95.4 million returns showed prepayments exactly equal to final liabilities (including returns of taxpayers who filed but were not subject to any tax). Of the remaining 93 million, 70 million received a refund check (or chose to credit the overpayment against the estimated tax for the following year), and 23 million had a balance of tax due (appendix table D-8).

Refunds greatly outnumbered balances of tax due for several reasons. (1) Withholding is based on the assumption that the employee works regularly (part time or full time), and thus the total amount of exemptions for the year is apportioned equally among pay periods; but employment is often irregular because of seasonality, changes of jobs, illness, and the like. (2) Employees may claim fewer exemptions for withholding purposes than they are entitled to. (3) The withholding tables allow only for the standard deduction, whereas many employees—particularly those who own homes—have large deductions, which they itemize when filing their returns. To moderate overwithholding on this latter score, those who have large itemized deductions are permitted to claim additional exemptions for withholding purposes, but they often fail to do so.

When the current payment system was adopted, great concern was expressed that overwithholding might be resented by taxpayers. Since the end of World War II, the number of returns with overpayments has never fallen below 30 million in any one year and it reached a high of 71.4 million in 1979 (appendix table D-8). But there have been few complaints. Apparently people would rather receive a check from the government than pay a tax bill, particularly since most of the refunds are mailed within two months after the tax return is filed.

Possible Modification of the Current Payment System

Proposals have been made to expand the withholding system to include incomes other than wages and salaries. On several occasions Congress has rejected plans for withholding on interest and dividends at a flat rate. A withholding system without exemptions was considered too burdensome for the aged and other nontaxable people; and corporations and other financial institutions paying interest and dividends argued that it would be too costly to administer a plan involving exemption certificates. However, in a quest for revenue in 1982, Congress extended withholding at a 10 percent rate to interest and dividend payments exceeding $150 a year, with an exemption for elderly married couples with income of less than about $22,000 a year ($14,000 for single persons). But the banks and saving and loan associations mounted a massive campaign to repeal the provision and Congress reversed itself in 1983. Instead, financial institutions and corporations were required to withhold 20 percent of interest and dividends of persons identified as having greatly underreported such income on their tax returns.

Economic Effects

Three issues are of particular importance in appraising the economic effects of the individual income tax: its role as a stabilizer of consumption expenditures, its influence on work incentives, and its effect on saving. In recent years, some economists who stress the "supply-side" view of economics have argued that reductions in marginal income tax rates would greatly stimulate work and saving incentives, increase the growth of output, and thus more than pay for themselves. The professional work on the effect of taxes on incentives is still in an early stage, but the studies completed so far indicate that the potential economic impact of tax cuts has been greatly exaggerated by the extreme proponents of the supply-side view.

Role as Stabilizer

Stability of yield was once regarded as a major criterion of a good tax. Today there is general agreement that properly timed changes in tax yields can help increase demand during recessions and restrain the growth of demand during periods of expansion. One of the virtues of the progressive individual income tax is that its yield automatically rises and falls more than in proportion to changes in personal income. Moreover, the system of paying taxes currently has greatly accelerated the reaction of income tax revenues to changes in income. An important by-product of current payment is that changes in tax rates have an almost immediate effect on the disposable income of most taxpayers. These features have made the personal income tax extremely useful for promoting economic stabilization and growth.

The automatic response of the individual income tax—its *built-in flexibility*—can be explained by the following example. Suppose a taxpayer with a wife and two children earns $15,000 a year when he is employed and uses the standard deduction. His taxable income is $7,600

($15,000 less $3,400 for the zero-bracket amount and $4,000 for personal exemptions), and the 1984 tax on that income is $959. The following table shows what the effect on his taxable income and tax would be if his income dropped to $10,000:

Adjusted gross income	$15,000	$10,000
Less exemptions	4,000	4,000
Less zero-bracket amount	3,400	3,400
Taxable income	7,600	2,600
Tax	959	291
Disposable income	14,041	9,709

Whereas adjusted gross income declined by 33 percent, taxable income was reduced 66 percent and the tax 70 percent.

Such examples are multiplied millions of times during a recession, while the opposite occurs during boom periods. Those with lower or higher incomes find that their tax is reduced or increased proportionately more than their income. As a result, disposable income is more stable than it would be in the absence of the tax. (In the above example, disposable income declined only $4,332 although income before tax dropped $5,000.) Since disposable income is a major determinant of consumption, expenditures of consumers are also more stable than they would be without the tax. On the other hand, if inflation occurs even when employment and output decline, tax receipts may actually rise as nominal incomes increase and the stabilizing effect of the income tax is reduced. If indexing takes place beginning in 1985, the stabilizing effect of the income tax will be limited to the reduction of tax liabilities resulting from changes in real income, and not from the inflation component of changes in income.

Changes in individual income tax rates or exemptions are also used to stimulate or restrain the economy. Substantial income tax reductions were made in 1964, 1971, and 1975 to raise consumer expenditures, while a special surtax was enacted during the Vietnam War to moderate the growth in private expenditures as wartime outlays rose. The tax cuts helped stimulate economic recovery, but the surtax did not restrain spending because monetary policy was relaxed prematurely and expectations of inflation were more pervasive than had been anticipated. Those who believe consumption is determined largely by what individuals regard as their "permanent" income argue that the surtax was not effective because it was a temporary tax change. Nevertheless, most economists are persuaded that income tax changes can contribute to regulating the rate of growth of private demand, but that permanent changes are more effective than temporary ones.

The 23 percent cut in income tax rates enacted in 1981, to take effect over a three-year period, was intended primarily as a long-run measure to reduce the burden of taxation and to stimulate work and saving incentives. The first and second rounds of the tax cut in October 1981 and July 1982 had no discernible effect on consumer spending, largely because monetary policy was tight and interest rates remained at extraordinarily high levels. (The July 1983 tax cut went into effect after this book went to press.) The 1981–82 recession was halted only after inflation had been sharply reduced and monetary policy was eased.

Work Incentives

The individual income tax affects work incentives in two different directions. On the one hand, it reduces the financial rewards of greater effort and thus tends to discourage work (the substitution effect). On the other hand, it may provide a greater incentive to obtain more income because it reduces the income left for spending (the income effect). There is no a priori basis for deciding which effect is more important.

Taxation is only one of many factors affecting work incentives. This makes it extremely difficult to interpret the available statistical evidence or the results of direct interviews with taxpayers. The evidence suggests that income taxation does not greatly reduce the amount of labor supplied by workers and managers who are the primary family earners. Work habits are not easily changed, and for most people in a modern industrial society there is little opportunity to vary their hours of work or the intensity of their efforts in response to changes in tax rates. Nearly all people who are asked about income taxation grumble about it, but relatively few say that they work fewer hours or exert less than their best efforts to avoid tax. The maximum 50 percent marginal tax rate on earned income, enacted in 1969, was justified on incentive grounds, but there is no evidence that it had a significant impact on labor supply.

Recent empirical work suggests that tax cuts would lead to an increase in labor supply, but the increase would not be nearly large enough to be self-financing. The effect of the present income and payroll taxes on the work effort of husbands is small (no more than about 8 percent), but the effect on the work effort of wives, who are usually the secondary earners in a family, is much more pronounced (as much as 30 percent on the average). Secondary earners have a much greater opportunity to vary their work effort than do primary earners, and econometric analyses have shown that they would respond to higher after-tax earnings by working longer hours. The special deduction for two-earner couples enacted in 1981 was justified in part as a method of encouraging spouses who might otherwise stay home to enter the labor force (see the section on the treatment of the family below). According to recent estimates, total labor supply might increase by about 5 percent if the present income tax were replaced by an equal-yield tax with a flat rate and a personal exemption.

Effect on Saving

The effect of taxes on saving is also ambiguous. Again, the substitution and income effects work against each other, and the net result cannot be predicted in advance. Some economists have made calculations suggesting that individuals save more if the after-tax return on saving increases, but other calculations suggest that the response, if any, is close to zero. The prevailing view is that saving does respond to an increase in the rate of return. The magnitude of the response is uncertain, but it would certainly not be large enough to increase output and the tax base enough to pay for a tax cut explicitly designed to increase the after-tax return on saving.

The individual income tax is often contrasted with a graduated consumption expenditure tax, which is an alternative method of taxing people on the basis of their "ability to pay." The income tax reduces the gain made when individuals save rather than consume part of their income, while an expenditure tax makes future consumption relatively as attractive as present consumption. Under the income tax, the interest reward for saving and investing is reduced by the tax; under the expenditure tax, the net reward is always equal to the market rate of interest regardless of the tax rate. Thus the consumption tax is neutral with respect to the consumption-saving choice, while the income tax distorts it. This means that an expenditure tax encourages saving more than does an equal-yield income tax that is distributed in the same proportions by income classes. The effect of substituting an expenditure tax for an income tax depends on how sensitive saving is to the interest rate; but, as already indicated, the interest elasticity of saving—and hence the magnitude of the effect—is not known. (For further discussion of the expenditure tax, see chapter 6.)

Numerous special provisions have crept into the U.S. tax law to promote particular types of saving (for example, investment in individual retirement accounts); other provisions permit individuals to "shelter" their income from tax (see the section on tax shelters below). Aside from providing unwarranted tax benefits in many cases, such provisions channel saving into assets yielding the highest after-tax returns, which are not necessarily the assets that yield the highest before-tax returns. In general, when faced with an array of assets with different degrees of preferential taxation, individuals will shift assets from the less to the more favored activities and equilibrium will be established when the after-tax returns are the same in all activities. As a result of this process, saving will be allocated to less productive uses than if the tax were uniform, and the distortions will reduce the productivity gains from investment.

Structural Problems

The personal income tax is determined by the definition of income, allowable deductions, personal exemptions, tax rates, and tax credits. These elements can be combined in various ways to produce a given amount of revenue. In recent years, there has been increasing recognition that the definition of taxable income under the U.S. tax law is deficient. Many of the exclusions and deductions are not essential for effective personal income taxation and have cut into the income tax base unnecessarily. This process of erosion has been halted in recent years, but only limited progress has been made in reversing it.

Erosion of the income tax base makes higher tax rates necessary. It puts a premium on earning and disposing of incomes in forms that receive preferential treatment, thus often distorting the allocation of resources. Under a progressive tax system, the tax value of any deduction or exclusion increases as the marginal tax rates increase, so that preferences (that are not in the form of tax credits) are most valuable to those with the highest incomes. Erosion also violates the principle that taxpayers with equal incomes should pay the same tax. These departures from vertical and horizontal equity, which often seem arbitrary, contribute to taxpayer dissatisfaction and create pressures for the enactment of additional special benefits—pressures that legislators find difficult to resist.

Most of the special provisions in the tax law are akin to direct government expenditures but are not explicitly included in the federal budget. For this reason they have been called "tax expenditures." In recent years, tax expenditures have amounted to over 40 percent of federal budget outlays (see appendix C).

Figure 4-2 shows the practical effect of the exemptions, deductions, and other special provisions of the income tax. If the total income reported by taxpayers were subject to the nominal tax rates, effective tax rates would begin at 11 percent and rise to almost 50 percent in the very highest brackets. But no taxpayers pay these rates on their entire income. The special provisions reduce the effective tax rates by about 12 percent at the $12,000 level and by over 20 percent at the higher income levels. Thus, after allowing for the special provisions, the *maximum average effective rate* for any income class is about 26 percent. Exemptions and the exclusions for unemployment compensation and social security benefits are most important in the low and middle income classes, and deductions are most valuable in the top classes. The capital gains and other preferences reduce taxes primarily for those in the top brackets. Income splitting and the 10 percent deduction for two-earner couples benefit those with incomes between $35,000 and $200,000 most. The effective rates shown in figure 4–2 are average rates, and there are wide variations in taxes paid at all income levels.

A personal income tax conforming strictly to the principle of horizontal equity is easily described but difficult to implement. It would include in the tax base all income from whatever source derived, permit deductions for the expenses of earning the income, and also make an allowance for taxpayers and their dependents through the personal exemptions. "Income" is defined by economists as consumption plus tax payments plus (or minus) the net increase (or decrease) in the value of assets during the taxable period. In practice, this definition is usually modified to exclude gifts and inheritances, which are subject to separate taxes, and, for practical reasons, to include capital gains only when realized or transferred to others, through gifts and bequests. In the discussion that follows, this comprehensive definition of income will be used as a basis for evaluating the major features of the income tax and the more important proposals for reform.

Personal Exemptions

The history of personal exemptions under the federal individual income tax in the United States since 1939 is summarized in figure 4-3. In constant dollars, exemptions for single persons and families show an

Figure 4-2. *Influence of Various Provisions on Effective Rates of Federal Individual Income Tax, 1985*

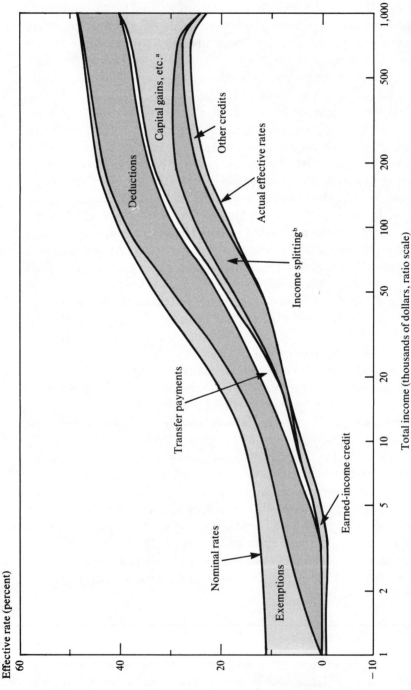

Effective rate (percent)

Total income (thousands of dollars, ratio scale)

Nominal rates

Exemptions

Earned-income credit

Transfer payments

Deductions

Capital gains, etc. [a]

Income splitting [b]

Other credits

Actual effective rates

Source: Appendix table D-11.
a. Includes effect of exclusions for capital gains, state and local bond interest, and other preference items.
b. Includes effect of income splitting on joint returns, special rates for single persons and heads of households, and special deduction for two-earner couples.

Figure 4-3. *History of Federal Individual Income Tax Exemptions in Current and 1939 Prices, 1939–82*[a]

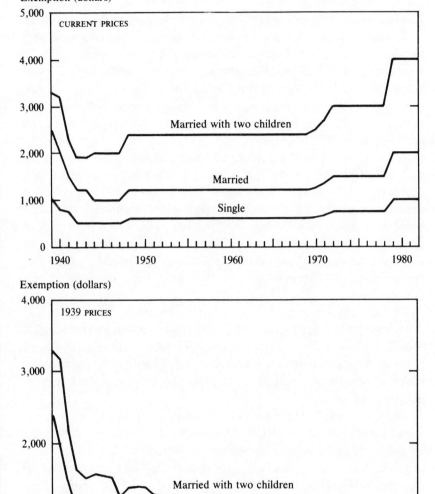

Exemption (dollars)

CURRENT PRICES

Married with two children

Married

Single

Exemption (dollars)

1939 PRICES

Married with two children

Married

Single

Sources: Appendix table A-1 and U.S. Department of Labor, Bureau of Labor Statistics, consumer price index, all items.

a. For 1944–45 exemptions shown are for surtax purposes only. For 1975–78 figures do not include the income equivalent of the per capita tax credit.

unmistakable downward trend. The value, in 1939 prices, of the 1982 personal exemptions was $148 for single persons, $295 for a married couple with no children, and $590 for a married couple with two children.

The basic justification for the personal exemption is that people with very low incomes have no taxpaying capacity. Taxation below minimum levels of subsistence reduces health and efficiency and results in lower economic vitality, less production, and possibly higher public expenditures for social welfare programs. The personal exemptions contribute to progressivity (mainly in the lower income brackets) and serve as an administrative device to remove from the tax rolls people with very low incomes, a function also performed by the zero-bracket amount (or standard deduction). At the higher income levels, personal exemptions differentiate tax burdens on the basis of the number of dependents, but the differences in tax for individuals and families of different sizes with equal incomes are small. Between 1964 and 1978, it was the policy of Congress to set the minimum taxable level under the income tax at or above the poverty level as officially defined by the federal government, but income tax adjustments since 1978 have been confined to rate changes.

Two questions must be discussed in evaluating the system of personal exemptions. First, are the allowances for single persons and for families of different sizes fair relative to one another? Second, is the general level of exemptions adequate? Recent calculations of the incidence of poverty, which are based on concepts of income adequacy, can shed light on these questions.

RELATIVE EXEMPTIONS FOR DIFFERENT FAMILY SIZE. If a family of two must spend x dollars to achieve a certain scale of living, what proportion of x would a single person spend, and how much more than x would families of three, four, five, or more people spend to maintain an equivalent standard? Clearly, the answer depends on the criteria used for measuring equivalence. The standard criteria used by the federal government, which are included in the official poverty-line estimates published annually by the Social Security Administration, are based on the amount of income needed to maintain an adequate diet.

As shown in table 4-3, the financial needs of a household do not increase in direct proportion to the number of people in the household. The relative incomes that would provide roughly equivalent standards of living appear to be in the ratio of 80:100:25 for single, married, and dependent persons, respectively. Income tax exemptions plus the zero-

Table 4-3. *Indexes of the Minimum Taxable Level under the Federal Individual Income Tax and Estimated Poverty-Level Budgets for Families of Various Sizes, 1985*
Two-person family = 100

	Index	
Size of family	Minimum taxable level	Poverty-level budget
1	61	78
2	100	100
3	119	120
4	137	151
5	156	178
6	174	200

Source: Table 4-4.

bracket amount give a ratio of approximately 60:100:20 for 1984. Although the per capita exemption has been too liberal for dependents and too small for single persons, the addition of the zero-bracket amount adjusts the ratio more nearly in line with the relative needs of families of different sizes except for single persons who maintain a separate household.

LEVEL OF EXEMPTIONS. The adequacy of the *level* of exemptions may be judged by comparing the incomes needed by families of different sizes with the minimum taxable level (see table 4-4). The minimum taxable levels equal the statutory per capita exemptions plus the zero-bracket amount. Unless Congress passes new legislation, these two elements will not be sufficient to raise the minimum taxable levels above the poverty lines for all family sizes in 1985.

It is clear from table 4-4 that the zero-bracket amount plays a useful role in correcting part of the inadequacy of the per capita exemption. The purpose of the zero-bracket amount is to augment the regular exemptions at the bottom of the income scale without incurring the heavy cost of raising the exemptions for all taxpayers.

TAX CREDITS IN LIEU OF EXEMPTIONS. Before 1975 income tax allowances for taxpayers and dependents were always given in the form of exemptions deducted from income in computing taxable incomes. An alternative method, now used in several states, is to convert the allowance to a credit computed by multiplying the value of the exemption by the first-bracket tax rate or some higher rate. With the present 11 percent first-

Table 4-4. *Minimum Taxable Level under the Federal Individual Income Tax and Estimated Poverty-Level Budgets for Families of Various Sizes, 1985*
Dollars

Size of family	Exemptions	Zero bracket	Minimum taxable level[a]	Poverty-level budget[b]	Difference
1	1,000	2,300	3,300	5,793	−2,493
2	2,000	3,400	5,400	7,455	−2,055
3	3,000	3,400	6,400	8,962	−2,562
4	4,000	3,400	7,400	11,292	−3,892
5	5,000	3,400	8,400	13,288	−4,888
6	6,000	3,400	9,400	14,878	−5,478

Sources: Minimum taxable levels are based on exemptions and zero-bracket amounts under the Economic Recovery Tax Act of 1981; poverty levels are 1981 data (Bureau of the Census, *Current Population Reports*, P-60 Series, no. 138, p. 181) projected to 1985.
a. Sum of the first two columns.
b. Poverty-level budgets for 1981 were adjusted for an estimated increase in the consumer price index of 22.5 percent from 1981 to 1985.

bracket rate, the $1,000 exemption would be converted to a credit of $110; at a 20 percent rate, the credit would amount to $200; and so on. The credit limits the tax value of the exemption to the same dollar amount for all taxpayers. It would increase the tax liabilities for those with taxable incomes above the bracket chosen to calculate the value of the credit and reduce them for those with taxable incomes below that level. The credit would also narrow the tax differences between families of different sizes above the break-even points and expand them below these points.

Carried to the extreme, the logic of a tax credit would lead to an exemption that vanished at some point on the income scale. A vanishing exemption is often supported on the ground that exemptions are not justified for persons with very large incomes, since expenditures for children are not a hardship at these levels. However, few people have seriously recommended a vanishing exemption for the United States.

Complete replacement of the exemption by a credit would be generous for large families in the lowest income classes and would reduce the tax differences by size of family in the higher classes. To avoid this effect, it has been proposed that a tax credit be allowed as an alternative to the exemption rather than as a substitute for it. Low-income taxpayers would use the credit, and those in the higher classes would continue to use the exemptions. But an optional credit would complicate the tax return and be confusing to many taxpayers. Moreover, roughly the same effect among income classes could be obtained without narrowing tax differences based on family size by retaining the exemption and adjusting the tax rates in the higher income classes. But proponents of the credit are not persuaded that the rate adjustments would actually be made.

Between 1975 and 1978, Congress departed from previous practice and provided a relatively small per capita credit ($30 in 1975 and $35 in 1976–78) instead of increasing the personal exemptions. The adoption of a small credit was a compromise between those who wanted to replace the entire exemption with a credit and those who preferred to increase the exemption. The credit was eliminated when it became clear that it added to the complexity of the tax return without accomplishing very much.

COST OF EXEMPTION INCREASES. For the first time in over a decade, Congress enacted major tax legislation in 1981 without providing for an increase in the minimum taxable levels. Continued adjustment of the personal exemption and the zero-bracket amounts will be necessary to avoid taxing people whose incomes are below the poverty line. The revenue effects of increasing the per capita exemption and zero-bracket amounts are illustrated in table 4-5. As would be expected, such adjustments concentrate most of the relief in the low and middle income classes.

The Negative Income Tax

Raising the exemptions or lowering the first-bracket tax rates would do little to alleviate the economic hardship of low-income families. In the first place, when poor families pay any income tax at all, the amount is small; even full relief from income taxation would not help much. Second, families with incomes below the present minimum taxable levels cannot be helped by income tax reduction that is confined to those who are taxable.

The traditional method of helping poverty-stricken families has been through public welfare and other direct transfer payments (for example, aid to families with dependent children, food stamps, supplemental security income and medical assistance for the aged, aid to blind and disabled persons, and general relief). Most of these programs reach specific categories of the poor; except for general relief, which is inadequate almost everywhere, they provide no assistance to families headed by able-bodied workers who, for reasons of background, training,

Table 4-5. *Revenue and Distributional Effects of Two Individual Income Tax Exemption and Zero-Bracket Plans, by Adjusted Gross Income Class, 1985*
Income classes in thousands of dollars

Revenue change and adjusted gross income class	$2,300 and $3,400 zero brackets[a]	$1,750 per capita exemption, $4,000 zero bracket[b]
Revenue change (billions of dollars)	−34.1	−33.7
	Percentage distribution of revenue change	
0–3	*	*
3–5	0.7	0.9
5–10	5.1	10.0
10–15	8.9	13.9
15–20	10.1	13.3
20–25	11.1	11.1
25–50	45.5	38.1
50–100	15.5	10.3
100–200	2.6	2.1
200–500	0.4	0.4
500–1,000	0.1	*
1,000 and over	*	*
All classes	100.0	100.0
	Percentage change in tax liabilities	
0–3	c	c
3–5	c	c
5–10	c	c
10–15	−23.9	−37.1
15–20	−18.6	−24.2
20–25	−17.3	−17.1
25–50	−13.7	−11.4
50–100	−7.4	−4.8
100–200	−3.0	−2.3
200–500	−0.8	−0.7
500–1,000	−0.4	*
1,000 and over	−0.1	*
All classes	−11.3	−11.2

Source: Brookings 1980 tax file, projected to 1985. Figures are rounded.
* Less than 0.05 percent.
a. $2,300 zero bracket for single taxpayers, $3,400 for married couples.
b. $4,000 zero bracket for all taxpayers.
c. Percentages are not shown because tax liabilities in these classes may be negative, reflecting the refundable earned-income credit.

or temperament, do not participate effectively in the modern industrial economy. Considerable thought has been given in recent years to the relation between the welfare system and the income tax system. The two developed side by side in response to different pressures, but it is recognized that one may be regarded as an extension of the other. Direct assistance to low-income people is an extension of progressivity into the lowest brackets, with negative rather than positive rates. Once this relation is understood, the next natural step is to consider the adoption of a negative income tax.

A negative income tax would provide assistance to families on the basis of how far their income fell below certain minimum standards, without inquiring into the reason for the deficiency. The various welfare programs conducted by government and private nonprofit agencies do not reach all the poor. The negative income tax is regarded by many as a way to supplement these welfare programs rather than replace them. However, a comprehensive negative income tax could be used to replace the entire categorical welfare system.

BASIC FEATURES. The negative income tax would involve the same computations of taxable income as does the positive income tax. Individuals and families would add up all their income and subtract their exemptions and deductions. If the result were negative, they would be entitled to a payment *from* the government. The amount of the payment would be computed by applying a new set of tax rates to the negative taxable income. The rates might begin with the first-bracket rate and increase as the amount of negative taxable income increased. But there is not necessarily any relation between the first-bracket rates of the positive and negative parts of the income tax. The rates on negative incomes could begin with, say, 30 percent and go as high as 70, 80, or even 100 percent. However, most negative income tax plans incorporate only one tax rate.

A negative income tax with only one rate would involve a fixed relation among three variables—the basic allowance (A), the break-even level (B), and the tax rate (t) on the family's income—and it would be impossible to change one variable without affecting at least one of the other two. The basic allowance is the payment made by the government when the family or individual receives no income; the break-even level is the income level at which no payment is received and no taxes are paid; and the tax rate is the rate at which the basic allowance is reduced

Table 4-6. *Illustrative Basic Allowances, Tax Rates, and Break-Even Levels under a Negative Income Tax Plan*

Basic allowance (A) (dollars)	Tax rate (t) (percent)	Break-even level (B) (dollars)
2,000	40	5,000
2,000	50	4,000
3,000	50	6,000
3,000	75	4,000
4,000	50	8,000
4,000	66⅔	6,000
5,000	66⅔	7,500
5,000	50	10,000
6,000	75	8,000
6,000	100	6,000

as income increases. The relation among the three variables is that the basic allowance is the product of the tax rate and the break-even level (or $A = tB$). Thus if the break-even level is $8,000 and the tax rate is 50 percent, the basic allowance is $4,000. Conversely, to keep the break-even level at $6,000 and have a basic allowance of $4,000, the tax rate must be 66⅔ percent. Examples of consistent As, Bs, and ts are shown in table 4-6; there are, of course, many other possibilities.

Because of these relationships, the negative income tax can be thought of in two ways. It can be regarded as providing a basic allowance to all persons, together with a special tax on the incomes of those who accept the allowance. Or it can be regarded as a payment that reduces the gap between income and the break-even level by the same percentage. The equivalence between these two approaches may be illustrated with the first combination of A, t, and B in table 4-6. According to the first approach, a family with an income of $4,000 would receive a basic allowance of $2,000 and would pay a tax of $1,600 on its income, which would leave it with a disposable income of $4,400. According to the second, the family would receive a payment of $400—40 percent of the difference between the $5,000 break-even level and its income of $4,000—leaving it with the same disposable income of $4,400.

The last entry in table 4-6 shows a basic allowance equal to the break-even level. This occurs whenever the income recipient must give up one dollar of the allowance for every dollar of income received: in other words, when the tax rate is 100 percent. The welfare system in the United States had this feature until the social security amendments of 1967 required the states to permit recipients to keep some part of whatever they might earn (this became fully operative in mid-1969).

It might also be noted that there is essentially no difference between a negative income tax and a guaranteed minimum income plan. Under the negative income tax, individuals would receive the basic allowance if they had no other income, and in this sense the basic allowance is a guaranteed minimum. Some guaranteed minimum income plans would impose a tax rate of 100 percent on any income a family might receive, but this is not an essential feature of such plans.

RELATION TO THE POSITIVE INCOME TAX. So long as the break-even levels are no higher than the levels at which the positive income tax begins to apply, the negative income tax can be operated quite independently. However, if the negative income tax is to provide more than a pittance as a basic allowance, the break-even levels may be higher than the levels at which the positive tax takes effect. For example, with a basic allowance of $5,000 and a tax rate of 50 percent, the break-even level would be $10,000 (see table 4-6). The minimum taxable level for a family of four in 1984 is $7,400. Thus the two systems would overlap in the range between $7,400 and $10,000.

The solution to this problem would be to give the family the option of choosing the system under which its disposable income was higher. In the above example, it is obvious that all families with incomes of $7,400 or less would choose the negative income tax. Some families with incomes above $10,000 would also choose the negative income tax, because the switch from the negative to the positive income tax at precisely $10,000 would raise the tax rate on an additional dollar of income above 100 percent. At $10,000, the positive tax for a family of four (at 1984 rates and exemptions) would be $291, leaving the family with a disposable income of $9,709 instead of the $10,000 it would have had without the additional dollar of income. Paradoxically, the option of paying the higher negative income tax rate would give a family of four a higher disposable income until its income exceeded $10,765 in this example (see figure 4-4). The exact location of the "tax break-even" point need not concern the individual taxpayer because the combined tax schedule for the positive and negative income taxes would automatically take the option into account. To operate the system efficiently, consistent definitions of income and filing unit under the two taxes would be necessary.

Negative income tax plans were proposed by Presidents Richard M.

Figure 4-4. *Illustration of a Negative Income Tax Plan for a Four-Person Family with a $5,000 Basic Allowance and a 50 Percent Tax Rate*

Disposable income (thousands of dollars)

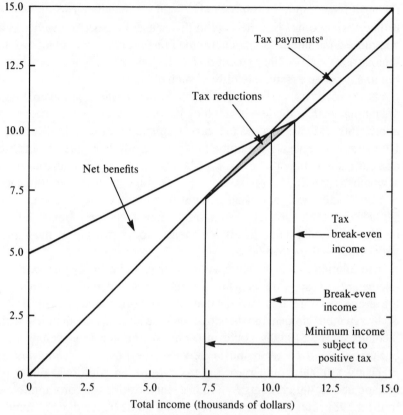

Total income (thousands of dollars)

a. Tax is based on rates, exemptions, low-income allowance, and credits applicable to 1984.

Nixon and Jimmy Carter, but were not approved by Congress partly because the negative income tax is a novel idea and partly because the American public does not understand why payments should be made to people with incomes above the poverty line. With the continued prolif-eration of overlapping programs for the poor, the negative income tax should be given more serious consideration.

Personal Deductions

Personal deductions itemized on taxable returns in 1981 amounted to $242 billion. Of this total, about $93 billion was subject to the zero-bracket rate. The tax savings from the additional $149 billion of itemized deductions amounted to about $30 billion.

The relative importance of the itemized deductions at different income levels is shown in figure 4-5. Because taxpayers had the alternative of taking the zero-bracket amount or standard deduction, it is not surprising to find that, at low income levels, those who itemize their deductions subtract much more than these minima provide. As a percentage of income, deductions decrease as incomes rise to $100,000, but increase in the highest brackets. In 1981 they averaged 24.1 percent of adjusted gross income on all taxable returns with itemized deductions (appendix table D-12).

The largest deductions at most income levels are interest and taxes, but medical deductions—which in the year shown here were subject to a 3 percent floor—are heaviest in the lowest income classes. Interest is particularly important for those with low incomes because of their high incidence of borrowing.

In 1981 the standard and itemized deductions combined amounted to 96.8 percent of adjusted gross income on all tax returns below $5,000, declined to 21.3 percent of income between $50,000 and $100,000, and rose to 27.1 percent above $1,000,000. The high percentage in the lower income classes reflects the importance of the standard deduction, which greatly exceeds itemized deductions for most persons in these classes. The rise at the top is due to an increase in the ratio of contributions to income, reflecting the importance of philanthropy among the wealthy and the incentive for giving provided by the tax deduction.

There is no recorded explanation of the justification for many of the personal deductions. Most of them have been allowed since the beginning of the income tax. Given the definition of income stated earlier, deductions would be allowed only for expenditures that were essential to earn income. An exception might be made for unusual personal expenditures that create hardships when incomes are low; but to avoid subsidizing personal consumption, the personal expense deductions should be kept to a minimum. The current tax law departs from these criteria to a substantial degree.

PURPOSES OF THE PERSONAL DEDUCTIONS. There are four major groups of itemized deductions under present law. The first is for large, unusual, and necessary personal expenditures. Deductions for extraordinary medical expenses are the best examples of this group. Such expenses are often involuntary and unpredictable and may exhaust a large proportion of the taxpayer's total income in a particular year. When a

Figure 4-5. *Itemized Deductions as a Percentage of Adjusted Gross Income, Taxable Federal Individual Returns, 1981*

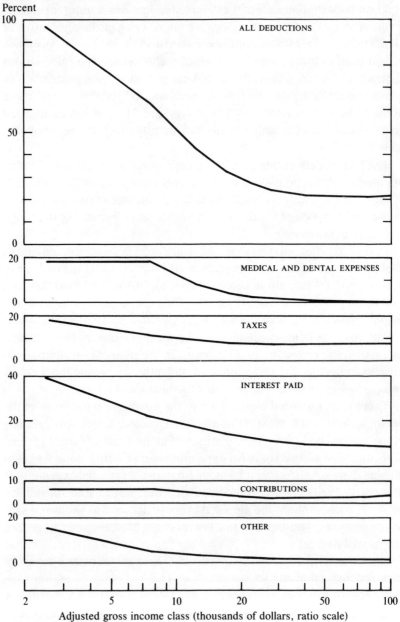

Adjusted gross income class (thousands of dollars, ratio scale)

Source: Appendix table D-12.

serious illness strikes a member of a family, that family's ability to pay taxes is clearly lower than that of another family with the same income whose members are healthy. For these reasons, taxpayers are permitted to deduct medical expenses in excess of 5 percent of their income. Other deductions for large, involuntary, and unpredictable costs are those for uninsured losses resulting from thefts, fires, storms, and other casualties. These deductions are limited to the amount of the losses during the year in excess of 10 percent of income.

The second group of deductions in effect subsidizes particular groups of taxpayers. For instance, deductions for taxes paid on owner-occupied residences and for interest on home mortgages help the homeowner. Since the rental value of an owner-occupied house is not included in the owner's income, the deduction of expenses connected with the home—including interest and taxes—is not warranted. In addition to the direct benefit from the deductions and the exclusion from taxable income of the rental value of their homes, homeowners also benefit indirectly from itemizing deductions. Tenants with low and middle incomes rarely accumulate deductions aggregating more than the standard deduction. The result is that homeowners are the primary beneficiaries of the remaining deductions. Moreover, when a new deduction is introduced, homeowners who already itemize ordinarily receive the full benefit. Other taxpayers must sacrifice the standard deduction before receiving any value from the new deduction.

Another deduction of the subsidy type is for contributions to religious, educational, and other nonprofit organizations, which may be deducted so long as they do not exceed 50 percent of a taxpayer's adjusted gross income (20 percent for foundations and other organizations not considered "public" charities). Taxpayers who do not itemize their deductions are to be allowed to deduct 25 percent of the first $300 of charitable contributions in 1984, 50 percent in 1985, and 100 percent in 1986. (This provision is scheduled to expire in 1987.) In effect, the charitable deduction requires the treasury to match private contributions and thus permits individuals to divert tax funds to the organizations they prefer. Some question whether private philanthropy should be encouraged at the expense of the federal treasury, but most people believe the activities of these organizations are in general socially desirable and that it is beneficial to promote pluralism in society.

The deduction for interest is justifiable when the interest is paid on a loan used to produce taxable income. The interest payment is in effect a negative income, which should be offset against the positive income produced by the asset purchased with the loan proceeds. Alternatively, an individual may prefer to borrow money and pay interest rather than sell an asset; in such cases, the interest deduction is also required to measure the individual's true net property income. A substantial proportion of the interest deducted on tax returns, however, is for loans on homes and consumer durables or for other purposes that do not produce taxable income. In addition, people with high incomes often deduct interest on debt incurred to carry investment assets that produce no current income, causing a mismatching of income and expenses. (See the section on tax shelters below.)

The most recent addition to the list of itemized deductions is the deduction for political contributions, which became effective in 1972. Originally, taxpayers were allowed a deduction or credit, whichever was to their advantage. Since 1979, the credit has been 50 percent of total contributions up to $50 ($100 on joint returns). In 1981 the credit for political contributions, reported on 5.2 million tax returns, amounted to $262 million. In addition, in fiscal 1982, a total of $39 million was placed in a special fund by individuals who exercised the option, also introduced in 1972, to set aside $1 ($2 on joint returns) of their annual tax liabilities for financing presidential campaigns.

The third group of deductions is for income, property, and sales taxes paid to state and local governments. A deduction for income taxes reduces the combined impact of federal, state, and local income taxes; it is also an effective way of moderating interstate tax differences in the higher income brackets. For example, if an income were subject to the highest state rate of 20 percent and also to the 50 percent rate for federal tax, the combined marginal rate would be 70 percent. By allowing taxpayers to deduct the state tax on their federal returns, the maximum combined rate is reduced to 60 percent. If the state also permits a deduction for federal taxes, the maximum combined rate is 55.5 percent. (Deductibility is discussed more fully in chapter 9.)

At one time, federal excises and many minor state and local taxes were allowed as deductions, but these were gradually eliminated. The deductions for general sales and property taxes survived because it was felt that some federal relief for these taxes was needed to encourage state and local governments to raise needed revenue without coercing them to use a particular source. The deduction for gasoline taxes was removed in 1979, after it became clear that a tax subsidy for gasoline consumption made no sense.

The fourth group contains the most theoretically defensible deductions, namely, those that make allowances for the expenses of earning income. These deductions are required to correct the deficiencies of the adjusted gross income concept. Expenses incurred in earning nonbusiness income (that is, wages and salaries, interest, and dividends) are generally not allowed as deductions in arriving at adjusted gross income, but some of these expenses are deductible in arriving at taxable income. Examples of these deductions are fees for investment counselors, rentals of safe deposit boxes used to store income-producing securities, custodian fees, work clothing, and union dues. Moving expenses and nonreimbursed travel expenses of employees are deductible in arriving at adjusted gross income, as are alimony payments, which are taxable to the recipient.

In lieu of a deduction for child care, single persons and married couples (with both husband and wife employed) are allowed a nonrefundable tax credit on expenditures of up to $2,400 for the care of a dependent while they are at work and up to $4,800 for two or more dependents. The credit is also available when one parent works full time and the other is a part-time worker or a full-time student, and to a divorced or separated parent with custody of the children. The credit is 30 percent of child care expenses for those with adjusted gross income of $10,000 or less and it phases down to 20 percent at $28,000. Congress justified this credit, which was introduced in 1976, on the ground that child care expenditures must be incurred by many taxpayers to earn a livelihood and are comparable to ordinary business expenses.

A major problem with using deductions to distinguish the taxpaying ability of different families and individuals is that the tax benefit depends on the tax rate. A person who would not be taxable even without the deduction receives no benefit; a 25 percent taxpayer receives a 25 percent benefit; and so on. Thus the deductions should be pruned to the minimum necessary for an effective and equitable income tax. Opponents of the deductions argue that, if they are not pruned, they should be converted to tax credits so that the tax benefit would be the same in all income classes. At the very least, a distinction should be made between deductions that help to refine income as a measure of ability to pay—such as unusual medical expenses and casualty losses—and those that provide an incentive to particular activities—such as charitable contributions.

POSSIBLE REVISIONS OF THE PERSONAL DEDUCTIONS. Revision of the personal deductions might begin with those that subsidize personal expenditures, which account for the major share of itemized deductions on taxable returns (appendix table D-12). The deductions that receive the most attention are those for charitable contributions, interest on personal loans, and state and local taxes other than income and sales taxes.

Proponents of the deduction for charitable contributions have persuaded Congress that the organizations benefiting from the deduction have such overwhelming social priority under present institutional arrangements that they warrant the use of tax incentives. Recent econometric analyses suggest that the tax deduction encourages charitable giving at all income levels, although the response in the lower income classes is uncertain. If an income tax deduction is considered necessary to encourage contributions, it might be better to allow the deduction only when the contribution is larger than some average amount. For example, the deduction might be allowed for the amount of contributions in excess of, say, 2 or 3 percent of adjusted gross income, with the total deduction limited to the present 50 percent of adjusted gross income. This revision was recommended by the Treasury Department in 1969, but was not accepted by Congress because of the strong opposition of tax-exempt organizations. The deduction for contributions by nonitemizers cannot be justified because they already benefit from the standard deduction, which was intended to substitute for itemized deductions; it should be allowed to expire in 1987. Especially unnecessary is the deduction for the full market value of contributed assets that have appreciated even though the gain on these assets has not been realized for tax purposes.

As for the 5 percent floor for the medical deduction, surveys indicate that 5 percent of income is about the median expenditure of families with incomes below $10,000. The median, however, is only an arbitrary dividing line between "usual" and "extraordinary." The lower limit could be increased, say to 10 percent, without violating its basic rationale. This would permit medical deductions by about 10 percent of all family units.

The interest deduction presents a special difficulty because interest is paid on both business and personal debts, and it is difficult to distinguish between the two. Clearly, the deduction should be allowed for interest on a loan made to the owner of a grocery store to carry inventory, while interest on a loan to purchase a consumer durable hardly merits a deduction. The inventory loan produces taxable income, while the consumer durable goods loan generates income in the form of services that do not enter into the tax base. But it is often difficult to identify the purpose of loans because owners of unincorporated enterprises take out personal loans to finance their business activities, and vice versa.

The best way to handle this problem would be to permit deductions (with carry-over privileges) for interest paid up to the amount of property and business income reported by the taxpayers, on the ground that interest paid must be subtracted to obtain net income from these sources.

The 1969 act adopted a variant of this approach by allowing taxpayers to deduct interest paid to purchase investment assets up to $25,000, plus their net investment income (dividends, interest, long-term capital gains, and so forth), plus one-half the amount of such interest in excess of net investment income. In 1976 the limit on deductible investment interest was reduced to $10,000 plus the taxpayer's net investment income other than capital gains. Any interest disallowed in one year may be carried over to offset investment income in subsequent years.

The omission of the rental value of owner-occupied houses from the tax base discriminates against renters; to redress the balance, the deductions for property taxes and interest payments on home mortgages (to the extent they exceed property income reported) might be eliminated. This would leave deductions for state and local income and sales taxes, which are justified as encouraging the use of general taxes for state and local purposes.

It may be concluded that the itemized deductions are too generous and that substantial increases in revenues might be gained by trimming them to the most essential items. Another alternative is to permit taxpayers to deduct only the amount of their itemized deductions exceeding, say, 20 percent of their adjusted gross income. The attractive feature of this approach is that it would greatly increase the yield of the tax at present rates and thus permit substantial reductions in these rates. A variant of this proposal was recommended by the Treasury Department in 1963, but it was virtually disregarded by the congressional tax-writing committees.

Estimates of the revenue gains from several revisions of the personal deductions are given in table 4-7. The gains would come mainly from the middle and higher income classes. On balance, equity would be better served by pruning the itemized deductions in these or other ways and using the revenues to reduce tax rates. But although it recognizes the inequity of the present system, Congress hesitates to remedy the situation directly for fear of alienating the large groups of taxpayers who benefit from the deductions. Some progress has been made in recent years by

Table 4-7. *Revenue Gains from Various Revisions of Personal Deductions under the Federal Individual Income Tax, 1985*
Billions of dollars

Revision	Revenue gain
Eliminate charitable deduction for nonitemizers	0.8
Introduce 2 percent floor on the charitable contribution deduction	5.5
Raise floor on medical expense deduction from 5 to 10 percent	7.2
Eliminate deduction for state and local sales tax	4.2
Eliminate deduction for personal interest (except for mortgage interest)	12.4
Limit interest deduction to the amount of business and property income	20.0
Introduce 20 percent floor on itemized deductions	19.6

Source: Brookings 1980 tax file, projected to 1985.

the removal of the gasoline tax (effective in 1979) and the increase in the floors for the medical expense and casualty loss deductions (effective in 1983).

Transfer Payments and Wage Supplements

The largest exclusions from the individual income tax base are receipts that are in the nature of transfer payments and wage supplements. The exclusion of transfers arises out of social insurance and relief programs enacted during the 1930s to alleviate personal hardship from unemployment, sickness, and old age. Since the original recipients were in general unable to pay taxes and were, in any case, not subject to tax under the relatively high personal exemptions in effect at the time, the exclusion of these payments did not create any substantial inequities. The situation has been altered completely by the conversion of the income tax to a mass tax during World War II, the increases in the average amounts of transfers paid, and the gradual expansion of the programs to include individuals who are not necessarily in dire straits. Recipients of such transfer payments are frequently much better off than their neighbors who cannot exclude any portion of their incomes in computing their tax liabilities.

War and postwar emergency conditions have also left a legacy of exclusions. Military personnel and veterans receive numerous nontaxable benefits primarily because it seemed unfair to tax those who risked their lives in the national service. These payments are in fact part of the remuneration for military service, but their value depends on the

Table 4-8. *Transfer Payments and Wage Supplements as a Percentage of Personal Income, Selected Years, 1950–82*

Year	Transfer payments	Wage supplements	Total
1950	2.8	1.5	4.3
1960	3.9	3.1	7.0
1970	7.4	5.8	13.3
1980	11.3	9.2	20.5
1982	12.2	9.7	21.9

Source: U.S. Department of Commerce, Bureau of Economic Analysis.

recipients' other income. Although an adequate salary scale is necessary to attract qualified personnel into the armed forces, the use of tax exemption is hardly the appropriate method of accomplishing this objective.

Since the end of World War II, employee compensation received in nontaxable form has grown rapidly. This includes contributions by employers to employee pension plans, which were specifically excluded from the tax base in 1942 to promote saving; employer-financed health and welfare plans; group life insurance; employee discounts; scholarships for the children of university faculty members; and other fringe benefits. New concessions are introduced periodically into the internal revenue code to correct inequalities arising from actions taken when these exclusions were relatively small, the most recent example being the individual retirement accounts (IRAs). The statutory authority for the exclusion of some employee benefits, such as discounts and free use of services, is ambiguous, but Congress has delayed implementation of attempts by the Internal Revenue Service to restrict their use for fear of alienating large employee groups and trade unions.

As measured in the national income accounts, the exclusions for transfer payments and wage supplements increased from 4.3 percent of total personal income in 1950 to 13.3 percent in 1970 and 21.9 percent in 1982 (table 4-8). These figures understate the leakage from the tax base because they exclude in-kind benefits, such as merchandise discounts, airplane tickets, company cars, free parking, and other employee privileges.

Progress has been made in recent years to introduce at least some part of the transfer payments and wage supplements into the tax base. Beginning in 1967, premiums paid by employers for life insurance in excess of the cost of $50,000 of such insurance have been included in the employee's taxable income. From 1979 to 1981, unemployment compensation benefits were included in taxable income for persons with other income over $20,000 ($25,000 for married couples). Beginning in 1982, such benefits became taxable for persons with other income over $12,000 ($18,000 for married couples). One-half of social security payments are to be made taxable, beginning in 1984, for persons with other income over $25,000 ($32,000 for married couples). In addition, the limit on the annual benefit payable under employer-financed pension plans was reduced from $136,425 (enacted in 1976) to $90,000 and the automatic cost-of-living adjustment for this limit was suspended until 1986.

In 1983 the Reagan administration proposed that employer premiums for employee health insurance in excess of $175 a month for a family plan and $70 a month for a single person's plan be included in taxable income of the employee. This proposal was intended to encourage more economical use of health care services, and it would also help to reduce income tax erosion. However, Congress has not acted on the proposal.

Congress has treated transfer payments and wage supplements so leniently because they benefit many members of the low and middle income classes. Relief for such taxpayers might be justified if the income tax were levied without exemptions and at a flat rate. If the exemptions are considered too low and rates too high, it would be far more equitable to discontinue the exclusions and use the revenues to raise the exemptions and lower the tax rates for all taxpayers.

The Family

During most of the history of the income tax, differentiation for family responsibilities was made among taxpayers through the personal exemptions. Since 1948, separate rate schedules for single people and married couples have been used to provide additional differentiation, particularly in the middle and higher tax brackets. In the United States and West Germany this has been accomplished by adopting the principle of "income splitting" between husband and wife. In France, income splitting among all family members is permitted. Other countries achieve a similar objective by providing separate rate schedules for families of different sizes.

The adoption of income splitting in the United States arose out of the historical accident that eight states had community property laws, which treated income as if divided equally between husband and wife. By virtue of several Supreme Court decisions, married couples residing in these eight states had been splitting their incomes and filing separate federal returns. Shortly after World War II, a number of other states enacted community property laws for the express purpose of obtaining the same advantage for their residents, and other states threatened to follow suit. In an effort to restore geographic tax equality and to prevent wholesale disruption of local property laws and procedures, Congress universalized income splitting in 1948.

The effect of income splitting is to reduce progressivity for married couples. The 1984 tax rates nominally begin at 11 and 12 percent on the first two $1,050 segments of taxable income above the zero-bracket amount and rise to 50 percent on the portion of taxable income above $81,200. A married couple with taxable income above the zero-bracket amount of $2,100 splits this income and applies the first rate to each half; without income splitting, the first two rates would apply to each $1,050 segment. Thus, whereas the nominal rate brackets cover taxable incomes up to $81,200, the actual rates for married couples extend to $162,400 (table 4-2). The tax advantage rises from $411 for married couples with taxable income of $10,000 to $9,300 for couples with taxable income of $162,400 or more (figure 4-6 and appendix table D-10).

The classic argument in favor of income splitting is that husbands and wives usually share their combined income equally. The largest portion of the family budget goes for consumption, and savings are ordinarily set aside for the children or for the enjoyment of all members of the family. Two conclusions follow from this view. First, married couples with the same combined income should pay the same tax irrespective of the legal division of income between them; second, the tax liabilities of married couples should be computed as if they were two single persons with their total income divided equally between them. The first conclusion is now firmly rooted in U.S. tax law and seems to be almost universally accepted. It is the second conclusion on which opinions still differ.

The case for the sharing argument is most applicable to taxpayers in the lower income classes, where incomes are used almost entirely for the consumption of the family unit. At the top of the income scale, the major rationale of income taxation is to reduce the economic power of the family unit, and the use made of income at these levels for family purposes is largely irrelevant for this purpose. Obviously, these objectives cannot be reconciled if income splitting is extended to all income brackets.

The practical effect of income splitting is to produce large differences

Figure 4-6. *Federal Tax Saving for Married Couples Filing Joint Returns, Heads of Households, and Single Persons, as a Percentage of the Basic Rate Schedule*[a] *Tax, by Taxable Income, 1984 Rates*

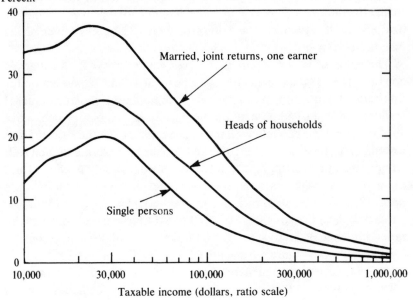

Percent

Source: Appendix table D-10.
a. Married, separate returns.

in the tax burdens of single persons and married couples, differences that depend on the *rate of graduation* and not on the level of rates. Such differences are difficult to rationalize on any theoretical grounds. It is also difficult to justify treating single persons with families more harshly than married persons in similar circumstances. As a remedy, widows and widowers are permitted to continue to split their incomes for two years after the death of the spouse, and half the advantage of joint returns is given (through a separate rate schedule) to single persons who maintain a household for children or other dependents or who maintain a separate household for their parents. This makeshift arrangement does not deal with the problem satisfactorily. For example, single taxpayers who support aunts or uncles in different households receive no income-splitting benefit; if they support an aged mother, they receive these benefits.

Pressures on Congress to treat single persons more liberally—by broadening the head-of-household provision, increasing their exemptions, and other devices—resulted in the adoption of a new rate schedule for single persons under the 1969 act. In this schedule, the single persons' tax never exceeds by more than 20 percent the tax for married couples filing joint returns (see table 4-2). In keeping with prior practice, the rate schedule for heads of households is halfway between the single-person and joint-return rate schedules. The result was the introduction of the so-called tax penalty on marriage: two persons with earnings split roughly 75–25, or more equally, between them paid more tax after marriage than the total tax they paid before marriage; under the pure version of income splitting, they would pay the same or less tax before and after marriage.

One of the major reasons for acceptance of the consequences of income splitting may well be that personal exemptions do not provide enough differentiation among taxpayers in the middle and top brackets. Single persons, it is felt, should be taxed more heavily than married couples because they do not bear the costs and responsibilities of raising children. But income splitting for husband and wife clearly does not differentiate among taxpayers in this respect since the benefit is the same whether or not there are children.

One problem with the income-splitting approach is that differentiation among families by size is made through the rate structure rather than through personal exemptions. It would be possible to differentiate among taxpayer units by varying the personal exemptions with the size of income as well as the number of persons in the unit with both a minimum and a maximum. This procedure could be used to achieve almost any desired degree of differentiation among families while avoiding most of the anomalies produced by income splitting. The tax rates for single persons and married couples could be equalized either by extending the rate advantages of income splitting to single persons or by requiring married couples to use the same tax rate schedule as single people. The revenue implications of this approach, illustrated in table 4-9, are large, but they can be offset by adjusting the tax rates.

Another problem with pure income splitting is that married couples pay the same tax whether there are two earners or one. The one-earner couple has more ability to pay, because the spouse who stays at home produces income (in the form of household services) that is not subject to tax. Some portion of the earnings of the two-earner couple is absorbed in providing such household services. Furthermore, the high marginal tax rate on the earnings of the second spouse may discourage some from seeking employment.

Elimination of income splitting would restore all the problems of the

Table 4-9. *Revenue Effects of Changes in Income Splitting and Allowances for Two-Earner Married Couples, by Adjusted Gross Income Class, 1985*

Income classes in thousands of dollars

Revenue change and adjusted gross income class	Extend rate advantages of income splitting to single persons		Eliminate rate advantages of income splitting for married couples	
	Deduction of 10 percent for two-earner couples[a]	Deduction of 25 percent for two-earner couples[a]	Deduction of 10 percent for two-earner couples[a]	Deduction of 25 percent for two-earner couples[a]
Revenue change (billions of dollars)	−16.5	−22.2	94.7	81.7
	Percentage distribution of revenue change			
0–3	*	*	*	*
3–5	1.7	1.3	0.4	0.4
5–10	11.2	8.3	1.8	2.0
10–15	14.4	11.1	3.4	3.9
15–20	14.7	11.9	5.3	5.8
20–25	14.7	12.9	7.1	7.3
25–50	30.6	39.0	46.4	45.1
50–100	7.1	10.5	26.4	26.4
100–200	3.8	3.4	6.7	6.9
200–500	1.0	0.8	1.8	1.9
500–1,000	0.4	0.3	0.2	0.2
1,000 and over	0.5	0.4	0.1	0.1
All classes[b]	100.0	100.0	100.0	100.0
	Percentage change in tax liabilities			
0–3	c	c	c	c
3–5	c	c	c	c
5–10	c	c	c	c
10–15	−18.7	−19.5	25.7	25.0
15–20	−13.2	−14.3	27.1	25.7
20–25	−11.1	−13.1	30.6	27.4
25–50	−4.5	−7.7	38.9	32.6
50–100	−1.7	−3.3	35.7	30.2
100–200	−8.0	−7.5	21.1	18.7
200–500	−0.9	−1.0	9.5	8.6
500–1,000	−1.1	−1.2	3.7	3.3
1,000 and over	−1.5	−1.4	1.0	0.9
All classes[b]	−5.4	−7.3	31.4	27.1

Source: Brookings 1980 tax file, projected to 1985. Figures are rounded.
* Less than 0.05 percent.
a. Deduction is based on earnings of spouse with lower earnings up to $30,000.
b. Includes negative incomes not shown separately.
c. Percentages are not shown because tax liabilities in these classes may be negative, reflecting the refundable earned-income credit.

pre-1948 law and would not adjust correctly for the understatement of the taxable income of the one-earner couple. Another approach would have been to permit married couples to file separately on their earned income, but this would have required arbitrary rules to calculate the tax on unearned incomes and to allocate deductions between spouses, and would have greatly complicated the tax return. Instead, in 1981, Congress decided to provide a special deduction for two-earner couples: 5 percent for 1982, and 10 percent thereafter, of the earnings of the spouse with the lower earnings, up to earnings of $30,000. The introduction of this deduction moderated, but did not eliminate, the marriage penalty; at the same time, it gave a tax deduction to some couples who did not suffer a marriage penalty.

The Aged

Personal exemptions and deductions for extraordinary medical expenses automatically allow for special circumstances of the taxpayer. Beyond this, the federal income tax structure has been particularly solicitous of the special circumstances of the aged. Taxpayers aged sixty-five or over have an additional personal exemption, pay tax on half their social security or railroad retirement pensions only if their other income is very high, and receive a 15 percent tax credit on the first $2,500 of their income (less any social security, railroad retirement, or other exempt pension income) for single persons and couples of whom only one is over sixty-five and the first $3,750 for couples of whom both are over sixty-five. The base for computing the credit is reduced by half of adjusted gross income above $7,500 for single persons and $10,000 for couples.

The exemptions for age and blindness, which amounted to over $13 billion on all tax returns in 1981, were justified on the ground that these taxpayers have less ability to pay than do other members of the community. The aged and the blind are in fact concentrated at the lower end of the income distribution. But the personal exemptions, the standard deduction, and the graduated income tax rates were specifically designed to differentiate among the taxpaying abilities of individuals with different incomes. The aged and the blind might have a claim for an additional exemption if it could be shown that they have to spend more out of a given income than other taxpayers. However, many other groups of taxpayers are handicapped in one way or another (for example, by physical or mental disability or lack of opportunity to receive training) or are required to spend more than others for geographical or other reasons, and it would be impractical and undesirable to take account of all these individual differences under an income tax.

Social security and railroad retirement benefits were omitted from the tax base by Treasury regulations soon after the original legislation was enacted in the 1930s. At that time, incomes were so low that it did not matter whether these payments were subject to tax or not. As incomes grew and social security was extended to almost the entire population, it became clear that the tax exemption for these benefits was extremely generous. Contributions by employees do not account for more than 10 to 20 percent of their benefits at present and will account for much less than 50 percent even when the systems mature. By contrast, recipients of pensions from other publicly administered retirement programs and from industrial pension plans are fully taxed on the portion of their benefits that exceeds their contributions. This discrimination was deeply resented by the recipients of taxable pensions. As a result, a credit against tax of 20 percent of the first $1,200 of retirement income (other than social security and railroad retirement benefits) was enacted in 1954. The maximum income subject to the credit was raised to $1,524 in 1962 and $2,500 in 1976, and the credit was lowered to 15 percent in 1965, when tax rates in the lower brackets were reduced.

The logjam on the taxation of social security and railroad retirement benefits was broken in 1983, when Congress enacted a comprehensive reform package to prevent the social security trust funds from being depleted (see chapter 7). The 1983 legislation subjects half of social security benefits and the corresponding railroad retirement benefits to tax, but only for single persons with other income (including tax-exempt interest) above $25,000 and married couples above $32,000.

Not only is special relief for the elderly questionable, but the preferences they receive give a tax advantage that increases with income. In principle, it would be fairer to remove the exemption for age and make all retirement income taxable (with an allowance, of course, for the portion contributed by the employee, on which tax was paid when earned). The additional revenue (which would amount to $11 billion in 1985) could be used to good advantage to raise social security benefits for all the aged or reduce the tax rates on those with low incomes generally.

Earned Income

An allowance for income earned from work rather than from property ownership was made in the United States in the years 1924–31 and 1934–43, and is still made in the United Kingdom and other countries. The earned-income allowance is justified by its supporters on the ground that earned income is not on a par with unearned income. In 1969 the top marginal rate on earned income was limited to 50 percent, but this special maximum was removed when the top-bracket rate was reduced to 50 percent in 1982. In 1975 a refundable earned-income tax credit was adopted to reduce the burden of the social security payroll tax for those in the lowest earnings classes and to increase their work incentives. Special deductions have also been added to the law for savings set aside for retirement purposes by the self-employed, workers not covered by a pension plan, and two-earner married couples.

THE EARNED-INCOME ALLOWANCE. In the United States the earned-income allowance was granted in the form of a deduction that ranged from 10 to 25 percent of earned net income. In some years the deduction was allowed for normal tax purposes only; in others it was allowed for both normal tax and surtax. In all years a certain minimum amount of income ($3,000 or $5,000) was presumed to be earned whether it actually was or not, and the deduction was limited to a maximum ranging from $10,000 to $30,000. The tax value of the deduction was always small. It was never worth more than $495 for a family of two (in the period 1928–31); immediately before it was eliminated in 1944 as part of the wartime simplification program, the maximum value was $84. One state—Massachusetts—still taxes earned income at a lower rate than unearned income.

The equity argument in favor of an earned-income allowance is that one person with a given income that is earned has less ability to pay than another who has the same amount of income that is unearned. Several reasons are cited to support this view. First, recipients of earned income do not have the benefit of an allowance for depreciation, and yet their productive capacities often decline as they grow older and are ultimately exhausted. Second, expenses of earning an income are not taken into account fully by the individual income tax deductions. Since 1964 the law has permitted a deduction for nonreimbursed moving expenses in connection with assuming a new job. But similar outlays such as commuting expenses, the additional cost of lunches and other meals away from home, office clothing, and laundry and dry cleaning make the costs of generating earned income higher than the costs of generating the same amount of income from property. Third, earning an income involves psychic costs and the sacrifice of leisure, warranting special income tax relief.

While these arguments appear to have some merit, there are good counterarguments. An earned-income allowance is at best only a rough method of correcting for the alleged inequities. To the extent that there are inequities, they should be corrected directly by adjustments either in the structure of the income tax or in other government programs. For example, the depreciation argument is essentially a question of recovering depreciation of human capital; if this is regarded as an important impediment to investment in education and training, the appropriate method would be to introduce a deduction for depreciation of such investments (although the amount would necessarily be arbitrary). If there are special costs involved in earning income, the rules for deducting such costs should be liberalized. Finally, to counter the view that recipients of earned income have greater psychic costs, it can be argued that the accumulation of capital that produces unearned income also involves costs and sacrifices.

On balance, the case for an earned-income allowance does not seem overwhelming. Where it has been employed, the allowance has been given to all people with incomes below a certain level and denied to those with incomes above a certain level, whether the income was earned or not. This means that, in practice, there was only a rough differentiation between earned and unearned income. There is also no basis for calculating the earned-income element of the incomes of the self-employed (for example, farmers and professional persons); in practice, this separation is made by an arbitrary formula. Furthermore, a substantial earned-income credit could be very expensive and would complicate the tax return form.

DEDUCTION FOR RETIREMENT SAVINGS. The law permits self-employed persons to deduct savings set aside for their retirement (called the Keogh plan after Congressman Eugene J. Keogh, who introduced the idea) up to 15 percent of earned income or $30,000, whichever is less. A deduction of $750 is allowed, regardless of the maximum limitation, up to the amount of the individual's earned income. This provision was adopted because it was felt that self-employed persons find it difficult to accumulate tax-free savings for purposes of retirement. By contrast, wage earners and salaried employees do not pay tax on the amounts contributed to qualified pension plans in their behalf by employers. The saving deduction for the self-employed was intended as an analogous provision for them, since they cannot participate in such plans.

When originally proposed, the Keogh plan did not have an upper limit on the allowable deduction for these contributions, and it also granted capital gains treatment to withdrawals from the retirement funds in which the savings were invested. As a result, it was regarded as a device to avoid taxes rather than to correct an inequity. These defects were corrected before the legislation was enacted, and there is no longer much concern about abuse. In 1981, 557,000 individuals reported deductions of $2 billion for Keogh plans.

Beginning in 1975 persons not covered by a pension plan were allowed to deduct 15 percent of their income up to a maximum of $1,500 for amounts invested in an individual retirement account (IRA). In 1976 the limit was raised to $1,750 for married couples with one nonworking spouse ($875 for each). In 1981 the limit was raised again to 100 percent of compensation up to $2,000 ($2,250 for married couples with only one earner) and, more important, the deduction was allowed even for persons covered by pension plans. Originally, the rationale for the IRA deduction was the same as the rationale for the Keogh plan: to allow those who are not active participants in a retirement plan to set aside their own savings for this purpose tax free. It was felt that the same deferral of tax on a modest amount of earnings should be allowed those who work for an employer who has not set up such a plan or who, because of the nature of their employment, cannot be covered. The additional $250 allowance for married couples with only one income was enacted in recognition of the household work done by the spouse who stays at home. In 1981 almost 3.4 million individuals reported $4.8 billion for this deduction.

The extension of IRAs to those already covered by pension plans goes beyond the retirement rationale. The purpose now is to reduce the marginal tax rates on saving for all taxpayers and thus to encourage saving generally. The provision is defective, however, because it provides a tax benefit even if the individual switches assets from another account to an IRA account or borrows the money for the IRA investment. The revenue loss from this provision will amount to about $3 billion in 1985. (See below for further discussion of saving incentives.)

THE EARNED-INCOME CREDIT. Another concession to those with earned income was the enactment in 1975 of a refundable tax credit for earned income of low-income persons with children. The credit is 10 percent of earned income up to $5,000 and is phased down to zero at $10,000. The credit is "refundable" because a payment is made when the amount of the credit exceeds the income tax liability of the wage earner.

The purpose of the earned-income credit is to moderate the burden of the social security payroll tax on low-income earners. During the congressional discussions of the negative income tax, it was emphasized that the working poor are required to pay social security tax even though they are not subject to the individual income tax. The credit against the income tax was devised to relieve the tax burdens of the poor in order to increase their work incentives without disturbing the social security tax arrangements. (See the discussion in chapter 7.) The credit is denied to persons without children to avoid making grants to students, retired people, and other part-time workers who have small amounts of earned income, even though they are also subject to the social security tax.

In 1985 the combined employee-employer social security tax rate will be 14.1 percent (7.05 percent each for the employer and employee) on earnings up to an estimated $39,600. Thus over 75 percent of their total social security tax paid will be refunded to those eligible to receive the full earned-income credit. The estimated cost of the credit for 1985 is $1.3 billion.

DEDUCTION FOR WORKING SPOUSES. Wholly apart from the treatment of earned income generally is the difficult question of taxing the income of working spouses. A special exemption is given working spouses under the British income tax system. In the United States, except for an allowance of up to $15 against the normal tax in 1944 and 1945, a working-spouse credit or deduction was not granted until 1982. The new provision permits married couples with two earners to deduct 10 percent of the earnings of the spouse with lower earnings up to earnings of $30,000 (5 percent for 1982). This deduction, described above, is allowed in addition to the credit for child care expenses.

As indicated in the discussion of income splitting, allowances for working spouses are supported partly on incentive grounds and partly on equity grounds. The incentive argument is that, if one spouse already earns income, the other spouse's earnings are taxable beginning at the first dollar. The higher the income of one spouse, the higher is the marginal rate of tax on the additional income of the other spouse. The high rate plus the additional costs of operating the household deter some spouses from seeking employment.

The equity argument is that the ability to pay taxes is not commensurate with the actual earnings of the working spouse. The services that a wife, for instance, performs at home (housework, care of children) may be performed by a domestic servant if she obtains gainful employment; moreover, clothing, laundry bills, and food are usually more expensive if she works, and the family purchases are, in general, less efficient. It is not fair to tax all the additional earnings of the wife since they are partly absorbed in meeting these extra expenses. In addition, many people object to the marriage penalty imposed on two-earner couples by the rate schedules enacted to modify the income-splitting arrangements. To a certain extent, however, the deduction for working spouses duplicates the effect of the credit for child care expenses, although the former is intended for married couples with or without children.

The estimated cost of the new deduction for married couples is $11 billion at 1985 earnings levels. Elimination of the marriage penalty by permitting two-earner couples to file separate returns for their respective earned incomes would have been even costlier and would have greatly complicated the tax return.

Indexing for Inflation

With prices rising at unsatisfactorily high rates, increasing attention has been given in recent years to the relation between inflation and the tax system. Inflation affects real tax burdens in two ways. First, it affects the measurement of several types of income for tax purposes, particularly capital gains, business profits, and interest. These problems will be discussed in the capital gains section below and in chapter 5. Second, the personal exemptions, the standard deduction, tax credits, tax rate bracket boundaries, and other structural features of the income tax are expressed in dollar terms. If the dollar value of such features remains unchanged as prices and incomes rise, taxpayers' incomes are thrown into higher tax brackets and effective tax rates increase even if there has been no increase in real income. This increase in effective rates is known as *bracket creep*.

The effect of bracket creep is illustrated in the first four columns of table 4-10, which compare the tax liabilities of a family of four at selected

Table 4-10. *Effect of a 5 Percent Inflation on the Tax Liabilities of a Family of Four, Selected Income Levels, 1984*
Amounts in dollars; effective rates in percent

							Effect of not indexing		
			Tax after 5 percent inflation				Per-	Percent	
	Tax before inflation[b]		Without indexing[b]		With indexing[c]		centage- point reduc-		
							Percent increase		tion in
Income before infla- tion[a]		Effec-		Effec-		Effec-	in- crease	in effec- tive	income after
	Amount	tive rate	Amount	tive rate	Amount	tive rate	in tax	rate	tax
10,000	291	2.9	351	3.3	306	2.9	14.7	0.4	0.4
12,000	539	4.5	623	4.9	566	4.5	10.1	0.4	0.5
15,000	959	6.4	1,064	6.8	1,007	6.4	5.7	0.4	0.4
20,000	1,645	8.2	1,777	8.5	1,727	8.2	2.9	0.3	0.3
25,000	2,353	9.4	2,541	9.7	2,471	9.4	2.8	0.3	0.3
30,000	3,201	10.7	3,465	11.0	3,361	10.7	3.1	0.3	0.4
50,000	7,660	15.3	8,320	15.8	8,043	15.3	3.4	0.5	0.6
100,000	23,316	23.3	24,996	23.8	24,482	23.3	2.1	0.5	0.6
200,000	61,130	30.6	65,100	31.0	64,187	30.6	1.4	0.4	0.6
500,000	181,100	36.2	191,100	36.4	190,155	36.2	0.5	0.2	0.3
1,000,000	381,100	38.1	401,100	38.2	400,155	38.1	0.2	0.2	0.1

a. Assumes all income is fully subject to tax and that one spouse earns all the income.
b. Assumes tax law applying in 1984. Tax liability computed on the assumption that the family deducts the zero-bracket amount of $3,400 or 20 percent of income, whichever is greater.
c. The exemptions, the zero-bracket amount, and the rate brackets of the 1984 law are increased by 5 percent.

income levels before and after a 5 percent inflation. Effective tax rates increase at all income levels as a result of the inflation. In percentage terms, those at the bottom of the income scale fare the worst. However, the increases in effective rates and the percentage changes in income after tax (shown in the last two columns of the table) are much more uniform throughout the income classes. The maximum effect occurs at the lower end of the income scale, where progressivity is determined primarily by the personal exemptions and the zero-bracket amount, and between $50,000 and $200,000 of income, where rate graduation increases most rapidly.

Several countries with high rates of inflation automatically index their income taxes for inflation. The technique is to raise the value of the personal exemptions, standard deductions, and rate brackets by the rate of inflation once a year on the basis of an overall price index, usually the consumer price index. As the inflation rate rose in the United States during the 1970s, proposals to index the income tax in this way received increasing support. From 1960 to 1975 discretionary changes in exemptions and tax rates more than compensated for inflation overall, but not evenly in all income classes. In 1981 Congress decided to index the personal exemptions and the rate brackets beginning in 1985. The adjustment will be based on changes in the consumer price index for the twelve months ending with September of the preceding calendar year.

The major argument for indexing is that the increases in effective income tax rates are unintentional by-products of inflation. Total tax receipts rise faster than incomes and the public sector grows more rapidly than it would in a noninflationary situation. Moreover, the increases in the real tax burdens are not selected by Congress but depend on the rate of progressivity and the rate of inflation.

An argument against indexing is that it reduces the built-in stabilizing effect of the income tax during periods of cyclical expansion and inflation. The rise in effective rates of a non-inflation-adjusted tax automatically reduces the growth of demand and thus contributes to the stability of the economy. However, indexing does contribute to stabilization when prices rise during periods of recession.

On balance, indexing seems to be justified in periods when inflation is running at a high rate, say, at 5 percent a year or more. At lower rates of inflation, some of the recorded increases in fixed-base price indexes may be illusory because of changes in buying patterns and quality changes of goods purchased. If indexing is to be retained, it would be more appropriate to adjust for bracket creep only for the excess of the inflation rate over some small percentage, say 2 or 3 percent, to avoid reducing real tax burdens under the guise of an adjustment for inflation. Even in a properly indexed system, it should be noted, average and marginal tax rates would still rise as real incomes increased.

Capital Gains and Losses

An economic definition of income would include all capital gains in taxable income as they accrue each year. To tax them in this way would be difficult for three reasons: first, the value of many kinds of property cannot be estimated with sufficient accuracy to provide a basis for taxation; second, most people would regard as unfair the requirement to pay tax on income that had not actually been realized; and third, taxation of accruals might force liquidation of assets to pay the tax. Thus capital gains are included in taxable income only when they are realized.

The United States has taxed the capital gains of individuals since it first taxed income. But this has not been the practice elsewhere until recently, when many countries began to tax capital gains, although generally at much lower rates of taxation than those applied to ordinary income.

HISTORICAL DEVELOPMENT. In the United States, realized capital gains were originally taxed as ordinary income, but since the Revenue Act of 1921 they have been subject to preferentially low rates. The provisions applying to such gains changed frequently during the 1920s and 1930s, but were stabilized beginning in 1942. In general, half of the capital gains on assets held for periods longer than six months were excluded in taxable income, and the amount of tax on such gains was limited to a maximum of 25 percent.

The 1969 act left all the old provisions intact, but added a new maximum rate of 35 percent on long-term capital gains of $50,000 or more and included in the base of the tax on preference income (see below) the half of capital gains excluded from taxable income. Gain on the sale of an owner-occupied house was exempt if the receipts from the sale were applied to the purchase of a new home of equal or greater value within eighteen months. For persons over sixty-five, such gains were entirely exempt up to $35,000 of the sale price. The holding period separating short- from long-term capital gains was lengthened from six to nine months in 1977 and twelve months beginning in 1978 (but the holding period for gains on farm commodity and other futures contracts remained at six months).

The thrust toward increased taxation of capital gains under the 1969 act was completely reversed by the 1978 act. The portion of long-run gains excluded from taxable income was raised from 50 to 60 percent, and the 35 percent maximum tax rate on gains of $50,000 or more became unnecessary because the 40 percent inclusion rate, combined with a top marginal rate of 70 percent, reduced the maximum rate to 28 percent. Taxpayers aged fifty-five or older were allowed a once-in-a-lifetime election to exclude $100,000 of gains from the sale of a permanent residence. The first $50,000 of long-term capital gains was excluded from the base of the tax on preference income.

The 1981 act continued the reduction of tax on capital gains by extending the rollover period for gains on sales of residences from eighteen months to two years and raising the exclusion for gains on sales of residences by elderly people from $100,000 to $125,000. The reduction of the top marginal rate on ordinary income to 50 percent, added to the 60 percent exclusion, reduced the maximum tax rate on long-term capital gains to 20 percent beginning in 1982.

THE ISSUES. From the standpoint of equity, it is well established that capital gains should be taken into account in determining personal income tax liability. Moreover, preferential treatment of capital gains encourages the conversion of ordinary income into capital gains. Business manipulation of this sort distorts patterns of investment and discredits income taxation. The low capital gains rates now apply to patent royalties, coal and iron ore royalties, income from livestock, income from the sale of unharvested crops, and real estate investments. The amount of ordinary income thus converted into capital gains is unknown, but a great deal of effort goes into this activity and it must be very substantial.

In addition to the overwhelming rate advantage, the law permits capital gains to escape income tax if they are passed from one generation to another through bequests, or if they are passed by gifts and are never realized by the recipient. The capital gain in assets transferred by gifts is taxed only if the assets are later sold. The result is that increases in the value of securities and real estate held in wealthy families may never be subject to income tax.

On the other hand, taxation on a realization basis requires some provision to moderate the effect of progressivity when large capital gains accumulated over many years are realized in a single year. Full taxation of gains is also criticized because it might have a substantial "locking-in" effect on investors and reduce the mobility of capital. It is also argued that preferential treatment of capital gains helps stimulate a higher rate of economic growth by increasing the attractiveness of investment generally and of risky investments in particular. In recent years, the principal argument for a reduced tax on capital gains has been that a considerable proportion of realized gains merely reflects inflation and is not real (see below for a discussion of the treatment of capital gains during inflation).

The "bunching" problem that would arise with full taxation of capital gains could be handled either by prorating capital gains over the length of time the asset was held or by extending the present general averaging system to the full amount of capital gains. (It now applies only to the portion of long-term gains that is included in taxable income.) Unless the present marginal rates were reduced, however, the tax might still discourage the transfer of assets. Part of the difficulty is that adherence to the realization principle permits capital gains to be taxed at declining effective tax rates the longer assets are held or to be transferred tax free either by gift or at death.

One solution to this problem is to treat capital gains as if they were constructively realized when given or bequeathed, with an averaging provision to allow for spreading the gains over a period of years. (This method was proposed by President Kennedy in 1963 and by President Johnson's Treasury Department in early 1969, but has not been seriously considered by Congress.) Under such a system, the remaining advantage to taxpayers from postponing the realization of capital gains would be the accumulation of interest on the tax postponed. Unless the assets were held for many years, this advantage for long-held assets would be small compared to the advantage of the tax exemption accorded to gains transferred at death; in any event, the interest on the tax postponed would be subject to income tax when the assets were transferred. In these circumstances, the incentive to hold gains indefinitely for tax reasons alone would be reduced.

ALTERNATIVE TREATMENT. In the quest to reconcile equity and economic objectives in the taxation of capital gains, tax experts differ about the best approach. Some believe that realized capital gains and those transferred by gift or bequest should be taxed in full, with a provision for averaging either over the period during which the asset was held or over an arbitrary but lengthy period. Others believe that present arrangements may be the best that can be devised, while still others insist that the capital gains rates are still too high. Most experts agree that there is little justification for granting preferential treatment to income that is not a genuine capital gain.

From 1948 through 1976 the preferential rates applied to capital gains on assets that had been held for longer than six months. This "holding period" was criticized as being both too long and too short. Investor groups urged that the holding period be reduced to three months, and some even recommended that it be eliminated entirely, maintaining that the resulting additional security transactions would increase capital gains tax revenues. On the other hand, if the purpose of the holding period is to differentiate between gains that are bunched and those that are not, there is no logical reason under an annual income tax to reduce the tax rate on incomes earned in less than a year. On this rationale, Congress raised the holding period from six to nine months in 1977 and to twelve months beginning in 1978. However, a proposal by representatives of the financial sector to restore the six-month holding period has considerable momentum.

The revenue effects of various revisions in the capital gains tax are shown in table 4-11. Since capital gains are heavily concentrated in the

Table 4-11. *Revenue Effects of Various Capital Gains Tax Revisions, by Adjusted Gross Income Class, 1985*

Income classes in thousands of dollars

Revenue change and adjusted gross income class	Constructive realization of gains at gift or death	Exclusion percentage reduced from 60 to 40 percent	Taxation at regular rates	
			Realized gains only	Realized and constructively realized gains
Revenue change[a] (billions of dollars)	2.4	4.9	15.7	23.0
	Percentage distribution of revenue change			
0–3	*	*	0.1	0.1
3–5	0.3	0.2	0.2	0.2
5–10	*	0.3	0.8	0.9
10–15	1.1	0.7	1.2	1.4
15–20	5.0	3.9	2.8	2.8
20–25	5.1	5.3	2.8	2.8
25–50	7.2	14.4	12.8	13.5
50–100	17.3	14.8	15.8	18.1
100–200	17.1	15.2	16.4	16.8
200–500	19.1	18.0	17.1	16.7
500–1,000	10.1	9.8	9.3	9.1
1,000 and over	17.7	17.3	16.4	16.0
All classes[b]	100.0	100.0	100.0	100.0
	Percentage change in tax liabilities			
0–3	c	c	c	c
3–5	c	c	c	c
5–10	c	c	c	c
10–15	0.2	0.3	1.5	2.6
15–20	0.7	1.0	2.4	3.5
20–25	0.6	1.2	2.0	2.9
25–50	0.2	0.6	1.8	2.8
50–100	0.6	1.6	3.5	5.9
100–200	1.4	2.6	8.8	13.2
200–500	2.6	5.0	15.3	21.7
500–1,000	4.7	9.4	28.4	40.5
1,000 and over	8.3	16.6	50.2	71.3
All classes[b]	0.8	1.7	5.3	7.7

Source: Brookings 1980 tax file, projected to 1985. Figures are rounded.
* Less than 0.05 percent.
a. Revenue effect for capital gains realizations estimated under the 1981 act rates.
b. Includes negative incomes not shown separately.
c. Percentages are not shown because tax liabilities in these classes may be negative, reflecting the refundable earned-income credit.

higher income classes, tax liabilities at the bottom of the income scale would not be much affected by changes in the capital gains tax, while those in the top classes would be substantially altered. The estimates assume that capital gains realizations would not be affected by the tax change, an assumption that may be unrealistic if present marginal tax rates remain unaltered. However, this effect could be moderated or completely offset if the revenue gains were used to substantially lower marginal rates in the top brackets.

CAPITAL LOSSES. In principle, capital losses should be deductible in full against either capital gains or ordinary income. However, when gains and losses are recognized only upon realization, taxpayers can easily time their sales so as to take losses promptly when they occur and to postpone gains for as long as possible. This asymmetry can be avoided under the U.S. system of capital gains taxation only by charging interest on the deferred tax on capital gains, a device that has never been seriously considered by Congress. The stopgap used in the United States is to limit the deduction of losses.

From 1942 through 1963, individuals were allowed to offset their capital losses against capital gains plus $1,000 of ordinary income in the year of realization and in the five subsequent years. In 1964 the loss-offset up to $1,000 of ordinary income was extended to an indefinite period. The loss-offset limit was raised to $2,000 for 1977 and $3,000 for 1978 and later years. In computing the offset, long-term losses were taken into account in full between 1952 and 1969; before 1952 and after 1969 only 50 percent of the net long-term loss could be offset against ordinary income up to the limit.

The annual limit on the amount of the offset is most harmful to people with modest investments, since they may not have large enough gains against which to subtract the losses they may incur. The only solution to this problem would be a pragmatic one that was reasonably liberal for the modest investor without opening the door to widespread abuse of the provision and large revenue losses. One practical approach would be to adjust the $3,000 limit on the loss-offset for the inflation that has occurred since it was last modified in 1978.

CAPITAL GAINS AND INFLATION. Capital gains cannot be treated on a par with current income flows when measuring income during a period of rising prices. An asset does not give the owner command over additional resources until the value of the asset exceeds its purchase price at prices prevailing when the asset is sold (or during the period of accrual, if the accounting is on an accrual basis). Thus, to measure the income from appreciated assets, the portion of the capital gain that results from inflation should be deducted from the nominal capital gain. The correction can be made by multiplying the purchase price of the asset by the ratio of a general price index (usually the consumer price index) on the date of sale to the value of the same index at the time of purchase. No correction is necessary for current income flows like wages and salaries, because they give the recipient command over resources in the prices of the period during which they are earned. (The bracket effect of inflation discussed in the previous section is a separate matter. Here the concern is with the measurement of income, which can be taxable under a fixed set of rates or rates that are indexed for inflation.)

A system corrected for inflation would have a dramatic effect on the distribution of taxable income. Many apparent capital gains would be converted to real losses, and real losses and gains that are now ignored would be recognized. For example, an individual who purchases an asset for $1,000 and sells it for $1,200 after holding it for a period during which prices have risen 50 percent would have a $200 nominal gain but a real loss of $300 at current prices. Assets that are fixed in money terms, such as bonds, mortgages, and bank deposits, generate real losses as prices increase. On the other hand, those who borrow money on fixed-dollar contracts repay their debts in depreciated dollars and thus gain from the rise in prices. All such gains and losses would have to be taken into account to calculate inflation-corrected income correctly.

The percentage of capital gains included in taxable income under an inflation-corrected system would not be a flat percentage, as it is under present U.S. tax law; it would vary with the rate of inflation and the length of time the asset was held. If the inflation rate were stable, the inclusion rate would actually rise with the length of time the asset was held. For example, suppose an asset purchased for $1 appreciated in real terms at the rate of 10 percent a year in a period in which prices also rose 10 percent a year. The real gain for a single year is just over half the nominal gain of 21 percent ($1.21 - 1.10 = 0.11$). After five years, the nominal value of the asset is 2.59 (1.21^5), the purchase price expressed in current prices is 1.61 (1.1^5), and the real gain measured in current prices is 0.98, or 62 percent of the nominal gain of 1.59.

The realization criterion would create problems if an inflation-corrected system were implemented on an equitable basis. If capital gains are taxed only when realized, the interest on the tax that is deferred during the period assets are held can be substantial. It would therefore be necessary to require taxpayers to correct nominal gains for the value of the tax deferral, as well as to permit them to adjust their gains for inflation. Such correction factors could be calculated in advance for different holding periods and provided in special tables to accompany the annual tax return.

Many proponents of the present treatment of capital gains favor an inflation adjustment for capital gains without making all the necessary refinements, including the adjustments for the real losses on assets fixed in money terms. Those who oppose the present treatment would argue against an inflation adjustment unless real capital gains were fully included in income, and some would insist on taking the value of tax deferral into account in computing tax liabilities even if real capital gains were taxed in full at realization.

Saving Incentives

Tax legislation in 1981 introduced a number of provisions specifically designed to increase saving. These include deductions for individual retirement accounts by employed and self-employed persons, which became effective in 1982, and an exclusion of 15 percent of net interest received (interest from all sources less interest paid on funds borrowed for purposes other than for a trade or business or a mortgage on the taxpayer's dwelling) up to $6,000 for married couples ($3,000 for single people), starting in 1985. The cuts in marginal tax rates made in 1981 were also justified on the ground that they would increase saving. Proposals are frequently made to permit additional deductions for savings set aside to accumulate the down payment for a house, to pay college tuition, or for other purposes.

The 1981 tax rate cuts and the deductions and exclusions for special types of savings have had no noticeable effect on the economy. The rate cuts were apparently allocated by households to consumption and saving approximately in the proportions they had allocated their disposable income before. The fatal flaw in the deductions and exclusions was that they rewarded people who borrowed money or switched existing savings into the tax-favored assets without necessarily doing any new saving. Moreover, the special deductions and exclusions have distorted savings decisions from their normal patterns. An exclusion of $400 of dividends and interest on joint returns ($200 for single persons), which was in effect for only one year (1981), also had little effect on saving.

As indicated in chapter 2, the most direct way to increase total national saving, and not merely private saving, would be to move toward a surplus in the federal budget. For each extra dollar the government reduces its borrowing, a dollar more of lendable funds is available for private investment. In contrast, each dollar of federal deficit drains a dollar from private lending, while only a small part of the tax cut dollar received by individuals is saved.

If it is agreed that individuals should be encouraged to save more by the tax system, the most appropriate solution would be to give people a deduction for net saving and let them decide how to invest it. This could be done by using the cash-flow approach designed for the consumption expenditure tax (see chapter 6). Taxpayers would list on a separate schedule their purchases of financial or business assets, payments on the principal of a home mortgage, and increases in bank and savings deposits during the year. From the total of these items, they would deduct sales of financial or business assets, reductions in bank and savings deposits, and increases in borrowing. The difference between these two sets of figures is net saving, which would be made deductible in full or up to a fixed amount. The same results could be achieved by substituting a consumption expenditure tax for part of the income tax.

State and Local Government Bond Interest

Interest received from state and local government bonds has been exempt from income tax ever since its enactment in 1913. The tax exemption has been criticized by secretaries of the treasury, tax experts, and others who believe that it is inequitable, reduces risk investment by high-bracket taxpayers, and costs the federal government an excessive amount. Interest rates on these bonds have increased as state and local debt has risen, and the relative advantage of the exemption to the top income classes has greatly increased. Proponents of the exemption argue that its elimination would make state and local borrowing costs prohibitive, which would be unwise in view of the mounting needs of these units of government. Bills to remove the exemption have reached a vote in Congress six times, but each time they have been defeated. Although Congress has not voted on the question since 1942, it is doubtful that a move to repeal the exemption would be successful today.

By discriminating between income from municipals and that from other securities, and by giving investors in the high income brackets an advantage (see table 4-12), the exemption violates the generally accepted

Table 4-12. *Revenue Effects of Taxing Interest on State and Local Government Bonds, by Adjusted Gross Income Class, 1985*

Income classes in thousands of dollars

Revenue change and adjusted gross income class	Individuals	Corporations[a]	Total
Revenue change[b] (billions of dollars)	4.1	11.6	15.7
	Percentage distribution of revenue change		
0–3	*	0.4	0.3
3–5	0.2	0.5	0.4
5–10	2.1	2.6	2.3
10–15	4.0	4.0	4.0
15–20	4.4	4.4	4.4
20–25	3.9	3.5	3.6
25–50	21.6	19.4	20.0
50–100	24.2	22.5	23.0
100–200	16.4	16.2	16.4
200–500	11.9	12.9	12.6
500–1,000	5.0	5.6	5.5
1,000 and over	6.4	7.3	7.1
All classes[c]	100.0	100.0	100.0
	Percentage change in tax liabilities		
0–3	d	d	d
3–5	d	d	d
5–10	d	d	d
10–15	1.3	3.7	5.0
15–20	1.0	2.5	3.5
20–25	0.7	1.8	2.5
25–50	0.8	2.0	2.8
50–100	1.4	3.7	5.1
100–200	2.3	6.3	8.6
200–500	2.7	8.2	10.9
500–1,000	3.7	11.7	15.4
1,000 and over	4.3	13.8	18.4
All classes[c]	1.4	3.8	5.2

Source: Brookings 1980 tax file, projected to 1985. Figures are rounded.
* Less than 0.05 percent.
a. Assumes corporation tax is borne by individuals in proportion to their divided income.
b. Does not take into account offsetting cost of alternative methods of subsidizing state and local government bond issues.
c. Includes negative incomes not shown separately.
d. Percentages are not shown because tax liabilities in these classes may be negative, reflecting the refundable earned-income credit.

principles that an income tax should apply equally to equal incomes and should be progressive. It also reduces investment in productive enterprises by diverting risk or venture capital from the private sector. It distorts the allocation of resources within the private sector, and between the public and private sectors, when state and local governments issue tax-exempt securities to finance such enterprises as public utilities, apartment developments, owner-occupied housing, and hospitals, or to subsidize local industry and student loans. Even many who favor the exemption agree that the use of so-called industrial development bonds to build tax-exempt facilities for private firms should be stopped. Since 1968 interest on large issues of such bonds has been subject to tax; the cutoff point is now $10 million. An exception to this limitation was provided for pollution control and airport construction bonds, and large numbers of these bonds have been issued in recent years. An explosive growth in the volume of tax-exempt mortgage subsidy bonds in the late 1970s led Congress to restrict the use of such bonds to low-income owner-occupied residential buildings with a maximum of four separate living units and to impose a cap on the amount that could be issued in any state. About half of the $86 billion of tax-exempt bonds issued in 1982 were used to finance private facilities or mortgages.

The exemption is an inefficient type of subsidy. Empirical studies suggest that the saving in interest payments by state and local governments is less than half the revenue loss to the federal government. There are not only less costly ways to assist or subsidize capital outlays by state and local governments, but also more equitable methods, since governmental units benefit not on the basis of need but on the basis of the amount of debt they issue.

Proposals to remove the exemption have usually been limited to new issues. This reflects the belief that taxing outstanding securities would be a breach of faith by the federal government, causing capital losses and the inequitable application of taxes to holders of existing securities.

Some lawyers have argued that taxing state and local bond interest is unconstitutional, whether the proposal is to apply the tax to new issues only or to existing ones as well. The majority opinion is that there is no constitutional bar to taxing state and local bond interest if Congress wants to do so.

Interest costs of state and local governments would rise if the exemption were removed. Municipals are more difficult to market than corporates and other securities. Many issues are too small to appeal to large institutional buyers, and lack of information about the finances of small units of local government discourages some investors. Thus, if municipals were fully taxable, they would have to bear higher interest rates than do corporate bonds of comparable quality. This would discourage borrowing by some localities and thereby reduce capital expenditures for public purposes. If total outlays were to rise in some areas, state and local taxes would ultimately be increased to meet higher interest charges. Since these taxes tend to be regressive, a greater burden might fall on the lower income groups. It has also been argued that the heavier financial burden on state and local governments, added to existing unmet needs for public facilities, would intensify pressure for federal aid, bring greater federal participation in local affairs, and further reduce the fiscal independence of states and localities.

Opponents of the exemption concede that some investment in social capital might be curtailed if the localities had to pay much higher interest rates on their borrowing. Consequently, they have often coupled suggestions for abolishing the exemption with proposals to provide alternative federal subsidies. These have generally taken one of two forms: (1) subsidies tied to state and local borrowing (for example, the payment of a portion of the interest on state and local debt by the federal government) as a quid pro quo for giving up the exemption or (2) subsidies tied to capital outlays rather than borrowing and thus not allocated strictly according to exemption benefits lost. In 1976 a House Ways and Means Committee bill included a provision that state and local governments could voluntarily relinquish the tax-exemption privilege for any specific bond issue and the treasury would pay 35 percent of the interest on the issue, depending on the value of the tax exemption in the market. The provision was not acted on by the House because of strong opposition by state and local officials and municipal bond dealers.

The major obstacle to reaching agreement on a more efficient subsidy to state and local governments is political. If the tax exemption is replaced by a generous subsidy, many people fear there will be an unhealthy increase in federal control over state and local fiscal affairs. Even the possibility of this is often sufficient to arouse opposition to removal of the exemption. Those opposed argue that the inefficiencies or tax inequities arising from the exemption are trivial compared with the dangers of more centralization of fiscal activity and possible disruption of the credit channels used by state and local governments. Others argue that efficiency and tax equity are important enough to justify exploring the possibility of substituting for the tax exemption an alternative formula that would not mean greater federal control.

Even if the tax exemption for state and local bond interest is retained, the case is weak for continuing the exemption for interest on bonds issued to finance private activities and housing. The revenue loss from these bonds will exceed $8 billion in 1984. Equity and economic efficiency would both be improved if the tax exemption privilege were limited to general obligation bonds assessed by state and local governments.

Income Averaging

The use of an annual accounting period, combined with progressive income taxes, results in a heavier tax burden on fluctuating incomes than on an equal amount of income distributed evenly over the years. For example, a single taxpayer who has a taxable income of $25,000 in each of two successive years pays a total tax before credit of $7,130 (1984 rates) in the two years. If $50,000 was received one year and nothing the next, the tax would be $12,014.

This type of discrimination is hard to defend on either equity or economic grounds. Taxpayers usually do not and cannot arrange their business and personal affairs to conform with the calendar. Annual income fluctuations are frequently beyond the control of taxpayers, yet they are taxed as if twelve months were a suitable horizon for decision-making. In addition, in the absence of averaging, there is great pressure for moderating the impact of the graduated rates on fluctuating incomes by lowering the rates applicable to them. As already indicated, reduced rates on capital gains have been justified on this basis although the rate reductions for such gains have more than compensated for the lack of averaging.

There is general agreement on the need for averaging, but the problem has always been administrative. Keeping an accurate account for a number of years is difficult for the government as well as for the taxpayer. It was therefore considered desirable to limit the averaging privilege to a relatively small number of taxpayers.

A start was made under the Revenue Act of 1964, which permitted averaging income over a five-year period if the income in the current year exceeded the average for the four prior years by one-third and if this excess was more than $3,000. Taxpayers who had been at least 50 percent self-supporting for the four prior years could average. The averaging technique is first to compute a tentative tax on one-fifth of the "averageable income" and then to multiply the tentative tax by five. The 1969 act increased the amount of income that can be averaged by permitting averaging if the current year's income exceeds the average of the four prior years by 20 percent and this excess is over $3,000. The 1969 act also permitted for the first time the averaging of the portion of capital gains included in taxable income.

The restriction of averaging to those who have an *increase* in income has benefited those with steadily rising incomes, not those with fluctuating incomes. Furthermore, it eliminated from the averaging system the millions of persons who have sharp reductions in income. It would be desirable to allow those with income reductions to average if a suitable way to avoid including retired persons in the averaging system could be devised.

In 1981 the averaging provision was used by 6.5 million taxpayers who saved $3.8 billion, or about 7 percent of the tax that would otherwise have been due.

Minimum Tax

An "add-on" minimum tax was introduced in 1969 in an attempt to obtain some tax contribution from wealthy people who had previously escaped income taxation on all or most of their income. The tax was levied at a 15 percent rate on a selected list of "preference" incomes to the extent that income from all the items exceeded $10,000 or half the regular income tax for the year, whichever was higher.

Beginning in 1983, the add-on minimum tax was replaced by an alternative minimum tax of 20 percent. The tax base for this tax is adjusted gross income plus the taxpayer's tax preferences less an exemption of $30,000 for single persons and $40,000 for married couples. The most important preference incomes in the alternative minimum tax base for individuals are the 60 percent of long-term capital gains excluded from taxable income, depletion deductions in excess of the amount that would be allowed on the basis of cost, intangible drilling costs for oil and gas to the extent they exceed the amount of deductions that would be allowed if these costs were capitalized and amortized, and accelerated depreciation on real property and equipment leases. The alternative minimum tax is paid when it exceeds the taxpayer's regular tax.

The alternative minimum tax has a number of deficiencies. First, the application of a low flat rate of tax violates the principle of progressivity. Since the tax applies only to wealthy people, the preference incomes would be taxed at or near the top-bracket rates if they were included in the regular income tax base. Second, the list of preferences is not comprehensive. The most important preferences omitted from the minimum tax base are tax-exempt interest and unrealized capital gains transferred by gift or at death. Third, the exemption restricts the applicability of the minimum tax to a small number of taxpayers.

An alternative method of accomplishing the same objective as the alternative minimum tax, proposed by the Treasury Department in 1973, would be to require that all individuals be taxable on no less than half their total income, including income from preference items. In computing the minimum taxable income subject to tax, allowances could be made for personal exemptions and essential deductions, such as extraordinary medical expenses and casualty losses. The advantage of this approach is that the regular progressive tax rates automatically apply to the minimum income subject to tax.

Another method of cutting down the benefits of tax-exempt income would be to allocate personal deductions proportionately between the individual's taxable and nontaxable sources and to permit a deduction only for the amount allocated to the taxable sources. This proposal is based on the reasonable assumption that personal outlays—whether deductible or not—come out of the taxpayer's total income, rather than out of his taxable income alone. The House version of the 1969 act included this provision, but it was eliminated by the Senate, largely because of the opposition of representatives of tax-exempt institutions and of state and local governments, who generally are against any proposal that would reduce the tax advantages of the charitable contribution deduction and of state and local securities.

Although allocation of deductions was rejected, the enactment of a minimum tax reflects an awareness on the part of Congress of the growing public resentment of unwarranted tax privileges. It is a weak compromise, but the minimum tax was a major break in the long struggle to achieve a more comprehensive income tax base. Mere publication of the amount of the tax preferences reported on tax returns has helped dramatize the inequities of the present tax structure. In 1981, $1.8 billion of additional tax on preference income was reported on 251,000 individual tax returns.

Tax Shelters

Tax shelters permit individuals to reduce drastically or even to wipe out tax liabilities on large incomes by taking advantage of preferential provisions in the tax law. A number of spectacular examples have been presented from time to time to the Ways and Means Committee by the staff of the Joint Taxation Committee. In one case, a man who participated in a real estate partnership reduced his economic income of $448,000 to an adjusted gross income of only $37,000 on the basis of an investment of $225,000 made by the partnership only three days before the end of the year. Many of these tax shelters are sold to individuals by promoters who misrepresent the tax law (these are called "abusive" tax shelters) and thus expose the individuals to audit and payment of deficiencies.

A tax shelter generally contains two basic elements: large current deductions for depreciation and interest on borrowed money, and deferral of inclusion of receipts in taxable income with possible capital gains treatment for such receipts when the investment is terminated. For example, a $1,000,000 investment with a depreciable life of five years would generate in the first year $400,000 of declining-balance depreciation at twice the straight-line rate plus interest on any funds borrowed to pay for the investment. If 80 percent of the $1 million were borrowed at a 10 percent rate, the interest deduction would amount to $80,000, and total deductions would come to $480,000 in the first year. Such deductions would ordinarily be sufficient to offset not only any current earnings from the investment, but also income from other sources. Ultimately, as the depreciation and interest deductions decline, the investor will sell the asset and can frequently apply capital gains treatment to most of the gain even though the depreciation was deducted at regular income tax rates.

Gains from the sale of property held for twelve months or less or of equipment regardless of the time held are treated as ordinary income up to the amount of depreciation previously taken, thus in effect "recapturing" the tax benefit of depreciation deductions. In the case of commercial, industrial, and unsubsidized residential buildings, the recapture provision applies only to the excess of accelerated depreciation over straight-line depreciation. In the case of housing projects subsidized by the government, excess depreciation is fully recaptured if the property is held less than 100 months (20 months for low-income housing) and the full gain, including excess depreciation, is taxable at capital gains rates after 200 months (100 months for low-income housing). However, tax shelters remain a serious problem because many other activities permit the conversion of ordinary deductions into capital gains, including equipment leasing, sports franchises, motion pictures, real estate, oil and gas drilling, and farming.

The proper way to remove the advantages of tax shelters would be to eliminate the favorable tax provisions and to tax "economic" income. This would require limiting depreciation deductions to economic depreciation and treating the gain on the disposition of assets as ordinary income. Alternatively, the artificial deductions arising in a tax shelter might be allowed only against the income generated by the shelter itself, thus limiting the loss offset to the earnings from the same project in future years. This provision, known as the limitation on artificial losses, was incorporated in the House tax reform bill of 1976, but was rejected by the Senate. Instead, Congress allowed taxpayers to take all the deductions available under the tax law up to the full amount of capital "at risk" (which is defined as the amount of cash or other property contributed to the business plus money borrowed on the taxpayer's personal liability or secured by personal assets). The provision applies to farming (except operations involving trees other than fruit or nut trees), oil and gas, motion pictures, and equipment leasing. Real estate investors are not subject to the at-risk provision, but are required to capitalize and amortize taxes paid during the construction period over ten years beginning in 1982 (1984 for residential housing). Subsidized housing projects were allowed current deductions for construction-period interest and taxes through 1981, and then amortized deductions over a four-year period starting in 1982 and rising to ten years in 1988. In 1982 new civil penalties were imposed on promoters of abusive tax shelters and the government was permitted to seek court injunctions to enjoin such activities.

Tax Simplification

Congress and every administration in recent years have paid lip service to the objective of tax simplification, but the income tax has become more and more complicated with the passage of every revenue act. The 1982 income tax return (Form 1040) contained, in addition to a two-page initial summary, nine separate schedules and thirty-five supplementary forms for detailed reporting of income receipts, deductions, and credits. The 1982 form listed eight adjustments that were allowed in arriving at adjusted gross income and eight tax credits. In 1960 there were only one adjustment to calculate adjusted gross income and one tax credit. The tax law and the tax return form were made even more complicated by the new tax preferences added in the 1981 tax act. There is no question that income tax reporting has become both aggravating and costly. Public opinion polls invariably report that millions of taxpayers feel they cannot cope with income tax reporting and must pay for assistance in the preparation of their forms.

The source of the complexity is the attempt by Congress and most administrations to do too much with the income tax. Whether it is promotion of jobs, energy saving, or incentives to work, save, and invest, the normal reaction is to add a special deduction or credit to the income tax to help achieve the allegedly urgent social objective. Every such departure from the normal structure of the income tax leaves its mark on the tax return and imposes additional burdens of record keeping for the taxpayer. The practice violates the principle that people with the same income should pay the same tax, narrows the tax base, and requires unnecessarily high marginal tax rates on the constricted base to raise the revenues needed from the income tax.

The solution to the complexity of the income tax is to simplify the tax law by repealing the special provisions and starting all over again. In the past, the forces arrayed against simplification through the elimination of tax preferences have been too powerful to permit any progress to be made in this way. But the idea of tax simplification has reappeared as the public has become fed up with the complications of the present income tax.

The idea is to tax all incomes without any exclusions, tax credits, or personal deductions (except for those that reduce ability to pay, such as unusual medical expenses and casualty losses); the increased tax base would then be used to reduce tax rates. Taxpayers would add up their income sources, subtract their personal exemptions and their unusual expenses, and calculate their tax liability from a tax table or the schedule of tax rates. With a fully comprehensive tax base, the tax rates could be cut by a minimum of 40 percent across the board.

The idea of a simplified, broad-based income tax has been supported recently by those who are interested in converting the income tax to a

Table 4-13. *Effective Tax Rates under Present Law and under a Comprehensive Income Tax Using Alternative Tax Rate Plans, by Income Class, 1984*

Income classes in thousands of dollars; rates in percent

Expanded adjusted gross income class[b]	Present law	Alternative plan[a]	
		Graduated rates, 9–28 percent[c]	Flat tax rate, 17 percent
0–5,000	0.7	0.0	0.0
5,000–10,000	4.0	1.6	3.0
10,000–15,000	6.0	4.2	7.1
15,000–20,000	7.7	6.5	9.2
20,000–25,000	9.1	8.3	10.6
25,000–35,000	10.0	10.0	11.8
35,000–50,000	11.4	12.4	13.0
50,000–100,000	15.5	16.3	14.2
100,000–500,000	23.0	22.1	15.4
500,000–1,000,000	26.4	25.4	15.9
1,000,000 and over	23.1	26.4	16.2
All classes[c]	12.0	12.0	11.9

Source: Joseph A. Pechman and John Karl Scholz, "Comprehensive Income Taxation and Rate Reduction," *Tax Notes*, vol. 17 (October 11, 1982), Brookings Reprint 390.

a. Assumes zero-bracket amount of $4,000 and exemption of $1,750 per capita plus an additional $1,750 for heads of households under both plans.

b. Adjusted gross income plus sick pay, excluded capital gains and dividends, interest on life insurance and state and local bond interest, all unemployment benefits, 50 percent of social security benefits, workmen's compensation, veterans' benefits, tax preferences reported for purposes of the minimum tax, one-third of employer-provided health insurance, employer-provided life insurance, and IRA deductions by those covered under private pension plans.

c. Rates are the same for all marital statuses: they rise from 9 percent on taxable income of less than $5,000 to 28 percent on the amount of taxable income in excess of $150,000. Married couples with two earners would receive a deduction of 25 percent of the earnings of the spouse with the lower earnings (for earnings up to $50,000).

"flat tax." The base of the flat tax would be the same as the broad-based tax just described. The only difference is that a single tax rate (between 15 and 20 percent, depending on how broad the base would become) would be substituted for a graduated rate schedule. However, the flat tax would do considerable violence to the distribution of tax burdens. As table 4-13 illustrates, it would increase average tax liabilities for the lower and middle income classes and reduce average tax liabilities for the highest income classes. At the top of the income scale, the flat tax would reduce average tax liabilities by 30 to 40 percent.

Most of the simplification that would be achieved under these approaches would come from the adoption of a comprehensive tax base. By removing the unnecessary deductions, exclusions, and tax credits, a comprehensive income tax would simplify the tax laws and the income tax return. Elimination of the distinction between capital gains and ordinary income alone would greatly reduce the size of the internal revenue code and simplify business decisions. The flat tax would eliminate the need for averaging and different tax rates for various marital statuses (see the sections on income averaging and income splitting above), but this added simplification would not justify the loss in equity resulting from the redistribution of tax burdens.

Summary

The individual income tax—the most important tax in the federal tax structure—is widely regarded as the fairest source of government revenues. Its yield expands or contracts more rapidly than personal income during a business cycle, imparting built-in flexibility to the revenue side of the federal budget. The tax is less burdensome on consumption and more burdensome on saving than a consumption or expenditure tax of equal yield would be. Its potential effect on work and saving incentives is unclear. There is little evidence to support the contention that the income tax has significantly retarded growth, or that a reduction in marginal tax rates would pay for itself.

Many unsettled problems remain regarding some of the major features of the individual income tax. These include the treatment of the family, the aged, earned income, special deductions for personal expenditures, capital gains and losses, the treatment of saving, tax-exempt interest, eligibility for averaging, the minimum tax, and tax shelters. Even in its present form, however, the individual income tax continues to be the best tax ever devised. Further improvement through broadening the tax base and lowering the tax rates would pay handsome dividends in still greater equity, simplification, and better economic performance.

CHAPTER FIVE

The Corporation Income Tax

THE CORPORATION INCOME TAX was enacted in 1909, four years before the introduction of the individual income tax. To avoid a constitutional issue, Congress levied the tax as an excise on the privilege of doing business as a corporation. The law was challenged, but the Supreme Court upheld the authority of the federal government to impose such a tax and ruled that the privilege of doing corporate business could be measured by the corporation's profits.

The corporation income tax produced more revenue than the individual income tax in seventeen of the twenty-eight years before 1941, when the latter was greatly expanded as a source of wartime revenue. From 1941 through 1967 corporation income tax receipts were second only to those of the individual income tax, but they were overtaken by payroll taxes in fiscal 1968 and have since been declining in importance. The corporation income tax accounted for about 6 percent of federal receipts in fiscal 1982, compared with 19 percent in 1968. Since the end of World War II, the corporate tax rate has been reduced from a peak of 52 percent in 1952–63 to 46 percent beginning in 1979.

A business enterprise enjoys special privileges and benefits when it operates in the corporate form. These include perpetual life, limited liability of shareholders, liquidity of ownership through marketability of shares, growth through retention of earnings, and possibilities of inter-corporate affiliations. Moreover, the modern corporation—particularly the large "public" corporation in which management and ownership are separated—generates income that nobody may claim for personal use. The growth of the corporate sector could not have taken place if the corporation had not been endowed with these valuable privileges. The Supreme Court's acceptance of the constitutionality of the corporation income tax was based on the view that the corporation owes its life, rights, and power to the government.

Few experts accept this rationale for a substantial tax on corporate profits. Instead, one justification seems to be that the corporation is a mechanism for accumulating capital that is managed by the corporate officers and directors, and is not really subject to the control of the owners—the stockholders. Proponents of the corporation tax believe that the earnings and economic power derived from this large stock of capital are a proper base for taxation.

Another reason for the corporation income tax is that it is needed to safeguard the individual income tax. If corporate income were not subject to tax, people could avoid the individual income tax by accumulating income in corporations. Short of taxing shareholders on their shares of corporate income whether the income is distributed or not (a method that has been proposed from time to time), the most practical way to protect the individual income tax is to impose a separate tax on corporate income. The existence of two separate taxes side by side creates other problems; these will be discussed at some length in this chapter.

Despite its long history in the United States, the corporation income tax is the subject of considerable controversy. In the first place, there is no general agreement about who really pays it. Some believe the tax is borne by the corporations and hence by their stockholders. Others believe it depresses the rate of return to capital throughout the economy and is therefore borne by owners of capital in general. Still others argue that the tax is passed on to consumers through higher prices, or may be shifted back to the workers in lower wages. Some believe that it is borne by all three groups—stockholders, consumers, and wage earners—in varying proportions. This uncertainty about the incidence of the tax makes strange bedfellows of individuals holding diametrically opposed views and often puts them in inconsistent positions. Some staunch opponents of a sales tax vigorously support the corporation income tax even though they profess to believe it is shifted to the consumer, while many who say that the corporation tax is "just another cost" (and is consequently shifted) demand that the tax be reduced and some form of consumption tax substituted for all or part of it.

Second, the proper relation between individual and corporation income taxes has never been settled. At various times, dividends have been allowed as a credit or deduction in computing the tax on individual income. Today, a $100 exclusion is allowed for dividends, which is intended to relieve the small shareholder from paying both individual and corporation income taxes on dividends. The present situation is makeshift and satisfies few people.

A third set of issues has to do with the impact of the corporation tax on the corporate sector and on the economy in general. It has been argued that, particularly during periods of inflation, the tax places a heavy burden on corporations and thus curtails business investment and reduces the nation's growth rate. Since interest paid is deductible in computing taxable corporation profits but dividends paid are not, the tax is said to favor debt over equity financing and to encourage the retention of earnings rather than paying them out in dividends. Some question the desirability of a tax that discourages the corporate form of business; others believe that alternative tax sources yielding the same revenue would be more harmful to the economy.

Fourth, the introduction of the investment tax credit and other preferences and the recent liberalization of depreciation allowances have sharply reduced the yield of the corporation income tax. Since corporate income is not measured or taxed uniformly, effective rates of tax vary widely among firms and industries. Under present circumstances, the major effect of the tax is to distort the allocation of investment funds rather than to reduce investment incentives generally.

Characteristics of the Tax

Since the corporation income tax is a tax on business, many of the refinements required in computing the taxable income of individuals do not arise. For example, the deductions allowed under the corporation income tax, with the exception of that for charitable contributions, are confined to expenses incurred in doing business. On the other hand, state and local bond interest is exempt from the corporation income tax as well as from the individual income tax. Capital gains and losses receive special treatment, but not the same as the treatment in the individual tax. Corporations are also required to pay taxes in quarterly installments as profits are earned during the year.

The Tax Base

The corporation income tax is a complicated instrument because it must be applied to a wide variety of organizations doing business in the corporate form or in a form that closely resembles a corporation. The major features will be discussed in later sections of this chapter, but at this point a number of the significant provisions may be noted.

1. As in the case of individuals, corporations may elect to be taxed on the capital gains they realize on assets held more than twelve months at a lower rate than that applying to ordinary income. But corporations are taxed at a rate of 28 percent on their long-term capital gains, while the maximum rate for individuals is 20 percent.

2. Whereas individuals may deduct half of net capital losses up to $3,000 from ordinary income and have an unlimited carry-forward, corporations are allowed to offset capital losses only against capital gains. The remaining capital losses may be carried back for three years and forward for five years to be offset against capital gains.

3. Net operating losses may be carried back and offset against taxable income of the three preceding years. If the income in these years is not sufficient, the remaining losses may be carried forward for fifteen years. In effect, this provides a nineteen-year period for offsetting losses against gains. These provisions are needed to avoid taxing corporations with fluctuating incomes more heavily than those with relatively stable incomes. Without carry-backs and carry-forwards of losses, corporations with losses in some years and net profits in others would have a higher taxable income than other corporations with the same average profits but no losses.

4. Very generous provision is now made for writing off the cost of capital in computing taxable income. In the case of plant and equipment, the original cost is depreciated or recovered over a specified period of years. Formerly, depreciation was based on the concept that the cost of an asset should be allocated over the period it was used to produce income. Since 1981 capital costs have been recovered over periods that are not only shorter than, but are generally unrelated to, useful lives. For minerals and gas and oil, the law allows deductions for the costs of exploration, discovery, development, and depletion, which often exceed the cost of the mine or oil or gas fields. In 1975 Congress limited the depletion deduction of integrated oil companies to recovery of cost.

5. An investment tax credit has also been allowed, with some interruptions, since 1962 for purchases of new equipment (new buildings are not entitled to the credit, but special credits are available for rehabilitation of structures). The credit was originally set at 7 percent of investment and was raised to 10 percent in 1975.

6. All current outlays for research and development may be deducted in full in the year they are made. Taxpayers may elect to capitalize such expenditures and, if regular depreciation cannot be used because the

useful life cannot be determined, the expenditures may be written off over a period of five years. In 1981 a tax credit of 25 percent was adopted for increases in research and development expenditures in the current year over the average of the three preceding years.

The provisions for net operating losses, recovery of capital, the investment credit, and research and development expenses (items 3, 4, 5, and 6 above) are also available to individuals and partnerships under the individual income tax.

7. Dividends paid by one corporation to another are subject to an additional tax at a low rate. Corporations are allowed to deduct 85 percent of the dividends they receive from other domestic corporations. This means that intercorporate dividends are subject to an extra tax of 6.9 percent (the regular 46 percent rate multiplied by 15 percent). The tax on intercorporate dividends is waived, however, if the two corporations are members of a group of affiliated corporations eligible to file a consolidated return.

8. Corporations are subject to U.S. tax on foreign as well as domestic income. Income earned by foreign branches (and certain corporations located in tax havens) is included in the corporation's tax return in the year it is earned. If the corporation operates through a foreign subsidiary, foreign earnings are subject to tax when they are distributed to the U.S. parent corporation as dividends. However, credit against the domestic tax is allowed for foreign income taxes and withholding taxes paid on earnings and dividends received from abroad. A domestic international sales corporation (DISC), which may be organized to handle the export business of a U.S. corporation, defers tax on part of its earnings until the earnings are returned to the parent corporation. Any domestic corporation can set up its own DISC subsidiary merely by electing to treat its export business separately from its domestic business.

9. Corporations with no more than thirty-five shareholders may elect to be treated as if they were partnerships for tax purposes. Such shareholders are subject to individual income tax on the entire earnings of the corporation, whether distributed or not, and may deduct any losses from other personal income. In 1979, 515,000 corporations reporting profits of $8.6 billion and deficits of $4.8 billion elected this treatment.

10. Financial institutions, including commercial banks, savings and loan associations, mutual savings banks, and insurance companies, are taxed, but they are permitted to accumulate substantial tax-free reserves

and some are allowed special deductions that are unrelated to the measurement of income. Religious, educational, and charitable organizations, trade associations, labor unions, and fraternal organizations are exempt from the corporation income tax, but the tax does apply to the "unrelated business income" of these organizations. Private foundations are subject to a special excise tax of 2 percent on their investment income. Cooperatives are subject to special provisions designed to tax their earnings at least once under the individual or corporation income tax, but the revenue collected from them is small. Investment funds that distribute at least 90 percent of their dividends and realized capital gains to their shareholders are not taxable on the distributed amounts.

Tax Rates

Since "ability to pay" does not apply to corporations as it does to individuals, the corporation income tax is levied at a flat rate on most corporate income. Lower rates are applied to the first $100,000 as a concession to small businesses; the remainder is taxed at one rate. The corporation tax is 15 percent on the first $25,000 of income, 18 percent on the second $25,000, 30 percent on the third $25,000, 40 percent on the fourth $25,000, and 46 percent on the excess over $100,000. About 83 percent of corporate taxable income is subject to the top rate.

A minimum tax is imposed on the preference items of corporations as well as individuals. The most important of these items for corporations are: 39 percent of long-term capital gains (that is, the proportion of gains not subject to the full corporation tax), accelerated depreciation on real property and equipment leases in excess of straight-line depreciation, depletion in excess of cost depletion, and bad-debt deductions of financial institutions in excess of loss experience. (Only a little over 70 percent of excess deductions for coal and iron ore depletion and bad debts of financial institutions are included in the minimum tax base, because they are among several preferences for which 15 percent was added back to the corporate tax base under the 1982 act.) The minimum tax is applied at a 15 percent rate to the amount of preference income above an exemption of $10,000 or the regular income tax paid, whichever is higher.

Tax Payment

Since 1967 large corporations and individuals filing declarations of estimated tax have paid tax on the same time schedule. The 1968 act extended the current payment system to all corporations, but permitted a phase-in for small corporations until 1977. Beginning in 1983, the estimated tax payments required from all corporations will increase from 80 to 90 percent of the current year's tax liability. However, exceptions based on prior years' income give considerable leeway to corporations with fluctuating income.

Shifting and Incidence of the Tax

There is no more controversial issue in taxation than the question, "Who bears the corporation income tax?" On this question, economists and businessmen alike differ among themselves. The following quotations are representative of these divergent views:

Corporate taxes are simply costs, and the method of their assessment does not change this fact. Costs must be paid by the public in prices, and corporate taxes are thus, in effect, concealed sales taxes. (Enders M. Voorhees, chairman of the Finance Committee, U.S. Steel Corporation, address before the Controllers' Institute of America, New York, September 21, 1943.)

The initial or short-run incidence of the corporate income tax seems to be largely on corporations and their stockholders. . . . There seems to be little foundation for the belief that a large part of the corporate tax comes out of wages or is passed on to consumers in the same way that a selective excise [tax] tends to be shifted to buyers. (Richard Goode, *The Corporation Income Tax*, Wiley, 1951, pp. 71–72.)

. . . The corporation profits tax is almost entirely shifted; the government simply uses the corporation as a tax collector. (Kenneth E. Boulding, *The Organizational Revolution*, Harper, 1953, p. 277.)

It is hard to avoid the conclusion that plausible alternative sets of assumptions about the relevant elasticities all yield results in which capital bears very close to 100 percent of the [corporate] tax burden. (Arnold C. Harberger, "The Incidence of the Corporation Income Tax," *Journal of Political Economy*, vol. 70, June 1962, p. 234.)

. . . An increase in the [corporate] tax is shifted fully through short-run adjustments to prevent a decline in the net rate of return [on corporate investment], and . . . these adjustments are maintained subsequently. (Marian Krzyzaniak and Richard A. Musgrave, *The Shifting of the Corporation Income Tax*, Johns Hopkins Press, 1963, p. 65.)

. . . There is no inter-sector inefficiency resulting from the imposition of the corporate profits tax with the interest deductibility provision. Nor is there any misallocation between safe and risky industries. From an efficiency point of view, the whole corporate profits tax structure is just like a lump sum tax on corporations. (Joseph E. Stiglitz, "Taxation, Corporate Financial Policy, and the Cost of Capital," *Journal of Public Economics*, vol. 2, 1973, p. 33.)

Unfortunately, economics has not yet provided a scientific basis for accepting or rejecting one side or the other. This section presents the logic of each view and summarizes the evidence.

The Shifting Mechanism

One reason for the sharply divergent views is that the opponents frequently do not refer to the same type of shifting. It is important to distinguish between short- and long-run shifting and the mechanisms through which they operate. The "short run" is defined by economists as a period too short for firms to adjust their capital to changing demand and supply conditions. The "long run" is a period in which capital can be adjusted.

THE SHORT RUN. The classical view in economics is that the corporation income tax cannot be shifted in the short run. The argument is as follows: all business firms, whether they are competitive or monopolistic, seek to maximize net profits. This maximum occurs when output and prices are set at the point where the cost of producing an additional unit is exactly equal to the additional revenue obtained from the sale of that unit. In the short run, a tax on economic profit should make no difference in this decision. The output and price that maximized the firm's profits before the tax will continue to maximize profits after the tax is imposed. (This follows from simple arithmetic. If a series of figures is reduced by the same percentage, the figure that was highest before will still be the highest after.)

The opposite view is that today's markets are characterized neither by perfect competition nor by monopoly; instead, they show considerable imperfection and mutual interdependence or oligopoly. In such markets, business firms may set their prices at the level that covers their full costs *plus* a margin for profits. Alternatively, the firms are described as aiming at an after-tax target rate of return on their invested capital. Under the cost-plus behavior, the firm treats the tax as an element of cost and raises its price to recover the tax. (Public utilities are usually able to shift the tax in this way, because state rate-making agencies treat the corporation tax as a cost.) Similarly, if the firm's objective is the after-tax target rate of return, imposition of a tax or an increase in the tax rate—by reducing the rate of return on invested capital—will have to be accounted for in making output and price decisions. To preserve the target rate of return, the tax must be shifted forward to consumers or backward to the workers, or be shifted partly forward and partly backward.

It is also argued that the competitive models are irrelevant in most markets where one or a few large firms exercise a substantial degree of leadership. In such markets, efficient producers raise their prices to recover the tax, and the tax merely forms an "umbrella" that permits less efficient or marginal producers to survive.

When business managers are asked about their pricing policies, they often say that they shift the corporation income tax. However, even if business firms intend to shift the tax, some doubts must be expressed about their ability to shift it fully in the short run. In the first place, the tax depends on the outcome of business operations during an entire year. Businessmen can only guess the ratio of the tax to their gross receipts, and it is hard to conceive of their setting a price that would recover the precise amount of tax they will eventually pay. (If shifting were possible, there would be some instances of firms shifting more than 100 percent of the tax, but few economists believe that overshifting actually occurs.)

Second, businessmen know that should they attempt to recover the corporation income tax through higher prices (or lower wages), other firms would not necessarily do the same. Some firms make no profit or have large loss carry-overs and thus pay no tax; among other firms, the ratio of tax to gross receipts differs. In multiproduct firms, the producer has even less basis for judging the ratio of tax to gross receipts for all products. All these possibilities increase the uncertainty of response by other firms and make the attempt to shift part or all of the corporation income tax hazardous.

THE LONG RUN. In the long run, the corporation income tax influences investment by reducing the rate of return on corporate equity. If the corporation income tax is not shifted in the short run, net after-tax rates of return are depressed, and the incentive to undertake corporate investment is thereby reduced. After-tax rates of return tend to be equalized with those in the noncorporate sector, but in the process corporate capital and output will have been permanently reduced. Thus, in the absence of short-run shifting, the burden of the tax falls on the owners of capital in general.

Where investment is financed by borrowing, the corporation tax cannot affect investment decisions because interest on debt is a deductible expense. If the marginal investment of a firm is fully financed by debt, the corporation tax becomes a lump-sum tax on profits generated

Figure 5-1. *Percentage of Business Income Originating in the Corporate Sector, 1929–82*[a]

Percent

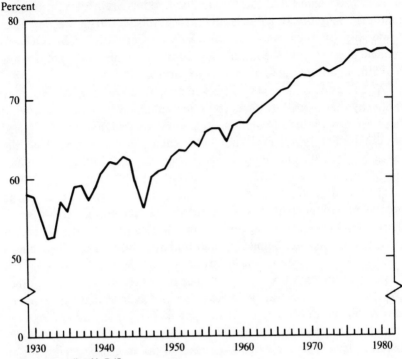

Source: Appendix table D-17.
a. Business income is national income originating in business enterprises.

by previous investments and is borne entirely by the owners of the corporation, the stockholders. In view of the recent large increase in debt financing (see the section on equity and debt finance below), a substantial proportion of the corporation income tax may now rest on stockholders and not be diffused to owners of capital in general through the shifting process just described.

The Evidence

The evidence on the incidence of the corporation income tax is inconclusive. The data do not permit a clear determination of the factors affecting price and wage decisions. Different authors examining the same set of facts have come to diametrically opposite conclusions.

Table 5-1. *Rates of Return and Debt-Capital Ratio, Manufacturing Corporations, Selected Periods, 1927–80*

Item	1927–29	1936–39	1953–56	1957–61	1964–67	1968–71	1977–80
Return on equity[a]							
Before tax	8.8	7.8	18.4	14.1	17.8	13.5	20.6
After tax	7.8[b]	6.4[b]	9.2	7.3	10.1	6.8	14.6
Return on total capital[a,c]							
Before tax	8.7	7.3	15.7	12.2	14.9	11.6	17.1
After tax	7.8[b]	6.2[b]	8.2	6.8	9.1	7.0	13.3
Ratio of debt to total capital[d]	15.2	15.0	19.0	20.5	25.1	32.7	34.5
General corporation tax rate[e]	12.2	17.0	52.0	52.0	48.5	50.7	47.0

Source: Appendix table D-18.
a. Equity and debt capital are averages of book values for the beginning and end of the year.
b. Rates of return are slightly understated (probably by 0.3 percentage point or less) because no allowance has been made for the foreign tax credit.
c. Profits plus interest paid as a percentage of total capital.
d. End of year.
e. Statutory rate of federal corporation income tax applicable to large corporations (average of annual figures).

Over the long run, unincorporated business has not grown at the expense of incorporated business in the United States. Corporations accounted for 58 percent of the national income originating in the business sector in 1929, 61 percent in 1948, 74 percent in 1975, and 76 percent in 1981 (figure 5-1). Much of the increase comes from the relative decline in industries, particularly farming, in which corporations are not important; but even in the rest of the economy, there is no indication of a shift away from the corporate form of organization. The advantages of doing business in the corporate form far outweigh whatever deterrent effects the corporation tax might have on corporate investment.

Beyond this, the data are conflicting. On the one hand, rates of return reported by corporations after tax have been slightly higher since the end of World War II than in the late 1920s, when the corporation income tax was much lower. After-tax rates of return on equity capital in manufacturing averaged 7.8 percent in 1927–29, 9.2 percent in 1953–56, 10.1 percent in 1964–67, and 6.8 percent in 1968–71, and then they rose to 14.6 percent in 1977–80, reflecting the effect of inflation. On total capital (equity plus debt), the returns for those same periods were 7.8 percent, 8.2 percent, 9.1 percent, 7.0 percent, and 13.3 percent, respectively (table 5-1). Before-tax rates of return were 50 to 100 percent higher than in the late 1920s.

On the other hand, except for recession years, the share of property income before tax (profits, interest, and capital consumption allowances)

Figure 5-2. *Property Income Share in Corporate Gross Product less Indirect Taxes, 1929–82*[a]

Percent

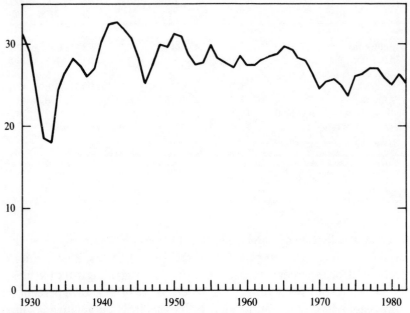

Source: Appendix table D-17.

a. Property income includes corporate profits before taxes after capital-consumption and inventory valuation adjustments, and net interest.

in the corporate gross product changed little over the same period (figure 5-2). Corporations have been able to increase their before-tax profits enough to avoid a reduction in the after-tax return without increasing their share of income in the corporate sector. This suggests that corporations have increased rates of return before tax not by marking up prices or lowering wages, but by making more efficient use of their capital. But what might have occurred without the tax is unknown, and its long-run effect remains unclear.

The burden of corporate taxation borne by individuals is strikingly different under the different incidence assumptions. The tax is regressive in the lower income classes and mildly progressive in the higher ones if as much as one-half is shifted forward to consumers in the form of higher prices and the remainder is borne by owners of capital in general. If the entire tax is borne by capital, progressivity increases in the higher income classes. The tax is even more progressive if it rests on stockholders (table 5-2).

Table 5-2. *Effective Rates of the Corporation Income Tax,*
by Income Percentiles, 1975
Percent

Household income percentile[a]	If half the tax is borne by owners of capital and half is shifted to consumers	If the tax is borne by owners of capital in general	If the tax is borne by stockholders
0–5	9.7	2.2	0.8
5–10	4.0	0.9	0.4
10–15	3.1	0.8	0.2
15–20	3.2	1.1	0.3
20–25	2.9	1.2	0.4
25–30	2.7	1.3	0.4
30–35	2.7	1.2	0.4
35–40	2.7	1.3	0.4
40–45	2.6	1.4	0.3
45–50	2.6	1.5	0.4
50–55	2.6	1.6	0.5
55–60	2.6	1.8	0.6
60–65	2.6	1.8	0.5
65–70	2.6	1.8	0.6
70–75	2.6	1.9	0.6
75–80	2.6	1.9	0.7
80–85	2.6	2.1	0.8
85–90	2.6	2.5	1.2
90–95	2.8	3.0	1.8
95–99	2.9	4.2	4.7
99–100	3.2	5.4	10.1
All classes[b]	2.8	2.6	2.2

Source: Brookings 1975 MERGE data file.
a. Ranked from low to high incomes. Income is defined as money factor incomes plus transfer payments, accrued capital gains, and indirect business taxes.
b. Includes negative incomes. The average burden of the corporation income tax is different under the different assumptions because the portion of the tax borne by the tax-exempt sector (and therefore not included in the household sector) varies.

Economic Issues

The corporation income tax has been subject to a continuous barrage of criticism on economic grounds. The most critical issues are its effect on investment and saving, equity and debt finance, resource allocation, built-in flexibility, and the balance of payments. The charges and countercharges reflect different assumptions about who bears the tax and the inherent difficulty of separating the effect of taxation from other factors.

Investment and Saving

The corporation income tax may affect investment in two ways: through investment incentives or through the availability of funds for investment.

INVESTMENT INCENTIVES. New investments will be undertaken by corporations if they promise to yield a satisfactory rate of return *after tax.* The higher the corporation tax, the higher the pre-tax rate of return must be to preserve the after-tax return. To remain equally attractive, an investment that promised a 10 percent return in the absence of the tax must yield a pre-tax rate of return of 18.5 percent with a tax rate of 46 percent. If 10 percent after tax is required to induce investments, corporations will defer the construction of new facilities and the purchase of new equipment unless there are projects that yield 18.5 percent or more before tax. This is the process, discussed earlier, through which the tax exercises its effect on investment; it depends crucially on the assumption that the corporation income tax is not shifted in the short run and that the marginal investment is financed out of equity rather than debt capital.

Is it possible to detect any reduction in the rate of investment that can be attributed to the corporation income tax? The answer is no, for three reasons. First, high tax rates were introduced during World War II, when wartime demands and support by government helped maintain investment at a high level. In the immediate postwar period, the rate of investment was extremely high because of the huge backlog of demand. Investment demand receded in the late 1950s, but this is attributed primarily to the slowdown in the rate of economic growth. The ratio of investment to the gross national product rose steadily during the 1960s and 1970s.

Second, the proportion of corporate capital financed by debt has been increasing since 1946 (see the section on equity and debt finance below). Since the corporation income tax is levied only on the residual after the payment of interest, the burden of the tax on investment has been declining.

Third, although the corporation tax rate has remained at a high level in recent years, its effect on investment has been cushioned by substantial increases in capital-consumption allowances. Whereas straight-line depreciation was the rule before World War II, the tax law has allowed more accelerated depreciation methods since 1954 and since 1981 has sharply reduced the period over which depreciation is taken. In addition, as was noted above, a tax credit has been allowed, with some interruptions, for investment in machinery and equipment since 1962. The effect of these changes may be illustrated by the following figures: in 1951 the corporation tax amounted to 44.3 percent of corporate profits before tax; it was reduced to 34.3 in 1965, 28.0 percent in 1975, 20.4 percent in 1981, and 13.1 percent in 1982 (table 5-3). This reduction in the effective rate occurred during a period when the general corporation income tax rate was reduced from 52 to 46 percent, or only 6 percentage points. (These are effective rates on nominal income. See below for a discussion of the effect of inflation on corporate tax burdens.)

AVAILABILITY OF FUNDS. All other things equal, the corporation income tax may be expected to reduce the amount of corporate funds available for investment, but other factors have been operating to maintain internal corporate funds at a high level. The high post–World War II individual tax rates on regular income and the preferential rate on capital gains stimulated a higher rate of corporation retentions (that is, lower dividend pay-out rates) than in the 1920s. In addition, the investment credit and the generous depreciation allowances enacted in later years have enabled corporations to set aside large amounts for investment purposes.

Since the end of World War II, dividends have been less than 25 percent of the cash flow of corporations (appendix table D-17). This is considerably lower than the rate in the late 1920s. As a result of the lower dividend rates and higher depreciation allowances, gross corporate saving has more than kept pace with the growth of the economy, rising from 7.3 percent of GNP in 1929 to 8.4 percent in 1982. During the large upswing in investment in the first half of the 1960s, internal sources of funds generally exceeded plant and equipment expenditures of corporations in each year; in the last half of the decade and in the 1970s, internal funds were insufficient to finance all corporate investment (appendix table D-19). This was due in part to the high level of investment demand and to a decline in the rate of corporate profits. After the burst of inflation beginning in 1973, corporation taxes were relatively high because profits were inflated by inventory gains, but the rate of investment continued to grow modestly. Thus the evidence suggests that the supply of corporate funds has not been impaired by the corporation income tax.

Table 5-3. *General Corporation Income Tax Rate and Effective Rate of the Federal Income Tax on Profits of U.S. Corporations from Domestic Operations, 1950–82*

Year	Corporation income tax rate (percent)	Corporation profits before tax[a] (billions of dollars)	Federal corporation taxes[b]	
			Amount (billions of dollars)	Percent of profit before tax
1950	42.00	41.1	15.6	38.0
1951	50.75	42.7	18.9	44.3
1952	52.00	37.9	16.7	44.1
1953	52.00	40.6	17.6	43.4
1954	52.00	38.3	16.6	43.3
1955	52.00	49.3	20.8	42.2
1956	52.00	49.2	20.5	41.7
1957	52.00	47.6	19.9	41.8
1958	52.00	43.4	17.5	40.3
1959	52.00	52.2	21.6	41.4
1960	52.00	50.2	20.5	40.8
1961	52.00	51.0	20.8	40.8
1962	52.00	57.8	21.7	37.5
1963	52.00	62.4	23.7	38.0
1964	50.00	69.1	24.5	35.5
1965	48.00	80.4	27.6	34.3
1966	48.00	86.5	29.8	34.5
1967	48.00	84.1	28.0	33.3
1968	52.80	92.7	30.2	32.6
1969	52.80	91.2	29.7	32.6
1970	49.20	78.5	26.3	33.5
1971	48.00	90.9	30.1	33.1
1972	48.00	106.8	33.4	31.3
1973	48.00	126.2	39.0	30.9
1974	48.00	134.3	40.0	29.8
1975	48.00	136.3	38.2	28.0
1976	48.00	168.0	48.7	29.0
1977	48.00	203.0	55.7	27.4
1978	48.00	237.7	64.3	27.1
1979	46.00	255.4	64.9	25.4
1980	46.00	254.8	58.6	23.0
1981	46.00	261.9	53.5	20.4
1982	46.00	238.3	31.3	13.1

Source: Appendix table D-15.

a. Profits before taxes as defined in the national income accounts plus accelerated depreciation over straight-line depreciation, dividends allocated by corporations to noninsured private pension plans, and net gains from sales of property, less taxable foreign income, state income taxes, Federal Reserve Board earnings, and Subchapter S income.

b. Federal corporation income tax as defined in the national income accounts less the Federal Reserve Board payment to the U.S. Treasury and the temporary surcharge of 1968–70. Excludes excess profits taxes.

Equity and Debt Finance

Corporations are allowed to deduct from taxable income interest payments on borrowed capital, but there is no corresponding deduction for dividends paid out to stockholders in return for the use of their funds as equity capital. At the present 46 percent tax rate, a corporation must earn $1.85 before tax to be able to pay $1 in dividends, but it needs to earn only $1 to pay $1 interest. This asymmetry makes the cost of equity more "expensive" for the corporation than an equal amount of borrowed capital. In fact, in combination with the accelerated cost recovery system and the investment tax credit, the allowance of an interest deduction provides a substantial subsidy to investment.

Large corporations borrow long-term capital funds at interest rates ranging from, say, 10 to 15 percent. With stocks selling at ten to fifteen times net earnings, corporate earnings *after* tax on equity capital range between 7 and 10 percent. Under these conditions, the earnings rate before tax (at the rate of 1.85:1) must range between 13.0 and 18.5 percent to prevent equity financing from reducing the rate of return. It is in this sense that equity capital costs more than borrowed capital.

Financial experts discourage large amounts of debt financing by corporations. Debt makes good business sense if there is a safe margin for paying fixed interest charges. But business firms may be tightly squeezed when business falls off, and the margin will evaporate rapidly. At such times, defaults on interest and principal payments and bankruptcies begin to occur. Even though borrowed capital may increase returns to stockholders, corporations try to finance a major share of their capital requirements through equity capital (mainly retained earnings) to avoid these risks.

The available data suggest that these reasons for caution have tended to restrain the use of borrowed capital despite its lower cost. However, the ratio of debt to total capital rose gradually immediately after World War II and increased rapidly during the 1960s and the 1970s. The ratio for manufacturing corporations was about 15 percent in 1927–29, 20.5 percent in 1957–61, 25.1 percent in 1964–67, 32.7 percent in 1968–71, and 34.5 percent in 1976–79 (table 5-1).

Resource Allocation

If the corporation income tax is not shifted in the short run, it becomes in effect a special tax on corporate capital. This does not necessarily mean that the tax permanently reduces rates of return on capital in the corporate sector relative to returns in the noncorporate sector. Capital may flow out of the taxed industries into the untaxed industries, and rates of return will tend to equalize. In the process, the allocation of capital between corporate and noncorporate business will be altered from the pattern that would have prevailed in the absence of the tax.

How much capital, if any, has left the corporate sector as a result of the corporation income tax is not known. It is possible that the corporate form of doing business is so advantageous for nontax reasons that, for the most part, capital remains in the corporate sector despite the tax. To the extent that corporate investment is financed by debt, the corporation income tax does not affect investment incentives because interest on debt is deductible as a business expense. The same is true if the capital-consumption allowances are so liberal as to be the equivalent of expensing (as under present law). In addition, the preferential treatment of capital gains under the individual income tax provides an offsetting incentive to invest in the securities of corporations that retain earnings for reinvestment in the business. These earnings show up as increases in the price of common stock rather than as regular income. In any case, the corporate sector has been getting larger, both relatively and absolutely, for decades (figure 5-1 and appendix table D-17). The discouragement of investment in the corporate form induced by the tax system, if any, must have been comparatively small. However, recent studies have shown that the tax preferences for home ownership have siphoned off some savings that might have been invested in plant and equipment, particularly during the inflation of the 1970s when housing prices rose much faster than the general price level.

Distortions may also take place if the tax is shifted in the short run. If prices increase in response to an increase in the tax, they rise in proportion to the use of corporate equity capital in the various industries. Consumers will buy fewer goods and services produced by industries using a great deal of corporate capital because the prices of these products will have risen most, and they will buy more goods and services produced by industries with less corporate capital. Within the corporate sector, profits will fall in the "capital-intensive" industries as a result of the decline in sales and will rise in the "labor-intensive" industries. In the end, not only will less capital be attracted to the corporate sector, but less will be attracted to the capital-intensive industries in that sector, and the economy will suffer a loss in efficiency as a result. The quantitative effect of this process is heavily dependent, of course, on the degree to which the noncorporate form of doing business can be substituted for the corporate form and production can be transferred from capital-intensive to labor-intensive industries. As in the nonshifting case, even a shifted corporate tax would tend to distort the composition of output.

Major distortions have been introduced by the allowances for investment and the deduction for interest on borrowed capital. The depreciation allowances under the accelerated cost recovery system (ACRS) plus the investment credit are equivalent on average to expensing of capital equipment, which can be shown to be equivalent to a zero tax on investment under certain conditions (see below). If the investment is financed by debt, the tax is actually converted to a subsidy. Moreover, the investment tax credit is allowed only for equipment and the depreciation allowances under ACRS are much less generous for buildings than for equipment. The result is that machinery is treated much more favorably than plant and other structures, inventories, and intangibles. Thus the effect of the capital allowances and the interest deduction differs greatly among different assets and industries, varying from large subsidies for some to positive taxes for others (see table 5-6 and discussion of ACRS below). The distortions thus introduced inevitably result in a misallocation of resources.

Built-in Flexibility

Receipts from the corporation income tax are volatile over the business cycle because corporate profits rise and fall more sharply than other incomes. However, this characteristic does not necessarily qualify the tax as an effective built-in stabilizer. To qualify, a tax must automatically moderate the changes in consumer disposable income or reduce fluctuations in investment. When profits fall, dividends are apt to be maintained, but this appears to be due largely to the dividend policy of corporations rather than to the reduction in tax paid by corporations. Similarly, corporate investments are determined largely by current and prospective sales volume and rates of return, although the reduced tax liability may have an effect through its impact on cash flow. Thus the corporation income tax is not one of the significant built-in stabilizers, despite its contribution to the large swings in federal surpluses and deficits during business cycles.

Table 5-4. *Changes in Real Gross National Product and Disposable Personal Income in Eight Postwar Recessions*
Billions of 1972 dollars

Pre-recession peak	Recession trough	Gross national product[a]	Federal receipts[a]	Federal corporation tax[a]	Undis-tributed corporate profits[a]	Disposable personal income[a]
1948:4	1949:2	−7.6	−5.5	−3.9	−7.8	−4.0
1953:2	1954:2	−20.2	−16.7	−8.5	−3.3	−3.5
1957:3	1958:1	−23.0	−10.7	−7.1	−8.8	−1.1
1960:1	1960:4	−8.6	−5.9	−6.8	−6.8	+3.7
1969:3	1970:4	−7.3	−20.4	−8.1	−8.5	+22.9
1973:4	1975:1	−60.7	−11.0	−10.1	−15.0	−30.7
1980:1	1980:3	−32.3	−4.6	−8.1	−14.4	−6.2
1981:3	1982:4	−45.1	−32.7	−14.6	−18.9	−1.4

Source: U.S. Department of Commerce, Bureau of Economic Analysis.
a. Current dollar magnitudes deflated by the GNP deflator.

The more important stabilizing feature of the corporate sector is the policy of cutting into saving rather than reducing dividends when economic activity declines. A reduction in retained corporate earnings prevents a corresponding decline in disposable personal income, thus maintaining spending on the part of consumers. Quantitatively, corporate saving is second only to the federal tax structure as a built-in stabilizer. In five of the eight recessions following World War II, undistributed profits of corporations declined about as much as or more than federal receipts; in the 1981–82 recession real undistributed profits fell $18.9 billion and total real federal receipts declined $32.7 billion (table 5-4). Largely because of the decline in corporate saving and federal receipts, real disposable personal income rose in the 1960–61 and 1969–70 recessions and declined much less than the real gross national product in the other six recessions since the end of World War II.

Balance of Payments

During the 1950s and 1960s, when the world operated under a system of fixed exchange rates, the corporation income tax figured prominently in discussions of ways to improve the U.S. balance of payments. It was contended that the United States should, for competitive reasons, reduce the corporation income tax, enact a value-added tax (see chapter 6) as a substitute, and rebate the value-added tax on exports.

Since a value-added tax is rebated for exports, it has no effect on prices in international markets, but a shifted corporation income tax would raise export prices and should be rebated. A corporation income tax that was not shifted would have no effect on prices and should not be rebated. Over the long run, however, removal of a nonshifted corporation income tax and substitution of a value-added tax would raise the net yield to capital. Assuming exchange rates are fixed, capital would be attracted from abroad and the outflow of capital from the United States would be discouraged. Larger investment would increase productivity and better the competitive position of U.S. industry, leading to an improvement in the balance of payments. However, the improvement would probably be small because the spread in effective corporation tax rates between the United States and most developed countries is small (appendix table D-5).

The analysis is different in a world where countries rely on flexible exchange rates to adjust external imbalances; this has been the case since 1973. When exchange rates are free to find their own levels in international financial markets, changes in tax rates or in the taxes used have little lasting effect on the competitiveness of the goods manufactured by a single country or its attractiveness as a place to invest. For example, if an unshifted corporation income tax were eliminated in the United States, rates of return would increase and the country would become temporarily more attractive to foreign investors. But the inflow of funds from abroad would raise the value of the dollar and make U.S. exports of goods less competitive in world markets. Ultimately, the advantage of eliminating the corporation income tax would be wiped out. Similarly, with a shifted corporation tax, the price of U.S. exports would decline if the tax were eliminated, but the increased trade balance would also raise the value of the dollar, make U.S. products more expensive on world markets, and soon wipe out the advantage gained by eliminating the corporation tax. In effect, floating exchange rates (without intervention to moderate fluctuations) permit countries to decide what type of tax structure they wish to have for domestic reasons, without being constrained by fear of foreign repercussions.

Structural Features

The structural features of the corporation income tax are highly technical and therefore rarely understood by the average taxpayer. The major features are (1) allowances for capital consumption; (2) depletion and other allowances for the mineral industries; (3) treatment of financial institutions; (4) treatment of tax-exempt organizations; (5) recognition of gain or loss on intercorporate asset transfers and on asset distributions to stockholders; and (6) treatment of foreign and export income. (The first, second, and sixth features also apply to individual income taxation, but they are treated here because their revenue and economic implications are much more important in the corporation income tax.) The purpose of this discussion is to show how these technical features affect particular firms and industries, the economy as a whole, and the equity and yield of the corporation income tax.

Capital-Consumption Allowances

The law has always permitted "a reasonable allowance for the exhaustion, wear and tear" of capital as a deduction in computing taxable income. A deduction for economic depreciation (the actual decline in the value of an asset as it ages) is necessary to avoid taxing capital rather than income. Capital-consumption allowances in excess of economic depreciation have been used in the United States and other countries as devices to stimulate investment.

DEPRECIATION. In most income tax systems, the annual deduction for depreciation is determined by spreading the cost of the depreciable asset over its "service life." Before 1954 the law and regulations were relatively strict, requiring fairly exact estimates of the period of use. Asset costs were amortized primarily by the "straight-line" method, which assumes a uniform amount of depreciation each year. The declining-balance method at 1.5 times the straight-line rate, while not specifically authorized by statute, was also permitted but seldom used. In 1954 the law was amended to permit the use of the declining-balance method for new property with an annual depreciation rate twice the straight-line rate or the sum-of-years'-digits method. The capital-recovery allowances enacted in 1981 are loosely based on the declining-balance method of calculating depreciation (see below).

The differences between the three methods are illustrated for a $1,000 asset with a service life of ten years in table 5-5. The straight-line method provides a uniform annual depreciation deduction of $100 a year. The declining-balance method permits the taxpayer to use a *rate* of depreciation and to apply this rate to the undepreciated amount each year. In the

Table 5-5. *Three Methods of Depreciation for a Ten-Year,*
$1,000 Asset
Dollars

| | Depreciation | | |
| | Straight-line | Double declining-balance | Sum-of-years'-digits |
Year	Straight-line	Double declining-balance	Sum-of-years'-digits
1	100	200.0	182
2	100	160.0	164
3	100	128.0	145
4	100	102.0	127
5	100	82.0	109
6	100	66.0	91
7	100	65.5	73
8	100	65.5	55
9	100	65.5	36
10	100	65.5	18
Total	1,000	1,000.0	1,000
Present value at 10 percent depreciation allowances	614	685	709
Tax value of depreciation allowances[a]	283	315	326

a. At a tax of 46 percent.

first year, the double declining-balance method provides a 20 percent allowance, or $200, leaving $800 undepreciated. In the second year, the 20 percent is applied to $800, giving an allowance of $160, and so on. Under the sum-of-years'-digits method, the fraction allowed as depreciation each year is computed by dividing the number of years still remaining by the sum of years in the useful life. With a ten-year asset, the sum of the years is 55 (10 + 9 + 8 · · · + 2 + 1), so that the depreciation allowance is ten fifty-fifths in the first year, nine fifty-fifths in the second year, and so on until it reaches one fifty-fifth in the tenth year. (The taxpayer is permitted to switch to straight-line depreciation at any time; as is shown in the example, this is profitable beginning in the seventh year under the declining-balance method but is not profitable at any time for a ten-year asset under the sum-of-years'-digits method.)

As table 5-5 shows, the two accelerated depreciation methods concentrate a larger percentage of the deductions in the early years. Under straight-line depreciation, half the original cost of a ten-year asset is written off in the first five years, compared with 67 percent under the double declining-balance method and 73 percent under the sum-of-years'-digits method. A useful way of comparing the value of the three methods is shown in the last line of the table. At a corporation income tax rate of 46 percent, the present value at the time of investment of the tax savings from the depreciation deductions (assuming a 10 percent interest rate) is $614 for straight-line depreciation, $685 for double declining-balance depreciation, and $709 for sum-of-years'-digits depreciation. In relation to the original cost, the tax saving amounts to 31.5 percent under the declining-balance method and 32.6 percent under the sum-of-years'-digits method.

SERVICE LIVES. A small pamphlet containing narrative material on useful lives for purposes of depreciation calculations was first published by the Bureau of Internal Revenue in 1920. Numerical useful lives for about 5,000 separate items were published in *Bulletin F* in 1942. *Bulletin F* remained substantially unchanged until 1962, when the Internal Revenue Service issued a new set of depreciation rules, Revenue Procedure 62-21, in a pamphlet titled *Depreciation Guidelines and Rules*. The new procedure assigned guideline lives to much broader classes of assets, numbering less than one hundred. These guidelines reduced the write-off period in manufacturing industries about 15 percent below those used earlier.

A second innovation made in the 1962 revenue procedure was a set of rules governing the determination of depreciation allowances, which was called the "reserve ratio test." This test required taxpayers to gear depreciation allowances to actual experience in replacing facilities. However, the unpopularity of the reserve ratio test led to its discontinuation in 1971 (it was never actually put into effect because of generous transition rules provided in 1962 and 1965). Instead, on the recommendation of the Treasury Department, Congress authorized the use of an "asset depreciation range" system that permitted taxpayers to use service lives for machinery and equipment that were within 20 percent (above or below) of the 1962 guideline averages. Most firms used the lower option to write off their investments at a faster rate. Unlike previous practice, the reduced service lives were made available for used as well as new investments.

In 1981 an even more liberal depreciation system—called the "accelerated cost recovery system" (ACRS)—was enacted. The act broke the precedent of prior laws by severing the connection between the useful life of an asset and the period over which it is depreciated for tax purposes. Under ACRS, capital costs may be recovered using an accelerated method (which is prescribed in the law) over specific recovery periods that are much shorter than useful lives. The write-off schedules for equipment are based on the 150 percent declining-balance method for the early recovery years and the straight-line depreciation method for the later recovery years. (The 1981 act provided for additional acceleration in 1985 and 1986, but this was eliminated in 1982.) The system, which is mandatory and applies to both new and used property, contains four different recovery periods for different kinds of assets. Most property is in the five-year class. Short-lived equipment, such as cars, trucks, and research and experimentation equipment, is in the three-year class. A ten-year class includes certain long-lived utility equipment, railroad tank cars, and coal utilization equipment. Other long-lived property and all buildings are in a fifteen-year class. The cost of this drastic revision is expected to exceed the cost of the prior system by $40 billion in 1985.

INVESTMENT CREDIT. The investment tax credit has been in effect since January 1, 1962 (except for two short periods). Under this provision, business firms are permitted to deduct as a credit against their tax 10 percent of the amount of new investment with recovery periods of more than three years. Sixty percent of the full credit is allowed for assets with recovery periods of three years. Qualified investments include all new tangible personal property and up to $150,000 of used property ($125,000 for 1981–84), and exclude all buildings except research and certain storage or special-purpose facilities. The credit is allowed to offset the first $25,000 of tax liability and 85 percent of the tax above $25,000. Unused credits may be carried back for three years and forward for fifteen.

The 1962 law required deduction of the credit from the cost of the asset before computing depreciation for tax purposes, but this require-ment was eliminated in the 1964 act. Thus taxpayers had the benefit of the full credit plus the liberalized depreciation allowances adopted in 1971 and 1981. In 1982 the law was revised to permit depreciation only on the cost of an asset less half the investment credit. In fiscal 1985 the revenue cost of the credit is expected to reach $27 billion.

The investment credit was originally enacted as a permanent feature of the tax system, but the rate of the credit could be raised, lowered, or eliminated entirely as a stabilizing measure. The credit was suspended from October 10, 1966, to March 9, 1967, and from April 19, 1969, to August 15, 1971, to counteract inflationary pressures, but it was increased to 10 percent in 1975 to help stimulate economic recovery and has remained at that level ever since.

The effect of an investment credit is similar to that of an increase in the depreciation allowances above 100 percent of the cost of the asset. For corporations subject to the 46 percent rate, the same results could be achieved by allowing the taxpayer to deduct an additional 21.8 percent in the first year. But a credit does not affect depreciation accounting (except for the reduction of basis by half the credit), and it provides the same tax benefit for all taxpayers regardless of their marginal rate. (It will be recalled that individuals are subject to rates ranging from 11 to 50 percent; profits of corporations are subject to rates ranging from 15 to 46 percent.)

Even though the credit seems small, it provides a sizable incentive for investment (assuming that the corporation income tax is not shifted through higher prices). In effect, the credit reduces the cost of the asset and hence increases the rate of return. For example, for an investment yielding 10 percent after straight-line depreciation and after the 46 percent corporation income tax, the credit increases the rate of return to 11.9 percent for an asset with a ten-year life. To increase the rate of return by an equivalent amount would require a reduction in the 46 percent corporate tax rate of 11.6 percentage points.

COMBINED EFFECT OF INCREASED CAPITAL-CONSUMPTION ALLOWANCES. It has already been noted that the liberalization of capital-consumption allowances beginning in 1954 reduced the effective rate of the corporation income tax, even though the tax rate remained constant through 1963 and has been reduced only moderately since then (table 5-3). Another measure of the benefits of the various provisions is given in figure 5-3, which shows their effects on the after-tax rate of return for an asset with a ten-year service life assuming the asset yields 10 percent on a straight-line depreciation basis.

The combined effect is dramatic. The rate of return is increased by ACRS and a 10 percent investment credit to 13.8. The investment credit accounts for half the increase in the rate of return. To reproduce the rate of return through a rate reduction alone, it would be necessary to reduce the corporation tax rate by 24.3 percentage points.

A major criticism of present law is that the investment allowances do not treat all business investments equally. ACRS is roughly neutral among assets eligible for the investment credit, assuming the appropriate discount rate is 10 percent (if, for example, the real rate of return on

Figure 5-3. *Effect of Various Investment Allowances on the Rate of Return on a Ten-Year Asset Yielding 10 Percent after Tax*[a]

Rate of return (percent)

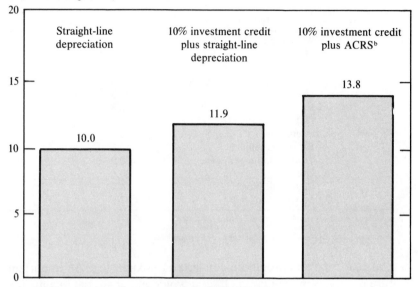

a. Assuming a constant stream of annual receipts during the life of the asset.
b. Assumes asset is "five-year property" under the accelerated cost recovery system (ACRS).

assets is 4 percent and the inflation rate is 6 percent). At lower inflation rates, the effect of ACRS is widely different among credit-eligible assets. Moreover, in combination, the investment credit and ACRS are more generous for equipment than for assets, such as buildings, inventories, and intangibles, which are not eligible for the credit. Thus the effective tax rates on assets vary among industries (see table 5-6) and, in some cases, they are negative (meaning that investment is subsidized in these industries). This differential treatment distorts investment incentives and leads to a misallocation of resources.

To achieve neutrality among assets, it would be necessary to restore economic depreciation and repeal the investment credit. If an incentive is desired, a uniform initial allowance could be provided and only the remaining cost depreciated. For example, if an initial deduction of 20 percent were allowed, economic depreciation would be taken on the remaining 80 percent. This would ensure the same reduction in effective tax rates for all assets.

In the extreme, if the initial deduction were increased to 100 percent,

Table 5-6. *Effective Tax Rates on New Depreciable Assets under the Accelerated Cost Recovery System, Selected Industries, 1982*
Percent

Industry[a]	Effective tax rate[b]
Agriculture	15.6
Mining	−3.4
Primary metals	7.5
Machinery and instruments	18.6
Motor vehicles	−11.3
Food	20.8
Pulp and paper	0.9
Chemicals	8.6
Petroleum refining	1.1
Transportation services	−2.9
Utilities	30.6
Communications	14.1
Services and trade	37.1

Source: *Economic Report of the President*, February 1982, table 5-7, p. 124.
a. Industries shown had at least $5 billion in new investment in 1981.
b. Assumes a 4 percent real after-tax rate of return and 8 percent inflation.

capital cost recovery would be converted to expensing. An important feature of expensing is that in effect it would eliminate the income tax on new investment. For example, assuming a 50 percent tax and economic depreciation, an asset with an expected rate of return of 10 percent would yield 5 percent after tax. If the asset was expensed, the investor would receive a rebate of half the cost of the asset. As a result, the 5 percent after-tax yield would be earned on half the cost of the investment, thus restoring the 10 percent before-tax yield. It has been estimated that the combined effect of ACRS and the investment credit for equipment (but not for structures) is roughly the same as expensing (assuming an inflation rate of 6 percent). If the investment is financed by borrowing, the tax is converted to a subsidy because the deduction for interest offsets the corporate tax a second time.

It would be possible to remove the distortions created by the present capital cost recovery system by substituting expensing of all new investment for ACRS and the investment credit. But it would still be necessary to remove the interest deduction if the subsidy for borrowing is to be eliminated. (Extension of expensing to structures would lose revenue; but elimination of the interest deduction would more than offset this loss. Thus the corporate tax rate could be reduced without cutting the yield of the corporation income tax.)

SAFE-HARBOR LEASING. Before the enactment of the 1981 tax act, the law contained safeguards to limit the use of leases in transferring the tax benefits of depreciation deductions and investment tax credit from one company to another. The 1981 act provided a new set of rules that were intended to facilitate the transfer of such tax benefits through leasing arrangements that did not alter the economic substance of ownership and operation of plants and equipment. Under these rules, a firm was able to sell part or all of the tax benefits associated with a particular property by entering into a nominal sale and safe-harbor leaseback. The purpose of the new provision was to permit corporations with insufficient taxable profits to sell their depreciation deductions and investment tax credits to other firms that could use them to offset their own tax liabilities. By so doing, the tax incentives would be realized immediately by the companies incurring losses, which would otherwise be required to wait until their operations generated enough profits to offset prior-year as well as current-year deductions and credits.

Immediately after the act was passed, safe-harbor leases were negotiated by well-known profitable corporations that purchased deductions that would not otherwise have been used by the actual owners of the property. Many of the corporations that sold such deductions were not able to use them because their profits had been wiped out by tax preferences (for example, oil companies). As a result of the public furor, in 1982 Congress reduced the safe-harbor leasing tax benefits for agreements entered into between July 1, 1982, and December 31, 1983, and terminated safe-harbor leasing at the end of 1983. Instead, it provided liberalized rules for leases with economic substance beginning in 1984.

Leasing would not be needed if the tax value of net operating losses and investment tax credits were made refundable in the year in which they are actually generated. Congress has not accepted the idea of refundability, largely because it does not wish to provide what appear to be subsidies to large corporations, especially those with a history of nonprofitability. Furthermore, the unused losses and investment tax credits are frequently the result of other tax preferences that convert economic income into tax losses.

Leasing is an inefficient substitute for refundability. Although the most egregious abuses will be eliminated when safe-harbor leasing expires at the end of 1983, consideration should be given to the proper treatment of firms which, for legitimate reasons, cannot use their net operating losses and investment tax credits. Unless the benefits of investment tax incentives are provided to such firms in some way, the law will discriminate against new and growing firms and older, less profitable firms attempting to revive their profit prospects through new investment. Such distortions should be avoided in an income tax if at all possible.

Allowances for the Mineral Industries

In computing their taxable income, firms engaged in extracting oil and gas and other minerals from the ground are entitled to a depletion allowance for exhaustion of the mineral deposit, just as other firms are entitled to a depreciation allowance for wear and tear on the capital they use.

Although there is little distinction in theory between depletion and depreciation, there are substantial differences in practice. First, it is difficult to estimate what proportion of a mineral deposit has been used up. Second, the value of a mineral deposit may be substantially larger than the amount invested in discovering and developing it. Some argue that depletion allowances should be based on the value of the deposit, rather than on the amount invested. Others argue that there is no reason to treat minerals differently from other investments and that only the original investment in bringing the mine or oil field into production should be amortized.

Historically, the capital-recovery provisions for the mineral industries have been generous. Allowances in excess of depletion based on costs were first permitted in 1918 in the form of discovery depletion to stimulate exploration for war purposes and to reduce the taxes of small-scale prospectors who often made discoveries after years of fruitless searching. (The 1918 act was not actually passed until after the war was over.) Discovery value proved difficult to estimate, and in 1926 Congress permitted the use of percentage depletion for oil and gas properties. Under percentage depletion, taxpayers deduct a fixed percentage of receipts from sales as a depletion allowance, regardless of the amount invested. The percentage depletion deduction for gas and oil, which was 27.5 percent from 1926 to 1969 and 22 percent from 1969 to 1975, has been eliminated entirely for the major oil companies and is being gradually reduced for unintegrated small producers to 15 percent on the first 1,000 barrels of oil or 6 million cubic feet of gas a day by 1984. Beginning in 1932, percentage depletion was extended to other products taken from the ground, at percentages ranging from 22 for sulfur, uranium, and other rare metals to 5 for gravel, sand, peat, pumice, and clay used in the manufacture of tile. In all industries, firms use cost depletion (depletion based on the actual cost of the property) if it is higher than percentage depletion. Percentage depletion cannot reduce the net income from the property (computed before taking the depletion allowance) by more than 50 percent, a constraint that applies in many cases because the income tax base has been greatly reduced by other tax preferences.

In addition to depletion, an immediate write-off is permitted for certain capital costs incurred in intangible drilling expenses and exploration and development, without limit for oil and gas and up to fixed dollar amounts for other minerals. Originally, the write-off was 100 percent, but it was cut back to 85 percent in 1982. This treatment of costs does not reduce percentage depletion, so a double deduction is allowed for the same capital investment for those eligible for percentage depletion. Studies made over the years by the Treasury Department indicate that the annual depletion deductions greatly exceed the deduction computed on the basis of the original investment. The tax benefits of these special provisions will be $8.6 billion in fiscal year 1985—$2.7 billion from percentage depletion and $5.9 billion from the expensing of intangible drilling costs and exploration and development costs.

Special treatment for oil, gas, and minerals is justified by its proponents on several grounds: there are unusual risks in exploration and development; national defense requires continuous exploration and development; the allowances are needed to finance new discoveries; and the present provisions serve as a strong impetus for taxpayers who discover new sources of supply to operate these properties rather than to sell them for the preferential capital gains rates.

On the other hand, the risks in these industries could be satisfactorily handled by the general deductibility of losses; the industries are no more strategic from a national defense standpoint than many other industries; and the large revenue cost of the benefits requires the imposition of higher tax rates than would otherwise be necessary to raise a given amount of revenue, thus penalizing other taxpayers. Moreover, the provisions lead to overinvestment in the favored industries and hence distort the allocation of resources.

The allowances for oil and gas and other minerals have been the subject of acrimonious debate for many years. In 1950 President Truman recommended the reduction of percentage depletion to a maximum of 15 percent. Congress took no action and in later years extended percentage depletion to other minerals and also raised percentage depletion rates. Bills were introduced frequently to curtail the allowances, but only minor changes were made until 1969, when the depletion allowance for oil and gas was reduced to 22 percent, and "excess" depletion was made subject to the minimum tax beginning in 1970. In 1975 percentage depletion was eliminated for the major oil and gas producers.

Financial Institutions

Financial institutions have always presented difficult problems for income taxation because many of them are organized on a mutual basis. At one time, mutuals were completely exempt from tax on the theory that they belonged to their members and were not corporations in any ordinary sense. But with the growth in number and size of mutuals, it became increasingly evident that the mutual status was not sufficient reason for exempting them from taxation. Attempts have been made to tax financial institutions—whether they organize as mutuals or not—like other corporations, but they are still paying relatively low taxes. Since the problems depend on the type of business conducted, it is necessary to discuss separately the thrift institutions (mutual savings banks and savings and loan associations), commercial banks, life insurance companies, and fire and casualty insurance companies.

THRIFT INSTITUTIONS. Mutual savings banks and savings and loan associations were made subject to the corporation income tax by the Revenue Act of 1951, which required them to pay the regular corporation income tax rate on retained earnings exceeding allocations to reserves. (Credit unions have never been subject to tax.) Payments of interest to depositors in savings banks and savings associations were allowed as a deductible expense, as is also true for ordinary commercial banks. However, the law permitted thrift institutions to build a reserve for bad debts of up to 12 percent of their deposits, while the regulations permitted commercial banks to set aside a reserve of three times their annual loss experience over a twenty-year period (less than 3 percent on the average). With steady growth in deposits, the amounts covered by the 12 percent ceiling increased steadily, and the result was that savings banks and building and loan associations paid very little tax.

The ineffectiveness of the 1951 law was partly remedied by a 1962 amendment that allowed thrift institutions to deduct an amount equal to 60 percent of their taxable income in lieu of actual additions to reserves for bad debts. While this fell far short of full taxation, the tax paid by savings and loan associations and mutual savings banks increased from $6.4 million in 1960 to $184 million in 1968. The 1969 act eliminated the 3 percent of assets rule and gradually lowered the deduction in lieu of additions to reserves from a maximum of 60 percent to 40 percent of taxable income over the period 1970–79. By 1979 the tax paid by savings and loan associations and mutual savings banks had increased to $2.3 billion.

COMMERCIAL BANKS. Commercial banks are regarded as ordinary business corporations for tax purposes and are subject to tax on their profits, after allowing for payment of interest on their deposits. One peculiarity of their taxation in the past was the treatment of capital gains and losses. Long-term capital gains of commercial banks were taxed at a maximum rate of 25 percent, as were the gains of ordinary business corporations. Capital losses of commercial banks, however, were deductible in full not only against capital gains but also against ordinary income. This treatment was justified on the grounds that dealings in securities are part of normal business operations in commercial banking, and losses should therefore be treated as ordinary losses. By this reasoning, capital gains from the sale of bonds should have been regarded as ordinary income and subjected to the ordinary corporation income tax rate. The 1969 legislation finally corrected this asymmetrical treatment, and such gains are now treated as ordinary income.

Commercial banks were also allowed to maintain a reserve for bad debts that was about three times their actual loss experience. Before 1969 the allowable reserve was set by regulation at 2.4 percent of outstanding loans. The 1969 law reduced this percentage to 1.8 in 1970–75, 1.2 in 1976–81, and 0.6 in 1982–87. Beginning in 1988, the actual loss experience for the current and the preceding five years will be the only criterion.

Another helpful feature of the corporation tax for commercial banks is the deductibility of expenses from taxable income, even though part of the expenses may be incurred to earn tax-exempt income. Commercial banks invest heavily in tax-exempt municipal securities and formerly were allowed to deduct all the interest they paid rather than allocate it between taxable and tax-exempt income. Under the 1982 act, however, banks are required to add 15 percent of the deductions for interest on assets to carry tax-exempt securities back to income, which still leaves them with a large tax advantage.

LIFE INSURANCE COMPANIES. Application of the corporation income tax to life insurance companies poses knotty problems because insurance companies earn income in two capacities: as fiduciaries for policyholders and as independent businesses. The treatment of income earned on behalf of policyholders is a problem for personal income taxation, but such income must be measured to determine the size of the remaining tax base on which the corporation income tax should be imposed. This problem is compounded in the case of mutual companies that are owned by their policyholders. The goal should be to tax the excess of total receipts of companies, less legitimate business expenses and less investment income clearly allocated for future liabilities to policyholders, at a rate that closely approximates the rate imposed on all other corporations. Methods of achieving these objectives have been considered periodically by Congress, but the treatment of life insurance company profits continues to be lenient.

FIRE AND CASUALTY INSURANCE COMPANIES. Stock companies selling fire and casualty insurance have long been taxed on both their investment and underwriting profits. Between 1942 and 1962, however, mutual fire and casualty insurance companies paid tax under special formulas that excluded underwriting profits. In 1963 underwriting profits were included in the formula for these companies, but they were allowed to set up a deferred income account that, in effect, permanently defers one-eighth of their underwriting gains from taxation and also defers taxation of another large portion of their underwriting gains for five years. In addition, these companies are allowed full deductions for interest paid to their policyholders even though they invest the funds in tax-exempt securities.

Tax-Exempt Organizations

The federal tax law exempts a variety of nonprofit organizations, including religious, charitable, educational, and fraternal organizations. Favorable tax treatment for these organizations dates from a time when the federal government assumed little responsibility for relief and welfare activities and the value of the tax exemption was relatively small. Today, the federal government has substantial responsibility for public assistance, and the revenue loss from the exemptions has become significant.

The tax status of these organizations might never have been altered had they remained small and not entered into business and public affairs. But numerous complaints were made against tax-exempt organizations for unfair competition with private profit-making businesses and for involvement in public activities that seem political in nature to those who disapprove of them. As a result, the permissible activities of private foundations have been spelled out in some detail in the internal revenue code, and the business income of all exempt organizations has been made taxable under the corporation income tax, even though they are still "exempt" under the internal revenue code. The special taxes apply to unrelated business income, rental income from "leaseback" arrangements, investment income of private foundations, and the income of cooperatives.

UNRELATED BUSINESS INCOME. The major change in the tax status of exempt organizations was made in 1950, when Congress decided to tax their "unrelated business income." This is defined as income from a business that is not substantially related to carrying out charitable, educational, or other exempt purposes. Unrelated business income is subject to the regular corporation income tax rates; and all exempt organizations except government agencies (other than publicly supported colleges and universities) are subject to tax on such income.

PRIVATE FOUNDATIONS. Private foundations are defined as tax-exempt organizations other than (a) religious, charitable, and educational institutions and (b) organizations that derive more than one-third of their income from contributions and less than one-third from investment income. These foundations were made subject to a new tax on investment income and to a variety of restrictions under the 1969 legislation; the tax was originally 4 percent of new investment income, but was reduced to 2 percent beginning in 1978. Foundations are also required to distribute at least 5 percent of the value of their assets each year; financial or "self-dealing" transactions between a foundation and persons with a direct or indirect interest in the foundation ("disqualified persons") or government officials are prohibited; and the amount of stock a foundation and disqualified persons may hold in any business enterprise is limited. These provisions are supported by a variety of sanctions for noncompliance.

COOPERATIVES. Farm, irrigation, and telephone cooperatives and like organizations are exempt from income tax. Other nonfinancial cooperatives are taxable. However, all cooperatives are allowed to deduct from their income amounts paid as "patronage dividends" to their patrons on the ground that they represent readjustments in prices initially charged patrons.

Originally, patronage dividends were deductible even if distributed in noncash form ("written notices of allocation"). The deductibility of noncash patronage dividends enabled cooperatives to expand from earnings not taxed at the cooperative level. Furthermore, patrons often were not taxed on such dividends until they were redeemed because the written allocations had no fair market value.

The law was revised beginning with the income year 1963. Earnings of taxable cooperatives distributed as written notices of allocation cannot now be deducted by the cooperatives unless at least 20 percent of the face amount of the allocation is in cash. Deductibility of noncash allocations is further limited to those that the patrons, at their option, can redeem in cash for the face amount within ninety days of the payment thereof or that the patrons have consented to include at face value in their income in accordance with the federal income tax laws. Thus taxable cooperatives may, in effect, retain 80 percent of their earnings by the use of noncash patronage dividends. At the same time, patrons are currently taxed on transactions entered into for business purposes. Dividends on purchases for personal consumption do not have to be included in a patron's income.

Corporate Acquisition, Reorganization, and Liquidation

The law permits the reorganization of corporations through acquisitions, mergers, divisions, and other arrangements without recognizing gains and losses as a result of the transaction. The purpose is to permit corporations to arrange their affairs in a flexible manner without incurring tax liability in the process. But the provisions are highly complicated and arbitrary, with the result that the unwary or ill-advised taxpayer may be subject to large amounts of tax for purely procedural rather than substantive reasons, while others escape paying taxes that ought to be paid. Under existing law, for example, corporations are often permitted to transfer appreciated assets to shareholders without recognizing the gains that have accrued. Simpler and consistent rules for the tax treatment of corporate transactions are needed to ensure that profits are subject to corporation income tax in full and at an appropriate time. Neither shareholders nor corporations should escape tax on corporate profits permanently.

Foreign and Export Income

The income earned by foreign subsidiaries of U.S. corporations is subject to tax when it is "repatriated" through the payment of dividends to the parent corporation. To avoid double taxation, the parent is allowed a credit against the U.S. tax for any tax paid on these dividends to a foreign government up to the U.S. tax liability on that income. Income of foreign branches is included in the taxable income of the parent in the year earned, but credit is allowed for any foreign tax paid on this income.

To encourage U.S. exports, the law was amended in 1971 to permit domestic manufacturers to create for their export businesses domestic international sales corporations (DISCs), which can defer tax on half their earnings. In 1975 the DISC privilege was removed for exports of energy products and natural resources subject to depletion. In 1976 deferral was permitted for only half the earnings in excess of 67 percent of the 1972–75 annual average (the four-year base moves forward one year at a time beginning in 1980). In 1982 the amount of the deferral as calculated under the 1976 law was reduced by 15 percent. The original estimate of the cost of the DISC provision was modest ($170 million a year), but the practice of funneling export earnings through DISCs mushroomed, and the revenue loss is expected to amount to $1.8 billion in fiscal year 1985 even after the restrictions enacted in 1976. The U.S. government recognizes that the DISC provision violates the prohibition against tax subsidies for exports under the General Agreement on Tariffs and Trade (GATT) and is expected to propose substitute legislation.

Corporations that take part in international boycotts based on race, nationality, or religion are denied the benefit of the foreign tax credit, deferral of earnings of foreign subsidiaries, and the DISC provision for profits earned in the boycotting countries.

Other less important provisions add to the favorable treatment for foreign income. A tax credit is provided for profits earned in U.S. possessions, such as Puerto Rico, which in effect exempts such profits from U.S. tax. Persons other than U.S. employees who live abroad for at least three years are permitted to exclude up to $75,000 of their earnings abroad in computing their U.S. income tax in 1982, $80,000 in 1983, $85,000 in 1984, $90,000 in 1985, and $95,000 in 1986 and later years.

The foreign tax credit is essential to prevent double taxation of foreign income. However, the other special provisions reduce revenues (see

Table 5-7. *Costs of Special Tax Provisions Applying to Foreign Income of U.S. Citizens and Corporations, Fiscal Year 1985*

Millions of dollars

Provision	Individuals	Corporations	Total
Deferral of tax on domestic international sales corporations	. . .	1,820	1,820
Exemption for certain income earned abroad by U.S. citizens	1,460	. . .	1,460
Deferral of income of controlled foreign corporations	. . .	655	655
Total	1,460	2,475	3,935

Source: Congressional Budget Office, *Tax Expenditures: Budget Control Options and Five-Year Budget Projections for Fiscal Years 1983–1987* (Government Printing Office, 1982).

table 5-7), complicate tax administration and compliance, and are of dubious value from an economic standpoint. Congress has been considering proposals to eliminate all or most of them in recent years, but they are staunchly defended by those who benefit from them as essential either to promote foreign investment or, in the case of DISCs, to protect employment at home. However, the economic benefits of these provisions tend to be exaggerated by their proponents.

Inflation Accounting

Business net income is calculated by subtracting from the gross receipts of a firm the expenses of generating these receipts. If all expenses were incurred at the time sales are made, the difference between the two would provide a correct measure of net income. But there are two complications: first, business outlays are frequently made long before sales are realized; and second, the outlays and expenses are expressed in different prices. The first of these problems is handled by estimating sales and expenses on an accrual basis. If the accounting methods match expenses and sales correctly, the difference between the two will accurately represent the net income of the firm—provided the general price level is stable. If prices change, accrual accounting alone will not suffice; a further correction is required to express sales and expenses in the same prices. (The tax rates and exemption, if any, that should apply to the price-corrected net income are another matter. Under a flat-rate tax without exemptions, there is no bracket creep. If the tax is graduated, bracket creep will increase the real tax burden as money income rises. Chapter 4 discusses whether, and how, a correction for this effect should be made.)

The elements in a set of business accounting statements that are affected by inflation are depreciation allowances, costs of goods sold, and financial assets and liabilities. Separate adjustments are required for each of these elements to arrive at a measure of real income expressed in prices of the current period.

Depreciation

As indicated earlier in this chapter, the purpose of the depreciation allowance is to write off the portion of the cost of a depreciable asset that is used up in producing the income of the enterprise. Even if the wear, tear, and obsolescence of plant and equipment could be measured, the funds accumulated in a depreciation reserve based on historical costs would not be adequate to maintain the value of the capital stock during periods of rising prices. The result would be an overstatement of profits and, thus, some tax on the capital itself. (If the general price level were stable, historical cost depreciation would be sufficient on the average, but not for particular assets because of changes in relative prices.)

Two types of adjustment are suggested by economists to correct depreciation for inflation. The first would permit firms to calculate depreciation on the basis of the replacement cost of each of its depreciable assets (or groups of like assets). The second would correct the deduction based on historical costs for the rise in the average of all prices. This could be done by multiplying the amount of historical-cost depreciation by the ratio of the general price level in the current period to the level in the period when the asset was purchased. Accelerated depreciation methods based on historical costs, which are used in many countries, are often justified on inflation grounds, but they can approximate direct adjustments for inflation only accidentally. (The ACRS system enacted in the United States in 1981 is an example of an unfortunate choice of depreciation methods that was justified in part on the ground of inflation.)

The basic difference between the two types of inflation adjustments concerns the treatment of accrued gains and losses resulting from changes in the relative prices of different depreciable assets. Depreciation at replacement cost permits the tax-free recovery of the cost of such assets as they wear out. Consequently, gains and losses on depreciable assets reflecting both changes in the general price level and changes in relative prices are ignored until the firm is liquidated or sold. Under the adjusted historical-cost approach, depreciation is corrected by the change in the average of all prices, with the result that gains and losses on depreciable assets exceeding those that reflect changes in the general price level are included in income as they accrue.

An innovative idea of adjusting the system of tax depreciation for inflation is to allow an immediate deduction for the present value of the future economic depreciation that firms could claim if there were no inflation. No adjustment for inflation would ever be needed because the depreciation deduction would be taken in the same year in which the asset was purchased. If a neutral stimulus were desired, the stimulus could be provided through the initial allowance described earlier. The results under this approach are consistent with the results under inflation-adjusted historical-cost depreciation because gains from changes in the relative prices of depreciable assets would be included in income.

Inventories

The tax law permits firms to use either the first-in-first-out (FIFO) or last-in-first-out (LIFO) methods of inventory valuation. Under FIFO, the deduction for the cost of materials is calculated on the basis of the earliest price paid for similar items in the closing inventory. Under LIFO, the valuation is based on the price last paid for similar items in the closing inventory. In a period of rising prices, the cost of materials is higher—and net income is lower—under LIFO than under FIFO and hence LIFO results in the lower tax.

As in the case of depreciation, gains and losses on items of inventory are taken into account at different times under FIFO and LIFO. Under FIFO, the change in the price of materials between date of purchase and date of use is treated as a realized gain or loss that is included in income for tax purposes. LIFO defers the date of realization of gains and losses on inventories so long as the number of units in stock does not decline.

LIFO is in effect the analogue to replacement-cost depreciation—inventory gains and losses are not included in income unless inventories are depleted or the firm is liquidated. FIFO treats the full gains and losses on inventories, including the gains and losses resulting from changes in the general price level and in relative prices, as realized on the date of use. An intermediate possibility, analogous to the use of inflated historical-cost depreciation, would be to modify FIFO by raising the historical cost of materials used by the percentage increase in the general price level between the date of purchase and date of use. This would protect the firm against taxation of inventory gains caused by general inflation, but would include in net income any gains or losses caused by changes in the prices of its inventories relative to all other prices.

Net Financial Assets and Liabilities

A business that lends $1,000 at a 10 percent interest rate realizes no real return on its investment if prices go up 10 percent a year. At the end of the first year, for example, it receives interest of $100 but the value of the loan has declined $100. The enterprise that borrows is in the exact opposite position. It is better off because the real value of the loan it must repay has declined by $100. Under the present tax laws, the lending firm is taxed on $100 of interest even though it has earned no income in real terms, while the borrowing firm is permitted to deduct the $100 of interest paid though the loan cost nothing in real terms.

In an inflation-corrected accounting system, real gains and losses on net financial assets and liabilities are taken into account in calculating business profits. Enterprises with net financial liabilities gain from inflation; their profits are increased by the reduction in the real value of their liabilities. Enterprises with net financial assets find that the value of these assets erodes during an inflation and their incomes are reduced by the fall in the value of their assets. In each case, the correction is calculated by adding to, or subtracting from, profits the increase or decrease in the nominal value of the assets.

Neither of these adjustments deals with the real gains or losses of issuers and holders of bonds when interest rates rise or fall. When interest rates rise, the market value of long-term bonds declines. This decline in value is a real loss to the bondholders, which they can realize by exchanging their holdings for similar bonds. The issuers of bonds enjoy a corresponding real gain as the value of their debt obligations declines (a gain that many corporations realize by redeeming their bonds at lower prices). When interest rates decline, the gains and losses are reversed—bondholders gain and bond-issuers lose. But there is substantial disagreement about whether such gains and losses should be taken into account in calculating the real income of business enterprises.

Choice of Adjustments

It is evident that, even if it is decided to convert the tax base to a measure of real income, no single set of adjustments can be regarded as "correct." The choice depends on which income concept is considered appropriate for taxing business profits.

One concept that is widely regarded by economists as the best measure of income but is not embodied in current tax law is the "accretion," or "economic power," concept. Applied to individuals, this is the sum of consumption plus the change in the value of their assets during the taxable period, including all accrued gains and losses (see chapter 4). Applied to business firms, it is equivalent to the change in the real market value of the firms during the taxable period before distributions to shareholders.

To correct for inflation on the basis of the economic power concept, nominal gains resulting from an increase in the general price level are eliminated from income, but all gains and losses resulting from changes in relative prices should be recognized in the period in which they accrue. Depreciation would be based on historical costs and adjusted for the increase in the general price level. Inventories would be valued on a FIFO basis and then adjusted for the increase in the general price level between the date of purchase and the date of use. Finally, real gains and losses on net financial assets and changes in the value of bonds would be recognized in the calculations of income.

An alternative concept of income, which is regarded as more appropriate for business accounting purposes by some economists, is the "capital-maintenance" concept. According to this concept, the purpose of the business entity is to produce or distribute a product or service. Changes in the value of the assets of the firm should not be taxed until the firm liquidates some of its assets or goes out of business entirely. There is thus a distinction between operating profits, which are measured on an accrual basis, and capital gains and losses, which are measured only when they are actually realized.

The capital-maintenance concept would defer until liquidation recognition of gains and losses on depreciable assets and inventories resulting from changes in relative prices as well as changes in the general price level. Depreciation would be calculated on a replacement-cost basis, and a strict form of LIFO, in which historical costs are disregarded even if inventories are liquidated, would be used in accounting for inventories. Real profits on net financial liabilities would be included in income, while changes in the real value of bonds would be ignored.

A major consideration in appraising real-income tax accounting, under either the economic power or the capital-maintenance concept of income, is that many provisions already provide generous treatment for business and property income, some of which are justified in part as an offset to the distortions caused by using historical prices during inflation. For example, the accelerated cost recovery system is not equivalent to replacement-cost depreciation or to adjusted historical-cost depreciation and would be hard to justify if prices were certain to remain stable. Preferential income tax treatment for capital gains would clearly be inappropriate if nominal gains from inflation were eliminated from the tax base. For these reasons, many believe that adjustment of the taxable-income concept for inflation should be considered only as part of a thorough revision of the tax law that reexamined all preferences and taxed income from all sources at the same rates.

Table 5-8 compares reported corporate profits of U.S. nonfinancial corporations for the years 1950 through 1979 with estimates of real profits under the two concepts of real income. The adjustments for depreciation and inventories reduce profits substantially, while the financial adjustments raise them. The net adjustments go in both directions, but the overall trend of profits is similar. In some years, the differences are substantial. Real profits are lower than reported profits in twenty years of the thirty-year period under the economic power concept and in twelve years under the capital-maintenance concept.

·The aggregates for the thirty-year period 1950–79 differ by 7 percent or less: total profits were $1,214 billion as reported, $1,259 billion under the economic power concept of real income, and $1,307 billion under the capital-maintenance concept. However, the inflation correction would have a significant effect on the relative distribution of taxes among various industries. In general, those that rely heavily on equity capital and use long-lived depreciable assets would benefit, while those that rely heavily on borrowed capital and use short-lived depreciable assets would be worse off.

Integration of the Corporation and Individual Income Taxes

Taxation of corporate earnings continues to be controversial. Some people regard taxation of total profits under the corporation tax and of

Table 5-8. *Reported and Real Corporate Profits after Taxes under Two Concepts of Real Income, U.S. Nonfinancial Corporations, 1950–79*

Billions of dollars

Year	Reported profits after tax[a]	Real profits after tax[b]	
		Economic power concept	Capital maintenance concept
1950	21.6	22.0	11.1
1951	17.9	16.3	17.3
1952	16.0	14.7	13.7
1953	16.4	14.1	14.3
1954	16.4	10.7	13.8
1955	21.8	31.5	19.6
1956	21.8	32.2	19.3
1957	20.7	15.7	19.2
1958	17.5	14.3	16.1
1959	22.4	22.0	22.5
1960	20.5	7.2	17.7
1961	20.1	16.0	21.4
1962	23.5	17.9	30.7
1963	26.2	17.9	31.6
1964	31.4	24.9	36.5
1965	38.0	37.2	42.6
1966	40.8	47.2	47.3
1967	38.6	46.9	47.0
1968	39.5	31.1	48.7
1969	36.2	65.5	53.9
1970	29.8	5.3	39.3
1971	35.6	−4.6	44.2
1972	43.0	39.9	48.9
1973	56.0	106.5	57.4
1974	63.3	169.3	89.9
1975	66.1	4.9	77.8
1976	82.3	21.0	75.3
1977	96.8	95.2	91.9
1978	111.5	144.8	114.1
1979	122.5	171.6	124.0

Sources: U.S. Department of Commerce, Bureau of Economic Analysis; and Jeremy I. Bulow and John B. Shoven, "Inflation, Corporate Profits, and the Rate of Return to Capital," in Robert E. Hall, ed., *Inflation: Causes and Effects* (University of Chicago Press, 1982).

a. As estimated in the official national income accounts.

b. Expressed in current dollars. For definitions of the income concepts, see the text.

distributed profits under the individual income tax as inequitable. Others believe that taxation of the corporation as a separate entity is justified. Whether something needs to be done depends on an evaluation of the economic issues discussed earlier and on the effect of the proposed changes on the distribution of tax burdens. Few people realize that the problem is tricky and that there is no easy solution.

The Additional Burden on Dividends

On the assumption that all, or a significant portion, of the corporation tax rests on the stockholder, the effect of the tax is to impose the heaviest burden on dividends received by persons in the lowest income classes. This can be seen by examining the illustrative calculations in table 5-9, which show the total and additional tax burden (ignoring the effect of the present $100 exclusion) on stockholders who receive $54 of dividends under present tax rates. Given the present rate of 46 percent, the corporation income before tax from which the $54 of dividends were paid must have amounted to $100. If this $100 had been subject to individual income tax rates only, the tax on these dividends would go from zero at the bottom of the income scale to a maximum of 50 percent at the top. With the corporation tax, the combined individual and corporation income tax increases from $46 for those subject to a zero rate to $73 for those subject to a 50 percent rate (table 5-9, column 6).

However, the *additional* burden resulting from the corporation tax falls as income rises. For example, the taxpayer subject to a zero individual rate would have paid no tax on the $54 of dividends; the additional corporation income tax burden in this case is the full $46 tax. By contrast, a taxpayer subject to the 50 percent rate pays an individual income tax of $27 on the dividend, and the total tax burden on the original $100 of corporate earnings is $73. But since the taxpayer would have to pay $50 under the individual income tax in any case, the additional burden is only $23 (table 5-9, column 7).

One test of an equitable method of moderating or eliminating the additional tax burden on dividends is to ask whether the method removes a uniform percentage of the additional burden shown in table 5-9. If the percentage removed is the same for all dividend recipients in every individual income tax bracket, the method deals evenly at all levels. Deviations from a constant percentage indicate the dividend recipients who are favored or penalized by the method.

Table 5-9. *Additional Burden of the Corporation Income Tax on $100 of Corporation Income*[a]

Dollars

Marginal individual income tax rate (percent) (1)	Corporate income before tax (2)	Corpora- tion tax at 48 percent (3)	Dividends received by stock- holders (4)	Stock- holder's individual income tax (5)	Total tax burden[b] (6)	Additional burden of the corporation tax (7)
0	100	46	54	0.00	46.00	46.00
10	100	46	54	5.40	51.40	41.40
20	100	46	54	10.80	56.80	36.80
30	100	46	54	16.20	62.20	32.20
40	100	46	54	21.60	67.60	27.60
50	100	46	54	27.00	73.00	23.00

Column 3 = 0.46 × column 2.
Column 4 = column 2 − column 3.
Column 5 = column 4 × column 1.
Column 6 = column 3 + column 5.
Column 7 = column 6 − column 1 × column 2.
a. Assumes that corporation income after tax is devoted entirely to the payment of dividends.
b. Does not take into account the effect of the exclusion of the first $100 of dividends from the individual income tax base.

A second test is whether the method increases or reduces the progressivity of the tax system as a whole. Since corporate ownership is heavily concentrated in the high income classes (see table 5-2), moderation or reduction of the additional tax burden on dividends alone would reduce progressivity, unless the change were accompanied by fundamental revisions in the individual income tax base to prevent windfalls for the minority of taxpayers who have large stockholdings.

Methods of Integration

Five methods of integrating the corporation and individual income taxes have been used at various times in different countries: (1) a dividend-received credit for individuals; (2) a deduction for dividends paid by the corporation in computing the corporation income tax; (3) a "split-rate" corporation income tax, which applies a higher tax rate to undistributed than to distributed corporate earnings; (4) a method that considers all or a portion of the corporation income tax to be withholding on dividends at the source; and (5) an exclusion of all or a portion of the dividends received from the individual income tax base. These methods would only partially integrate the corporation and individual income taxes because the relief would be given only to distributed earnings. A

Table 5-10. *Portion of the Additional Burden of the Corporation Income Tax Removed by the 4 Percent Dividend-Received Credit*

Marginal individual income tax rate (percent) (1)	Additional burden resulting from corporation tax (dollars) (2)	Dividend-received credit (dollars) (3)	Percentage of additional burden removed by the dividend credit (4)
0	46.00	0.00	0.0
10	41.40	2.16	5.2
20	36.80	2.16	5.9
30	32.20	2.16	6.6
40	27.60	2.16	7.8
50	23.00	2.16	9.4

Column 2 = column 7 of table 5-9.
Column 3 = 4 percent of $54.
Column 4 = column 3 ÷ column 2.

sixth method would be to treat all corporations like partnerships and tax their income to the stockholders whether distributed or not. This is the only method that would fully integrate the corporation and individual income tax on both distributed and undistributed corporate earnings and would rely entirely on the individual income tax for the taxation of corporate profits. Of the various methods, 2, 3, 4, and the partnership plan would remove the same proportion of the additional burden of the corporation tax at all individual income levels. All the methods except the sixth would make the federal tax system less progressive without offsetting changes. It is assumed that there is no shifting of the corporation income tax.

THE DIVIDEND-RECEIVED CREDIT. Under this method, dividend recipients are allowed to deduct a percentage of their dividends as a credit against their individual income tax. Between 1954 and 1963, U.S. taxpayers were allowed a credit of 4 percent for dividends in excess of a $50 exclusion ($100 for joint returns).

Although the credit grants the same relief on a dollar of dividends at all income levels, it removes an increasing proportion of the additional burden of the corporation tax as incomes rise. For those subject to a zero rate, the credit is worthless. For a taxpayer subject to a 10 percent rate, the 4 percent credit would remove 5.2 percent of the additional burden, and for a taxpayer subject to the maximum 50 percent rate, the credit would remove 9.4 percent (table 5-10). This regressive pattern of relief led to its repeal.

Table 5-11. *Portion of the Additional Burden of the Corporation Income Tax Removed by the Dividend-Paid Deduction*

Assuming the corporation deducts 20 percent of dividends paid

Marginal individual income tax rate (percent) (1)	Additional burden resulting from corporation tax (dollars) (2)	Tax benefit of dividend-paid deduction (dollars)			Percentage of additional burden removed by the dividend-paid deduction (6)
		Reduced corporation tax (paid to stock-holders as additional dividends) (3)	Tax on additional dividends (4)	Net benefit (5)	
0	46.00	5.47	0.00	5.47	11.9
10	41.40	5.47	0.55	4.92	11.9
20	36.80	5.47	1.09	4.38	11.9
30	32.20	5.47	1.64	3.83	11.9
40	27.60	5.47	2.19	3.28	11.9
50	23.00	5.47	2.74	2.73	11.9

Column 2 = column 7 of table 5-9.
Column 3 = amount of additional dividends corporations could pay out with a 20 percent dividend-paid deduction.
Column 4 = column 1 × column 3.
Column 5 = column 3 − column 4.
Column 6 = column 5 ÷ column 2.

THE DIVIDEND-PAID DEDUCTION. This is the simplest method of dealing with the problem; it was used in the United States in 1936 and 1937. Corporations deduct from their taxable income all or a portion of the dividends they pay out, and the corporation tax applies to the remainder. Table 5-11 shows the relief that would be granted under this method if the corporation were allowed a deduction of 20 percent of dividends paid. As shown in column 6, the relief would be 11.9 percent of the additional tax imposed by the corporation income tax at all income levels.

Aside from granting the same proportionate relief at all income levels, the dividend-paid credit has the merit of treating dividends more like interest. (If a full deduction were allowed, the treatment would be identical.) This would increase the attractiveness of equity financing by corporations.

The dividend-paid deduction raised a storm of protest when it was used briefly in the United States during the 1930s. Corporations complained that by encouraging payouts of earnings it reduced their ability to save and invest at a time when the market for corporate equities was almost dried up. The method is also criticized on the ground that it discourages internal financing by corporations and might reduce total saving and investment. On the other hand, some believe it unwise to permit corporations to avoid the capital markets for financing their investment programs. Forcing them "to stand the test of the marketplace" might exercise a desirable restraint on bigness and also give investors more control over the disposition of their funds.

An alternative method of equalizing the treatment of dividends and interest would be to eliminate the deduction for interest in computing the taxable income of corporations. Since the base of the tax would be raised, the tax rate could be reduced substantially. (At 1982 income and borrowing levels, the 46 percent rate could be reduced by over half.) Such a plan has merit if a separate tax on corporate capital—whether financed by debt or equity capital—is justified. Such a tax has not been seriously considered in the United States because it would drastically alter the distribution of the corporation tax burden among firms and industries. In general, manufacturing corporations, which rely mainly on equity capital, would benefit; utilities and transportation and financial companies, which rely heavily on borrowed capital, would pay much higher taxes.

THE "SPLIT-RATE" CORPORATION INCOME TAX. A number of countries tax undistributed earnings at a higher rate than distributed earnings. This split-rate plan is similar in effect to a reduction for dividends paid. For example, a 50–25 percent split rate would be equivalent to a 50 percent tax on total corporate earnings with a deduction of 50 percent for dividends paid. The percentages actually used by various countries differ greatly, reflecting the absence of accepted criteria for establishing the split rates. The split-rate system is used in Austria, Japan, Norway, and other countries.

THE IMPUTATION METHOD. Under this method, all or a portion of the individual income tax is regarded as having been paid at the source (through the corporation tax). For example, if 10 percent of the dividend were regarded as having been withheld, a shareholder receiving a $54 dividend would "gross up" the dividend by adding $5.40 (0.10 × 54) to taxable income and then take the $5.40 as a credit against tax. In this illustration, the portion of the additional burden of the corporation income tax removed is 11.7 percent at all income levels (table 5-12). Thus, with a corporate rate of 46 percent, a dividend gross-up of 10 percent at the individual level is roughly equivalent to a 20 percent dividend would "gross up" the dividend by adding $5.40 (0.10 × 54) to 5-11 and 5-12).

The imputation method achieves the same result as the dividend-paid

Table 5-12. *Portion of the Additional Burden of the Corporation Income Tax Removed by the Imputation Method*
Assuming 10 percent of dividends received regarded as withheld

Marginal individual income tax rate (percent) (1)	Additional burden resulting from cor- poration tax (dollars) (2)	Withholding credit (dollars)			Percentage of additional burden removed by the dividend credit (6)
		Amount withheld at source (3)	Tax on amount withheld (4)	Net credit (5)	
0	46.00	5.40	0.00	5.40	11.7
10	41.40	5.40	0.54	4.86	11.7
20	36.80	5.40	1.08	4.32	11.7
30	32.20	5.40	1.62	3.78	11.7
40	27.60	5.40	2.16	3.24	11.7
50	23.00	5.40	2.70	2.70	11.7

Column 2 = column 7 of table 5-9.
Column 3 = 10 percent of $54.
Column 4 = column 1 × column 3.
Column 5 = column 3 − column 4.
Column 6 = column 5 ÷ column 2.

deduction for corporations but is likely to discourage corporate saving somewhat less. This advantage frequently makes the imputation method more attractive, even though it is more difficult to understand and would also complicate the individual income tax return. Variants of the imputation method are used in a number of countries, including the United Kingdom, France, Italy, and West Germany.

THE DIVIDEND EXCLUSION. This method, adopted in the United States in 1954, permits individual income taxpayers to exclude all or a portion of their dividends from taxable income. In the United States, there is an individual exclusion of $100 ($200 on joint returns), which is a vestige of the compromise adopted when the 4 percent dividend credit was repealed in 1964. Like the dividend-received credit, the exclusion grants an increasing amount of relief on a dollar of dividends as incomes rise. Accordingly, it cannot remove the same proportion of the additional tax burden at all levels of income.

THE PARTNERSHIP METHOD, OR "FULL" INTEGRATION. The most far-reaching solution is to regard the income of corporations as belonging to their stockholders in the year in which it is earned, regardless of whether the earnings are distributed. The corporation income tax as such would be abolished, but a tax would be retained at the corporate level as a withholding device for the individual income tax. Stockholders would pay individual income tax on their prorated share of the earnings of corporations in which they held stock and would receive credit for the amount of tax withheld at the source, just as in the case of wages and salaries.

This method would automatically apply the correct individual income tax rates to all corporate earnings and thus equalize the tax rates on corporate and noncorporate earnings. It would also be more progressive and less costly than partial integration for dividends alone, because retained as well as distributed corporate earnings would be subject to the individual income tax.

A major drawback of the plan is that, unless the withholding rate was set at a very high level, some stockholders would not have funds to pay tax on earnings they did not receive. This would force them to liquidate security holdings or apply pressure on corporations to distribute a much larger portion of their retained earnings. In the former case, stock ownership among people with modest means would be discouraged; in the latter, corporate saving would be reduced.

Treatment approximating this method is available under present law for closely held corporations with no more than thirty-five shareholders. These corporations operate much like partnerships and can arrange to distribute enough earnings to the partners to avoid forced liquidations. The decision to be treated like a partnership for tax purposes is made only if it is advantageous to the shareholders. Experts agree that it would not be practical to extend the partnership method to large, publicly held corporations with complex capital structures, frequent changes in ownership, and thousands or millions of stockholders.

A procedure that would approximate the effect of the partnership method and avoid its liquidity problems would be to permit corporations to allocate all or a portion of their undistributed earnings to their shareholders. The corporation income tax would be converted to a withholding tax for the individual income tax, and the corporate rate would be set at the top-bracket individual income tax rate. Shareholders would include the allocated dividends as well as cash dividends in their taxable income and would deduct the amount of tax withheld as a credit against their income tax. The only difference between this procedure and the original partnership method is that the allocation of earnings by corporations to shareholders would not be mandatory. But since shareholders would be denied immediate credit for the withheld tax, the pressure on corporate management to allocate all undistributed earnings would probably be irresistible. The procedure, which was originally proposed by a Canadian Royal Commission in 1966, has merit (if a separate corporation tax is considered inappropriate), but it has not been seriously considered anywhere.

PRACTICAL PROBLEMS. Integration of the corporation and individual income taxes raises a number of difficult issues. First, it would be inappropriate to assume that all corporate earnings were subject to a 46 percent rate in crediting individuals with the amount of tax paid on their corporate earnings. For one thing, all corporations are taxed at reduced rates on the first $100,000 of earnings. For another, numerous special provisions (such as accelerated depreciation, the investment credit, the deduction for intangible drilling and development costs, and so on) reduce the effective rate of the corporation tax. If an attempt were made to distinguish such sources of earnings from taxable sources in designing the integration scheme, the mechanics would be extremely complicated. Moreover, the objectives of the special provisions would be thwarted by making such distinctions and the groups affected would object strongly. On the other hand, if distinctions are not made, relief from the corporate tax would be provided when in fact the tax was not paid. As already noted in this chapter, the present combination of accelerated depreciation and the investment credit effectively wipes out the corporate tax on new equipment purchases, so that integration is unnecessary for such investments (or alternatively relief would have to be denied for dividends from the earnings of such investments).

Second, it would be difficult to decide how to treat foreign shareholders and tax-exempt organizations under an integration plan. The corporation income tax now applies to the earnings of the entire corporation, including those that would be allocated to foreign shareholders and tax-exempt organizations under an integration plan. If foreign shareholders and tax-exempt organizations were not eligible for refunds, the cost of the plan would be greatly reduced.

Third, the partial integration schemes—imputation or the split-rate integration schemes, particularly the latter—would have the effect of encouraging larger dividend payouts by corporations. The retained earnings of corporations are a large source of saving in the United States; many would regard it unwise to encourage a reduction in this source of saving. A reduction in the corporation income tax rate would be simpler than partial integration and might do less damage to saving and investment.

Fourth, full integration through the partnership method is impractical for a number of reasons. An adjustment of the basis of all shareholdings for the amount of corporate tax withheld would be required so that individuals would be able to calculate capital gains and losses. It would be virtually impossible to allocate losses satisfactorily among part-year and full-year shareholders and to attribute adjustment of tax through audits or amended returns to the right shareholders. Furthermore, many, if not most, taxpayers would resent paying full tax on income they did not receive.

Summary

The corporation income tax ranks third in the federal tax system. It now produces a relatively small amount of revenue, but this revenue would not be easy to replace with another tax. Moreover, without a corporation tax, a substantial part of the individual income tax would be permanently lost from the tax base through retention of earnings by corporations.

The arguments that are made against the corporation income tax are largely economic. The tax may reduce the saving capacity of corporations and their incentives to invest; encourage debt financing by discriminating against equity financing, thus exposing many corporations to unnecessary risks; protect marginal producers by keeping up the prices of more efficient producers; and distort the allocation of resources both between the corporate and noncorporate sectors and between capital- and labor-intensive industries. There is no evidence in the available data, however, that the corporation tax has impaired the growth of the corporate sector or of the U.S. economy as a whole.

Numerous changes have been made in the structure of the corporation income tax since the end of World War II. Foremost among these are the liberalization of depreciation and the adoption of the investment credit to encourage investment. Revisions have also been made to prevent tax avoidance by tax-exempt organizations, financial institutions, and cooperatives. A minimum tax now applies to income items that receive special treatment and some tax preferences have been cut back. Nevertheless, many difficult problems remain. The accelerated cost recovery system is regarded by many as excessively generous and discriminatory among different types of assets. Debt-financed investment is now heavily subsidized as compared with equity-financed investment. The treatment of oil and gas and other mineral industries is still a major issue. The loss of revenue from the DISC provision is difficult to justify on economic grounds.

In periods of inflation, the reported profits of most corporations are not representative of their real incomes. Depreciation is understated, inventory profits may be overstated, and accrued gains and losses on financial assets are not taken into account. Correcting for all the distortions would radically alter the distribution of the corporation income tax among different firms and industries.

Dividends paid out by corporations are taxed at both the corporation and the individual levels. Even if it were agreed that something needs to be done about this double taxation, there is no easy solution. Among the various alternatives, the only theoretically correct method is the partnership method, which would fully integrate the two taxes, but this is impractical. The partial integration methods (a deduction for dividends at the corporate level and the imputation method) would be complicated if relief were denied to dividends from untaxed sources and would tend to discourage corporate saving.

The major task in corporate income taxation today is to eliminate the large differences in effective tax rates—and subsidies—on investment in different assets and industries. These differences distort the allocation of resources and reduce the contribution of capital to productivity and growth.

CHAPTER SIX

Consumption Taxes

CONSUMPTION TAXES are not very popular in the United States. It is true that general sales taxes are used by state and local governments (see chapter 9), but even when they are taken into account, consumption taxes are less important here than anywhere else in the world. In 1981 consumption taxes accounted for 15 percent of total federal, state, and local tax revenues.

Types of Consumption Taxes

There is a bewildering variety of consumption taxes. An *expenditure* tax is levied on the total consumption expenditures of the individual; a *sales* tax is levied on the sales of goods and services; and a *value-added* tax is levied on the difference between a firm's sales and its purchases. Expenditure taxes may be proportional or progressive; sales and value-added taxes may be imposed at a uniform rate on all commodities or at differing rates on various groups of commodities. Expenditure taxes are collected from the consumer; sales and value-added taxes, from the seller. Sales taxes are in use throughout the world; the value-added tax, a relative newcomer, is now widely used in Western Europe and many other countries. A graduated consumption expenditure tax was in effect briefly in India and Sri Lanka, but it is not now in use anywhere.

The sales tax can be a single-stage or a multistage tax. Canada levies its sales tax at the manufacturers' level, and U.S. state and local governments levy it at the retail level; Australia and New Zealand use the wholesale sales tax. The *turnover* tax is so called because the tax is levied every time a commodity "turns over" from one firm to another. The value-added tax is also a multistage tax, but it is figured on the *net* value added by each firm.

A common form of consumption tax is the *excise* tax on the sale of a particular commodity or group of commodities. Most excises are levied at *specific* rates (for example, cents per gallon or per pack of cigarettes), but some are levied at *ad valorem* rates (for example, 20 percent of the sales price). Excises are levied almost everywhere on alcoholic beverages and tobacco products, but they apply to many other products as well. They are also employed as "user charges" to collect part or all of the cost of government services enjoyed by specific groups of taxpayers. Gasoline taxes and taxes on motor vehicles, for instance, are used to pay for highway construction and maintenance. Appendix table A-8 summarizes the major excises imposed by the federal government since 1913.

Customs duties, which are levied on imports, are often used to protect domestic industries against foreign competition as well as to raise revenues. The policy of the U.S. government is to reduce trade barriers in the interest of promoting world trade, but the size and pace of the reductions depend on international negotiations, which are complicated and time-consuming. The negotiations are concerned with the role of customs duties in the nation's foreign economic policy rather than with their role as taxes to produce revenue. Customs duties are therefore not discussed in this book.

A major issue regarding consumption taxes in this country is equity. Because the poor consume more of their income than do the rich, the burden of a flat-rate sales tax falls as incomes rise. The sales tax also bears more heavily on families that have larger expenditures relative to their incomes, such as families with a large number of children or those just starting a household. Some excise taxes may be progressive (if levied on luxury goods), but since they are usually levied on mass consumption items, they tend to be regressive on balance.

Sales and excise taxes are also criticized on economic grounds. Consumption taxes are never levied at a uniform rate on all goods and services, and thus they interfere with the freedom of choice of consumers and misallocate the nation's resources (except, as will be discussed below, when they are employed as pollution and user charges or to discourage consumption of items, such as narcotics, that lead to increased social costs). They rank low as automatic stabilizers because they respond no more than in proportion to changes in income. Moreover, purchasers may be charged more than the amount of the tax through *pyramiding* when successive markups are applied to the same goods as they move through the channels of production and distribution. On the other hand, sales and excise taxes are often supported for their relative stability of yield, a characteristic that is important for financing state and local government activities, but not federal.

Because of the equity and economic shortcomings of sales and excise taxes, other forms of consumption taxation have been proposed as substitutes. Some economists are partial to a graduated expenditure tax, but this tax is not well understood by the public and policymakers alike. Value-added taxation, on the other hand, has spread rapidly in recent years, particularly among countries that relied heavily on turnover and selective excise taxes and have come to recognize their economic deficiencies.

In the United States, forty-five states and many local governments levy retail sales taxes, and the trend is toward greater use of this tax at the state and local levels. Federal consumption taxes are restricted to selective excises, while the state and local governments levy general sales taxes as well as excises. In 1965 all but a few major federal excise taxes were eliminated. A federal tax on automobiles, graduated inversely to the models' fuel efficiency, was enacted in 1978, and a special excise tax on the domestic production of oil—called the "crude oil windfall profit tax"—was enacted in 1980.

Issues in Excise Taxation

The imposition of taxes on particular commodities alters the results of the market mechanism. Such interference should be avoided, but there are circumstances in which excise taxes are useful and even necessary.

Economic Effects of Excise Taxes

The immediate effect of an excise tax is to raise the price of the taxed commodity. The consumer will respond by buying less of the taxed commodity, purchasing other commodities, or saving more. The burden of the tax is thus borne in part by consumers and in part by producers (and distributors) of the taxed commodity. If demand is relatively inelastic (that is, if consumers do not reduce their consumption of the particular item as much as its price increases), most of the burden is

Table 6-1. *Federal Excise Tax Revenues, by Major Sources,*
Fiscal Year 1982

Major source	Amount (millions of dollars)	Percentage of total
Alcohol	5,382	14.8
Tobacco	2,537	7.0
Highway	6,744	18.6
Gasoline	4,228	11.6
Trucks, buses, and trailers	725	2.0
Tires, inner tubes, and tread rubber	672	1.9
Diesel fuel used on highways	594	1.6
Other[a]	525	1.4
Crude oil windfall profits tax	18,881	52.0
Telephone and teletype services	920	2.5
Airport and airway	1,169	3.2
Other[b]	678	1.9
Total	36,311	100.0

Source: *The Budget of the United States Government, Fiscal Year 1984*, pp. 9-14, 9-15. Figures are rounded.
a. Includes taxes on lubricating oils, truck parts and accessories, and use tax on certain vehicles less refunds.
b. Includes taxes on firearms, shells, cartridges, fishing equipment, wagering, sugar, gaming devices, investment income of foundations, foreign insurance policies, and undistributed excise tax collections less refunds.

borne by the consumers. On the other hand, if supply is relatively inelastic (if the producer does not or cannot reduce production as price declines), the burden is borne mainly by the producer.

In general, the objective of excise taxation is to place the burden of the tax on consumers, and most excise revenues are derived from taxes imposed on articles for which the demand is relatively inelastic. For example, taxes on alcohol, tobacco, and gasoline accounted for one-third of federal excise revenues in fiscal 1982 (table 6-1). Supply is generally so highly elastic in the taxed industries that, even where demand is relatively elastic, very little of the burden of consumer taxes is borne by the producers. However, the crude oil windfall profit tax was intended to be a tax on producers, rather than on consumers of oil (see below).

BURDEN OF EXCISES. The effects of excise taxes on the allocation of economic resources depend on the sensitivity of consumption to a rise in price. If consumption is not reduced much by the higher price, consumers respond by cutting their consumption of other commodities as well as the taxed commodity. The effect is much like that of an income tax, which reduces disposable income, leading the consumer to reduce consumption of a wide range of commodities. There is little incentive for labor and capital to move out of the taxed industry, and the allocation of resources elsewhere in the economy is not altered significantly.

When consumption is fairly sensitive to price, however, production and employment decline in the industry producing the taxed commodity. Demand for other products increases at the expense of the taxed industry, and over time the labor and capital will move to other industries (if high employment is maintained). In this case, the tax substantially alters the pattern of production and consumption in the private economy. It also may create hardship for the employees and owners of capital in the industries affected (at least for a temporary period until they move to other industries).

Thus an excise tax imposes a burden on the economy because consumers are not as well off as they would have been if the same revenue had been raised by another tax that did not change patterns of consumption. The loss resulting from this distortion is called the *excess consumer burden* of the excise tax. The amount of the excess burden is the difference between the value placed by consumers on the consumption they give up and the yield of the tax. Excess burden is, in other words, the loss in economic efficiency caused by the imposition of the tax.

This analysis holds only in a world in which the allocation of resources before the imposition of the commodity tax is optimal. In the real world there are substantial departures from the conditions necessary for this optimum for reasons other than taxes, and there is no a priori basis for making the judgment that a new excise tax necessarily involves a loss in consumer welfare. Consumers may value the newly taxed commodity less highly than other commodities they consume in its place after the tax is imposed, particularly if the new tax makes them shift their consumption to commodities that are already heavily taxed.

Nevertheless, the case for selective excise taxes is weak. Conceivably, there are excise taxes that would not reduce consumer welfare, but there is no basis for making such a selection. Excise taxes should be avoided unless there is a compelling reason for altering the allocation of resources and for discriminating among individuals and families on the basis of their consumption preferences.

EXCISE TAXES IN WARTIME. One situation in which the government has a definite interest in changing the pattern of resource use is in wartime or in a similar national emergency. Many materials are needed for production in war industries. Excise taxes may be helpful both as a rationing device and as a selective way of reducing consumer demand. By increasing the prices of the taxed commodities, the government can reduce demand and divert it to other, more plentiful commodities or to saving. In extreme cases, as in the two world wars, the government can not only impose excises to discourage consumption, but can also replace the market mechanism with direct rationing and halt production of items that conflict with the war effort.

Excises are among the first taxes to be increased in a national emergency. Criticism of this practice usually arises because the taxes chosen are hard to justify on economic and equity grounds. And the rationale of discouraging consumption on a selective basis is quickly forgotten once excises are imposed and the revenue objective becomes paramount. Even in wartime, excise taxes should be used sparingly; first, because there are better ways to raise general revenues and, second, because wartime taxes are apt to linger on—and do considerable damage—for many years. For example, the excises levied by the federal government on many electric, gas, and oil appliances in 1941 were not repealed until 1965.

USER CHARGES AND POLLUTION TAXES. Selective excise taxes may be used to good advantage to obtain payments from individuals and businesses that benefit from particular public services or that impose special costs on society. If no charges are made, demand is stimulated for public services that are provided at less than cost or for private activities that result in uncompensated damages to others, and too many resources may be used in carrying them out. An excise tax, or some other means of charging for the service or compensating for damage, is needed to maintain economic efficiency.

Despite the sound theoretical justification for such excise, or benefit, taxes, they are not employed nearly enough for this purpose at any level of government in the United States. Specific excise taxes are allocated to the federal Highway Trust Fund, which was established in 1956 to finance the interstate highway system, and to the Airport and Airway Trust Fund, established in 1970 to finance airport and airway development. The Highway Revenue Act of 1982 raised the highway taxes (mainly an increase in the excise taxes on gasoline and diesel fuel from four to nine cents a gallon) for the period April 1, 1983, through September 30, 1988. The act also raised the taxes imposed on sales of trucks and truck parts and on the registration of highway vehicles so as to increase the share of highway tax revenues paid by heavy vehicles in order to bring them more closely in line with the costs they impose on the highway system. The Airport and Airway Trust Fund taxes expired on October 1, 1980, but were reinstated for the period from September 1, 1982, to September 30, 1987.

The pollution of water and air by private individuals and businesses imposes heavy costs on society, which should not be borne by the general taxpayer. Two types of antipollution taxes have been proposed: taxes on products that pollute the air or water, and taxes on processes or enterprises based on the costs they impose. Such taxes and charges would discourage consumption of products that generate the most pollution and would give producers incentives to use production processes and equipment that reduce pollution. Economic efficiency and equity would be improved and the burden of other taxes could be eased. But successive administrations have had little success in persuading Congress to accept this approach. Recent presidents have recommended the adoption of a wide range of special taxes or user charges, including taxes on sulfur emissions and payments for the use of air and inland waterway transportation facilities, recreation facilities, and many other federally financed benefits. Such taxes and user charges are strongly resisted by the groups that would be required to pay, and past experience suggests that this resistance is politically potent and difficult to overcome.

A breakthrough occurred in 1978 when special automobile excise taxes were imposed by the federal government on the basis of fuel efficiency. These "gas guzzler" taxes, which are paid by automobile manufacturing companies, became effective in 1980 and increase annually through 1986. In that year, there will be no tax on cars averaging more than 22.5 miles per gallon; the tax will then rise from $500 for cars averaging 21.5 to 22.5 miles per gallon to $3,850 for those averaging less than 12.5 miles per gallon. Through 1982, the automobile companies had generally met the minimum standards and virtually no revenues had been collected from this tax. In addition to the gas guzzler tax, a fine is imposed on automobile manufacturers by the Environmental Protection Agency for failing to meet its fleet economy standards, but so far the companies have also met these standards.

In 1980 special excise taxes were levied on crude oil and on forty-two hazardous chemicals or chemicals that may create hazardous products or wastes when used, with rates of seventy-nine cents per barrel of crude oil and twenty-two cents to $4.87 per ton for chemicals. These taxes are used to finance the Hazardous Substance Response Trust Fund, which pays for chemically created damages where the specific source of the damages cannot be identified or held accountable for cleanup. The efficiency effects of these taxes will be minimal, however, because they are levied on current production of chemicals to pay for damages of past chemical pollution. The taxes will terminate after September 30, 1985, or earlier if the balance of the trust fund exceeds $900 million, or when cumulative receipts from these taxes reach $1.38 billion.

THE CRUDE OIL WINDFALL PROFIT TAX. An unusual excise tax was imposed by the federal government in 1980 as a result of President Carter's decision to phase out controls on crude oil. The decontrol of oil was intended to raise the price of oil in the United States to the world price to encourage energy conservation and production of domestic oil and alternative energy sources. With oil prices set by the world market, this is one of the few excise taxes expected to be paid by producers and not shifted forward to consumers in any significant degree.

The crude oil windfall profit tax is an excise tax on the difference between the current price of oil and a base price, depending on the type of oil produced. The tax is 70 percent for oil already discovered ("first-tier" oil), 60 percent for stripper oil or production from a National Petroleum Reserve ("second-tier" oil), and 30 percent for newly discovered oil ("third-tier" oil). Newly discovered oil is defined as oil from wells not producing in calendar year 1978. The tax will phase out over a thirty-three-month period after December 31, 1987, or when cumulative revenues reach $227.3 billion, whichever is later. However, the phaseout will begin no later than January 1991.

Although the crude oil windfall profit tax was strongly opposed by oil producers, it was approved by Congress in order to capture for the federal government part of the extra sales revenues generated by the decontrol of oil prices. Such a tax was defended on the ground that the price increase for oil already discovered would have a minimum effect on output and would not provide much incentive for exploration and development. The tax on newly discovered oil was intended to raise revenues, but it was levied at a reduced rate to avoid discouraging investment in oil exploration and development.

SUMPTUARY TAXES. Excises on commodities or services that are considered socially or morally undesirable are known as *sumptuary* taxes. The best examples are the excises on liquor and tobacco. The rationale for sumptuary taxes is that the consumption of some products creates additional costs for society that are not borne by the producers and are not reflected in the prices they charge. For example, consumption of liquor generates costs in the form of lost working time, accidents, broken homes, and increased delinquency; and consumption of cigarettes has been shown to be associated with higher frequencies of a wide range of illnesses. An excise tax raises prices on such commodities to a level that more nearly reflects total social costs as well as private costs and discourages consumption of such commodities.

In some cases, the costs imposed by certain items or activities are so great that society prohibits them. This is true, for example, of narcotics and gambling. The federal government prohibits the sale of narcotics except under very strict rules; most states either outlaw or regulate gambling, but some run their own lotteries and impose taxes on betting at racetracks. Taxes are imposed on these items to aid in regulation and law enforcement and, in the case of lotteries and taxes on gambling, to raise revenue.

In a democratic society, complete prohibition of the use of any commodity or service requires virtually unanimous agreement that it is harmful or immoral. Where this unanimity does not exist, the majority expresses its view by levying a tax that will discourage consumption without eliminating it entirely. Those who place a high value on such items are allowed to purchase them but at a higher price. This is why gambling is illegal in some states and is subject to regulation and to special taxes in others. Similarly, since opinion on the harmful effects of alcoholic beverages and cigarettes is not unanimous, purchases of these items are permitted but are heavily taxed by the federal and state governments and even by some local governments. However, the main effects of these taxes as levied in the United States are to tax smokers and drinkers while curtailing their consumption modestly and to intro-duce an element of regressivity into the system.

Sumptuary taxes in the United States have not increased since 1951, except for a temporary increase in the tax on cigarettes from eight cents to sixteen cents a pack for the period January 1, 1983, through September 30, 1985.

Equity Considerations

Excise taxes rank low in terms of equity on a number of grounds. First, consumers of the taxed commodities probably bear the major burden of the excise taxes that have been levied in the United States.

Table 6-2. *Effective Rates of Federal Excise Taxes and of a Hypothetical General Sales Tax, by Income Percentiles, 1975*
Percent

Household income percentile[a]	Federal excise taxes	5 percent general sales tax
0–5	3.5	12.8
5–10	1.8	5.0
10–15	1.7	4.0
15–20	1.5	3.7
20–25	1.4	3.2
25–30	1.4	3.1
30–35	1.4	3.0
35–40	1.4	2.9
40–45	1.3	2.7
45–50	1.3	2.6
50–55	1.2	2.5
55–60	1.2	2.5
60–65	1.2	2.5
65–70	1.2	2.4
70–75	1.1	2.4
75–80	1.1	2.3
80–85	1.0	2.2
85–90	1.0	2.1
90–95	0.8	1.8
95–99	0.6	1.4
99–100	0.3	0.7
All classes[b]	1.0	2.2

Source: Brookings 1975 MERGE data file.
a. Ranked from low to high incomes. Income is defined as money factor incomes plus transfer payments, accrued capital gains, and indirect business taxes.
b. Includes negative incomes.

How this burden is distributed depends on what proportion of income is allocated to consumption of the taxed items at the various income levels. For example, excise taxes on beer and cigarettes are regressive, while those that were formerly levied on furs and some consumer durables were progressive. The present federal excise tax structure is clearly regressive (table 6-2).

Second, excise taxes are unfair for different people with the same income. Families whose preferences for the taxed commodities are high are taxed more heavily than those who prefer to spend their income in other ways or who save. This violation of horizontal equity is not justified unless there are overriding social reasons for discouraging the use of particular goods or services. However, the imposition of a selective excise tax can improve equity and the allocation of resources where special costs or benefits associated with the production or distribution of a particular commodity are not borne or paid for by the individuals and firms creating the costs or receiving the benefits.

Third, while most of the pre-1965 excise taxes were levied on goods and services used by consumers, some applied to items that were used primarily or exclusively by business (such as business and store machines, lubricating oils, long-distance telephone services, and trucks). Taxes levied on such items enter into business costs and are generally reflected in higher prices for consumer goods. Since people with low incomes spend a larger proportion of their income than those in the higher income classes, taxes that enter into business costs are regressive. Furthermore, they often create unfair competitive situations by discriminating against firms that use the taxed commodity or service and distorting the choice of production methods. The classic example of a bad excise tax was the one on freight, since it discriminated against firms with distant markets. It was eliminated in 1958.

The Excise Tax Reduction Act of 1965 eliminated most federal excises, except for a few regulatory taxes and highway taxes that recover the costs of services or facilities directly benefiting individuals and business firms. The act reduced the tax on passenger cars in stages from 10 percent to 1 percent on January 1, 1969. It also reduced the 10 percent telephone tax in stages until it was to be completely eliminated by January 1, 1969. However, the scheduled reductions were postponed in 1966, 1968, 1969, and 1970. The repeal of the automobile tax became effective December 11, 1971. The repeal of the telephone tax was postponed even longer; it is now set at a 3 percent rate for 1983, 1984, and 1985 and is scheduled to expire on January 1, 1986.

A General Consumption Tax?

The major drawback of selective excise taxes is that they are not neutral; that is, they discriminate among different items of consumption. A broadly based tax is much more appropriate for taxing consumption. The three broad-based taxes mentioned most often are the general sales tax, the value-added tax, and the expenditure tax.

The General Sales Tax

Sales taxation has been used extensively throughout the world, and there is almost no limit to the variations in the structure of these taxes. On the whole, experience suggests that a single-stage tax is preferable to a turnover tax and that the scope of the tax should be as broad as possible. Among single-stage taxes, the retail sales tax is preferable on economic and equity grounds, but it is somewhat more costly to administer than either a manufacturers' or a wholesalers' tax.

SINGLE-STAGE VERSUS TURNOVER TAXES. The advantage of a turnover tax is that any particular revenue goal can be realized at the lowest possible rate. This makes the turnover tax politically attractive, but it is highly objectionable on other grounds. A turnover tax levied at a uniform rate results in widely varying total rates of tax on different goods, depending on the complexity of the production and distribution channels. This means that the total tax burden differs among commodities, much as it does under a selective excise tax system. But, unlike excises, it is complicated to rebate turnover taxes on exports and to tax imports equally with domestic production. Moreover, the multistage tax gives firms a strong incentive to merge with their suppliers and contributes to greater concentration in industry and trade.

Even the uniform rate turns out to be a will-o'-the-wisp whenever the turnover tax is tried. The discriminatory effects of the uniform rate soon become very serious, and the government finds it difficult to resist pressures to moderate the tax load where it is demonstrably out of line. Once introduced, modifications of the uniform rate proliferate, and the tax becomes a maze of complications and irrational distinctions. Thus a tax that was originally intended to be relatively simple turns out to be an administrative monstrosity and highly inequitable. For these reasons, the turnover tax has generally been replaced by other forms of consumption taxes and is little used today.

WHOLESALERS' AND MANUFACTURERS' SALES TAXES. Administrative complications are reduced if the tax is levied at the wholesale or manufacturing level. The number of firms is smaller, their average size larger, and their records more adequate. These advantages are offset, however, by the difficulty of identifying taxable transactions and of determining the price on which the tax is based.

The most troublesome feature of the wholesalers' tax is the determination of wholesale values when manufacturers sell directly to retailers.

To avoid discrimination among industries with differing degrees of integration, these manufacturers' prices are usually raised to include a normal wholesale markup. The adjustment goes the other way in the case of the manufacturers' tax: the price a manufacturer charges a retailer must be lowered to eliminate the value of the wholesale services.

Both taxes are subject to the criticism that the rate tends to pyramid as goods move to the retail level. A 10 percent manufacturers' tax may become a 20 percent tax on the price at the retail level after the wholesaler and the retailer have applied their customary markups. There is less pyramiding under a wholesalers' tax, but the problem is by no means avoided. In time, competition tends to wipe out the effect of pyramiding, but the adjustment process may be slow.

On balance, there is little to choose between the wholesalers' and the manufacturers' tax. The wholesalers' tax is more practical when the wholesale and retail stages are fairly distinct; on the other hand, complications arise if there is much integration between manufacturers and retailers. The manufacturers' tax is more practical when there is either a high degree of integration in most consumer lines or none at all; the mixed situation raises the most difficulties.

RETAIL SALES TAX. A retail sales tax is meant to apply uniformly to most goods and services purchased by individual consumers and is basically much less complicated than a wholesalers' or manufacturers' tax. Retail sales taxes are usually imposed on a broader base, but they are rarely completely general. It is difficult to reach many consumer services, although it is possible to tax the services of public utilities and such other services as admissions, repairs, laundry, and dry cleaning. The retail sales tax does not apply to housing—the largest service in most consumer budgets—but housing is subject to the property tax. Many state sales taxes in the United States exempt food, medicine, and other commodities that are regarded as necessities.

Although the retail sales tax often falls short of complete generality, it is in many ways better than the taxes levied at earlier stages of the production or distribution process. Its most important advantage is that there is little or no pyramiding. For goods purchased by consumers, wholesale and retail markups are not inflated by the tax since it applies only to the final price. An attempt is sometimes made to exempt from the retail sales tax investment goods purchased by business firms, but taxes on business purchases often run as high as one-fifth of sales tax receipts, making such exemptions expensive. These taxes enter into business costs and are probably pyramided, but the extent of this pyramiding must be only a small fraction of the pyramiding under a manufacturers' or wholesalers' sales tax.

The broad base of the retail sales tax means that lower rates can be used than with other single-stage taxes to yield a given amount of revenue. And this difference in rates is not small, since prices may be 50 or 100 percent higher at the retail level. Thus a retail tax of 5 percent may yield the same revenue as a manufacturers' tax of 7.5 or 10 percent.

On administrative grounds, the retail sales tax has both advantages and disadvantages. It is more difficult to deal with the larger number of small retailers than with the less numerous and more sophisticated manufacturers or wholesalers. On the other hand, the problems of defining a transaction and of determining the base of the tax are more easily handled at the retail level, although even there the problems are not insignificant. State governments have had retail sales taxes for many years, and most of them have learned that they are not easy to administer and enforce.

The introduction of a retail sales tax by the federal government would involve duplication of existing state and local taxes. The state and local governments would interpret this as unwarranted interference with their freedom of action concerning the rates and coverage of their own taxes. At a minimum, some effort would have to be made to coordinate the definition of the tax bases and perhaps also to administer collection of the taxes on a cooperative or joint basis.

The strongest objection to a retail tax, which also applies to wholesale and manufacturers' taxes, is its regressivity. In 1975 a 5 percent sales tax on all consumption, including food, would have amounted to 2.5 percent of income for families at the median level and less than 1 percent for those in the top percentile (table 6-2). These figures, based on income and consumption in a one-year period, overstate the regressivity of the sales tax, since persons temporarily in the lower income classes do not reduce their consumption by the entire amount of the reduction in their income, and those temporarily in higher classes do not raise their consumption by the entire increase in their income. Some economists have suggested that the burden of the sales tax should be measured against income over a longer period. On this basis, a retail sales tax would be less regressive and might even be proportional, but it is unlikely that it would turn out to be progressive to any significant degree, regardless of the time period examined.

Many units of government have exempted food and certain other items of consumption from the sales tax to alleviate its burden on the poor. Although these exemptions moderate the regressivity of the tax, they do not eliminate it. As an alternative, experts have long suggested refunding the estimated tax paid by people with low incomes. This suggestion was ignored until 1963, when Indiana introduced a retail sales tax and adopted a small tax credit against the income tax as a relief measure for the sales tax paid by low-income recipients. Since then, Indiana has repealed its sales tax credit, but Hawaii, Idaho, and Nebraska have adopted it. New Mexico provides a credit for all state and local taxes and a food credit of $45 per capita for low-income families.

The Value-Added Tax

The value-added tax, first proposed in 1918 by a German industrial executive, was discussed sporadically for more than three decades before it was actually put to use. A modified version was adopted in 1953 by the state of Michigan and repealed in 1967; in 1954 the central government of France imposed such a tax, and most European countries and many other countries have since followed suit. Some people have advocated the inclusion of a value-added tax in the U.S. federal tax system to provide a revenue source to supplement the income tax or substitute for part of it.

FORMS OF VALUE-ADDED TAXATION. For any given firm, value added is the difference between receipts from sales and amounts paid for materials, supplies, and services purchased from other firms. The total of the value added by all firms in the economy is equal to total wages, salaries, interest, rents, and profits and is therefore the same as the national income.

There are two types of value-added taxes, which differ only in the way outlays for investment purposes are treated. The first type permits business firms to subtract purchases of capital goods in computing the tax base. Total value added is thus equal to total retail sales of final consumer goods. With the second type, purchases of capital goods are not deducted; instead, firms are permitted to deduct an allowance for depreciation over the useful life of the asset. Thus the second type is equivalent to a tax on the national income; the first, which is now widely used in Europe, is a general consumption tax.

There are two methods of computing the allowance to be made for purchases from other firms. Under the "tax credit" method, the tax rate is applied to the total sales of the firm, and the tax paid on goods purchased is then deducted. Where this method is used, the tax on all goods shipped must be shown separately on each invoice. Under the second, the "calculation" method, purchases are subtracted from sales, and the tax rate is then applied to the net figure.

The two methods may be illustrated as follows. Suppose a retailer who pays $52.50 for an item (including a 5 percent tax of $2.50) applies a markup of 100 percent. Under the tax credit method, he charges his customer $105 ($100 plus $5 tax) and takes a credit of $2.50 in computing the amount to be paid to the government, leaving a net tax of $2.50. If the calculation method is used, the retailer deducts from the $100 the $50 paid to his supplier and then applies a tax rate of 5 percent to the remainder to obtain the same $2.50 net tax. The customer pays the same total price of $105, which consists of the $100 price net of tax, the $2.50 tax paid by the supplier, and the $2.50 paid by the retailer.

Although both approaches have the same result, some administrators believe that noncompliance is easier to control under the tax credit method. In addition, the tax credit method automatically provides an accounting of the tax to be rebated on exports (the standard practice to avoid putting domestic firms at a competitive disadvantage in foreign markets) and solves some of the problems raised by the inclusion or exclusion of various items, such as charitable contributions, that are troublesome under the calculation method. In general, however, the taxation of goods and services produced in the tax-exempt and government sectors presents difficult problems under a value-added tax.

ECONOMIC EFFECTS OF THE VALUE-ADDED TAX. The value-added tax reduces or eliminates the pyramiding that would occur under the turnover tax or the manufacturers' and wholesalers' sales taxes. Since a firm receives credit for the tax paid by its suppliers, it is unlikely to apply a markup to its purchases in computing the price to be charged.

The base of the consumption-type value-added tax is the same as that of a retail sales tax and is confined to goods for consumption. On the other hand, the income-type value-added tax is equivalent to a proportional income tax. Whether the patterns of distribution of the burden of the two types of value-added taxes are the same is in dispute, reflecting a difference of opinion about the impact of a proportional income tax and a general tax on consumption. The income-type value-added tax is paid on capital goods at the time the purchase is made, and the tax is presumably recovered as they are depreciated. Under the consumption-type value-added tax, purchases of capital goods are free of tax. Thus, at any given time, the income-type value-added tax imposes an extra tax on net investment. Some argue that prepayment of the tax under the income-type tax reduces the return on capital; others believe that it is reflected in higher prices for final consumption goods and has no effect on the rate of return.

THE VALUE-ADDED TAX VERSUS THE RETAIL SALES TAX. The consumption-type value-added tax and the retail sales tax are similar on both economic and equity grounds. Both are taxes on general consumption. The retail sales tax involves fewer administrative problems because the determination of tax liability is somewhat less complicated and the number of taxpayers is smaller. But in practice retail sales taxes always exclude many items of consumption, while a value-added tax could probably be levied on a more general basis.

Sales or Value-Added Taxes versus Income Taxes

Following World War II, the major argument for adoption of a sales or value-added tax by the federal government was the arbitrariness of the excise tax system. Except for sumptuary and benefit taxes, the excises that were in effect between 1944 and 1965 could hardly be defended on rational grounds. If revenues from consumption taxes were needed permanently, it would have been better to replace the miscellaneous excises with a general low-rate tax on consumer goods.

This argument was eliminated by the enactment of the Excise Tax Reduction Act of 1965. It can be said that, for all practical purposes, the federal government has reduced consumption taxation to a minimum. The appeal of a low-rate consumption tax must now rest on the substantive ground that it would be better national policy to replace part of the income tax with a tax on consumption.

Heavier reliance on a sales or value-added tax by the federal government is opposed for several reasons. First, the shift from income taxes to a consumption tax would impair the built-in flexibility of the tax system. The automatic reductions in income tax revenues during the post–World War II recessions helped moderate the declines in disposable income and contributed to the brevity and mildness of the recessions. Maintenance of built-in flexibility is good insurance against the possibility of a serious business contraction.

Second, a sales or value-added tax would bring the federal government into an area that is now the most important source of state revenue and is also becoming important at the local level. Federal use of this tax source would almost surely restrict its use by the state and local governments, and their fiscal capacities would be impaired.

Third, the load of federal, state, and local taxes on low-income recipients is already heavy. Additional consumption taxes at the federal level would make the combined structure less progressive. Such a policy would be particularly inappropriate in light of attempts by the federal government to lessen poverty in the United States.

On the other hand, several arguments are advanced in support of greater use of consumption taxes by the federal government. First, even though income tax rates were lowered in 1964, 1969, and 1981, they are still considered high by some people, particularly for individuals with high incomes. These rates may reduce incentives and the willingness and capacity to save.

Second, built-in flexibility does not require that all elements of the federal tax system be highly sensitive to changes in income. A large automatic growth in tax receipts has the effect of promoting higher federal expenditures. If these revenues were not so easily obtained, federal expenditures might be much lower.

Third, the federal government need not impair the fiscal capacities of the state and local governments to build up its own consumption tax revenue. If a value-added tax were adopted, the federal government would not encroach on state and local revenue. Since practically all business enterprises already file income tax returns, the administrative and compliance problems of a value-added tax should not be insurmountable.

Fourth, it is argued that a general consumption tax in lieu of part or all of the corporation income tax would improve the U.S. balance of payments. As explained in chapter 5, this substitution would improve either the trade surplus if the corporation income tax were shifted in the form of higher prices, or the capital account, if the tax were borne by the owners of capital and exchange rates were fixed. Either possibility is unlikely because the assumption that the corporation income tax is shifted is doubtful, and because floating, rather than fixed, exchange rates are now the rule.

While there are a number of important peripheral considerations, the major issue in the controversy over the income tax versus the consumption tax concerns the degree of progressivity. Proponents of a general consumption tax rarely recommend a graduated expenditure tax (see the next section) as an alternative to income taxation. Their concern is to reduce progressivity, and they propose a flat-rate sales or value-added tax as a way of accomplishing this objective. On the other hand, those who oppose a general consumption tax either defend the present degree of progressivity or believe it is inadequate. Most of them would support a graduated expenditure tax if a new consumption tax were necessary, but oppose the adoption of a sales or value-added tax.

The Expenditure Tax

The consumption expenditure tax has long been discussed in the economic literature but was not seriously considered until the Treasury Department recommended it during World War II. It was also recommended by a minority of the British Royal Commission on the Taxation of Profits and Income in 1955, by a British committee of experts chaired by Professor J. P. Meade in 1978, and by the U.S. Treasury Department in 1977. Although these recommendations were not adopted, the tax has come to be regarded as a respectable possibility.

Unlike the consumption taxes already discussed, the consumption expenditure tax is levied on the consumer rather than on the seller of goods and services. In practice, there is little difference in the methods of administering the expenditure tax and the individual income tax. Individual taxpayers submit a form at the end of the year estimating the amount of their expenditures. Personal exemptions and deductions for selected expenditures may be allowed. The rates may be proportional or graduated, although it is usually suggested that the expenditure tax be graduated.

The consumption expenditure tax is proposed to either replace or supplement the income tax. Such a shift is supported strongly by those who believe that the income tax has a large adverse effect on the incentive to save and invest (see chapter 4) and that private saving must be increased to increase the level of output and income.

COMPARISON WITH THE INCOME TAX. The individual income tax and a graduated consumption expenditure tax are alternative methods of taxing people in accordance with ability to pay. In the case of the income tax, the measure of ability to pay is income; in the case of the expenditure tax, the measure is consumption.

Some have argued that an income tax is inequitable because it taxes income when it is saved and then again when the savings earn additional income. It is now generally agreed that double taxation is not the real issue. Both the expenditure tax and the income tax may be progressive and redistributional in effect. If income is considered the better measure of ability to pay, the expenditure tax is inferior. On the other hand, some believe that it is fairer to tax individuals on what they take out of the common pool (consumption) rather than on what they contribute to it.

Some economists believe that the expenditure tax is superior to an income tax because current expenditures reflect normal or permanent income better than current income does. But it is far from obvious that current taxation should be related to income earned in the distant past or future.

Inflation would be much less of a problem under the expenditure tax than it is under the income tax. In general, there would be no need to adjust the tax base for inflation, as consumption is appropriately measured in current dollars. Under the income tax, an inflation adjustment is required to measure real income (see chapter 4).

To avoid a reduction of progressivity, the expenditure tax rates would have to be much higher than the income tax rates. For example, if in a given taxable income bracket the income tax rate was 50 percent and the marginal saving rate on income before tax was 25 percent, the marginal expenditure tax rate on income less saving would have to be 66⅔ percent to raise the same revenue from the bracket (if there were no change in the marginal propensity to save). Furthermore, there is no guarantee that the expenditure tax base would not be eroded as much as, or more than, the income tax base. Deductions for contributions, interest payments, and state and local taxes might be regarded as essential under the expenditure tax as they are under the income tax, and these would greatly restrict the revenue productivity of an expenditure tax.

DISTRIBUTION OF TAX BURDENS. On the assumption of equal yields, an expenditure tax would distribute the burden of taxation very differently from an income tax. Tax burdens would be heavier under an expenditure tax for households with high consumption ratios relative to income, such as young and large families and elderly persons, and lower for those with relatively low consumption ratios, such as families whose children have finished school and single persons in general. Tax rates on outlays for "big-ticket" items such as automobiles, furniture, and homes would be extremely high, and would probably be regarded as excessive by many people.

A tax that omits saving from the tax base is the same as a tax applying only to labor income and exempting all property income. For example, suppose a person in the 25 percent bracket earns and saves $4,000, on which the annual return is 10 percent. At the end of the year he withdraws his savings plus interest and consumes it all. Under a consumption tax, he pays a tax of $1,100 on the $4,400 he withdraws, leaving $3,300 to consume. Under a wage tax that does not tax interest income, he would pay a tax of $1,000 right away, deposit $3,000 and earn $300 interest tax-free. At the end of the year, he would also have $3,300 to consume. Most people would regard a tax that exempts property income as unfair.

Aside from the question of equity raised by an expenditure tax, it is clear that the exemption of saving from tax would permit the accumulation of vast fortunes, which would give the owners the ability to exercise great power over the economic and political life of the nation. To prevent excessive concentration of wealth, the expenditure tax would have to be accompanied by high death and gift taxes.

Graduated expenditure taxes are often proposed as a method of avoiding or correcting the defects of the income tax base, particularly in the top brackets, where the preferential treatment of capital gains, tax-exempt interest, and depletion allowances and other favorable provisions (see chapters 4 and 5) permit the accumulation of large fortunes with little or no payment of income tax. An expenditure tax would reach such incomes when they were spent without resort to regressive taxation.

FISCAL EFFECTS. Consumption expenditures are over 60 percent of the gross national product, so that a consumption expenditure tax would have a large tax base. The base would probably be somewhat smaller than the base of a comprehensive income tax, but in practice the revenue productivity of the two taxes depends on the specific deductions and exclusions that would be allowed.

Because expenditures tend to be relatively more stable than incomes, an expenditure tax would have less built-in flexibility over a business cycle than an income tax of equal yield. On the other hand, discretionary changes in tax rates for countercyclical purposes would be more effective under the expenditure tax, since expenditure tax changes would directly affect the net cost of current purchases (relative to future purchases) and would therefore have a much greater effect on consumption than income tax changes of equal amount.

ADMINISTRATION AND COMPLIANCE. Taxpayers cannot estimate their expenditures directly, since almost no one keeps adequate expenditure records. They must be estimated by subtracting investment outlays made during the year from total receipts. This calculation requires taxpayers to furnish information on the proceeds of dispositions of assets, the costs of newly acquired assets, and changes in cash holdings and bank and savings accounts, as well as on the ordinary income receipts now reported on income tax returns.

Administration and compliance would be more difficult under the expenditure tax than under the income tax in some respects and easier in others. Changes in cash holdings, personal debts, and purchases and dispositions of personal assets (such as jewelry and paintings) would be hard to trace. On the other hand, the expenditure tax would avoid the weakness of the income tax created by the use of the realization principle for calculating capital gains and losses; and since capital outlays would be treated as an expense when the outlays were made, the complications of accrual accounting adjustments for depreciation and depletion would be eliminated. In distinguishing between business and personal expenditures, both taxes are subject to somewhat similar problems, and both are subject to tax base erosion through the proliferation of personal deductions.

On balance, the administrative and compliance problems of a consumption expenditure tax are difficult but probably not insuperable for advanced countries that have effective income tax administration. But most countries would find it difficult to enforce such a tax with the present state of administrative know-how. Although it is hard to imagine total replacement of the income tax by an expenditure tax in the advanced countries, the latter might be a useful supplement if it became necessary to discourage consumption.

Summary

The federal government has relied exclusively on selective excises for consumption tax revenues. These taxes have been increased during every major war and subsequently de-emphasized as the need for revenue declined. The cycle lasted somewhat longer during and after World War II, but the last vestige of the wartime excises was eliminated by the 1965 Excise Tax Reduction Act. The excise taxes now levied by the federal government are sumptuary taxes on alcohol and tobacco, benefit taxes for highways, airways, and some recreational activities, a tax on domestically produced crude oil, a tax on telephone usage, and certain regulatory taxes.

Sumptuary taxes help offset the additional cost to society of the consumption of certain commodities; taxes imposed on those who benefit from particular government services are needed to prevent excessive use of such services; and special charges may be used to discourage private activities that lead to pollution. Otherwise, excise taxes are bad taxes: they discriminate arbitrarily against the consumption of the taxed commodities and distort the allocation of resources in the economy.

If consumption taxes are needed to boost revenue, economic and equity considerations suggest that a general consumption tax would be more appropriate than a series of selective excise taxes. A general tax does not discriminate against particular forms of consumption and therefore produces less distortion in the economy.

Among general consumption taxes, manufacturers' and wholesalers' sales taxes are easiest to administer, but they are pyramided through the markup of prices as goods go through production and distribution channels. Retail sales taxes and the value-added tax involve much less pyramiding, if any. All these taxes are regressive or, at best, proportional. Progressivity can be achieved by adopting a credit for sales taxes paid against the individual income tax or by taxing consumption through a graduated expenditure tax. The graduated consumption expenditure tax has a number of attractive features, but the nature of this tax and its implications for the distribution of tax burdens are not well understood.

Broad-based consumption taxes, such as the retail sales tax or the value-added tax, are more burdensome on the low income classes than income taxes and have less built-in flexibility. Adoption of a general consumption tax by the federal government would interfere with a revenue source that has become a mainstay of state and some local tax systems. However, consumption taxes are vigorously supported by those who believe either that the federal tax system is too progressive or that income taxation has severely impaired the incentive to save. More recently, there has been some support for the adoption of a graduated consumption expenditure tax to replace part or all of the individual and corporation income taxes in order to help increase the national saving rate and thus to promote a higher rate of investment.

CHAPTER SEVEN

Payroll Taxes

TAXES ON PAYROLLS, first introduced into the federal revenue system by the Social Security Act of 1935, have grown markedly since the end of World War II. They rank second to the individual income tax in importance, accounting for 33 percent of federal budget receipts in fiscal 1982 (figure 7-1). Payroll taxes will continue to rise as scheduled rate increases go into effect. Unlike most other taxes, payroll taxes are "earmarked"—through trust funds—to finance the nation's social security program.

The Development of Payroll Taxes

Most countries levy special taxes on payrolls (or income) to finance social security. When the United States passed its Social Security Act, twenty-eight countries had well-developed national retirement systems. The depression of the 1930s demonstrated that the state and local governments and private industry did not have the capacity to develop and finance a stable and adequate retirement program for the general population.

The 1935 act established two social insurance programs: a federal system of old-age benefits (now old age, survivors, disability, and health insurance—OASDHI—commonly called "social security") and a federal-state system of unemployment compensation. The first is financed by payroll taxes collected from employees and employers in equal amounts; the second is financed mainly by payroll taxes on employers (a few states tax both employers and employees). The major characteristics of these programs are summarized in table 7-1.

The original programs have undergone considerable change in coverage, benefits, and tax rates. Old-age benefits were supplemented by survivors' benefits in 1939, disability benefits in 1957, and hospital and medical benefits for persons sixty-five and over in 1966. The tax rate,

Figure 7-1. *Payroll Taxes as a Percentage of Gross National Product, Federal Budget Receipts, and Individual Income Tax Receipts, Fiscal Years 1955–82*

Percent

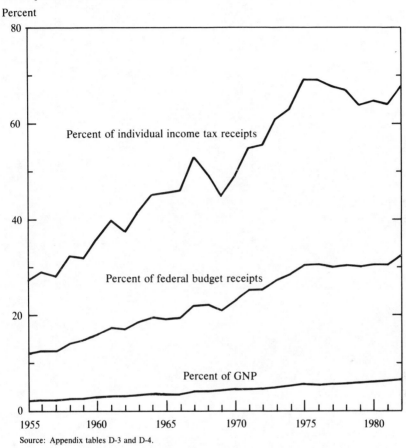

Source: Appendix tables D-3 and D-4.

initially 1 percent each on employers and employees for wages and salaries up to $3,000 annually, is scheduled to rise from 7 percent each in 1984 to 7.65 percent in 1990. Since 1975 the top limit on earnings subject to tax has been automatically increased by the rise in average wages (except for 1979–81, when ad hoc adjustments were made); in 1984 the maximum taxable earnings limit is $37,800. Self-employed persons with net earnings of $400 or more a year were added to the social security system in 1951, with a tax rate 1.5 times the rate applied to employees. From 1966 to 1983, the self-employed tax rate was somewhat less than 1.5 times the employee rate, but it was raised to twice the

Table 7-1. *Major Characteristics of the Social Insurance Programs as of January 1, 1984*

Program	Contribution rates (percent except as indicated) Employer	Employee	Maximum earnings subject to tax (dollars)	Eligibility requirements for benefits	Benefits
Old age, survivors, and disability insurance	5.7[a]	5.7[a]	37,800[b] a year	OASI: 1½ to 10 years of coverage; age 62 and over for men and women workers and wives; age 60 for widows	Individual: maximum $703 a month[b] Family: maximum $1,232 a month[b]
				Disability: insured status for OASI and recent employment; 5-month waiting period following total disability	Individual: maximum $853 a month[b] Family: maximum $1,280 a month[b]
Hospital	1.3[c]	1.3[c]	37,800[b] a year	Age 65 and over; entitled to disability benefits under OASDI or railroad retirement for at least 24 consecutive months; or chronic renal disease	60 days (with $356 deductible) plus 30 days at $89 a day; also posthospital services; and a lifetime reserve of 60 days with a $178 daily coinsurance[b]
Supplementary medical	$14.70 monthly premium[d]	...	...	Age 65 and over; entitled to disability benefits under OASDI or railroad retirement for at least 24 consecutive months; or chronic renal disease	$75 deductible and 20% coinsurance

Unemployment compensation	. . .	3.5[e]	7,000 a year	3–6 months of covered employment, depending on state law	Typically 50% of weekly wage; from 26 to 36 weeks, with additional weeks of extended and emergency benefits payable in states with high unemployment rates
Railroad retirement					
Tier I	6.7[f]	7.0[f]	2,975 a month	10 years of coverage, reduced at age 62 and full at age 65; 30 years of coverage, full at age 60	Maximum: $1,316 for workers retiring at age 65, with spouse $1,924 (in December 1983)
Tier II	2.0	11.75	2,225 a month		
Railroad unemployment compensation	. . .	8.0[g]	400 a month	Compensation of at least $1,000 in base year[h]	Typically 60% of daily pay for last employment in base year (subject to maximum of $25 a day), up to 130 days; extended benefits payable to long-term employees and to others during periods of high unemployment[i]

Source: Social Security Administration.

a. Scheduled to increase to 6.06 percent in 1988–89 and 6.2 percent in 1990. During 1984 a tax credit for employees is allowed to offset the increase of 0.3 percentage point over the 1983 OASDI tax rate. The self-employed pay the combined employee and employer contribution rates, with a tax credit of 2.7 percent in 1984, 2.3 percent in 1985, and 2.0 percent in 1986–89.

b. Based on a projection utilizing the II-B (intermediate) assumptions in the 1983 Trustees Report on Social Security. The OASI maximums assume the worker always had the maximum earnings subject to tax and became 65 in January 1984. The DI maximums assume a worker aged 24 or less who had maximum earnings subject to tax in 1982–83 and became disabled in January 1984.

c. Scheduled to increase to 1.35 percent in 1985 and 1.45 percent in 1986. The self-employed pay the combined employee and employer contribution rates.

d. Increases annually on the basis of increases in the cost of the program. Participation is voluntary. Based on a projection in the 1983 Trustees Report on Social Security.

e. Scheduled to increase to 6.2 percent in 1985.

f. Scheduled to increase to 7.05 percent in 1985, 7.15 percent in 1986–87, 7.51 percent in 1988–89, and 7.65 percent in 1990.

g. Statutory rates vary between 0.5 percent and 8.0 percent depending on balance in the trust fund.

h. Base year is calendar year preceding the beginning of the benefit year, which runs from July 1 to the following June 30.

i. Benefits may be extended 13 weeks with 10–14 years of coverage, and 26 weeks with 15 or more years of coverage.

employee rate beginning in 1984. (However, a credit against the income tax will be allowed for 2.7 percent of self-employment income in 1984, 2.3 percent in 1985, and 2.0 percent in 1986–89. Thereafter, the credit will be replaced by special provisions that will treat the self-employed in much the same manner as employees and employers are treated for social security and income tax purposes.)

The federal unemployment compensation tax rate started at 1 percent of payrolls of employers of eight or more persons; the 1984 rate is 3.5 percent for employers of one or more persons on wages and salaries up to $7,000 (rising to 6.2 percent in 1985). Lower rates (with a minimum stipulated by the federal government) are permitted in most states, depending on the stability of the employer's past record of employment.

Railroad workers are covered, though at much higher tax rates, for both retirement and unemployment under their own systems. Originally, employers and employees each paid half the railroad retirement tax; now the employers' rate is more than twice the employee rate. As under the federal-state system, the employer has always paid all the railroad unemployment insurance tax. (See appendix tables A-9 and A-10 for historical summaries of the social security and railroad payroll taxes.)

The employee's share of payroll taxes is withheld at the source by employers, but these taxes differ from the pattern established by the individual income tax in other respects. First, they are levied at a flat rate on wages and salaries up to a certain maximum amount each year, with no exemptions or deductions. Second, the employee—even though liable for half the OASDHI tax—does not file a return. The reporting of earnings, which provide the basis for calculating benefits, is handled entirely by the employer. Taxes are paid quarterly by the self-employed on an estimated basis.

In 1983 the federal old age, survivors, disability, and health programs covered more than 91 percent of all persons in paid jobs; 90 percent of the population sixty-five and over drew benefits. The hospital insurance program covered 27 million people sixty-five and over. Unemployment insurance covered 87 million people, or 97 percent of the total number of wage and salary earners.

The Insurance Analogy

When the social security program was enacted in 1935, considerable emphasis was placed on its resemblance to private insurance: "contributions'' were paid by the worker and the employer into a trust fund, interest was credited on trust fund balances, and benefits were based on the worker's previous earnings. This emphasis promoted public acceptance of the system as a permanent government institution. But the insurance analogy does not apply to the system as it has developed. Beneficiaries have received larger benefits than they would have been entitled to by the taxes they have paid, plus a reasonable rate of return, and this situation will continue into the twenty-first century. In recent years trust fund balances have not been large enough to finance even one year's worth of benefits (see appendix table D-20), so the payroll taxes paid by workers are not stored up or invested but are paid out currently as benefits. When the benefits promised to current workers become due, they will be paid from the tax revenues of that future date. Thus social security is really a compact between the working and nonworking generations that is renewed as each successive cohort retires and claims benefits.

In this concept of social security, payroll taxes are not insurance premiums but rather a financing mechanism for a large, essential government program. Many who hold this view believe that payroll taxes should be evaluated like any other major tax of the federal government. According to this view, increases in benefits should not be financed automatically by higher payroll taxes as they have been in the past, but by the best tax source or sources available to the federal government. On the other hand, since the retirement and disability benefits are related to past wages, many believe that the system has sufficient insurance elements to justify taxing payrolls to finance it.

Features of Payroll Taxes

As the second largest source of federal revenue, payroll taxes significantly affect the distribution of tax burdens and influence economic activity. From the standpoint of tax analysis their important features are their regressivity; their built-in flexibility; their effect on prices, employment, and wages; and their effect on personal and public saving.

Regressivity

A flat payroll tax on earnings up to a maximum is progressive for income at the bottom of the income scale, roughly proportional for some

Figure 7-2. *Effective Tax Rates of the Payroll Tax and of Alternative Methods of Raising the Same Revenue, 1977*[a]

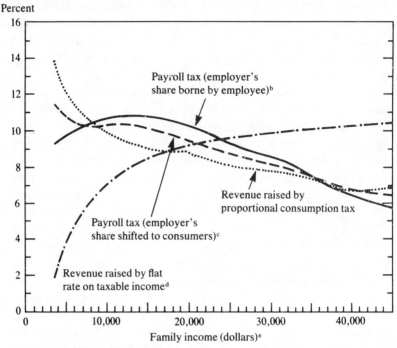

Percent

Family income (dollars)[e]

Source: Brookings 1970 MERGE data file projected to 1977.

a. Tax is 11.7 percent for wage earners and 7.9 percent for the self-employed. Maximum earnings subject to tax are $16,500.

b. Both the employer and the employee portions of the tax are assumed to be borne by the employee; the self-employment tax by the self-employed.

c. The employer tax is distributed in proportion to consumption by income class; the employee tax and self-employment tax by the employee and the self-employed, respectively.

d. The tax is applied to taxable income as defined in the income tax law for 1977.

e. Family income is a comprehensive definition of income, which includes estimated accrued capital gains.

distance, and regressive thereafter (figure 7-2). This pattern of tax incidence reflects the changing importance of covered earnings as incomes rise. In the lower part of the income scale, the ratio of covered earnings to total income increases; the ratio begins to fall at higher levels because the payroll tax applies to earnings in excess of the maximum and because property income, which is not subject to this tax, becomes increasingly important as incomes rise above this point.

The payroll tax is more progressive than a proportional tax on consumption up to the maximum taxable earnings level and less progressive thereafter (figure 7-2). On the other hand, the income tax is much more progressive than the payroll tax throughout the income scale. These conclusions are the same if the employer and employee portions of the OASDHI taxes are assumed to be borne entirely by the wage earners or if it is assumed that only the employee tax is borne by wage earners and the employer tax is shifted to consumers.

Payroll taxes are a significant part of the tax payments of the lowest income groups. In 1984 the employee and employer taxes for social security, disability, and hospital care will reach 14 percent of wages up to $37,800, or a maximum of $5,292 (table 7-2). The 1984 payroll tax will exceed the income tax liabilities of single persons with incomes up to $18,656, married persons with incomes up to $28,955, and married persons with two children and incomes up to $33,500. In 1979 the federal payroll tax for OASDHI purposes was the highest tax paid by over half of those covered by social security (assuming backward shifting of the employer's tax).

To moderate the burden of the social security tax on low incomes, Congress introduced in 1975 a "refundable" income tax credit of 10 percent of earnings up to $4,000 (phasing down to zero between $4,000 and $8,000 of income) for persons with children. Since 1979 the credit has been applied to the first $5,000 of earnings (phasing down to zero between $6,000 and $10,000 of income). The credit is "refundable" because cash payments are made to those who are not subject to the income tax. About 71 percent of the combined employer-employee payroll tax is eliminated for eligible workers earning less than $5,000.

Built-in Flexibility

Payroll taxes are less sensitive than the federal individual income tax to fluctuations in national income and employment. Since the social security tax is levied at a flat rate up to a limit that increases with average covered earnings, its yield (if the tax rate is constant) fluctuates no more than in proportion to earnings, unlike the individual income tax, which fluctuates more than proportionately to income over a business cycle. Automatic increases in the payroll tax rates enacted for many years ahead have occasionally come at the wrong time. Such increases went into effect when the country was in the midst of the 1953–54 recession, and only a few months before the onset of recessions in 1957, 1960, and 1981. The automatic escalation of the maximum taxable earnings ceiling raised payroll taxes during the 1974–75 and 1981–82 recessions. How-

Table 7-2. *Maximum Combined Employer-Employee Taxes and Maximum Taxes on Self-Employed under the OASDI and Hospital Insurance Programs, 1970–84*

Year	Maximum employer-employee tax			Maximum tax on self-employed		
	OASDI[a]	Hospital insurance	Total	OASDI[b]	Hospital insurance[b]	Total[b]
1970	655.20	93.60	748.80	491.40	46.80	538.20
1971	717.60	93.60	811.20	538.20	46.80	585.00
1972	828.00	108.00	936.00	621.00	54.00	675.00
1973	1,047.60	216.00	1,263.60	756.00	108.00	864.00
1974	1,306.80	237.60	1,544.40	924.00	118.80	1,042.80
1975	1,395.90	253.80	1,649.70	987.00	126.90	1,113.90
1976	1,514.70	275.40	1,790.10	1,071.00	137.70	1,208.70
1977	1,633.50	297.00	1,930.50	1,155.00	148.50	1,303.50
1978	1,787.70	354.00	2,141.70	1,256.70	177.00	1,433.70
1979	2,326.64	480.90	2,807.54	1,614.45	240.45	1,854.90
1980	2,631.44	543.90	3,175.34	1,825.95	271.95	2,097.90
1981	3,177.90	772.20	3,950.10	2,376.00	386.10	2,762.10
1982	3,499.20	842.40	4,341.60	2,608.20	421.20	3,029.40
1983	3,855.60	928.20	4,783.80	2,873.85	464.10	3,337.95
1984[c]	4,309.20	982.80	5,292.00	4,309.20	982.80	5,292.00

Source: Social security statutes enacted in 1969 and later years.
a. During 1984 a tax credit is allowed to employees to offset the increase of 0.3 percentage point over the 1983 OASDI tax rate.
b. Starting in 1984 the self-employed will pay the same taxes as the combined employer and employee taxes for OASDI and HI. During 1984 a tax credit of 2.7 percent is allowed to the self-employed to provide a transition to the new higher rates.
c. Based on a projection utilizing the II-B (intermediate) assumptions in the 1983 Trustees Report.

ever, benefits have usually been raised along with or shortly after tax increases, offsetting their deflationary impact. Beginning in 1975 benefits have been raised automatically each year on the basis of increases in average covered earnings.

Pressure for increasing payroll taxes at inappropriate times in the business cycle has also been experienced in state unemployment compensation programs. When the trust funds are threatened by a lack of reserves, the states are forced to raise tax rates regardless of the level of economic activity. Almost all states have adopted the "experience rating" system, which reduces tax rates for firms with stable employment. As a result, state unemployment taxes may fluctuate *inversely* with national income and employment levels.

By contrast, the expenditure side of the social insurance trust accounts is extremely effective as a countercyclical instrument. Unemployment

insurance benefits increase automatically as demand slackens and unemployment increases; they decline automatically as employment picks
up. This automatic effect is supplemented (by advances from the federal
government's general fund, if necessary) during periods of high national
or state unemployment by the payment of additional weeks of benefits
to workers who have exhausted their benefits under the regular state
programs. In addition, older workers fall back on old-age insurance
when they cannot find employment during slack periods.

On balance, despite the regressivity of the taxes and the inappropriate
timing of tax rate increases, the social insurance system has contributed
to the nation's economic stability since the end of World War II.

Effect on Prices, Employment, and Wages

It is popularly assumed that the employee's share of the payroll tax is
borne by wage earners and that the employer's share is shifted forward
to the consumer in the form of higher prices. But most economists
believe there is no difference in incidence between the payroll taxes
legally imposed on employers and those imposed on employees.

The OASDHI tax is a proportional tax on wages and salaries up to a
given ceiling. Although a few categories of workers are excluded, the
tax covers virtually all private-sector workers; public employees have
their own contributory retirement systems, but federal employees hired
after January 1, 1984, and military personnel are also covered by social
security. State and local employees may also be covered at the option
of the state and local governments. Since the social security tax is paid
in almost every occupation and industry, employees have no incentive
to move elsewhere to avoid it. Thus, like the personal income tax, the
payroll tax is not shifted.

In the short run, producers treat the payroll tax like any other
production cost and try to recover it through higher prices. At the higher
prices they do not sell as much as they did at pre-tax prices, and output
and employment tend to decline. This effect can be offset if the government maintains real demand at the old level (through a combination of
monetary and fiscal policies), but relative prices and output of labor-
intensive and capital-intensive goods will be altered in any event.

In the long run, the impact of the payroll tax depends on the reaction
of wage earners to reduced wages. Business firms aim at using just the
right combination of labor and capital to produce at lowest cost. A

payroll tax does not make labor any more productive, so employers have no reason to pay higher total compensation after the tax is imposed unless some wage earners react to their reduced earnings by withdrawing from the labor force (that is, unless the supply of labor is less than completely inelastic with respect to wages). If some wage earners do withdraw, employers will have to offer higher wages to attract additional employees or to keep those that remain; wages will rise as a result of the tax (though not necessarily by the exact amount of the tax), and the ratio of capital to labor will increase.

But it is generally agreed that the aggregate supply of labor is relatively inelastic with respect to wages: lower wages do not induce many wage earners to withdraw from the labor force or to cut their hours of work significantly. (This is not true of secondary family workers—see chapter 4.) In these circumstances, the supply of labor will not decline very much as a result of the imposition of a payroll tax, and workers will bear much of the tax burden. Although wages may not actually fall, they will increase less rapidly than they would have without the payroll tax, and the shifting process takes place over the long run.

It is also possible that workers will bear the tax even if the supply of labor is not completely inelastic with respect to wages. Employees may be willing to accept a lower wage after the tax is imposed if they regard the benefits financed by the tax as an adequate quid pro quo. If this were the prevailing attitude, the tax would be similar to a user charge, the supply of labor would not be altered, earnings would fall by the amount of the tax, and the full burden would be borne by wage earners. On the other hand, for workers retiring in the next twenty years, presently scheduled social security benefits generally exceed scheduled tax payments plus accumulated interest. If workers are knowledgeable about benefits and take them into account in their work decisions, the payroll tax may actually raise perceived wages and thus increase hours of work or attract workers into the labor force.

One qualification must be applied to the economic analysis of the burden of payroll taxes. The model on which the analysis is based assumes competitive behavior in labor markets and excludes the possible effect on wages of collective bargaining agreements between large firms and labor unions. Labor unions will resist any cut in the wages of their members and may succeed in inducing management to raise wages by an amount sufficient to offset the effect of the payroll tax. In such circumstances, part or all of the employer and employee portions of the tax may be transferred to the consumer. Critics of this view argue that, if such market power existed, labor and management could have exercised it to raise wages and prices before the tax was imposed. Nevertheless, one cannot dismiss the possibility that the adoption of a new payroll tax or an increase in an old one may be the occasion when labor and management choose to exercise this power.

Effect on Personal and Public Saving

National social insurance provides protection against loss of income resulting from retirement, death, unemployment, permanent disability, and illness. Before these government programs were enacted, people's savings and contributions from other family members were their only protection against these hazards. Social insurance may encourage individuals to set aside a smaller amount of personal savings on the ground that a major reason for saving has been removed. On the other hand, the availability of social insurance gives people an incentive to retire earlier, and this encourages them to save more. So far these tendencies have probably offset one another and total personal saving has not been greatly affected on balance. In fact, the ratio of personal saving to disposable income has been somewhat higher in the post–World War II years than it was in 1929, but many other factors have influenced this ratio. Econometric studies of time series and cross-country data have been inconclusive, but they do not support the conclusion that personal saving has been reduced by the social security program.

The effect of the social security program on government saving is also not clear. From the inception of the program in the 1930s until mid-1976, the balances in the OASDI trust funds rose to a total of $43.5 billion, but since then the balances have been drawn down as benefits paid out have exceeded the receipts from the payroll tax. Had the balances in the funds not been accumulated in the first thirty years, other taxes might have been raised to yield the same revenue, outlays might have been reduced, or additional debt might have been issued to the public. Similarly, if the OASDI trust funds had not been drawn down during the late 1970s and early 1980s, other taxes might have been reduced, outlays might have been increased, or the public debt might have been reduced. Nevertheless, it seems fair to say that federal surpluses were somewhat larger, or deficits were smaller, during the buildup stage of the trust funds, while the deficits in the more recent period have been aggravated by the condition of the trust funds.

Concern about the condition of the trust funds led to the establishment of a bipartisan National Commission on Social Security Reform in 1981. On January 15, 1983, this commission proposed a combination of reduced benefits and accelerated tax increases, which was accepted virtually intact by the Congress and approved by President Reagan in April 1983. On the basis of this legislation, it is expected that the OASDI funds will accumulate large balances in the 1990s upon the retirement of the generations born when birth rates were low in the 1920s and 1930s. Whether these balances will in fact be accumulated or will instead be reduced by benefit increases, payroll tax cuts, or transfers to the hospital insurance fund (see below) remains to be seen. If the balances are not dissipated and if real wages grow at a modest rate, the OASDI fund balances should be adequate to pay benefits stipulated under current law at least until 2025 or even later without tax increases beyond those now scheduled by law.

The hospital insurance trust fund will face similar problems in the late 1980s as hospital costs continue to rise rapidly. Under present projections, the fund will be depleted by 1990. Although benefits can be reduced and taxes raised to prevent insolvency, the major issue in hospital insurance will be how to reform the nation's health care system so that the rate of growth of health costs will be reduced generally. (See below for a discussion of the unemployment insurance trust fund.)

Taxation of Benefits

The retirement and unemployment insurance benefits were originally not subject to tax (because at that time benefit recipients would usually not be taxable). However, in response to the need for revenues, Congress has recently begun taxing benefits of workers with high incomes from other sources. In 1984 taxable income includes unemployment compensation benefits received by persons with other income over $12,000 ($18,000 for married couples) and one-half of social security benefits received by persons with other income over $25,000 ($32,000 for married couples). The receipts from the taxation of unemployment benefits go into the general fund, while those from the taxation of social security benefits are earmarked for the social security trust funds.

Financing Social Security

In view of the multiple objectives of the social security program, it is not surprising to find disagreement over financing methods. Some advocate recourse to general revenues to finance future increases in benefits; others favor continued use of payroll taxes; still others prefer a combination of the two.

The Contributory System

Financing social security through contributory taxes on payrolls is well established in most countries. Although the benefits are not based on the actuarial value of taxes paid, they are related to the earnings record of the individual worker. Receipts are earmarked to make workers feel they are receiving benefits as a right rather than as a gift from the government. The earmarked taxes emphasize the statutory nature of the benefit and discourage reduction in benefits when the budget is tight.

Those who oppose financing social security through the contributory system point out that benefits are not closely tied to the tax payments. There are both minima and maxima to the level of benefits. Congress has been lenient in extending eligibility to people with minimum periods of covered employment. Under the circumstances, the benefit payments do not approximate contributions even loosely. The regressivity of the taxes adds to the dissatisfaction with the contributory system. Nevertheless, the possibility of departing from payroll tax financing in the near future seems remote, especially since such financing was endorsed by the bipartisan National Commission on Social Security Reform and by the legislation enacted in 1983.

In practice, the financing of OASDHI in the United States is a compromise between conflicting points of view. Although the taxes are regressive, the social security system does give to the lowest-paid workers the largest benefits relative to their contributions. Moreover, the existence of a reserve fund and earmarked taxes gives assurance to the millions of covered workers that their rights to benefits are protected. (The social security system could be administered without the trust fund device, but every impartial commission that has ever examined this question has concluded that the trust funds should be continued. In 1983, on the recommendation of the National Commission on Social Security Reform, Congress decided to remove the OASDHI trust funds from the unified budget beginning in 1992.)

A significant departure from the precedent of relying entirely on payroll taxes to finance social security benefits occurred in 1965, when Congress added medical and hospital insurance to the OASDI system. Hospital care for the insured aged is funded by payroll tax contributions from employers and employees; the general fund pays for those not insured. Medical insurance was made available to aged persons who voluntarily paid a fee of $3 a month; an equal amount was transferred to a new trust fund by appropriation from the general fund. The premium rate for medical insurance was subject to change after 1967, depending on actual experience, but the general fund now contributes much more than the individual's payment, which rose to $14.70 a month on January 1, 1984.

Another departure from payroll tax financing was made in 1966, when all those reaching the age of seventy-two before 1968 were granted a small special benefit, regardless of whether they were covered by social security. This extension of coverage, which now affects few individuals, was financed out of general funds.

In 1972 the federal supplemental security income (SSI) program was enacted to provide a uniform minimum income guarantee for the aged, blind, and disabled. (This program replaced the federal and state programs that had been established by the Social Security Act of 1935.) Some states supplement SSI payments for beneficiaries who were receiving higher benefits under the earlier system of public assistance, but the basic SSI payments are made entirely by the federal government out of general revenues. The 1984 SSI supplement raises the monthly income of those eligible up to a maximum of $314 for single persons and $472 for married couples, plus $20 from another source. It has been proposed that social security benefits be converted to a flat percentage of earnings and that benefits similar to those paid under SSI be relied on to bring the lowest benefits up to an adequate level (some propose means testing the lower tier, others do not).

Proposals for Reform

Suggestions for changing the method of financing social security fall into four categories.

REDUCE REGRESSIVITY. One way to reduce regressivity would be to raise the amount of earnings subject to tax and eventually to remove the limit entirely. The taxes would then become proportional taxes on payrolls and would still be regressive for total income but much less so than under present law. The earnings base is now increased annually in proportion to the increase in average covered earnings, but there is little support for going beyond the automatic increase.

A major share of the burden of the payroll tax at the lower end of the income scale would be eliminated if the 10 percent refundable earned-income tax credit enacted in 1975 were increased to the 14 percent social security tax rate and if people without children were made eligible for the credit.

CONVERT TO A PROGRESSIVE EARNINGS TAX. The payroll tax could be converted to a progressive tax on earnings by introducing personal exemptions and a standard deduction (or zero bracket) to approximate the poverty levels, as in the income tax, and eliminating the maximum taxable earnings ceiling. The exemption and standard deduction would eliminate taxes paid by earners who were below the poverty levels, and with no taxable earnings limit the regressivity at higher earnings levels would be eliminated. At 1984 price levels, a per capita exemption of $1,750 and a $4,000 zero-bracket amount would closely approximate the poverty levels. It would be necessary to raise the employer and employee tax rates to yield the revenues now produced by the social security tax.

INTEGRATE THE PAYROLL AND INCOME TAXES. Another way to moderate regressivity would be to incorporate the employee contribution into the individual income tax, either directly or through a tax credit. With coverage now available to 91 percent of workers (in the case of OASDHI), the income tax population for any given generation of workers is not very different from the payroll tax population. The differences that do exist between the two taxes—the exemptions, personal deductions, and broader income concept—argue in favor of using the income tax rather than the payroll tax. The psychological advantage of having a special earmarked tax to finance the social security program can be duplicated either by the credit device or by allocating some percentage of the income tax receipts, or a given number of percentage points of the income tax rates, to the trust funds.

The decision to integrate the employee tax with the individual income tax would not necessarily require a change in the employer tax, although the two would undoubtedly be considered together. One method might be to replace the employer tax by adding the necessary number of percentage points to the individual and corporation income taxes. For example, the OASDHI tax paid by employers on 1984 payrolls is equivalent to a 10-percentage-point increase in all individual and corporation income tax rates.

USE THE GENERAL FUND. As indicated, precedent exists for using general fund receipts to finance social security. With the combined employer-employee OASDHI tax scheduled to be 15.3 percent in 1990 and later years, use of the general fund might be considered as a substitute for at least part of the social security payroll taxes. Since the general fund relies primarily on progressive taxes, this would automatically improve the equity of the overall tax system.

One way to introduce general revenue financing would be to adopt the recommendation of the 1975 and 1979 Quadrennial Advisory Councils on Social Security that general revenue receipts be used to replace the payroll tax receipts in the hospital fund. The benefits under the hospital program for the aged are not related to wages and consequently there is no justification for using a payroll tax to finance these benefits. However, because of the large, continuing deficits in the general fund, Congress has taken no action on this proposal.

EFFECT ON BENEFITS. Since the basic objective of the system is to moderate the decline in earnings at retirement, the relation between benefits and past earnings can be preserved whatever the structure of the tax used to finance the benefits. Under the present system, benefits are calculated by declining percentages up to the taxable earnings ceiling. A ceiling on benefits is considered appropriate because it is generally agreed that the national retirement system should be used to guarantee benefits based on earnings up to some reasonable level, beyond which private pension arrangements and personal saving could be expected to take over.

The decision to eliminate the earnings ceiling entirely or to replace the payroll tax by the income tax or general revenues would require an explicit decision on the point at which earnings replacement would terminate. Those who wish to protect the insurance image of the system would oppose any move to divorce the maximum benefit from the maximum earnings or income subject to tax. Those who do not regard the system as insurance see no practical difficulty in establishing maximum benefit levels without tying them to a tax limit.

Financing Unemployment Insurance

Two major financial features of the unemployment insurance system have been debated in recent years: the variation of tax rates among firms in accordance with their employment experience and the inadequacy of trust funds in states suffering heavy and prolonged unemployment.

Experience rating was adopted to induce employers to stabilize their employment and also to avoid the criticism that firms with stable employment would be subsidizing those with irregular employment records. Some believe that each firm should bear the full cost of its own unemployment. The major argument against experience rating has been that individual firms have little control over unemployment, particularly of the cyclical variety. It has also been suggested that, since the contribution rates of firms vary, only the lowest tax paid by any firm can be shifted to consumers or wage earners. This may well account for the resistance of employers to increases in coverage and benefits. Despite these objections, there is considerable reluctance to abandon experience rating, partly because it gives individual employers an incentive to prevent abuse of the system and partly because there is strong objection to changing the distribution of tax burdens among firms. On the other hand, there seems to be little support for basing the tax entirely on the actual experience of each firm.

The concentration of unemployment in particular industries and regions has had an uneven effect on the state trust funds. The federal government has extended coverage beyond the basic twenty-six weeks for workers who have exhausted their benefit rights in every recession. In 1970 Congress enacted permanent legislation to provide the automatic extension of benefits beyond twenty-six weeks when unemployment becomes serious. Such extended benefits are funded equally by state and federal payroll taxes.

The severe recessions of 1974–75 and 1981–82 have had a major impact on the financial viability of the federal and state unemployment insurance system. From fiscal 1976 through 1982, total receipts exceeded outlays in only two years (1978 and 1979) and in mid-1983 over half of the state systems were insolvent. Several state programs have been financed by loans from the federal program, which has also needed loans from the general fund. Since 1981 the federal government has imposed interest charges on outstanding loans in order to prevent abuse of the borrowing authority by the states.

Proposals to improve the financial situation of the state programs include increases in payroll taxes or reductions in benefits. In addition, the federal taxes paid on unemployment benefits since 1979 might be returned to the unemployment insurance trust fund; benefit extensions during recessions could be financed from federal general revenues; and the loans from the general fund might be forgiven. To improve the effectiveness of the program, proposals have been made to expand unemployment insurance beyond its current income-support role to help workers find jobs.

Summary

Payroll taxes paved the way for the enactment of a comprehensive system of social security and unemployment compensation that protects workers against income losses from retirement, disability, and unemployment. Legislation passed in 1965 also provided protection for retired workers against the costs of hospitalization and medical care. The payroll taxes that are used to finance these programs are regressive. In the long run, most of the payroll taxes are probably paid by the worker; it makes no difference whether the law imposes the tax on the employee or on the employer.

The existing payroll taxes and the increases in tax rates already scheduled will have a major effect on the distribution of tax burdens. The equity of these taxes would be increased by improvement of the earned-income tax credit, introduction of personal exemptions and a standard deduction into the payroll tax and removal of the maximum taxable earnings ceiling, integration of the payroll and income taxes, or use of the general fund for financing future social security benefits.

The financing of the social insurance system has been endangered in recent years by slow productivity growth and high unemployment. However, legislation enacted in 1983 promises to provide adequate financing for the old-age, survivors', and disability system for at least forty years. But hospital insurance and unemployment insurance are still not adequately financed, either for the near term or for the long term. Reductions in benefits, increases in payroll taxes, contributions from the general fund, or a combination of all three will be required to restore the financial viability of these two essential programs.

CHAPTER EIGHT

Estate and Gift Taxes

TAXES ON PROPERTY left by individuals to their heirs are among the oldest forms of taxation. In societies in which property is privately owned, the state protects the property rights of the individual and supervises the transfer from one generation to the next. Consequently, the state has always regarded property transfers as appropriate objects of taxation.

Transfer taxation can take several forms, depending on when the transfers are made and how the tax base is figured. The federal government imposes an *estate* tax on the privilege of transferring property at death, while most states impose *inheritance* taxes on the privilege of receiving property from the dead. In general, both taxes are graduated, the former on the basis of the size of the entire estate and the latter on the basis of the size of individual shares in the estate. Usually the inheritance tax is also graduated on the basis of the relationship of the heir to the decedent, the rate being lowest for the closest relative.

Taxes at death could be avoided simply by transferring property by gift *inter vivos* (between living persons). Accordingly, the federal estate tax is associated with a *gift* tax, which is imposed on the donor. (However, only nine of the forty-nine states with death taxes levy a gift tax.) In the United States, the estate and gift taxes were originally separate taxes, but the rate schedules and exemption levels of the two taxes were unified by the Tax Reform Act of 1976, effective January 1, 1977.

The Role of Wealth Transfer Taxes

Opinions about death taxes vary greatly in a society relying on private incentives for economic growth. Some believe that these taxes hurt economic incentives, reduce saving, and undermine the economic system. But even they would concede that death taxes have less adverse effects on incentives than do income taxes of equal yield. Income taxes

225

reduce the return from effort and risk taking as income is earned, whereas death taxes are paid only after a lifetime of work and accumulation and are likely to be given less weight by individuals in their work, saving, and investment decisions.

Death taxes have been supported by people in all wealth classes. One of their strongest supporters was Andrew Carnegie, who had doubts about the institution of inheritance and felt that wealthy persons are morally obligated to use their fortunes for social purposes. In his *Gospel of Wealth,* Carnegie wrote that "the parent who leaves his son enormous wealth generally deadens the talents and energies of the son, and tempts him to lead a less useful and less worthy life than he otherwise would." He applauded the growing acceptance of estate taxes and said: "Of all forms of taxation this seems the wisest." According to Carnegie, it is the duty of a wealthy man to live unostentatiously, "to provide moderately for the legitimate wants of those dependent upon him, and, after doing so, to consider all surplus revenues which come to him simply as trust funds . . . to administer in the manner . . . best calculated to produce the most beneficial results for the community."

Bequests and gifts, like income from work or investments, are a source of ability to pay. In theory, therefore, they should be taxable as income when received. However, bequests and gifts are taxed separately from income, partly because death taxes antedate the income taxes and partly because it would be unfair to tax these transfers at the full graduated income tax rates in the year of receipt. Of course, the impact of income tax rate graduation could be moderated by averaging, but this approach to transfer taxation has never been seriously considered in this country (although the income tax levied in 1894, which was held unconstitutional, included in the definition of income "money and the value of all personal property acquired by gift or inheritance"). In 1966 a Canadian Royal Commission on Taxation recommended that the Canadian estate and gift taxes be repealed and that gifts and inheritance be included in the recipient's taxable income. Although many people began to think seriously about this alternative method of taxing transfers, the Canadian government did not follow the commission's recommendation.

Despite the appeal of estate and gift taxes on social, moral, and economic grounds, taxes on property transfers have never provided significant revenues in this country and have been reduced to an insignificant proportion in recent years. The federal government used an inheritance tax briefly for emergency purposes from 1862 to 1870 and an estate tax from 1898 to 1902; the present tax was enacted in 1916. The gift tax was first levied for two years in 1924 and 1925 and then was enacted permanently in 1932. During and after World War II, income and excise tax rates were increased substantially; but the estate and gift tax rates and exemptions remained unchanged from 1942 through 1976, and structural changes made in 1948 reduced their importance in the federal revenue system. In 1976, the estate and gift tax rates and exemption levels were unified and the exemption levels were increased. Estate and gift taxes accounted for 1.4 percent of budget receipts in fiscal 1955, 1.7 percent in 1976, and 1.3 percent in 1982 (appendix table D-4). The 1981 legislation, which increased the exemption levels still further and reduced the top rate from 70 percent to 50 percent, will cut the yield of the unified estate and gift tax to 0.5 percent of budget receipts by 1988.

One can only guess why heavier reliance has not been placed on estate and gift taxes. A possible explanation is that equalization of the distribution of wealth by taxation is not yet accepted in the United States. In some countries, economic classes tend to be fairly stable, with little crossing-over by succeeding generations. In the American economy, membership in economic classes is fluid. The average family in the United States still aspires to improved economic and social status, and the estate and gift taxes are erroneously regarded as especially burdensome to the family that is beginning to prosper through hard work and saving.

Moreover, wealth transfer taxes are not considered equitable by many people. A surprising number resent even the relatively low taxes now imposed on estates as large as $1,000,000. This may be because the base of the wealth transfer taxes in certain respects includes more than what the public considers "wealth" properly subject to tax. The family home, the family car, Series E bonds, savings bank deposits, and similar property are not regarded as appropriate objects of taxation. The public generally is not aware that the major part of the estate tax base consists of stocks, bonds, and real estate, and that the exemption removes the wealth from the estate tax base in all but a small minority of estates.

Characteristics of the Taxes

The calculation of the estate and gift taxes follows the pattern established by the income taxes. The total amount of property transferred is reported, deductions are subtracted, and the graduated rates are applied to the remainder, but there are many complications.

The Estate Tax

The gross estate consists of all property owned by a decedent at the time of death, including stocks, bonds, real estate, mortgages, and any other property that technically belonged to the decedent. (The property is valued either on the date of death or on an alternate valuation date, generally six months later, at the option of the estate's executor.) The gross estate also includes gifts made after December 31, 1976, insurance owned by the decedent, and the value of any trusts created by the decedent while alive that could have been revoked or even modified by the decedent. Deductions are allowed for funeral expenses and expenses of settling the estate, debts, legal fees, charitable bequests, and property passing to a surviving spouse. The marital deduction applies without limit to most property transferred between spouses.

The unified estate and gift tax rates begin at 18 percent on the first $10,000 of the taxable transfer and rise to 55 percent on the amount of the taxable transfer in excess of $3,000,000 in 1984 and 50 percent in excess of $2,500,000 in 1985 and later years (appendix tables A-11 and A-12). Credits are provided for any gift tax paid and for state death taxes up to 80 percent of the tax imposed by the 1926 federal tax rate schedule. In addition, a credit is deducted from the tax liability computed from the official rate schedule. The credit for both estate and gift tax purposes—called the *unified credit*—is $96,300 in 1984, $121,800 in 1985, $155,800 in 1986, and $192,800 in 1987 and later years. These credits provide the equivalent of a complete exemption for estates valued at less than $325,000, $400,000, $500,000, and $600,000, respectively. As a result of the use of the credit rather than an exemption, the estate and gift tax rate is zero up to the exemption level and 37 percent above that level.

For example, assume that a married man who made no taxable gifts during his life dies in 1985 owning $2,000,000 in securities and bequeaths half his wealth to his wife and half to his children. Assume also that the expenses of settling the estate amount to $50,000 and his debts at the time of his death amount to $50,000. If this decedent had been single or had not left anything to his spouse, the net estate would be $1,900,000. But the marital deduction reduces the net estate to $950,000.

The tax rates would produce a tax before credits of $326,300 on a taxable estate of $950,000. From this, two credits are deductible: the unified credit in lieu of an exemption and the credit for state death taxes. The former is $121,800 and the latter, in this case, is $30,400. Thus the net tax payable to the federal government would be $174,100 ($326,300 minus $121,800 and $30,400). If the decedent had made taxable gifts after 1976, the gifts would be taken into account in computing the estate tax and a credit would be allowed for any gift tax paid.

The Gift Tax

The gift tax is calculated in much the same way, except that the exemptions are more complicated and the tax is computed on the basis of total gifts made after 1932. The tax due in any particular year is the additional tax resulting from the gifts made in that year. The unified credit is used first against the tax on gifts; the remainder is used against the tax on the estate of the same person. In addition to the credit, which is the same as the estate tax credit, there is an annual exclusion for gifts of $10,000 per donee.

As in the case of bequests, gifts from one spouse to another are not subject to tax. For married persons, a gift to third persons can be treated as if half were given by the husband and half by the wife. Although the gift tax rates are the same as the estate tax rates, the gift tax is actually lower because the property given to the government in payment of tax (except for the tax paid on gifts made during the three years prior to death) is excluded from the gift tax base, but not from the estate tax base.

Suppose a married man with an estate of $2,000,000 decides to distribute it to his two children systematically over a period of ten years beginning in 1987. The law gives him and his wife an annual exclusion for each child of $10,000. The annual exclusions amount to $20,000 a year for each child or a total of $400,000 for the two children over the ten-year period. The total amount remaining for additional gifts and gift taxes by each spouse is $800,000, of which $745,985 can be allocated for gifts and the remaining $54,015 would be used to pay the gift tax. By contrast, if the same amounts (including the gift tax paid) were retained until death, the estate of each spouse would pay a tax of $153,000. Thus, disposition of the estate through gifts would reduce the taxes on the estate of each spouse by $98,985, or 65 percent.

The Tax Base

Estate and gift taxes are levied on only a small proportion of privately owned property in the United States. When the increased exemptions enacted in 1981 become fully effective, less than 1 percent of the estates of those who die in any one year will be subject to estate or gift taxes.

The total number of estate tax returns filed in 1976 was 200,747; of these, 139,115 were taxable. The value of the gross estates reported on taxable returns was $40.6 billion. Exemptions and deductions reduced this amount by about 50 percent, leaving an estate tax base of $20.3 billion. The estate tax after credits was $5.0 billion, or 25 percent of the taxable base (see appendix tables B-10 and D-21).

Sixty-one percent of the taxable returns reported total estates of less than $200,000, but these accounted for only 9 percent of the tax after credits. Returns on estates of $1,000,000 or more, on the other hand, accounted for almost 44 percent of the total tax and only 3 percent of the number of taxable returns. The tax after credits ranged from 4 percent of gross estates for taxable gross estates of less than $200,000 to 16 percent for estates of $10,000,000 and over.

Gifts reported for the year 1966 (the last year for which gift tax data were tabulated) amounted to $4.0 billion, of which $2.4 billion was reported on 29,547 taxable returns. Taxable gifts totaled $1,455 million, and gift tax paid amounted to $413 million, or 17 percent of the total gifts on taxable returns and 28 percent of the taxable gifts (appendix table D-22).

Structural Problems

Since wealth transfers can take many forms, estate and gift taxation is inherently complicated. Many of the structural features of the estate and gift taxes have unequal impact, depending on how and when dispositions of property are made. Such disparities are hard to justify because many people—for personal or business reasons or because of early death—cannot avail themselves of the opportunity to minimize the tax on their estates. Because property can be transferred in many different ways, it is difficult to devise one solution that will be equitable in all cases. The major problems are (1) the treatment of transfers by husband and wife, (2) imperfect unification of the estate and gift taxes,

(3) the use of trusts to escape taxation for one or more generations, (4) outright transfers to escape taxation for one or more generations, (5) charitable contributions, and (6) small businesses and farms.

Transfers by Husbands and Wives

Transfers by married couples present a difficult problem because it is hard to decide whether they should be taxed as if their property is part of one estate or two. Since the estate and gift taxes are excises on transfers of property, the concept of legal ownership plays an important part in determining the amount of tax to be paid. The distinction between community and noncommunity property has been crucial in this respect.

COMMUNITY AND NONCOMMUNITY PROPERTY. Under the community property system, which prevails in eight states, all property acquired during marriage by a husband and wife (except property acquired by gift or inheritance) belongs equally to each spouse. The community property states vary on whether the income from property owned before marriage or acquired during marriage by gift or inheritance belongs to both spouses equally or to the original owner or recipient alone. In noncommunity property states, each spouse retains ownership of all property acquired or accumulated out of his or her separate earnings or inheritance even after marriage.

Before 1942 federal estate and gift taxes recognized the community property system: only half the community property was taxable under the estate tax at the death of a spouse, and gifts to third parties were treated as if half were made by each spouse. In noncommunity property states the entire amount of property accumulated by a spouse was taxable to him or her.

To equalize estate and gift taxes for residents of community and noncommunity property states, the Revenue Act of 1942 made transfers of community property taxable to the spouse who had earned it. In effect, the 1942 law treated community property as if it were noncommunity property.

THE MARITAL DEDUCTION. The Revenue Act of 1948 attempted to achieve equalization by moving in the opposite direction. In the spirit of income splitting for income tax purposes, transfers of community property were made taxable under the pre-1942 rules, while for transfers of noncommunity property a deduction was allowed for the amount of the property transferred to the surviving spouse, up to half the separate property in an estate. In the case of a gift of noncommunity property by one spouse to another, only half of the gift was made taxable. Gifts to third persons were to be treated, if so elected, as though half were made by each spouse. The 1981 act increased the marital deduction to 100 percent of property transfers between spouses, and retained gift splitting between spouses for gifts to third persons.

The marital deduction greatly increases the amount of property that married persons may transfer free of tax. Beginning in 1987, when the effective transfer tax exemption will be $600,000, the total exemption for married couples will amount to $1,200,000, provided the first spouse who dies transfers half the estate to a third person. Gift splitting also in effect doubles the annual personal exclusion from $10,000 to $20,000, thus increasing the transfer tax exemption even further if gifts are made.

Transfers between spouses are subject to tax at the death of the recipient or when the recipient makes gifts, but the total tax of the couple can nevertheless be significantly reduced through the use of the marital deduction. Under progressive rates, the total tax on two estates of equal size is less than that on one large and one small estate. For example, a net estate of $5 million will be subject to a tax of $2,083,000 in 1987 and later years. If half the estate is left to a surviving spouse, the tax is reduced to $833,000. If the $2.5 million received by the spouse is later taxed in full, the subsequent tax will also be $833,000, and the total tax on the original $5 million will be $1,666,000, involving both a deferral of the tax and a tax decrease of $417,000, or 20 percent (table 8-1).

AGGREGATION OF HUSBAND AND WIFE TRANSFERS. Complete exemption of transfers between husband and wife suggests that the husband and wife are a single unit, yet the total tax paid by the couple depends on the amounts transferred by each to one another and to third parties. To achieve total equality among married couples, the combined estates would have to be cumulated for estate tax purposes. The initial installment on the combined tax would be collected on the death of one spouse, and the remainder (figured on the basis of the cumulated estates) would be collected on the death of the second spouse. The attractive feature of this proposal is that it would equalize the taxes paid by married couples in all states regardless of the order in which they disposed of the estate.

However, estate cumulation may produce inequitable results where the wealth of the husband or wife was separately inherited or accumulated. For example, a woman married to a wealthy man for a relatively short period might be taxed at the maximum estate tax rates even though

Table 8-1. *Estate Taxes Paid by a Married Couple, by Net Estate Level, 1987*[a]

Dollars unless otherwise specified

Net estate before exemption	Tax on husband (assuming he leaves no bequest to wife) (1)	Tax on husband (assuming he leaves half of estate to wife)		Tax on husband and wife (assuming bequest from husband is taxed in full at wife's death)	
		Amount (2)	Percent of column 1 (3)	Amount (4)	Percent of column 1 (5)
600,000	0	0	. . .	0	. . .
750,000	35,500	0	. . .	0	. . .
1,000,000	153,000	0	0.0	0	0.0
2,000,000	588,000	153,000	26.0	306,000	52.0
5,000,000	2,083,000	833,000	40.0	1,666,000	80.0
10,000,000	4,583,000	2,083,000	45.5	4,166,000	90.9
20,000,000	9,583,000	4,583,000	47.8	9,166,000	95.6

a. Assumes the husband owns all the property and dies first. Effective rates are before the credit for state death taxes.

the amount of property she owned was small. This objection could be met by cumulating only as much of the property transferred by the wife (during life or at death) as was originally acquired from the husband. Tracing difficulties could be avoided by cumulating transfers of the wife only up to the dollar amount of property received from the husband. Such a compromise, however, would fail to take into account any increase in the value of the property after the interspousal transfer. Estate cumulation would also require the solution of some intricate problems involving the treatment of gifts made before marriage and the taxation of transfers by widowed or divorced persons who had married again.

Imperfect Unification of Estates and Gifts

Even though the estate and gift tax rates have been unified, wealthy people are well advised to transfer a substantial part of their property by gift during their lifetime rather than by bequest for two reasons. First, the annual exclusion of $10,000 per donee under the gift tax permits tax-free transfers in addition to the unified estate and gift tax exemption. Second, the amount paid as gift tax three years before death does not enter into the gift tax base, whereas the estate tax is computed on the basis of the decedent's entire property, including that part used to pay the tax. Furthermore, by transferring part of the estate to a spouse, a testator splits the estate into two parts, moderating the full impact of transfer tax graduation.

To minimize tax liability, a person would have to take these factors into account as well as the tax that would be due at the death of the spouse. Although there are many uncertainties, it is clear that a carefully drawn plan of wealth distribution during the life of a wealthy person can pay handsome dividends in lower tax burdens (see table 8-1).

USE OF GIFTS. Information on the distribution of wealth during life and at death has been collected by the Treasury Department on the basis of the estate and matched gift tax returns of the wealthiest decedents for whom estate tax returns were filed in 1945, 1951, 1957, and 1959. Information on gifts made before 1932 was available from the 1945 and 1951 estate tax returns. Thus it was possible to build up an aggregate figure for the property distributed by each decedent during life and at death for the two earlier years, and a total, excluding gifts made before 1932, for the two later years.

The figures (table 8-2) show clearly that wealthy people prefer to retain the bulk of their property until death and fail to use gifts to maximum tax-saving advantage. There are a number of reasons for the small proportion of gifts. First, most people are reluctant to contemplate death. Uncertainty regarding time of death encourages delay in making estate plans even by those with considerable wealth. Second, many wish to retain control over their businesses. Disposal of stock or real estate frequently means loss of control over substantial enterprises. Third, donors may wish to delay transfers of property until their children have had an opportunity to make their own careers. Fourth, many people— even those who are wealthy—do not know the law and often do not take the advice of their tax lawyers on such personal matters.

Whatever the reason, the actual use of gifts has resulted in less erosion of the tax base than might have taken place, and the recent unification of the estate and gift tax rates has reduced further the incentive to make gifts. The major criticism of the law is that it discriminates against those who, for business or personal reasons, do not dispose of a substantial portion of their wealth during their lives. And among those who do make gifts, the law discriminates in favor of wealthier donors by rewarding them with larger tax savings than those available to less wealthy donors

Table 8-2. *Frequency of Gifts and Percentage of Wealth Transferred by Gift during Life among Millionaire Decedents, 1945, 1951, 1957, and 1959*

Total wealth transferred during life and at death (millions of dollars)	Percent of decedents who made gifts during life				Percent of wealth transferred by gift			
	1945	1951	1957	1959	1945	1951	1957	1959
1.00–2.15	77	74	52	56	14	12	5	5
1.25–1.50	76	65	57	58	17	7	6	8
1.50–1.75	83	74	55	67	21	12	7	8
1.75–2.00	89	70	67	71	28	10	6	8
2.00–3.00	84	88	65	68	20	14	6	8
3.00–5.00	88	84	69	84	20	14	7	11
5.00–10.00	100	95	75	84	20	18	10	11
10.00 and over	91	100	92	100	38	25	15	17
Total	83	77	60	66	24	16	9	10

Source: Special tabulations by the Treasury Department. Includes only returns with total transfers before tax during life and at death of $1,000,000 or more. Data for 1945 and 1951 include gifts before 1932; those for 1957 and 1959 exclude such gifts.

on gifts of the same value. This feature stems from the exclusion of the gift tax from the base of the tax.

COMPLETE UNIFICATION OF ESTATE AND GIFT TAXES. The remedy for the inequalities resulting from the separate taxation of gifts and estates is to complete the unification of the two taxes begun in 1976. A truly unified system would have a single marital deduction for lifetime transfers and bequests. In addition, any gift tax paid would be included in the base of the final transfer tax. Unification to this extent is opposed by those who believe that gifts should be encouraged. It is argued, in fact, that gifts tend to reduce the concentration of wealth by dispersing property among a relatively larger number of donees.

Generation Skipping through Trusts

The most difficult problems in wealth transfer taxation have arisen from the existence of the *trust*, a legal institution used to administer funds on behalf of individuals or organizations. Suppose A wants his wife to have the income from his estate as long as she lives. He may place his property in a trust, the income of which would go to her for life; the trust might be dissolved at her death and the property distributed to the children. The trust is administered by a *trustee*—usually a relative or associate, the family lawyer, or a bank—who is the legal owner. He is required by law to manage the trust property strictly in accordance with the terms of the trust instrument.

Legal terms are used as shorthand in trust language for the various beneficiaries of a trust. In the above example, A's wife, who is entitled to receive the income from the trust, is the *life beneficiary*. Any number of life beneficiaries may be designated, and they need not be confined to members of the same generation. The creator of the trust may designate his wife and children as joint or successive life beneficiaries and prescribe the proportions in which the income is to be distributed among them. When the trust is terminated, the trust property is legally transferred to the *remaindermen,* who then own the property outright. More often than not, children are the remaindermen of family trusts; but grandchildren or other relatives as well as unrelated persons may also be remaindermen. In some cases, the trust is created with the wife and children as life beneficiaries and the remainder is distributed, after the last one dies, to one or more charities. In all but a few states, all interests in a trust must vest not later than twenty-one years after the death of the last survivor among persons who were alive when the trust was created (*lives in being*). This rule has the effect of restricting most noncharitable trusts to a duration of less than a century.

The trust has a profound influence on the taxation of property transfers. Before 1977, if the trust was properly planned, the trust property was not subject to transfer tax when one life beneficiary was succeeded by another or when the property was received by the remaindermen. An estate or gift tax was paid when the trust was created, but tax was not paid again until the remaindermen transferred the property. Given these characteristics, the trust was frequently used by wealthy people to avoid estate and gift taxes for at least one generation and sometimes more. In extreme cases, trusts were set up to last for the lives of the children and grandchildren, with the remainder going to the great-grandchildren, thereby skipping two estate and gift tax generations.

USE OF TRUSTS. The trust device has been used frequently by the wealthy to transfer property to later generations. The data from the Treasury studies of 1945, 1951, 1957, and 1959 returns indicate the following patterns:

1. In the 1940s and 1950s more than three of every five millionaires transferred at least some of their property in trust. Transfers in trust accounted for at least one-third of noncharitable transfers by millionaires

Table 8-3. *Frequency of Noncharitable Transfers in Trust and Percentage of Wealth Transferred in Trust by Millionaire Decedents, 1945, 1951, 1957, and 1959*[a]

Total wealth transferred during life and at death (millions of dollars)	Percent of decedents with noncharitable transfers in trust				Percent of non-charitable transfers made in trust			
	1945	1951	1957	1959	1945	1951	1957	1959
1.00–2.15	75	72	57	56	44	39	28	26
1.25–1.50	75	78	53	61	48	44	25	29
1.50–1.75	80	77	53	62	38	44	25	30
1.75–2.00	71	80	63	69	37	49	37	31
2.00–3.00	89	69	61	64	55	39	34	34
3.00–5.00	84	87	63	70	42	51	32	35
5.00–10.00	87	74	77	67	44	44	43	30
10.00 and over	91	100	73	92	58	59	33	30
Total	80	76	59	63	47	46	32	31

Source: Special tabulations by the Treasury Department.
a. Includes only returns with total transfers before tax during life and at death of $1,000,000 or more. Data for 1945 and 1951 include gifts made before 1932; those for 1957 and 1959 exclude such gifts.

in this period (table 8-3). The data also indicate that trusts were used primarily by wealthy people. Those with smaller estates gave much more of their property outright.

2. There was little difference in the eventual disposition of property transferred outright and property transferred in trust. Outright transfers were received in the first instance largely by the wife and children; these properties were in turn transferred to grandchildren and great-grand-children. In the case of trust transfers, wives, children, and grandchildren frequently received only a life interest, so the grandchildren and great-grandchildren received the property undiminished by estate or gift taxes. As table 8-4 indicates, about half the trust property of wealthy decedents escaped estate and gift taxes until the death of the grandchildren or great-grandchildren. Only a very small proportion of the property transferred outright escaped tax for a similar period.

THE 1976 LEGISLATION. There are legitimate reasons for trusts, and it would be unwise to abolish them altogether. On the other hand, since trust transfers and outright transfers go to the same people, it seems unfair to impose lower taxes on trust transfers. Equity suggests that the two types of transfers should be treated equally. Moreover, trust property is managed more conservatively than property owned outright. Some economists have pointed out that it is unwise to encourage

Table 8-4. *Timing of Next Estate Taxes on Outright and Trust Transfers of Millionaire Decedents, 1945, 1951, 1957, and 1959*

Persons at whose death the next estate tax falls due	Outright transfers		Trust transfers[a]	
	Amount (millions of dollars)	Percentage of total	Amount (millions of dollars)	Percentage of total
1945				
Spouse	77	24	. . .	. . .
Children	154	48	. . .	. . .
Grandchildren	9	3	. . .	. . .
Great-grandchildren	b	b	. . .	. . .
Other	80	25	. . .	. . .
Total	320	100	. . .	. . .
1951				
Spouse	164	41	2	1
Children	137	34	95	28
Grandchildren	11	3	124	37
Great-grandchildren	b	b	20	6
Other	89	22	96	28
Total	400	100	337	100
1957				
Spouse	405	39	2	*
Children	362	35	90	18
Grandchildren	56	5	209	43
Great-grandchildren	b	b	24	5
Other	212	21	162	33
Total	1,034	100	487	100
1959				
Spouse	468	42	4	1
Children	366	33	91	18
Grandchildren	68	6	208	42
Great-grandchildren	b	b	37	7
Other	214	19	160	32
Total	1,117	100	500	100

Source: Special tabulations by the Treasury Department. Figures are rounded.
* Less than 0.5 percent.
a. Data not available for 1945.
b. Outright transfers to great-grandchildren were not tabulated separately, but the amount is negligible and is included in transfers to "other."

excessive use of the trust device because it reduces the supply of capital available for risky investments.

Several methods have been devised to remove or reduce the tax advantage of trust transfers. The 1976 legislation, which is effective for transfers in trust beginning June 12, 1976 (except transfers pursuant to a will in existence on June 11, 1976, of a decedent dying before January 1, 1983), used the direct method. Under this legislation, life estates are treated as if the property generating their income is owned by the income beneficiaries, a procedure followed in Great Britain. The capital from which the life estate is supported is taxed as if it had been included in the life beneficiary's gross estate. In effect, the trust property is taxed at the marginal transfer tax rate of the life beneficiary. The tax is paid from the assets of the trust.

The mechanism for taxing life estates in the 1976 legislation is a new tax imposed on "generation-skipping" transfers of trust property, equivalent to the estate tax that would be imposed if the property had been actually transferred outright to each successive generation. A generation-skipping trust is one in which income or remainder interests are given to two or more generations that are younger than the generation of the grantor of the trust. The tax applies when the trust assets are distributed to a generation-skipping heir (for example, a great-grandchild of the transferor) or when an intervening interest in the trust terminates (for example, when the life interest in a trust is transferred from a child to a grandchild); but an exclusion of $250,000 is provided for transfers to each grandchild of the grantor. For trust transfers outside the family, individuals not more than twelve and a half years younger than the grantor are treated as members of his generation; those who are twelve and a half to thirty-seven and a half years younger than the grantor are regarded as members of his children's generation; and so on. In the case of a discretionary trust, the tax is postponed until the death of the last member of an intervening generation.

The 1976 legislation was an effort to plug the former generation-skipping loophole under the estate and gift taxes. The provisions are complex and there have been difficult problems of compliance and administration. Moreover, by setting up separate trusts for children and grandchildren (as opposed to a single trust in which each has a partial right to benefit from the same property), the wealthiest individuals can escape all or a major part of the generation-skipping tax. The remedy is to eliminate the exclusion for grandchildren and to apply the generation-skipping tax on trust transfers to persons more than one generation younger than the grantor's generation. But there is considerable pressure to eliminate the generation-skipping tax entirely or to further weaken it, rather than to improve its effectiveness.

Generation Skipping through Outright Transfers

Transfers in trust and outright transfers are to some degree substitutes for one another. If they are subject to taxes of unequal size, many persons will avoid the more heavily taxed kind of transfer and will make the one that is taxed more lightly. It is just such an inequality in tax burdens that caused many wealthy people to tie up property in trust for one or two generations rather than have it taxed each time it passed from one generation to the next. Now that a tax is imposed on generation-skipping transfers in trust, some people who would otherwise create such trusts may instead make generation-skipping outright transfers, which are not subject to an additional tax under the 1976 legislation. Instead of establishing a trust and naming the children as life beneficiaries and grandchildren as remaindermen, a donor could transfer property outright to them in amounts equal to the present value of the interests in trust they would otherwise receive. The gift of property to a grandchild is the generation-skipping component of the outright transfer. The similarity between the outright transfer and single transfer in trust has led some to argue that a tax imposed on generation-skipping trusts ought to be accompanied by an equivalent tax on generation-skipping outright transfers, in order to preserve fairness in the tax system and to prevent tax avoidance.

It is easier to reach generation-skipping outright transfers than generation-skipping transfers in trust, because property given outright can ordinarily be valued exactly at the time it is transferred, whereas interests in trust are often difficult to value at the time the trusts are created. Many state inheritance taxes already incorporate some form of relationship discrimination in their rate schedules, and the same principle could be used in designing a generation-skipping tax on outright transfers under the federal estate tax. Arbitrary rules based on the age and relationship of the transferor and the recipient could take care of transfers to persons outside the transferor's direct line of descent. The tax rate could be set in any one of a number of ways. It might be set at some fraction above the transferor's average tax rate on all other transfers. Or the transfer might be taxed according to a separate rate schedule whose rates were graduated according to the total of all generation-skipping transfers that the transferor had ever made. Whatever method was adopted, the additional tax clearly would add features of the inheritance tax form of death taxation to the federal estate tax.

Charitable Contributions

Unlike the deductions allowed under income taxes, charitable bequests and gifts are deductible without limit from the estate or gift tax bases. (Contributions are deductible up to 50 percent of income in the individual income tax and up to 5 percent in the corporation income tax.) Although a minority of people allocate substantial portions of their estates to charity, the charitable deduction does stimulate giving at death. Slightly over half the estate tax returns of millionaire decedents in 1957 and 1959 reported no contributions above the annual exclusion during life or at death, and about 15 percent of their total transfers were given to charitable organizations. Nevertheless, the total amounts deducted are significant; they rose from $254 million on all 1945 estate and gift tax returns to $3.0 billion on 1976 estate tax returns.

The large growth of private foundations, some of which have been suspected of abusing the tax exemption privilege, has led to concern about the charitable deduction. Owners of closely held corporations may avoid the impact of the estate tax by dividing the stock into voting stock, which is retained in the family, and nonvoting stock, which is transferred to a foundation. In this way, the family continues to control the assets without being subject to the full estate and gift tax rates when control passes from one generation to the next. In many cases, the economic power of the family grows rapidly as the enterprise continues to expand; the estate tax does not encroach on the property because the property belongs to the foundation and has been permanently removed from the estate tax base. This type of transfer amounts to giving up the income from the property rather than the property itself, yet the transfer is treated as if control of the property has also been relinquished by the donor.

Private foundations were not even required to file financial statements until 1950, when the tax law was amended to require public information returns on their assets, earnings, and expenditures. These reports did not completely eliminate shady dealings on the part of a few donors and foundation officials. Investigations by congressional committees revealed abuses ranging from excessive salaries for foundation officials to the use of loans from foundation funds for personal investment purposes.

Although the large majority of foundations operate in the public interest, by 1969 there was substantial agreement that their affairs should be subject to stricter public controls. As a result, the Tax Reform Act of

1969 included prohibitions against loans to contributors, officers, and directors and rules to prevent accumulation of income and the use of foundation funds to influence legislation. The legislation also included a 4 percent tax on the investment income of private foundations, which was reduced to 2 percent beginning in 1978. These measures appear to have curbed abuses of the foundations' tax exemption privilege.

Small Business and Farm Property

A perennial problem in estate taxation is its effect on small businesses and farms. Small businessmen and farmers have always felt that the estate tax is especially burdensome. Often their estates consist of little more than the business. Heavy taxation or a rule requiring payment of taxes immediately after the death of the owner-manager would necessitate liquidation of the enterprise and loss of the business by the family.

As the previous discussion indicated, a little advance estate planning would be sufficient to prevent or mitigate most of these problems. Furthermore, liberal provisions for installment payments of estate taxes were enacted in 1976 and made even more generous in 1981. The 1976 and 1981 legislation also permitted small businesses and farms to be valued substantially below their market value for estate tax purposes if used by the decedent's family for a number of years following the death of the decedent.

First, tax payments on estates of which a small business or a farm is a large proportion may be made in installments over a period of fourteen years. There is a special 4 percent interest rate for the first million dollars of closely held property. Only interest is paid the first four years; thereafter the tax plus interest is payable in equal installments over the next ten years. This option, which is exercised by the executor, is available if the value of the business exceeds 35 percent of the gross estate. Installment payments are limited to the portion of the estate tax accounted for by the business. A special lien is provided for payment of the deferred taxes, and when this lien procedure is followed, the executor is discharged from personal liability.

Second, redemptions of stock in closely held corporations to pay death taxes and administrative expenses are taxed as capital gains rather than dividend income. To qualify for this treatment, the value of the decedent's stock in the closely held corporation must exceed 35 percent of the gross estate. The allowable redemption period is four years for all estates and fifteen years when an election has been made for the deferred payment of taxes. Such stock redemptions are, of course, indistinguishable from ordinary distributions of profits by private corporations, which are subject to tax.

Third, spokesmen for farm interests have alleged that farmland was often assessed for estate tax purposes at a value far in excess of its value in agricultural production. As a result, heirs to the property, who frequently wanted to keep it in family hands and continue to farm it, purportedly were forced to sell to pay the tax. Under the 1976 legislation, farmland and other closely held business real property may be assessed at its "current-use" value rather than at its market value, but this valuation may not be used to reduce the decedent's gross estate by more than $750,000.

It is hard to estimate how far the difficulties described are attributable to an estate tax squeeze. Prices of farmland have been rising rapidly, and the increase must be due in most cases to mounting demand for the land for nonagricultural uses, particularly when it is located on the fringes of metropolitan areas. If decedents' assets are included in their estates at fair market value, it must be expected that the estate taxes will often encourage heirs to sell to people who will put the property to more profitable use. The generous liberalization of payment provisions enacted in 1976 should have been sufficient to avoid the liquidation of farms to pay the estate tax. In fact, most estates benefiting from the special valuation have liquid assets in excess of the tax due. Current-use valuation was once in effect in the United Kingdom, but it was recently repealed because wealthy people were encouraged to shift their investments into agricultural property to reduce their death duties.

Other Methods of Taxing Wealth

Some have argued that, instead of trying to improve the present estate and gift tax, it would be better to start afresh. The alternatives most often recommended are based on the inheritance or accessions tax principle. Another type of wealth tax, which has been enacted in a number of European countries, is an annual tax on net wealth. This tax is regarded primarily as a supplement to, rather than a substitute for, the estate and gift taxes.

Inheritance or Accessions Taxes

Although widely used by the states, the inheritance tax is rarely considered at the federal level. Its most serious deficiency in its unmodified form is that each receipt of a gift or inheritance is taxed separately. Thus two individuals would pay the same tax on equal inheritances received from the same decedent. However, if one received the inheritance in a lump sum and the other received it from several decedents, they would pay different taxes.

This deficiency would be remedied by the modern modification of the inheritance tax principle—the *accessions tax*. This is a progressive, cumulative tax on the total lifetime acquisitions of an individual through inheritances and gifts. The tax in any one year would be computed by subtracting the tax paid on earlier acquisitions from the tax on total acquisitions received. There would be small annual exclusions and a lifetime exemption. Although tax rates could be varied on the basis of the relationship of donor and donee, there is little support for such differentiation under an accessions tax.

The accessions tax has appeal for those who advocate a more equal distribution of wealth than the present estate tax provides. It would also be more equitable than the estate tax since it would be graduated according to the total wealth received by any one person. It is probably true that the accessions tax would encourage individuals to distribute their property among a larger number of heirs, but the result would not necessarily be a different distribution of wealth, since property is ordinarily kept in the immediate family. Moreover, in practice, only the wealthiest could afford to divert property from their wife and children to more distant relatives to take advantage of the tax savings offered by an accessions tax. To the extent that the accessions tax did encourage a wider distribution of estates, it might do so by shifting some of the burden of the wealthiest estates to the smaller estates.

The accessions tax offers some practical advantages. For one thing, it would equalize the taxes on transfers during life and at death. Some of the proponents of the accessions tax also claim that it would facilitate the inclusion in the tax base of property settled in trust. For example, receipt of trust property by remaindermen would automatically be subject to the accessions tax, but not to the estate tax. On the other hand, the estate tax collected when the trust is created would not automatically be recovered by the accessions tax. To include such transfers in the accessions tax base, the benefits received by the life beneficiaries would have to be valued—a problem that has not been solved satisfactorily even after years of experience with the estate tax.

A practical argument against the accessions tax is that it would not raise as much revenue immediately as the estate and gift taxes unless the tax rates were raised substantially. Ultimately, the accessions tax base in a stationary population should build up to the estate and gift tax base, but the transition is very long. To obtain a given yield in the transition period, accessions tax rates would have to be higher and exemptions lower than under the present transfer taxes. In view of the recent reductions in estate tax rates and increases in exemptions, the revisions necessary to preserve the revenue yield might be difficult to obtain.

The Annual Wealth Tax

Annual taxation of wealth is fairly common among the advanced industrial countries. The tax is now levied in eight European countries—Austria, Denmark, Finland, Ireland, the Netherlands, Norway, Sweden, and West Germany. In all these countries, estate or inheritance taxes are levied in addition to an annual net wealth tax.

The base of the wealth tax is the value of assets less the liabilities of the individual or household. Exemptions are high in order to exclude all but the top wealthholders. Tax rates are graduated, but the top rates are very low compared with income tax rates. The maximum rate in the European countries is 2.5 percent, but most countries tax at much lower rates. Many assets are not included in the tax base, and as a result the effective tax rates are very low.

A major objective of an annual tax on wealth is to reduce the concentration of wealth directly. A wealth tax would also be an effective method of taxing people who have not paid tax on large, unrealized capital gains. Even with a low rate, the wealth tax may be a significant fraction of the income from property. For example, the Swedish top wealth tax rate of 2.5 percent is a 25 percent tax on the income from assets yielding 10 percent; a 10 percent rate might be confiscatory of the income of most assets. For this reason, a moderate wealth tax rate is often proposed as a substitute for high individual income tax rates.

Since the wealth tax is paid on the value of an asset regardless of its rate of return, people in ventures yielding low rates of return have an incentive to shift into risky enterprises that could yield high rates of return if successful. On the other hand, since a wealth tax would fall more heavily on accumulated savings than an equal-yield income tax on earnings from all sources, substituting a wealth tax for an income tax might reduce the incentive to save.

The possibility of adopting an annual net wealth tax at the federal level in the United States has never been seriously considered. Local governments, which rely heavily on property taxes, might regard federal entry into this field as an unwarranted invasion of a revenue source that has been reserved exclusively for them. Questions about the constitutionality of a national wealth tax might also arise, since the Constitution requires apportionment of all direct taxes other than income taxes on the basis of population. Nevertheless, the experience of the European countries is worth watching to see whether a wealth tax can be used effectively in a modern tax system.

Summary

In theory, estate and gift taxes are among the better taxes; in practice, their yield is disappointing, and they have little effect on the distribution of wealth. In recent years, exemptions have been increased, the top tax rate has been cut, and new ways have been provided to escape the taxes. The major avenues are the distribution of estates by gifts during lifetime, use of the tax-free charitable foundation to maintain control without paying tax on the bulk of the estate, and undervaluations of farms and small businesses for estate tax purposes. Generation skipping through trusts was at one time a major tax avoidance mechanism, but the 1976 legislation has closed this loophole somewhat. The revenue potential of further estate tax reform is, however, relatively modest.

Although tax theorists almost unanimously agree that taxation of wealth transfers should play a larger role in the revenue system, they have not been successful in convincing Congress. The public does not appear to accept the desirability of a vigorous estate and gift tax system. The major obstacles to the increased use of these taxes are public apathy and the difficulty of understanding their major features and how they apply in individual circumstances. The merits of wealth transfer taxes will have to be more widely understood and accepted before they can become effective revenue sources.

CHAPTER NINE

State and Local Taxes

STATE AND LOCAL TAXES are important components of the national revenue system. These governments spent $406 billion in fiscal 1981, which is 18 percent more than federal nondefense expenditures and 78 percent of total federal expenditures. Whereas the federal income tax rates are at their lowest levels in more than forty years, state and local tax rates continue to increase.

The growth in expenditures and taxes during the 1950s, 1960s, and 1970s reflected the persistent demand for more state and local services to meet first the large backlog of unmet needs at the end of World War II and later the requirements of a rapidly growing population. The mobility of the people accentuated the problems of population growth. Entire new communities were developed, with schools, roads, sewers, police and fire protection, and other public services. The rate of growth of state and local expenditures declined in the 1970s in part because population growth subsided, but there has been a continued fiscal squeeze as a result of inflation, high rates of unemployment, reductions in federal grants-in-aid, and, most recently, years of poor performance of the economy. In addition, beginning in 1978 when Proposition 13 was passed in California, a number of states imposed limits on the growth of property taxes and other taxes, which seriously restricted the resources available to state and local governments.

The major characteristics of the state and local tax system are its regressivity and sluggish response to income growth. Fear of driving out commerce and industry and discouraging the entry of new business restrains the use of most taxes; this is true particularly of the individual income tax, which is the most equitable and most responsive to growth. At constant tax rates, state and local tax receipts rise barely in proportion to the gross national product, while expenditure demands grow at a faster rate than GNP.

The federal government filled a major part of the gap until 1980, but the growth of federal grants has been declining since then. They rose from $6.8 billion in fiscal 1959 to $20.3 billion in 1969, $91.5 billion in 1980, and an estimated $93.5 billion in 1983. In constant dollars, federal grants peaked in 1978 and declined about 17 percent by 1983. Most federal grants finance expenditures for education, health, welfare, and roads. In addition, revenue sharing was enacted in 1972 to link the state and local governments more directly to the superior tax resources of the federal government.

Economic instability and the pressure for larger revenues have generated a great deal of fiscal activity throughout the country. Many states have adopted new taxes, increased rates on old taxes, adjusted their personal exemptions and income tax rate brackets for inflation, introduced withholding for income tax payments, and reformed their tax administrative machinery. Under pressure from the states, local governments have improved property tax administration. Some large cities have adopted municipal income and sales taxes. But much remains to be done to satisfy state and local financial needs.

The State and Local Structure

In the three years ending June 30, 1981, annual state and local expenditures for general purposes (all activities other than public utilities, liquor stores, and insurance trust funds) rose from $295.5 billion to $405.6 billion, an increase of $110.1 billion or 37 percent. In real terms, expenditures rose 10 percent during the three years, or at an annual rate of 3.4 percent. In the same period, state and local revenues rose from $316.0 billion to $423.4 billion, an increase of $107.4 billion or 34 percent. Only 19 percent of the revenue increase came from federal grants; 81 percent came from state and local sources. State and local debt rose from $280.4 billion to $363.9 billion during the period (appendix tables D-23, D-24, and D-25).

The state and local governments relied on all their major sources to produce their share of the additional revenue raised between 1978 and 1981: 17 percent came from sales and excise taxes, 16 percent from individual and corporation income taxes, 8 percent from property taxes, 7 percent from other taxes, and the remaining 33 percent from user charges, fees, and other miscellaneous sources (figure 9-1). The heavy

Figure 9-1. *Sources of Growth of State and Local Revenue, 1978–81*

Billions of dollars

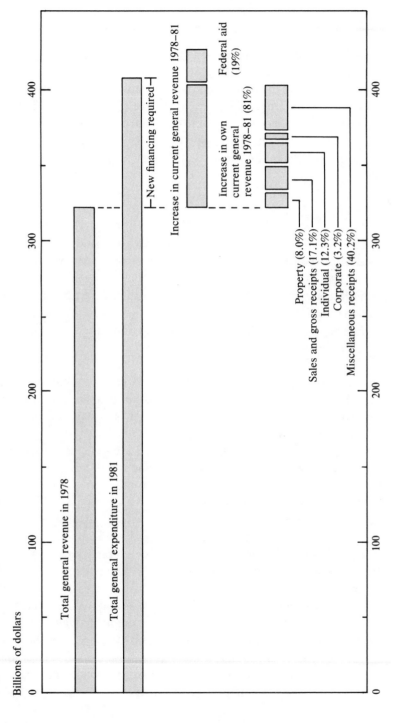

use of user charges and fees is partly a response to the constraints imposed by Proposition 13 and tax limitations enacted in other states as an aftermath.

While state and local tax sources are often considered together, the two levels of government have very different tax systems. The state governments rely heavily on consumption and income taxes; local governments are dependent largely on the property tax, but they have also been increasing their reliance on user charges and fees in recent years.

State Taxes

State tax structures have changed dramatically since the turn of the century. In 1902 almost half of state revenue came from property taxes and the rest from selective excise taxes. Today, the general sales tax is the largest single source of state revenue, with income taxes next. Most states have relinquished the general property tax to their local governments; only Arizona, Kentucky, and Washington raise 5 percent or more of their revenues from this tax.

SALES AND EXCISE TAXES. State legislatures have been irresistibly attracted to the productivity and stability of revenues from consumption taxes. Selective excise taxes on gasoline, cigarettes, and liquor are also in extensive use throughout the country. But the retail sales tax is the largest source of consumption tax revenues.

The retail sales tax emerged as a major state revenue source in the 1930s. It is now in use in forty-five states and the District of Columbia, at rates ranging from 2 to 7.5 percent. To moderate its regressivity, twenty-seven states exempt food, and forty exempt drugs. Another possibility is to provide a credit against the state personal income tax for sales tax paid. For example, a per capita credit of $10 might be allowed for individuals and families whose taxable income does not exceed $10,000. (For a family of four, the $40 credit is equivalent to a 5 percent tax on $800 of purchases.) Hawaii, Idaho, and Nebraska have such a provision. Cash refunds are paid to individuals and families who do not pay enough income tax to recover the entire credit. In New Mexico, an income tax credit is provided for all state and local taxes for those with incomes of $10,000 and under; in addition, the state provides a credit of $45 per capita for food purchases and $7.50 for medical expenses for all persons regardless of income.

INCOME TAXES. State individual and corporation income taxes in their modern form began in Wisconsin in 1911. (Hawaii had adopted both taxes in 1901, but this experience apparently had no influence on the states.) General individual income taxes are now in force in forty states and the District of Columbia, and the corporation income tax in forty-five states and the District of Columbia. New Hampshire and Tennessee tax only dividends and interest (though interest on savings deposits is excluded in New Hampshire), and Connecticut taxes only capital gains. State tax rates are much lower than the federal rates, and personal exemptions are generally higher. Tax brackets used for the individual income tax are narrower, and graduation is steeper but terminates at a much lower income level, usually between $5,000 and $25,000. The highest individual income tax rates are levied in New York, where the top rate on unearned income is 14 percent (the top rate on earned income is 10 percent). West Virginia taxes both earned and unearned income at a top rate of 13 percent. Minnesota has the highest corporation income tax, with a rate of 12 percent (6.5 percent after allowing for the deductibility of the federal tax). Since 1978 ten states have indexed the personal exemptions and the individual income tax rate brackets for inflation, but Iowa's indexing provision was effective only in 1979, and Colorado and Wisconsin have suspended indexing, the former for 1983–84 and the latter for 1983–85.

The nominal tax rates overstate the net impact of the state income taxes because these tax payments are deductible from taxable income in computing federal taxes. In addition, fifteen states permit the deduction of all or part of the federal tax in computing taxable income for state tax purposes. In most cases the net effect of deductibility is to make the burden imposed by state individual income taxes heavier on the lower and middle income classes than on the higher income classes (see the discussion of deductibility below).

State income taxes are generally patterned after the federal taxes. Thirty-three of the personal income tax states have an optional standard deduction. Thirty-two states start with the items reported on the federal income tax return in calculating taxable income for state tax purposes. All states modify the adjusted gross income concept by subtracting interest on federal securities, and most states add interest on out-of-state state or local bonds. Despite the interest in uniformity with federal definitions, many states have not followed the federal government in providing special savings incentives, the deduction for two-earner couples, and the generous depreciation allowances adopted in 1981. Withholding for individual income tax purposes was introduced by Oregon in 1948, and all the states except North Dakota now withhold from wages and salaries. Most of the states complement withholding by requiring declarations of estimated tax for income on which tax is not withheld.

SEVERANCE TAXES. Until the energy crisis of the 1970s, severance taxes—that is, taxes on the extraction of minerals, oil, and gas—were of little importance in state revenue systems. However, state severance tax revenue has risen sharply in recent years—from $733 million in 1971 to $7.4 billion in 1981, or 5 percent of total state tax collections.

DEATH AND GIFT TAXES. Death taxes were levied by states long before the federal government enacted an estate tax in 1916. Pennsylvania taxed inheritances as early as 1825, and Wisconsin set the modern pattern by adopting a progressive inheritance tax in 1903. Only Nevada does not tax bequests. Ten states levy a tax that picks up only the equivalent of the credit for state death taxes under the federal estate tax. The gift tax is levied in nine states. For the United States as a whole, death and gift taxes amount to less than 1 percent of total state tax collections.

LOTTERIES. During the 1970s, the states began using lotteries in their quest for new sources of revenue. Lotteries were used early in American history, but fell into disuse when it was found that they generated crime and corruption. Recent experience, which began with the New Hampshire Sweepstakes in 1964, has been more acceptable from the social point of view. As of mid-1983, sixteen states had adopted a lottery. In fiscal year 1982 net revenues from lotteries amounted to about $1.5 billion, or about 5 percent of the revenues from these states' own sources. Aside from the danger of encouraging criminal activity, lotteries are criticized on the ground that they appeal too often to people who cannot afford to participate and are therefore regressive.

Local Taxes

The tax sources of municipal and county governments are limited. They have always relied heavily on the property tax, and despite persistent efforts to diversify their sources of funds, the majority of local governments assign nonproperty taxes a relatively unimportant place in their finances.

PROPERTY TAX. In fiscal 1981 the property tax provided 49 percent of the general revenues from all local sources (76 percent of tax revenue).

Dependence on this tax reflects the reluctance of many state governments to give localities authority to levy other taxes. It also reflects fears that high local income or sales taxes might induce emigration to or purchases in neighboring communities. Taxation of real property may have significant effects on the price and use of land but not on its location.

Although critics have long predicted the demise of the property tax, it performed creditably in the postwar period until 1978, when California voters started a trend by approving Proposition 13, which reduced the rates of the property tax and limited its growth. State and local property tax collections rose from about $6 billion in fiscal 1948 to $66.4 billion in 1978, an annual rate of growth of 8.4 percent during a period when the gross national product (in current dollars) grew at a rate of 7.3 percent. From 1978 to 1981, the annual growth rate of the property tax was only 4.1 percent, when the nominal gross national product grew 8.3 percent a year. In 1976 the median effective rate for single-family homes in 144 cities with a population of 100,000 or more was 1.6 percent, and only 19 cities had an effective rate for houses of 3 percent or more.

To moderate the burden of the property tax on the poor, thirty-two states and the District of Columbia have provided credits for property tax payments against the personal income tax. In most of these states, the credit is also given to renters on the basis of an assumed relation between property taxes and rental payments. Like the sales tax credit, the property tax credit is paid directly to the taxpayers if they are not subject to income tax or if the income tax does not cover the entire credit.

NONPROPERTY TAXES. Some large cities in a limited number of states have successfully diversified their revenue sources. Sales taxes are the most productive nonproperty taxes, with taxes on earnings or income next. Local general sales taxes are now used in twenty-six states by over 4,700 local governments. Local income taxes are levied in eleven states but are widespread only in Indiana, Kentucky, Maryland, Michigan, Ohio, and Pennsylvania.

NONTAX REVENUES. Nontax revenues are most important at the local level and, as already noted, they are being used more heavily since the passage of Proposition 13. In 1981 they accounted for 35 percent of local revenues from own sources and for 20 percent of comparable state revenues. Such nontax sources include charges for water, electric power, and gas, special assessments, license and other fees, and user charges for transportation, medical care, and housing. Payments for most government services that yield measurable benefits are substantially below marginal cost, primarily because it is feared that user charges will hurt low-income families. To moderate the impact of such charges on low-income families, the cities have been using such measures as reduced-fare cards, admission on vouchers, and senior citizen discounts.

State and Local Fiscal Performance, Capacity, and Effort

The fiscal performance and tax capacity of the fifty states are summarized in figure 9-2. Performance is measured by per capita revenue collected from state and local sources; capacity is measured by a representative, or national average, tax system; and revenue effort is the ratio of performance to capacity, or the ratio of revenue collected to the revenues that would be collected if each state used the representative tax system.

When the states are arrayed by size of per capita tax capacity, the per capita revenue obtained from state and local sources increases from low- to high-capacity states. In fiscal 1980 the ten states with the lowest tax capacity raised only $720 per capita, whereas the ten states with the highest capacity raised $987 per capita. This pattern of performance cannot be attributed to a lack of effort on the part of the states with low capacity. In fact, the average revenue effort in the poorest one-fifth of the states is greater than the average effort made in the top two-fifths. Even if the states with the lowest capacity increased their revenue effort from their 96.3 percent to the 102.0 percent of the fifth with the highest effort, they would raise only $762 per capita—still far below the amount raised by other states. These figures indicate that the states with low tax capacity cannot provide average levels of public services just by increasing their revenue effort.

Major Issues

The state and local tax systems are still in transition. The fiscal squeeze from inflation, unemployment, and the recent reductions in federal grants requires higher taxes, which create equity and economic problems. These problems are not new, but they have become acute as tax burdens have increased.

Figure 9-2. *State and Local Revenue and Revenue Effort,*
by Quintiles of State per Capita Tax Capacity, Fiscal Year 1980[a]

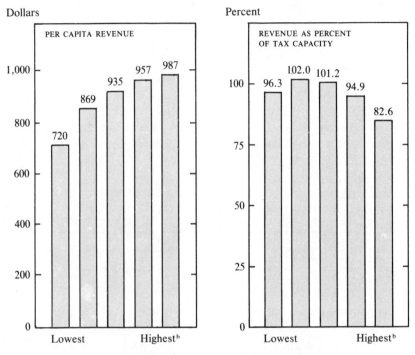

Quintiles of state per capita tax capacity

Source: Advisory Commission on Intergovernmental Relations, 1980.
a. State and local revenue excludes federal grants.
b. Excludes Alaska.

Income Taxes versus Sales Taxes

The relative merits of an individual income tax and a sales tax for
state use continue to provoke emotional responses in many areas of the
country. The debate is primarily over equity, but other considerations
enter into it.

The major argument in favor of the income tax is its progressivity.
Proponents of the income tax believe that state as well as federal taxes
should be based on ability to pay. Moreover, the deductibility of state
income taxes in calculating the federal income tax greatly moderates the
impact of the top state rates on high-income taxpayers (see the discussion
of deductibility below). The income tax is also much more responsive to
economic growth than the sales tax.

Table 9-1. *Combined Federal and State Income and Sales Tax Liabilities, Married Couple with Two Dependents, Oregon and Washington, 1982*
Dollars

Adjusted gross income	Federal income tax[a] plus		Difference (income tax less sales tax)
	Oregon income tax[b]	Washington sales tax[b,c]	
3,000	− 303	− 129	− 174
5,000	− 500	− 326	− 174
8,000	13	2	11
10,000	670	561	109
15,000	1,905	1,392	513
20,000	3,300	2,379	921
25,000	4,893	3,546	1,347
35,000	7,474	6,071	1,403
50,000	12,836	10,931	1,905
75,000	23,362	20,714	2,648
100,000	35,127	31,514	3,613

a. After the refundable earned-income credit, indicated by minus signs.
b. After taking into account deductibility of the state income or sales tax in computing the federal income tax. All other deductions were assumed to be equal to the Oregon standard deduction of 13 percent of income.
c. Sales tax for 1982 as estimated by the Internal Revenue Service for purposes of federal deductibility. See Commerce Clearing House, *1983 U.S. Master Tax Guide* (1982), p. 39.

Proponents of the sales tax believe it is undesirable to pile a state income tax on top of the federal tax. Even with deductibility, they fear that high-income taxpayers will emigrate to avoid the state income tax. They feel that tax progressivity is not essential at all levels of government, provided the entire federal, state, and local tax system is progressive on balance.

Both the income and the sales taxes can be productive revenue sources for state governments if they are levied on a broad base. Most states levying both sales and income taxes derive more revenue from the sales tax. While it is possible to devise an income tax with a yield equal to that of almost any sales tax, sales taxes of 3 to 5 percent are generally more productive than income taxes with rates graduated up to 10 percent. These are the ranges currently used in most states. The balance, of course, swings toward the income tax as incomes increase.

Whether an income tax would drive wealthy residents to sales tax states is difficult to determine. For example, in 1983 Oregon had an income tax and neighboring Washington had a sales tax. Table 9-1 compares the combined federal and state income and sales tax burdens of families with different incomes, after taking into account the effect of the deductibility of state taxes in computing the federal income tax. A married person with two children residing in Oregon would have paid $174 less tax on an income of $5,000 than a person residing in Washington, but $1,905 more tax on an income of $50,000. Reactions to such differences depend heavily on individual attitudes toward equity, the need for state revenues, and the benefits of improved public services. In any case, the opposition to state income taxes is often vocal and influential and succeeds in delaying the introduction of income taxation. For instance, New Jersey, Ohio, and Pennsylvania finally enacted income taxes in the 1970s, but only after long struggles.

There is little to choose between income and sales taxes on administrative and compliance grounds. Costs of administration are somewhat lower for the income tax than for the sales tax. Compliance is more difficult for the taxpayer in the case of the income tax, while the sales tax imposes a burden on retailers. Sales tax revenues are more stable than income taxes, but both taxes are responsive to changes in income and employment. Some support the sales tax because its revenues come partly from tourists and other visitors who use the facilities of the state temporarily. On the other hand, income taxes can be, and usually are, imposed on employees who live outside the state and work within the state. These differences may be significant in a few places where interstate travel and commuting are important.

In recent years, the need for revenue has tended to soften attitudes on both sides of the controversy. At one time most states had either an income tax or a sales tax, but the number of states with both has been increasing. On January 1, 1984, thirty-seven states had both, eight had only a sales tax, three had only an income tax, and two (Alaska and New Hampshire) had neither (appendix table D-26). Credits for sales taxes against state individual income taxes, adopted in four states, make it possible to eliminate the burden of the sales tax on the lowest incomes. There are few remaining objections on equity grounds to the use by states of either type of tax, or both, if such credits are allowed.

Deductibility

The discussion in chapter 4 of the deductibility of state taxes in calculating the federal income tax base implied that simultaneous use of the same tax source by two (or even three) levels of government is acceptable provided the combined rates are not excessive. Deduction from the federal tax base of income, sales, and property taxes paid to state and local governments is considered desirable to encourage state and local use of these taxes and to narrow interstate and intercommunity net tax differences.

Most states with income taxes have borrowed the deductibility features of the federal law. While practices vary, state and local sales and excise taxes are deductible in arriving at taxable income in most states. In addition, fifteen of the forty-one states with an individual income tax permit deduction of the federal individual income tax (four on a limited basis), and four permit deduction of the state individual income tax itself; six of the forty-five states with a corporation income tax permit deduction of the federal corporation income tax, and seven allow deduction of the state corporation income tax.

Deductibility of any tax from the base of another (or from its own base) has two effects: first, the extra burden on the taxpayer of the deducted tax is reduced by the marginal rate of the tax against which it is deductible; and second, the net yield of the tax with the deductible feature is reduced, requiring higher nominal rates to obtain any given amount of revenue. The net marginal burdens of state taxes with federal and federal plus state deductibility are illustrated in table 9-2.

For example:

1. A proportional 2 percent state income tax is converted to a regressive tax by the deductibility feature of the federal income tax. Such a tax would impose a net burden of 1.78 percentage points on a taxpayer subject to the lowest federal rate of 11 percent, 1.4 points on a taxpayer subject to a 30 percent federal rate, and only 1 point on a taxpayer subject to the top federal rate of 50 percent. If the state allowed its income tax to be deducted from its own income tax base, the regressivity would be even greater.

2. Federal deductibility of state income taxes already greatly reduces the burden of the top state income tax rates. As the following shows, state deductibility accomplishes little more for the taxpayer at a substantial cost to the state:

	Tax collected as a percentage of income (50 percent federal rate, 10 percent state rate)		
	Federal	Federal	
Level of	deductibility	and state	
government	only	deductibility	Difference
Federal	45.00	47.37	2.37
State	10.00	5.26	−4.74
Total	55.00	52.63	−2.37

Table 9-2. *Marginal Burden of State Income Taxes under Federal Tax Deductibility*[a] *and under Federal and State Tax Deductibility,*[b] *at Illustrative Marginal Rates*

Percent

Marginal federal tax rate	Type of deductibility	Marginal state tax rate				
		2	3	5	7	10
11	Federal only	1.78	2.67	4.45	6.23	8.90
	Federal and state	1.58	2.38	3.98	5.55	7.78
20	Federal only	1.60	2.40	4.00	5.60	8.00
	Federal and state	1.29	1.93	3.23	4.54	6.53
30	Federal only	1.40	2.10	3.50	4.90	7.00
	Federal and state	0.99	1.48	2.49	3.50	5.05
40	Federal only	1.20	1.80	3.00	4.20	6.00
	Federal and state	0.73	1.09	1.84	2.59	3.75
50	Federal only	1.00	1.50	2.50	3.50	5.00
	Federal and state	0.51	0.76	1.28	1.81	2.63
60	Federal only	0.80	1.20	2.00	2.80	4.00
	Federal and state	0.32	0.49	0.82	1.17	1.70
70	Federal only	0.60	0.90	1.50	2.10	3.00
	Federal and state	0.18	0.28	0.47	0.66	0.97

a. State income taxes paid are deducted in computing federal income taxes.
b. Same as note a; in addition, federal income taxes paid are deducted in computing state income taxes.

With federal deductibility of the state tax, a top state rate of 10 percent imposes a net additional burden of only 5 percentage points on a taxpayer subject to a federal rate of 50 percent. With state deductibility of the federal tax, the net additional burden of the same 10 percent state tax is only 2.63 points. The 2.37-point net reduction in the taxpayer's total burden costs the state 4.74 points, or two times the taxpayer's saving.

3. Federal deductibility reduces the progressivity of the state tax and may actually convert it to a regressive tax. Adding state deductibility of the federal tax aggravates matters. For example, if the state rates are paired with the federal rates along the diagonal in table 9-2, the net impact of the state tax on an additional $1 of income is as follows:

Marginal federal rate	Marginal state rate	Net impact of the state tax (percent)		
		Federal deductibility only	Federal and state deductibility	Difference
11	2	1.78	1.56	−0.22
20	3	2.40	1.93	−0.47
30	5	3.50	2.49	−1.01
40	7	4.20	2.59	−1.61
50	10	5.00	2.63	−2.37

If the federal income tax allows deductibility of the state tax, the state tax adds 1.78 percentage points to the federal tax in the lowest federal bracket, rising to 5 points in the 50 percent bracket. If, in addition, the state permits the federal income tax to be deducted against its own tax, the additional tax reaches a maximum of only 2.63 points.

Although the income tax rates in the top brackets raise only a fraction of their nominal values in many states, very high rates at the high income levels act as a psychological barrier to further use of the income tax for needed revenues. Since deductibility of the state tax in computing the federal tax already protects taxpayers against excessive rates, removal of the deductibility of the federal tax against the state tax would provide some additional revenue for the states and improve and simplify state income taxes.

The Property Tax

In spite of widespread and vehement criticism, the property tax continues to be the major revenue source for local governments. Its survival is due to the continued need for revenues by local governments, which have few other productive revenue sources at their disposal. Recent economic analysis suggests that the tax is borne largely by owners of capital and is, therefore, a progressive element of the tax system.

Although the property tax was at one time intended to be a tax on all wealth, it is no longer general in coverage. While practices vary from community to community, the tax falls chiefly on real estate and often, though not universally, on business equipment and inventories. The tax rate is frequently determined as a residual. Local governments assess the value of property subject to the tax, estimate the revenue needed from this source, and calculate the tax rate required to obtain the predetermined result. When employed in this manner, the property tax is a more reliable tax source for local governments than are income or sales taxes, whose rates vary only with legislative action, and whose yield is uncertain. The ease with which rates can be raised has probably contributed to its durability.

ADMINISTRATION. Administration of the property tax has been subject to universal criticism. Because the value of the tax base for any particular property cannot be determined directly by a market transaction, property assessments are often arbitrary and result in an erratic distribution of

Table 9-3. *Distribution of States by Percentage Ratios of Assessed Value to Sales Price of Real Property, 1956, 1961, 1966, 1971, and 1976*

Assessed value as percent of sales price[a]	Number of states				
	1956	*1961*	*1966*	*1971*	*1976*
0–9.9	2	3	1	5	7
10.0–19.9	16	15	17	11	15
20.0–29.9	16	13	10	9	7
30.0–39.9	4	6	7	10	5
40.0–49.9	7	10	5	7	5
50.0–59.9	2	2	6	4	3
60.0–69.9	1	1	2	1	5
70.0 and over	0	0	2	3	3
Total	48	50	50	50	50
Average assessment (percent)	30	29.5	32.5	32.7	31.3

Source: Bureau of the Census, *Census of Governments*.
a. Total assessed value of all properties sold that were included in the census samples expressed as a percentage of their sales prices.

the tax burden. Substantial underassessment is the rule rather than the exception, even in the twenty states that require full valuation. Between 1956 and 1976, for example, property was assessed at an average of about 30 percent of its market value in all states and at less than 50 percent in at least three-quarters of the states (table 9-3). Moreover, there is great variability in assessments of properties of equal value, creating irritating inequities among taxpayers and among different communities within the same state. Yet errors are much less visible when properties of similar value are assessed at only a fraction of their true value. The variability of local assessments requires state agencies to "equalize" the assessments before they are used for allocating state grants to local governments. In some places, property tax limitations are based on assessed valuations; in such cases, underassessment may impair the ability of the local government to finance its needs.

Uniform assessment can be attained at any assessment ratio, but assessors seem able to achieve more uniformity at the higher assessment ratios (table 9-4). Between 1956 and 1971 average assessment ratios increased somewhat, while the variability of assessments declined significantly. However, between 1971 and 1976, the last year for which such data are available, average assessment ratios declined and the variability of assessments increased.

Table 9-4. *Property Tax Assessment Ratios and Coefficients of Intra-Area Dispersion, Nonfarm Houses in Selected Local Areas, 1956, 1961, 1966, 1971, and 1976*
Percent

Assessment ratio and dispersion coefficient	1956	1961	1966	1971	1976
Median assessment ratio[a]	*Median coefficient of intra-area dispersion*[b]				
Under 20	37	33	26	27	31
20–30	32	27	21	21	24
30–40	25	23	19	21	19
40 and over	22	19	16	17	17
All areas	30	26	19	20	22
Coefficient of intra-area dispersion[b]	*Percentage distribution of local areas*				
Under 15	8	14	28	25	22
15–20	12	16	25	24	20
20–30	30	32	27	30	29
30–40	21	19	10	12	15
40 and over	29	19	10	9	14
All areas	100	100	100	100	100

Source: Bureau of the Census, *Census of Governments.*
a. Median ratio of assessments to sale prices for the census samples of nonfarm houses in each local area.
b. The average deviation of assessment ratios from the median expressed as a percentage of the median ratio in the area.

The poor quality of assessments is partly due to the difficulty of valuing property that is sold infrequently. In addition, local assessors are often not capable of making assessments, or the local taxing jurisdiction lacks the staff and resources to take advantage of market evidence on property values. Support for high-quality, frequent assessments is often lacking because politicians and their constituents tend to resist shifting property tax burdens from year to year.

Good administration is possible despite the inherent difficulties. The Advisory Commission on Intergovernmental Relations (ACIR)—a permanent commission created by act of Congress to make recommendations on intergovernmental relations—has recommended centralization of property assessment in one state agency to take advantage of the states' superior technical resources; appointment rather than election of assessors to remove the assessment process from political influence; full information on property assessments and easy procedures for appeal so that taxpayers can help enforce good administration; publication of the value of property that is exempt from local property taxes by state action; and elimination of unnecessary and inequitable property tax limitations.

Many state governments have taken the initiative to improve local property tax administration along the lines proposed by the ACIR. The reforms involve more state participation in the administration of the tax, greater reliance on professional personnel, and reorganization of local assessment districts into larger and more efficient units. Most states collect comparative statistics on assessment ratios, which reveal the diversity in assessment practices and permit state officials to locate the major areas of administrative weakness. Many states are also taking an active part in supervising local assessment practices, training assessment personnel, and providing technical assistance where needed.

INCIDENCE AND ALLOCATION EFFECTS. Practically every economist since Ricardo has agreed that a property tax on unimproved land is borne by the landowners. Since the supply of land is fixed, the value of sites will fall by the capitalized value of the tax when it is first imposed or increased. More recently, it has been pointed out that a property tax on land may be shifted if, as a result of the reduced value of the land, investors accumulate a larger amount of reproducible capital. In these circumstances, the productivity of land would increase and interest rates would decline, and the tax would be shifted in the form of a lower rate of return on capital in general.

The incidence of a uniform property tax on reproducible capital has been disputed by economists for many years. If the supply of saving is not responsive to the rate of return, the tax will not affect the supply of capital and will be borne entirely by the owners of capital. (See chapter 5 for this analysis as it applies to the corporation income tax.) If the supply of saving responds at least to some extent to the rate of return, the tax will discourage new investment and reduce the supply of new buildings (and other capital, such as inventories, to the extent that it is taxed). The prices of services produced by such capital will rise and the tax will be borne partly by the consumers of these services and partly by the owners of capital.

The property tax on improvements could also be shifted forward in the form of higher prices under two conditions. First, property owners may have sufficient market power to set prices and may exercise this power when the property tax is imposed or increased, although this possibility is remote because the real estate industry is highly competitive throughout the country. Second, where rents are subject to control, property tax increases are usually considered justification for rent increases.

On the assumption that the property tax on improvements is borne entirely by capital, the distribution of the burden of this tax is progressive throughout most of the income scale. On the other hand, if the property tax on improvements is shifted forward to users, the property tax is regressive (table 9-5). In both calculations it is assumed that the property tax on land is borne by landlords.

It is also assumed that the property tax is a uniform tax levied on all property at the average rate for the country as a whole, although, in fact, taxes vary substantially among local areas and industries. Returns to owners of land and reproducible capital will fall on the average, but the interarea differences will also have significant effects. If labor and reproducible capital are not perfectly mobile, workers, property owners, and consumers will have higher real incomes in low-tax areas than those in high-tax areas.

On the other hand, property taxpayers may consider at least part of the tax payment as a charge for local services, such as police and fire protection, education, and roads. To this extent, the property tax is a benefit tax and allocates the burden of local services in a rough way to those who use it.

The property tax also affects land use. In a city surrounded by farmland, the property tax will have no effect on land development if the farm property is taxed at the same rate as urban land. On the other hand, taxes on urban real estate often exceed taxes on farms; land development for urban use will be retarded where this occurs. Similarly, heavy taxation of improvements discourages rebuilding in urban areas.

Residential property is one of the major sources of property tax revenue. The taxes on housing might be expected to discourage the demand for housing. For many, however, the income tax advantages of homeownership and the exclusion of housing services from the state sales tax bases offset the property tax's deterrent effects.

CIRCUIT BREAKERS. Credits against state income taxes for property tax payments by the elderly and the poor are a recent development that has swept the country. By the beginning of 1983, thirty-two states and the District of Columbia had enacted such a program, but the programs are significant only in Michigan, Minnesota, Oregon, Vermont, Wisconsin, and the District of Columbia. The credits are called "circuit breakers,"

Table 9-5. *Alternative Estimates of the Incidence of the Property Tax, by Income Percentiles, 1975*
Percent

Household income percentile[a]	Effective rates of tax, assuming property tax on improvements is borne in proportion to	
	Housing expenditures and consumption[b]	Income from capital[b]
0–5	11.4	1.8
5–10	5.0	0.9
10–15	3.7	1.0
15–20	3.6	1.1
20–25	3.2	1.3
25–30	2.9	1.4
30–35	2.9	1.3
35–40	2.9	1.4
40–45	2.9	1.5
45–50	3.0	1.7
50–55	2.9	1.7
55–60	3.0	1.9
60–65	3.0	1.9
65–70	3.1	1.9
70–75	3.1	2.0
75–80	3.1	2.2
80–85	3.1	2.2
85–90	3.3	2.5
90–95	3.3	3.3
95–99	3.2	4.3
99–100	2.8	5.6
All classes[c]	3.2	2.7[d]

Source: Brookings 1975 MERGE data file.
a. Ranked from low to high incomes. Income is defined as money factor income plus transfer payments, accrued capital gains, and indirect business taxes.
b. It is assumed that the property tax on land is borne by landlords.
c. Includes negative incomes.
d. The average burden of the property tax is lower because, under these assumptions, part of the tax is borne by the tax-exempt sector and is not included in the household sector.

the analogy being that they protect the family against a property tax overload in the same way that a circuit breaker protects an electrical line against an overload of current.

The circuit breaker is triggered when the income of a property taxpayer falls below certain levels. Some states provide a credit against the state income tax or a refund if the income tax is not large enough to absorb the entire credit (or if the individual is not subject to income tax) for the entire amount of property tax paid that exceeds the statutory percentage of income. In others, the credit is given on a sliding scale, with the highest percentage of relief at the lower end of the income scale. Some states assume that the property tax accounts for an arbitrary percentage of rental payments. In some states, only elderly homeowners are eligible; in others, relief is provided for elderly renters as well as homeowners; in a few states, all homeowners and renters, regardless of age, are eligible. The benefits under these programs amount to less than 2 percent of the revenue generated by the property tax.

Proponents of the circuit breaker idea believe that it is an effective device to cushion the impact of heavy property taxes on poor families, especially the elderly, many of whom go on living in the family home even after their children have left and their incomes have declined. The benefits are financed by the state government and thus do not erode the fiscal resources of the local government. Moreover, to the extent that the circuit breaker makes the property tax more acceptable, it helps to strengthen the major tax source of local governments.

On the other hand, although the circuit breaker is justified primarily on the ground that the property tax is regressive, economists have increasingly come to believe that the property tax is borne largely by owners of capital and is therefore progressive. If the property tax is actually borne by owners of capital, renters are not entitled to relief. Furthermore, the relief is given to those who have unusually large amounts of property in relation to their income or who spend an unusually large percentage of their current annual income on housing because their income is temporarily depressed. Where there are current difficulties in paying, provision can be made for delayed payments of property taxes without paying benefits to those who are not entitled to them.

The relief provided by circuit breakers is far less efficient than a general income maintenance system in helping the poor. If relief for housing is desirable, a system of housing allowances to those with low incomes and low net worth would be more appropriate. Without such programs, circuit breakers will continue to be attractive because they provide apparently needy people with relief from an unpopular tax at relatively modest cost.

ALTERNATIVES. Other forms of real estate taxation have been proposed as alternatives to the general property tax. One is to use annual returns rather than capital values as a base, a measure often advocated by those who wish to increase the tax on high-rent, low-capital-value housing. Such a system would favor properties in low-return uses and, like the present tax, would discourage improvements to increase annual income from properties.

A second alternative is site-value taxation: taxing the value of the sites themselves while exempting the value of improvements. Site-value taxation has merit on equity grounds; since the value of land is increased by population growth and general improvements are financed by the community at large, the community has the right to tax this "unearned increment." Site-value taxation would also discourage the hoarding of land for speculative purposes and encourage more efficient use of land in and around the nation's cities. On the other hand, the supply of sites is not fixed, as the supporters of site-value taxation assume; in these circumstances, the tax on sites will be shifted in part to improvements. This is especially applicable to the fringes of city areas that are bordered by annexable land not subject to taxation. Moreover, shifting from the present system to site-value taxation would create losses for present property holders who paid the full current value, or close to it, for their land and who therefore have not received large unearned increments.

A third proposal, with similar equity and economic advantages, is to tax land-value increments. This would avoid the transitional problems of the site-value tax, but would yield much less revenue than the property tax if it were levied at moderate rates only at the time of transfers of ownership.

A different approach to property taxation is that of a user charge. It is argued that the distribution of taxes based on property values has little relation to the distribution of services to property provided by local governments. A series of user charges would be more clearly linked to the benefits received. For some services, like fire protection, the appropriate benefit charge would be easy to determine because the area of service is well defined; others, like transportation, would be more difficult to allocate. This proposal, however, would not deal with the bulk of the current tax revenues that finance services to persons, rather than to property.

Other methods of financing local governments could be devised, but the alternatives to the property tax would not yield comparable revenues at reasonable rates. This will probably preserve the property tax as a major source of local government revenue, making the need for improved administration especially urgent.

With the growing sophistication of assessment techniques, it should be possible to further reduce administrative inequities. Participation in the administrative process by state governments, with their superior financial and technical resources, would accelerate the adoption of improved techniques to the fiscal advantage of local governments.

PROPOSITION 13. In 1978 the voters of California approved an amendment to the state constitution that imposes strict limits on local property tax rates and growth in property tax revenues. The California revolt was triggered by a sharp rise in property taxes as assessed valuations increased to reflect the inflation of housing prices in the mid- and late 1970s. Before the amendment was approved, the average California property tax rate was about 2.5 percent of actual market value. Proposition 13 reduced the tax to 1 percent of the 1975 market value.

Proposition 13 had an enormous influence on tax and expenditure policies in other states, as well as at the federal level. Since 1978 twenty-one states have imposed limits on local taxes or expenditures and fifteen states have imposed limits on state taxes or expenditures. The tax limitation movement has also spurred efforts, so far unsuccessful, to pass a balanced-budget amendment to the federal Constitution.

Proposition 13 has had a powerful effect on state and local finance. Many states have used up their surpluses to provide state aid as a substitute for the lost property tax revenues. In many parts of the country, expenditures have been shrinking in real terms for several years, partly as a result of the tax limitation movement and partly because of reduced fiscal resources during the recession. Other taxes are gradually being increased, but the fiscal condition of many states and local governments continues to be stringent.

The desirability of limits on taxes and expenditures depends on one's view of the effectiveness of taxpayer control of the size of the public sector. Some economists believe that the collective choice mechanism inevitably leads to excessive growth in government spending. Others argue that the evidence to support such assertions is not persuasive. In any case, tax and expenditure limits introduce great inflexibilities in governmental fiscal decisions and prevent rational consideration of revenue and expenditure options. Budgetary procedures can be improved without imposing arbitrary limits on tax and expenditure policies (see chapter 2).

Tax Coordination

Tax overlapping among different levels of government was at one time considered a major drawback of the national tax system of the United States, but attempts to divide revenue sources have had little success. The state and local governments failed to pick up the electrical energy tax, which was repealed by Congress in 1951, although they had urged the federal government to relinquish this tax for their use. The same was true of reductions in the federal admissions tax during the 1950s. In 1958–59 the Joint Federal-State Action Committee (consisting of state governors appointed by the chairman of the Governors' Conference and representatives of the federal government appointed by the president) could not reach agreement on a proposal to eliminate some federal grants in return for relinquishment of the local telephone tax by the federal government. Similarly, a far-reaching proposal by President Reagan to reallocate programs and tax sources between federal and state governments has languished for lack of support by state and local authorities. Such attempts fail because it is difficult to devise a plan that all states regard as equitable and because the state and local governments are likely to view the specific federal taxes relinquished with the same reservations that motivated Congress to give them up as revenue sources in the first instance.

One successful transfer of a tax source did occur when federal excise taxes were reduced in 1965. At the request of the ACIR and the states, Congress delayed the effective date of the repeal of the federal stamp tax on realty title transfers to give states time to enact a replacement tax that would assure continuity of the sales information used in computing assessment-sales ratio data for property tax equalization and state school aid programs. In this case, states were motivated more by the need for the tax-record information than by a desire for revenue.

Tax overlapping was moderated slightly by the 1965 federal excise tax reductions, but these cuts were made for other reasons. Moreover, in 1982, federal excise taxes on cigarettes were doubled and those on motor fuels were more than doubled; both of these excise taxes are used extensively by the states. Experience to date suggests, therefore, that the major cases of duplication—in income and estate taxation as well as excise taxation—will persist.

But the situation is not as serious as it appears. In recent years new methods of administrative cooperation between federal and state governments have been developed. State income taxes resemble the federal taxes in major respects; many, in fact, start with the federal definition of adjusted gross income for individuals and taxable income for corporations. Several states have simplified their tax returns. Most experts accept some tax overlapping as inevitable, and even desirable if the taxes used in common are good taxes. The present approach is to relieve major taxpayer compliance problems, remove inequities resulting from tax overlapping, and extend the area of intergovernmental administrative cooperation as much as possible.

ESTATE TAX COORDINATION. The administrative and compliance problems raised by overlapping estate and gift taxation are out of proportion to their revenue yield. Most of the states use inheritance taxes, but they have a wide variety of exclusions, deductions, and exemptions. The federal credit for state death taxes (enacted in 1924 and enlarged in 1926) placed a floor under state taxes but did not produce uniformity in state taxation of property transfers. The states left their own taxes unchanged and later added special levies to pick up the difference between these taxes and the maximum allowable credit. Today, twenty-nine states have inheritance taxes, twenty-eight with pickup taxes; ten have estate taxes, nine with pickup taxes; and ten have only pickup taxes. Only Nevada levies no state death tax.

The states have long felt that the estate tax should be left to them, but they do not want the credit arrangement repealed. They recognize that, without the protection of the federal credit, interstate competition for wealthy taxpayers would quickly dry up state death tax revenues. The credit ensures that any state can tax up to the amount of the credit without running the risk of losing its taxpayers to other states, but in its present form the credit provides no incentive for states to adopt uniform definitions of the tax base. (A credit for gift taxes is not needed because only nine states now tax gifts.)

There is little interest in Congress or the executive branch in increasing the state estate tax credit, partly because federal revenues from this source have been greatly reduced in recent years and partly because the degree of coordination this might achieve does not seem to justify additional revenue loss. The federal government might be more receptive to modernizing the credit if such action were accompanied by provisions that achieved greater uniformity in estate and inheritance taxation among the states.

STATE TAXATION AND INTERSTATE COMMERCE. For years the states have been reaching out to exact taxes from activities that cross state lines. On the whole, their claims have been sustained by the Supreme Court. In 1959 the Court upheld a state corporation income tax on a firm whose activities consisted solely of the solicitation of sales within a state. A few months later the Court held that an out-of-state business could be required to collect and pay over to a state a use tax on sales made to customers within the taxing state even if it maintained no facilities in the state and its sales were made entirely through independent contractors. In response to the threat of unrestricted state taxation of interstate commerce, Congress enacted Public Law 86-272, which established minimum criteria for determining when out-of-state sales become taxable in a state, but these criteria still give the states wide latitude in taxing interstate sales.

Federal control over state taxes on corporations is also minimal. The states have always taxed multistate corporations on the basis of various formulas, which may lead to more tax base being claimed by all states together than if a corporation were strictly a one-state operation. In 1983 the Court permitted the states to tax corporations on the basis of their worldwide income, thus sanctioning the nonuniformity in corporate taxation among the states.

After years of study, very little has been done to coordinate state taxation of interstate (and, more recently, foreign) commerce. The major issues are (1) the division of the income of multistate and multinational firms among the states, and (2) requirements for the collection of use taxes by firms shipping into a state.

1. The District of Columbia and the forty-five states that impose a corporation income tax have various formulas to compute the allocation for state tax purposes of profits of multistate firms from their domestic and foreign operations. Twenty-six states have adopted uniform laws for allocation purposes patterned after a 1957 proposal of the National Conference of Commissioners on Uniform State Law. Twenty states have joined the Multistate Tax Compact, which was established in 1966 as an alternative to proposed interstate taxation bills then pending in Congress. Eighteen states generally follow the regulations of the compact, but only fourteen have officially adopted them. Most states have incorporated the commissioners' or the multistate compact rules piecemeal, while twenty states have not agreed to the rules of either association.

At present, the states give varying weights to property, payroll, and sales in allocating corporate earnings by states. This diversity produces anomalous results: some interstate corporations are taxed lightly; others claim they pay state taxes on an aggregate tax base that exceeds their net income. Reporting for state income tax allocation is time-consuming and costly, especially for small and medium-sized businesses with small accounting and legal staffs. Agreement is widespread that states should adopt uniform rules, but there is disagreement on what factors should be considered and who should administer the rules.

Under some legislative proposals, businesses subject to taxation would have the option of computing their state income tax liability under the existing state formula or under an optional federally prescribed tax apportionment formula (presumably either the three-factor payroll, property, and sales formula or the two-factor payroll and property formula). No business would have to pay a state tax greater than that calculated under the optional prescribed formula.

The theory of the two-factor approach is that income should be apportioned according to the factors used in producing it, and sales should be taken into account only to the extent that they involve the use of company facilities or labor in a particular state.

The three-factor approach is advocated on the ground that no income is realized without sales. Sales reflect the relative importance of each state as a market for the output of any particular company and should therefore be given recognition in the division-of-income rules. Supporters of this approach hold that the elimination of the sales factor would create a competitive environment that discriminated against local firms.

There is support for federal legislation to coordinate state taxation of corporate profits, particularly by small firms whose accounting and legal staffs are not prepared to cope with the diversity in state apportionment formulas. But the states are reluctant to give the federal treasury the responsibility for making administrative interpretations that have traditionally been within their own purview. And most of the business community has been unwilling to forgo direct negotiations with state tax officials over the details of the business tax structure.

The corporation income tax accounts for less than 5 percent of state and local revenue in all but three states, so that the overall revenue consequences for the states of either approach are small. Nonetheless, shifts in tax burden could be significant for states with heavy concentrations of particular industries. This gives rise to concern about a state's ability to retain its industrial base if changes in the allocation formula were mandated by the federal government.

2. All forty-five states with sales taxes levy use taxes on out-of-state purchases to complement their sales taxes. The use tax is imposed on the buyer for the privilege of using the commodity in the state and is designed to ensure that tangible personal property used in the state is subject to tax, wherever it may have been purchased. As a rule, states cannot enforce such taxes by collecting them from the purchasers except for registered automobile owners and business purchasers who are registered vendors.

To eliminate tax avoidance in connection with out-of-state purchases, states began to require in-state sellers to out-of-state customers and out-of-state sellers to in-state customers to collect the use tax for them. In 1941 the Supreme Court permitted Iowa to require a mail order house with retail stores in Iowa to collect a use tax on mail order sales sent to its out-of-state customers; and in 1960 it upheld Florida's right to require use tax collections by a Georgia corporation that had representatives in Florida but no office or place of business there.

Although the volume of interstate sales in relation to local sales is small, sales across state lines create some of the most troublesome problems in sales taxation. Interstate sellers object to the requirement that they collect use taxes. The tax base is not uniform from state to state, and interstate sellers sometimes find compliance with use tax collection requirements as burdensome as compliance with state corporation income tax laws. As states rely more and more on these taxes and as rates rise, state tax officials feel an increasing obligation to protect local firms from competition by enforcing the use tax on out-of-state sellers.

Resolution of the issues in state taxation of multistate business involves a balancing of the values of state tax sovereignty against the advantages of, and constitutional requirement for, the free flow of commerce across state lines. With the increasing interdependence of all regions of the country, a higher degree of uniformity and certainty in state taxation of interstate activities is desirable, but the process of accommodation to economic realities by the states and the federal government is painful. The states have recently been more defensive over their tax sovereignty as a result of cutbacks in federal grants and proposals to decentralize government responsibilities.

Although only minimal constraints have been enacted by Congress, the threat of federal legislation has triggered state action. Most of the states have amended their laws or regulations to eliminate practices that were criticized—for example, failing to allow the taxpayer a deduction for the cost of sending a tax auditor to an out-of-state headquarters, or forbidding a trade-in allowance on out-of-state purchases but allowing it on local sales. The multistate tax commission, which has been in existence for almost twenty years, seeks to promote the acceptance of uniform laws, regulations, and procedures, to conduct audits of taxpayers on behalf of a number of states, and to settle disputes that involve a single taxpayer and two or more states by an arbitration procedure. Nevertheless, much remains to be done to improve interstate uniformity and reduce taxpayer costs of complying with the diverse and often conflicting state tax laws.

STATE TAXATION OF NONRESIDENTS. It is a settled rule of law that the states, like the federal government, have the right to tax all the income of their residents, wherever earned, and the right to tax all income originating in the state. Most states have eliminated multiple taxation of the same income by allowing credits for income taxes that must be paid by their residents to other states, provided the other states grant reciprocal credits. In addition to the resident credit, a number of states grant credits to nonresidents for income taxes they pay to their home states, provided those states reciprocate. In 1975 the Supreme Court outlawed the brazen attempt by New Hampshire, a state with no income tax, to take advantage of the resident credit available in its neighboring income tax states by imposing a tax on the income earned in New Hampshire by nonresidents.

The likelihood of an individual's owing tax to two states on the same income is now slight, although situations of multiple taxation do arise when two states, because their definitions of residence vary, claim the same person as a resident.

The problem is more acute when residents of a state without a personal income tax work in a state with such a tax. In these cases, the employees pay income tax to the state in which they are employed but receive no credit in their home states, where their principal tax payments are sales or property taxes. This problem would be solved, of course, if all states taxed personal income, as has been recommended by the ACIR. This group has also recommended the elimination of the nonresident credit and the adoption of a uniform definition of residence. The latter might be required as a condition either for continuing the deductibility feature of the federal income tax or for the enactment of a federal credit in lieu of, or as a supplement to, deductibility (see the discussion of federal assistance below).

COOPERATIVE TAX ADMINISTRATION. Formal federal-state cooperative tax administration dates back to the Revenue Act of 1926. The earliest form of cooperation involved examination of federal income tax returns by state tax officials; in 1950 a plan for coordinated federal-state use of income tax audits was developed. While the states benefited from these arrangements, the federal government received little in return.

In 1957 a new series of agreements on the coordination of tax administration was launched to extend cooperation to other taxes and activities. These agreements, which had been negotiated with forty-eight states by 1983, provide for examination of federal tax returns by state officials and of state returns by federal officials, including the exchange of automatic data processing tapes and information disclosed by federal and state audits. In addition, special enabling legislation permitted the Internal Revenue Service to perform statistical services for state agencies on a reimbursable basis and to enroll state enforcement officers in its training programs. In 1952 a Treasury Department regulation permitted federal agencies to withhold income taxes for state governments. In 1974 Congress passed a bill authorizing federal agencies to withhold income taxes for major cities.

These examples of federal-state cooperation suggest that federal, state, and local tax officials are willing to coordinate their activities in the interest of greater efficiency. In the revenue-sharing legislation enacted in 1972, Congress authorized the federal government to enter into agreements with the states for federal collection of state income taxes if at least two states with 5 percent of the federal individual income tax returns elected to have their income taxes "piggybacked" on the federal system. States showed no interest in this because of the high degree of federal conformity required, the widespread feeling that the federal income tax base may not be the perfect income tax instrument, and the lack of any interest at the federal level in assuming the responsibility for administering state income taxes. In 1976 Congress reduced the number of states needed to start the piggyback system to one, eliminated the requirement for 5 percent of federal returns, and made it explicit that no costs of collection would be charged to any state. With this legislation in place, most of the administrative and compliance benefits of unitary administration (including the same or similar tax returns for all units of government for any one tax, joint audits, and joint collection of taxes other than income taxes) could be achieved by agreement between the federal and state governments rather than through federal coercion. Nevertheless, not a single state has accepted the option to piggyback its income tax on the federal tax, largely because state officials jealously guard their tax prerogatives and view piggybacking as a wedge to undermine their independence. Recent federal legislation that has introduced controversial new tax deductions (such as universal individual retirement accounts and the special deduction for net interest) as well as generous depreciation allowances has strengthened the conviction of many state officials that it would be unwise to accept the federal tax base on both equity and revenue grounds, even in the interest of reducing administrative and compliance costs.

State and Local Fiscal Relations

Most public services enjoyed directly by a resident of the United States—education, health, sanitation and sewerage facilities, welfare aid, and police and fire protection—are provided by local governments. Yet local governments derive all their powers, including fiscal powers, from their parent state governments. Fortunately, the states recognize that local governments cannot be left to their own devices to finance an adequate level of public services.

INCREASING LOCAL TAX CAPACITY. There are limits to the freedom that can be given local governments in the field of taxation. Unless they were restrained by the state governments, they might soon find themselves with a maze of complicated, burdensome, and inefficient local taxes that would impair economic growth. However, several techniques permit local governments to take advantage of the revenue productivity and growth potential of the major nonproperty taxes—sales and personal income taxes—within limits set by the state governments for purposes of control.

Tax supplements. Under this arrangement, the local rate is added to the state rate and the state collects the two taxes and then remits the local share. The tax supplement has the advantages of simplicity, elimination of duplicate administrative costs, and ease of compliance for the taxpayer. It also retains the local governments' freedom to select local tax rates. Local tax supplements on sales taxes are now used in twenty-two states.

Maryland requires its local governments to add their own income tax to the state tax, with a minimum of 20 percent of the state tax and a maximum of 50 percent. Practically all local governments were close to the maximum within three years of the enactment of the legislation. The principal result has been that local property tax increases have been modest compared to increases in other states.

Tax sharing. Most state governments earmark one or more taxes for partial or total distribution to the local governments. The state government decides the tax to be shared, the rate to be imposed, and the formula for allocating receipts. Taxes are frequently returned to the communities where they were collected, but other methods of distribution are also used. Tax sharing imposes statewide uniformity in tax rates and automatically eliminates intercommunity competition. Like the tax supplement, it does away with duplicate tax administration and relieves local governments of unnecessary administrative costs. The device is widely used for automotive taxes, but it may be applied to the entire gamut of state taxes, including income, sales, and cigarette taxes and other excises and fees.

Tax credits. This is a little-used device to force local governments to use a particular tax. The state levies a statewide tax but gives a credit to the taxpayer for a specified portion (sometimes as much as 100 percent) of the tax paid to a local government. In California and Utah tax credits are used to divide the sales tax revenues between counties and cities. The states require the counties to credit sales taxes levied by the cities within their jurisdictions. Florida credits municipal cigarette taxes and Virginia credits municipal taxes on bank shares against the corresponding state taxes. The tax credit is similar to the shared tax, except that local governments may exceed the credit if the state permits. However, the tax credit perpetuates duplicate tax administration, although local governments often benefit from the experience under the state tax.

There is no a priori basis for judging which of these three devices is most appropriate in given circumstances, although each has advantages for particular objectives. In states where a specific tax is not widely used by the local governments, the tax supplement may be the best alternative. Tax sharing will be more acceptable where local taxes tend to be uniform or where the tax to be shared is not widely used at the local level. The tax credit provides the least coordination between state and local governments, but it may be the only alternative in states where the diverse interests of the local governments are difficult to reconcile.

Beyond these alternatives, there is always the possibility of authorizing local taxes even when the state does not levy a similar tax. For example, some states permit their local governments to levy their own

Figure 9-3. *Federal Aid to State and Local Governments and State Aid to Local Governments, Selected Fiscal Years, 1902–50; Annually, 1952–81*

Percent

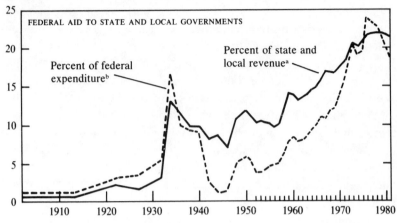

Percent

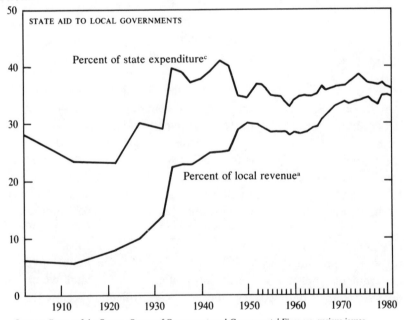

Sources: Bureau of the Census, *Census of Governments* and *Governmental Finances*, various issues.
a. Includes intergovernmental revenue and excludes utility, liquor store, and insurance trust revenue.
b. Includes intergovernmental expenditure and excludes insurance trust expenditure.
c. Includes intergovernmental expenditure and excludes liquor store and insurance trust expenditure.

payroll taxes. Such a tax is particularly appropriate when a tax on commuters is desired.

STATE GRANTS-IN-AID. Grants are similar in many ways to shared taxes. However, instead of distributing funds according to the local tax base, grants provide financial aid to local governments according to some predetermined formula. The source of the revenue may be specified in the legislation, but the grants are often appropriated from general funds. Distribution formulas give weight to such factors as population, number of schoolchildren, income, property tax base, miles of paved street, and so on. The grants are usually for specified purposes (such as schools, roads, and health services), but in recent years general revenue sharing, under which the grants are provided unconditionally for general local use, has become widespread.

State assistance to local governments is not a new phenomenon. It amounted to 6 percent of local general revenue in 1902 and rose to 23 percent in 1934, 30 percent in 1950, 34 percent in 1970, and 35 percent in 1981. Since the early 1930s, state transfers to local governments have amounted to more than one-third of all state expenditures (figure 9-3).

Most state grant systems have grown without systematic planning. They are often complicated and inequitable, and may even defeat the purposes for which they were designed. Distribution formulas remain unchanged for decades despite huge population shifts. Some of the nation's largest cities are denied their appropriate shares of state grants by suburban-dominated state legislatures. The states have become more sensitive to the needs of their counties and cities, however, and this sensitivity is increasing as urban problems multiply. Although there are entrenched interests to overcome, state grant systems are gradually being revamped to meet current requirements.

Federal Aid

State and local governments have received some federal financial assistance since early in the nineteenth century. The early grants, financed by the sale of federal lands, were used for road construction and later to establish and operate the land grant colleges. The amounts were relatively modest until the 1930s, when the desperate financial condition of the states and localities led to the development of a great variety of grants to help finance their programs in education, health, welfare, transportation, housing, and other fields. Federal grants have risen from less than 1 percent of state and local general revenue in 1902 to 11 percent in 1948, 22 percent in 1978 (the peak), and 21 percent in 1981 (figure 9-3).

CONDITIONAL GRANTS-IN-AID. Federal aid is now provided mainly through grants for specific government services. Such grants stimulate increased state and local action in particular areas that serve the national interest. In effect, the grants are used to enlist state and local governments as subcontractors for national programs, such as financing health care for the poor or job training for the disadvantaged.

Conditional grants may also be justified on the ground that the benefits of many public services "spill over" from the community in which they are performed to other communities. For example, an individual may be educated in one state and migrate to another when entering the labor force. In such circumstances, investment in education will be too low if it is financed entirely by state funds, because each state is willing to pay only for benefits likely to accrue to its citizens. Federal assistance would be needed to raise the level of such expenditures closer to the optimum from the national standpoint.

Conditional grants permit the federal government to tailor its assistance to those activities that have the largest spillover effects. It can set minimum standards and require matching funds to assure state or local government support and participation. It can also allocate funds to states and communities where the need for a particular program is greatest or where fiscal capacity is least. The spillover rationale suggests that the assistance should be provided through an open-ended cost-matching grant, but special-purpose federal grants are generally not open-ended.

Conditional grants help finance state and local services without transferring their operation to the federal government. However, the proliferation of grants in the 1950s and 1960s made them increasingly subject to criticism. Critics charged that many specific grants involved excessive federal direction and rigidity, diverted large sums from other urgently needed state and local programs, and were apt to be perpetuated long after their original objectives were met. On the other hand, the ability to control the use of funds and to require state and local financial participation appealed to Congress and private groups that trusted the federal government more than the state and local governments, but were unable to win support for nationally operated programs.

Since 1971 all presidents have recommended consolidation of categorical grants into block grant programs in order to give state and local governments more discretion in the management and allocation of grant funds. Wholesale consolidation of categorical grants into block grants has been rejected by Congress, but elements of the block grant system have been adopted for grants to finance community development, manpower training, urban mass transportation, health care, social services, and child nutrition. President Reagan proposed a swap program between the federal and state governments under which the federal government would assume sole responsibility for medicaid and the states would be given sole responsibility for aid to families with dependent children (AFDC) and food stamps. He also proposed to turn back responsibility for forty-four other grant programs to state governments. He coupled these proposals with an interim trust-fund arrangement consisting of excise and other revenues; after four years, the trust fund was to disappear, a selected list of federal excise taxes would be rolled back, and states would be responsible for financing and operating any of the programs they wished to retain. These proposals were made against a background of sharp cutbacks in federal grant levels. The states objected to the structural features of the program, as well as to the reduction in the grant amounts, and Congress took no action on it.

GENERAL-PURPOSE GRANTS. The federal government first appropriated funds to be given the states for any state or local purpose in 1836, when federal surplus revenues were large enough—partly as a result of receipts from the sale of public lands—to retire the entire national debt and to accumulate a treasury balance besides. Beginning January 1, 1837, the funds were distributed quarterly on the basis of the number of congressmen and senators from each state, which was very nearly the same as a per capita distribution. The federal surplus disappeared before the end of 1837, a recession year, and the grants were terminated after three installments. From 1837 to 1971, all federal grants were conditional.

General-purpose grants are justified on two grounds. First, all states do not have equal capacity to pay for public services. Even though the poorest states make a relatively larger revenue effort (see figure 9-2), they are unable to match the revenue-raising ability of the richer states and cannot provide the range or quality of services offered elsewhere. While on balance conditional grants have an equalizing effect (figure 9-4), the assistance they provide is inadequate for the total needs of the poorer states. Within states, conditional grants have widened fiscal disparities slightly among metropolitan areas rather than narrowing them.

Figure 9-4. *State and Local General Revenue from Own Sources and from Federal Grants, by Quintiles of State per Capita Personal Income, Fiscal Year 1980*

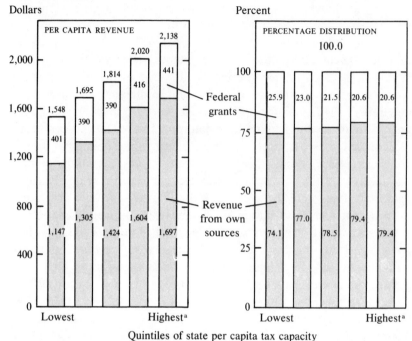

Dollars   Percent

Quintiles of state per capita tax capacity

Source: Bureau of the Census, *Governmental Finances in 1980–81*.
a. Excludes Alaska.

Second, federal use of the best tax sources leaves a wide gap between state and local need and state and local fiscal capacity. Moreover, no state can push its tax rates much higher than those in neighboring states for fear of placing its citizens and business enterprises at a disadvantage. On this line of reasoning, all states need some federal assistance even for purely state or local activities, with the poorer states needing more help because of their low fiscal capacity.

As federal revenue increased during the 1960s, considerable support developed for some way to use part of the increasing federal receipts for general-purpose grants. Several proposals were considered in Congress, including one that was originated by a task force created by President Johnson and later became the central element of the New Federalism program of the Nixon administration. In the end, a general revenue-sharing program was enacted in 1972 for the five years ending December 31, 1976, to provide financial assistance to the states and local governments with few strings attached. In 1976, the legislation was extended to September 30, 1980. It was extended again in 1980 to the end of 1983, this time, however, with assistance to the local governments but not to the states. The major features of the program are:

1. For the first five years a total of $30.2 billion was set aside in a special federal trust fund, with annual amounts ranging from $5.3 billion in the first year to $6.8 billion in the fifth. The annual rate was cut to $5.1 billion in fiscal 1981 and $4.6 billion in 1982 and 1983. The appropriations are automatic and are not subject to the annual budget process.

2. Originally, one-third of the revenue-sharing funds were paid to the states and the other two-thirds to over 38,000 general-purpose local governments; since 1980 all funds have gone to local governments. Allocations among local governments are made on the basis of a formula that gives weight to population, per capita income, and tax effort.

3. Few constraints are imposed on the use of funds. States were permitted to spend the revenue-sharing funds for any purpose. Local governments were originally permitted to spend their revenue-sharing funds on a selected list of items, but the 1976 legislation eliminated these restrictions. Thus the local governments are given considerable flexibility in budgeting their total financial resources.

4. Each state and local government is required to report to the secretary of the treasury on the planned and actual use of the funds and to publish a copy of the reports in a newspaper covering the geographic area of the government making the report.

5. The funds cannot be used for any program that discriminates on the basis of race, color, national origin, or sex. Where such discrimination is found, the secretary of the treasury is directed to withhold all revenue-sharing funds to which the unit of government would be entitled.

In actual practice, the revenue-sharing program has helped equalize the fiscal resources of the states, though not by much (table 9-6). Metropolitan central cities receive more shared revenues than other areas on a per capita basis, but the advantage is not significant if the shared revenues are compared with the total expenditures of the various units of government. As a percentage of nonschool revenues, the assistance to the large urban counties is smaller than to the other counties. Thus far, the revenue-sharing program has not altered the pattern of spending by the state and local governments and has had a limited effect

Table 9-6. *Relation of Revenue-Sharing Grants to State and Local Revenues from Own Sources and to State Personal Income, by States Ranked by 1980 per Capita Personal Income, 1981*

	Revenue-sharing grants in 1981 as a percentage of	
States ranked by 1980 per capita income quintile	*State and local revenues from own sources, 1980–81*	*Personal income, 1980*
Top	1.7	0.23
Second	1.8	0.27
Third	1.7	0.24
Fourth	1.8	0.29
Lowest	2.2	0.33

Source: Bureau of the Census, *Governmental Finances in 1980–81.*

on the decisionmaking processes and institutional structure of state and local governments.

Reaction to the revenue-sharing program depends on attitudes toward the relations between the federal and the state and local governments. The program is opposed by those who wish to control the use of federal funds in great detail, have little faith in the willingness or ability of state and local governments to use the funds wisely, and believe that general-purpose grants will weaken the role of conditional grants. It is supported by those who wish to strengthen the role of the state and local governments and to limit federal control over state and local spending and believe that conditional grants are overworked in the federal system. Some oppose the expansion of federal assistance on the ground that separation of the expenditure and financing functions will lead to excessive and wasteful expenditures. It is also difficult to persuade federal budget officials that revenue sharing should have a high priority when large federal deficits are in the offing for years to come.

The categorical and revenue-sharing grants have very different functions. Categorical grants ensure that the states do not neglect areas where the "spillover" effects are clearly in the national interest. Revenue sharing, on the other hand, gives the states and localities a share in the superior revenue resources of the federal government. If properly designed, revenue sharing could help poorer states and localities provide services of the same scope and quality as those of the wealthier ones without putting far heavier tax burdens on their citizens.

Restriction of revenue-sharing grants to local governments is justified primarily as an economy measure in an era of tight budgets. However, there is no basis in the rationale of the program to deny assistance to the states. Many important local activities are financed entirely, or to a major degree, by state governments (for example, welfare assistance, higher education, and health). The equalization objective of revenue sharing cannot be achieved by a program that denies assistance to the level of government that finances such activities.

In addition to a continuing revenue-sharing program, special financial assistance for state and local governments is needed during recession periods. The programs and activities supported by these units of government should not be turned on and off in response to changes in tax receipts. Moreover, periods of slow growth or recession have a major impact on the ability of the states and local governments to finance their expenditure commitments. In periods of stagflation particularly, local government revenues cannot keep up with the rising costs caused by inflation. Only the federal government can moderate cyclical changes in state and local receipts. On the basis of these considerations, legislation was enacted in 1976 to provide payments automatically to the states and local governments when national unemployment exceeded 6 percent of the labor force. This legislation was enacted after the 1974–75 recession was over, but it did serve to moderate the curtailment of needed state and local programs during the early stages of the recovery. The legislation was not renewed in the 1980 and 1981–82 recessions because of budgetary stringency and the poor timing of the 1976 program.

OTHER METHODS OF FEDERAL ASSISTANCE. Alternatives for accomplishing the objectives of federal grants involve the reduction of federal revenues. These include (1) reducing federal taxes or relinquishing specific types of federal taxes; (2) sharing federal tax collections with the states; and (3) granting credits against federal taxes for state and local taxes. These are the same methods that state governments use to provide assistance to local governments. Such measures would help state and local governments in varying degrees, but they would not achieve the broad objectives sought through the grant device, especially fiscal equalization.

If the objective of reducing federal taxes is to increase state and local fiscal resources, the response of the state and local governments, which depends on action by many different executive and legislative bodies, is bound to be spotty. State and local revenues would rise mainly through the indirect effect of the increased national income resulting from federal tax reduction, but this would amount to only a fraction of the released federal revenues. To the extent that state and local tax receipts increased, the richer states and localities would benefit most.

As has been indicated, tax sharing is a common arrangement at the state and local level, but not at the federal and state level. Since the federal government relies heavily on income taxes, the tax-sharing alternative would greatly reduce federal revenues unless the states were willing to relinquish these taxes or the federal government raised its tax rates to finance the shared revenues.

Tax credits would not automatically increase state and local revenues: state and local governments now imposing the tax that could be credited would have to raise their rates. Since this could be done without raising the total taxes paid by their citizens, they might be encouraged to do so, but there would be strong opposition from groups that would prefer the tax reduction provided by the credit. If the credit applied to income taxes, the ten states without individual income taxes would benefit only after they imposed such a tax. This might be regarded as federal coercion, however, and in some states would face formidable constitutional barriers. The earlier discussion of the estate tax credit suggested that the tax credit could be used as a coordinating device, but it would not redistribute resources to the neediest states.

The Plight of the Cities

In recent years, city finances have emerged as a major fiscal problem. The resources of many of the nation's largest cities, particularly those in the northeast and north central regions of the country, are inadequate to pay for their rapidly growing expenditures. In general, the problems are most acute in the old core cities, which have been losing population to the suburbs, have a high proportion of low-income families, and cannot improve their finances through annexation of or amalgamation with more affluent surrounding communities.

The distress of the old, declining core cities results from several factors.

1. The tax base has been moving from the central city to the suburbs for many years, and the expenses of operating public services for residents and commuters have been rising sharply. The poor, who cannot pay taxes, are concentrated in the cities, while the middle- and high-

income recipients are in the surrounding suburbs. Some of the large cities and counties and urban states have been carrying a major share of the welfare burden, even though poverty is a national problem.

2. State legislatures are often controlled by representatives of the suburbs and small towns who believe that it is in their interest to prevent the cities from levying taxes on suburbanites to pay for the costs they impose on the city. The result is that many cities are shortchanged in state grant programs and others are prohibited from levying taxes on the earnings of commuters. This impoverishes the cities even more and leads to further deterioration of their fiscal capacity.

3. Many cities overextend themselves. Salaries of local government employees rose sharply in the early 1970s, and public employee unions extracted unusually generous pension benefits from city governments. Although inflation may on balance improve the fiscal position of the cities (because property values generally rise faster than the average inflation rate and property tax receipts respond accordingly), frequent recessions and relatively high unemployment in recent years have greatly reduced the fiscal viability of the cities, particularly in areas where large industries are undergoing major structural decline. Budgetary controls are also lax in many cities. Some cities borrow in the short-term market to cover current expenses, a practice that backfires as soon as receipts slacken during a recession. In 1975 New York City forced holders of some of its maturing note issues to accept longer maturities and lower interest rates, and it needed massive state and federal assistance to avoid bankruptcy.

Since the cities are creatures of the states, the states have the responsibility of supervising the city budget and debt procedures to enforce sound fiscal practices. In some states, city budgets or borrowing plans are subject to approval by the state government, but often the procedure has not been taken seriously by either side. To prevent fiscal distress in the cities, state governments should exercise stricter supervision over city fiscal procedures.

In addition to their supervisory role, the state governments also have the responsibility of providing adequate revenue resources for the cities, but most large cities are hamstrung in their efforts to tax suburbanites, who rarely pay their fair share of the costs they impose on the cities. In the absence of metropolitan government, the state governments could solve the problem by making special or block grants to the cities out of state funds and by increasing financial support of such local functions as hospitals and education. Another possibility is to require the suburbs to share their taxes with the cities. One such arrangement is operating in the Minneapolis-St. Paul area, where the central cities share in the growth of property tax bases of the surrounding suburbs under a program approved by the state government.

Since poverty is a national problem, the federal government has been urged to assume the full financial burden of the welfare system. Release of state and local fiscal resources now used to pay welfare benefits would ease the burden of a few of the cities and counties directly and would provide elbow room throughout the country for additional state support of city activities. The program of countercyclical revenue sharing discussed earlier would help prevent the erosion of city tax receipts during periods of high unemployment.

The cities of this country are centers of industry and commerce, education, arts and letters, theater and sports, and other economic, cultural, and recreational activities. These benefits accrue to the residents of the entire area in which the cities are located and, to a lesser extent, to the people throughout the country. Part of the costs of the cities should therefore be shared by residents of other parts of the country. This is the reason both the states and the federal government must be concerned with city finances.

Summary

Despite the sluggish response of their taxes to economic growth, state and local governments have made a good fiscal record since the end of World War II. But they will continue to be hard pressed in the foreseeable future as their financial needs grow.

Most of the additional revenue needed must be raised by the state and local governments themselves. At the state level, the trend is toward the use of both income and sales taxes. In some states, there are long-standing traditions against one or the other of these two major taxes, but historical precedents have broken down under the pressure for more revenue. The adoption in four states of a credit against the income tax for sales taxes paid suggests that the objection to sales taxes on equity grounds can be dealt with effectively. The deductibility of state income taxes under the federal income tax makes income taxation at the state level more acceptable. However, states that permit the deduction of federal income taxes from their own income tax bases should recognize that they lose much more revenue than their taxpayers save and reduce the equity of their income taxes.

At the local level, strengthening of property tax administration is needed. According to the modern theory of incidence, this tax is borne by owners of capital and is therefore progressive. The tax will continue to be the main revenue source of local governments; state governments should take a strong hand in promoting improvements in the professional quality of assessment personnel and assessment procedures. The circuit breaker technique for moderating the property tax burdens of the poor and the elderly is based on the older notion that the property tax is regressive. In actual operation, the circuit breakers use up scarce revenues and are poor substitutes for an effective and equitable program to help the poor. The property tax limitations spawned by Proposition 13 have reduced the capacity of local governments to meet their growing revenue needs and have made them more dependent on the state governments.

The states should supervise local budgetary and debt practices closely to prevent fiscal mismanagement and should expand their use of the tax-sharing or general revenue-sharing device. They might also consider the feasibility of permitting local governments to supplement the property tax with revenues from income or sales taxes. Allowing local governments to levy such taxes has some dangers, but unnecessary complications and inefficiencies can be avoided if local income and sales taxes are levied as supplements to the corresponding state taxes.

Even if they make a substantial effort of their own, state and local governments are unable to meet their needs without federal assistance. Part of this assistance comes from conditional federal grants, which help finance activities in which the federal government has a strong interest. The federal revenue-sharing program, which now gives aid only to local governments with few strings attached, provides assistance for other local programs. The state share of general revenue funds should be restored, since general-purpose as well as categorical grants are essential ingredients of a federal grant policy. Renewal of special countercyclical grants by the federal government to the states and local governments would help cushion the decline in their receipts during recessions.

Historical Summary
of the Major Federal Taxes

THE FEDERAL TAX SYSTEM as we know it today is of fairly recent origin. From 1789 to 1909 the federal government relied almost exclusively on excise taxes and customs. An income tax was used for emergency purposes during the Civil War, and rudimentary death taxes were levied in the years 1797–1802, 1862–70, and 1898–1902. The corporation income tax was enacted in 1909 and the individual income tax—now the backbone of the federal revenue system—was enacted in 1913. The modern estate tax was first levied in 1916 and the gift tax in 1924; the two taxes were unified in 1977. Payroll taxation—now the second largest federal tax source—was introduced by the Social Security Act of 1935.

The Individual Income Tax

The Civil War tax on individual incomes was in effect from 1862 through 1871. The tax contained a flat $600 exemption with no allowance for children, was graduated up to 10 percent (in 1865 and 1866), and was collected at the source on wages, salaries, interest, and dividends. Total revenues under this tax amounted to $376 million. At its peak in 1866, it accounted for almost 25 percent of internal revenue collections. The tax was allowed to lapse in 1872, when the urgent need for revenue disappeared.

For almost twenty years after the expiration of the Civil War tax, there was only isolated support for the reenactment of an income tax. As the country grew and prospered, great industries and fortunes were established, and inequalities in the distribution of income became more disturbing. The income tax was reenacted in 1894, when the country was in a mood for reform against the evils of monopolies and trusts, but it was declared unconstitutional by the Supreme Court in 1895.

The high court held that the portion of the personal income tax that fell on income from land was a "direct" tax, which the Constitution stipulated must be apportioned among the states according to population. The decision was assailed by many groups, and agitation for a change in the Constitution continued until the Sixteenth Amendment was ratified in 1913. This amendment stated that "Congress shall have power to lay and collect taxes on incomes, from whatever source derived, without apportionment among the several States, and without regard to any census or enumeration."

The 1913 tax, which was enacted shortly after the Sixteenth Amendment was ratified, applied to wages, salaries, interest, dividends, rents, entrepreneurial incomes, and capital gains. It allowed deductions for personal interest and tax payments, as well as for business expenses. It exempted federal, state, and local government bond interest and the salaries of state and local government employees; it also exempted dividends from the normal tax but not from surtax. Taxes were collected at the source on wages and salaries, interest, rents, and annuities, with an exemption of $3,000 for single persons and $4,000 for married couples. A normal tax of 1 percent was applied to income above the exempted amounts, with a surtax of 1 to 6 percent.

The most significant changes made since the original 1913 act are the following: an allowance for dependents and a deduction for charitable contributions were introduced in 1917; collection at the source was eliminated in 1916 and was reenacted for wages and salaries in 1943; preferential rates on long-term capital gains were adopted in 1921; in 1939 the exemption of the salaries of state and local government employees was eliminated; the sale of tax-exempt federal bonds was discontinued in 1941; the standard deduction and the per capita personal exemption were adopted in 1944; income splitting for married couples was enacted in 1948; an averaging system and a minimum standard deduction were introduced in 1964; in 1969 the minimum standard deduction was replaced by a low-income allowance, and a minimum tax on selected preference incomes and a top marginal rate on earned income of 50 percent were adopted; in 1975 a refundable earned-income credit was introduced to alleviate the burden of the payroll tax on low-income recipients; in 1977 the low-income allowance was replaced by a zero-rate bracket; in 1982 the top marginal rate on unearned income was reduced to the 50 percent rate applied to earned income, and a 10 percent deduction (5 percent for 1982) was provided for two-earner couples on the first $30,000 of earned income of the spouse with lower earnings for 1983 and later years; and beginning in 1985 the rate brackets and the personal exemptions will be adjusted annually for inflation.

Rates and exemptions have changed frequently (tables A-1 through A-5). Maximum marginal rates reached 77 percent during World War I, 94 percent during World War II, and 92 percent during the Korean War. They declined to 24 percent in the 1920s and rose to 79 percent in the 1930s; in the late 1950s and early 1960s, the maximum rate was 91 percent. From 1965 to 1980 the permanent maximum rate was 70 percent. A special Vietnam War surcharge was in effect at 7.5 percent of tax in 1968, 10 percent in 1969, and 2.5 percent in 1970. The permanent maximum rate was reduced to 69.125 percent in 1981 and then to 50 percent beginning in 1982. Exemptions showed a downward trend during the first three decades of income taxation in this country, reaching a low of $500 per taxpayer during World War II, and then rose to $600 for each personal exemption in 1948, $625 in 1970, $675 in 1971, $750 in 1972, and $1,000 in 1979. Since 1975 low-income families with children have been permitted to deduct as a credit against their tax (with refunds for those who are not taxable or whose tax does not equal the credit) 10 percent of their earned income. From 1975 to 1978, the credit applied to $4,000 of earned income, phasing down to zero at $8,000; beginning in 1979 it applies to the first $5,000 of earned income, phasing down to zero at $10,000.

The Corporation Income Tax

The general corporation income tax rate began at 1 percent in 1909 and reached 12 percent during World War I, 13.5 percent in the 1920s, 40 percent during World War II, and 52 percent during the Korean War. The Revenue Act of 1964 reduced the rate to 50 percent for 1964 and 48 percent beginning in 1965 (table A-6). The Vietnam War surcharge also applied to corporations at 10 percent of tax in 1968 and 1969 and 2.5 percent in 1970. The current rate of 46 percent became effective in 1979.

Between 1909 and 1935 the tax was levied at a proportional rate on taxable income. A small exemption was allowed in computing taxable income for sporadic periods: $5,000 in the years 1909–13; $2,000 in 1918–

27; and $3,000 in 1928–31. Graduation was introduced for the first time in 1936, with rates ranging from 8 percent on the first $2,000 of taxable income to 15 percent on income over $40,000.

Beginning in 1938 graduation was limited to corporations with incomes of $25,000 or less. Above this point, a flat rate applied to all the taxable income of the corporation, on the theory that rate graduation in the corporation income tax cannot be defended on equity grounds as in the case of individuals. The limited graduation was intended as a concession to small business. This rationale produced a peculiar rate schedule, which persisted until the end of 1949. For example, between 1942 and 1945 the rates began at 25 percent on the first $5,000 of taxable income and rose to 53 percent for taxable incomes between $25,000 and $50,000 (table A-7); beginning at $50,000, the rate was a flat 40 percent on total taxable income. The 53 percent rate—called the "notch" rate—was just enough to raise the corporation rate to 40 percent at $50,000 and thus avoided a discontinuity in effective rates at that point.

While it produced the desired result, the notch rate was regarded as a penalty on small business. After considerable agitation, the 1950 act removed the notch rate and restored a simple two-bracket system of graduation. This was accomplished by enacting a normal tax applying to all corporation profits and a surtax applying to profits in excess of $25,000. For the years 1952–63 the combined rates were 30 percent on the first $25,000 and 52 percent on the amount in excess of $25,000. They were reduced to 22 percent and 50 percent in 1964 and to 22 percent and 48 percent in 1965. Including the Vietnam War surcharge, the rates were 24.2 percent and 52.8 percent for 1968 and 1969 and 22.55 percent and 49.2 percent for 1970. They returned to 22 percent and 48 percent in 1971. In 1975 graduation was extended to $50,000, with rates of 20 percent on the first $25,000 and 22 percent on the next $25,000. In 1979 graduation was extended further to $100,000, with rates of 17, 20, 30, and 40 percent on successive $25,000 segments; the top rate of 46 percent applies to the amount of taxable income above $100,000. The rates on the first two $25,000 segments were reduced to 16 and 19 percent in 1982 and to 15 and 18 percent beginning in 1983.

Dividends distributed by corporations were excluded from the individual *normal* tax before 1936 and were subject to the *surtax* (which was the progressive element of the individual income tax). In 1936 this exclusion was removed, and a tax on undistributed profits was imposed at the corporate level. This tax was intended to force corporations to distribute most of their earnings as dividends. The tax was vigorously attacked as a deterrent to corporate growth and was repealed after being in operation for only two years.

Between 1939 and 1954 the individual and corporation income taxes were levied without any attempt to integrate the two taxes as they applied to dividends. In 1954 individuals were allowed to exclude the first $50 of dividends from their taxable income ($100 for joint returns) and to subtract as a credit from the tax 4 percent of the dividends received in excess of the exclusion. After a decade of debate, Congress reduced the credit to 2 percent in 1964 and eliminated it entirely beginning in 1965; at the same time, the exclusion was increased to $100 ($200 for joint returns). The exclusion was raised to $200 ($400 for joint returns) for dividends and interest income for 1981 and then reverted back to $100 ($200 for joint returns) for dividends only in 1982.

The corporation income tax was supplemented by an excess profits tax during World Wars I and II and the Korean War. The method adopted was to tax at a very heavy rate (as high as 95 percent in World War II) the excess of a corporation's profits over a prewar base period or over a "normal" rate of return (specified in the statute) on invested capital. For example, the base period for the World War II excess profits tax was 1936–39. The excess profits tax creates difficult economic, equity, and administrative problems; taxation of even a portion of a corporation's net profits at rates close to 100 percent tends to be unfair. To relieve the most glaring inequities, the law provided alternative methods of computing excess profits and also permitted adjustments for hardship cases. But such provisions made a complicated law even more difficult to administer. Experience to date indicates that excess profits taxation is appropriate only for wartime use.

Excise Taxes

Immediately after the ratification of the Constitution, the new government introduced a fairly elaborate system of excise taxes, including taxes on carriages, liquor, snuff, sugar, and auction sales. Even at that time, these taxes were considered unfair and burdensome to the poor. The Whiskey Rebellion of 1794 was a revolt by farmers against the federal tax, which ran up to thirty cents a gallon. Except for the tax on salt, the early excises were abolished by the Jefferson administration in

1802, revived during the War of 1812, and then terminated again in 1817, not to reappear until the Civil War.

The Civil War excise tax system foreshadowed what was to happen during every major war thereafter. Liquor and tobacco taxes, which remained as permanent parts of the federal revenue system after the war, were supplemented by taxes on manufactured goods, gross receipts of transportation companies, advertising, licenses, legal documents, and financial transactions. During World War I, the list was again expanded, this time to include special occupational taxes and taxes on theater admissions, telephone calls, and retail sales of jewelry, toilet preparations, and luggage. After the war, tobacco and stamp taxes remained as the major excise taxes. The liquor taxes remained in effect throughout the Prohibition era.

A break with peacetime precedent was made during the early 1930s, when Congress enacted a series of manufacturers' excise taxes on such items as automobiles, trucks, buses, appliances, and other consumer durables; also taxed were long distance calls. These taxes were to be continued at varying rates and with varying degrees of comprehensiveness until 1965. The Depression taxes were enacted after an attempt to introduce a general manufacturers' sales tax was defeated in Congress. During World War II, the rates of most of the then existing excise taxes were increased, and new excise taxes were introduced on retail sales of furs, jewelry, luggage, and toilet preparations, local telephone service, and passenger and freight transportation.

A bill to reduce the excise taxes was passed by the House just as the Korean War began. These changes were quickly eliminated from the Revenue Act of 1950, which was enacted three months after the beginning of hostilities. In the following year, the excise taxes on liquor, tobacco, gasoline, automobiles, consumer durables, and other products were increased, and new taxes on wagering and diesel fuel were adopted.

A major innovation in excise taxation was introduced in 1956, when a number of excise taxes were earmarked for the specially created Highway Trust Fund to finance the construction of the federal highway system. The earmarked taxes included the old taxes (with increased rates) on gasoline, diesel, and special motor fuels, trucks, and tires, and new taxes on tread rubber and the use of heavy trucks and buses on the highways. The Airport and Airway Trust Fund was set up along similar lines in 1970 to finance construction of airports and improvements in the airway system. The taxes earmarked for this fund included those on passenger tickets, air freight, gasoline used by general aviation aircraft, tires and tubes used on aircraft, a special tax on international air trips, and an annual aircraft user tax.

The Korean War excise tax structure was dismantled beginning in 1954; the process took more than a decade. The original Korean War tax increases had been enacted for a period of three years, but most of them were extended each year as revenue requirements forced continued postponements of their repeal. The first significant break came in 1954, when all excise tax rates in excess of 10 percent were reduced to 10 percent, with the exception of the 20 percent cabaret tax. The freight tax was repealed in 1958; the cabaret tax was reduced to 10 percent in 1960; and in 1962 the railroad and bus passenger tax was eliminated and the air transportation tax was reduced from 10 percent to 5 percent. An interest equalization tax was enacted in 1964 (retroactive to July 1963) for balance-of-payments reasons and was allowed to expire on June 30, 1974. In 1965 Congress scaled down the Korean War excises to all but a few major taxes levied for sumptuary and regulatory reasons and as user charges. The telephone tax, levied at a 10 percent rate during the Korean War, was scheduled to be phased out gradually and to expire at the end of 1981, but it was later extended to the end of 1984 and then to the end of 1985.

A special excise tax on crude oil production—called a "windfall profits" tax—was enacted in 1980 as part of the program to deregulate oil prices. This tax is imposed on the difference between the selling price of oil and the price in May 1979. The tax is scheduled to expire over a thirty-three-month period beginning on January 1, 1988.

The Tax Equity and Fiscal Responsibility Act of 1982 doubled the cigarette excise tax from January 1, 1982, to September 30, 1985, and increased the local telephone tax for the years 1983–85. It also increased the airway user taxes and extended them to the end of 1987. The Highway Revenue Act of 1982 raised the gasoline and other motor fuels taxes and extended them to October 1, 1988.

Federal excise taxes are now confined to five general categories: (1) alcohol and tobacco taxes; (2) manufacturers' excises on automobiles, gasoline, tires and related items, as well as firearms, sporting goods, and mined coal; (3) retailers' excises on certain fuels and on trucks and trailers; (4) a windfall profits tax on domestically produced crude oil; and (5) miscellaneous excises on such diverse items as telephone services, air transportation, foreign insurance policies, and the use of certain highway vehicles (table A-8).

Payroll Taxes

The Social Security Act of 1935 imposed payroll taxes to finance the old age insurance system and unemployment compensation benefits. Later the tax was used to finance survivor, disability, and health insurance. Railroad employees are covered under a separate system of taxation, which is similar to, but not identical with, the general social insurance system.

The OASDHI Taxes

The 1935 act established the principle that the retirement system would be financed by equal taxes on employers and employees. Under the original act, the tax was 1 percent for employer and employee on covered wages up to $3,000 per employee. The act also provided a schedule of rate increases for subsequent years, reaching a maximum of 3 percent for 1949 and later years. However, the original increases were deferred when the social security trust fund accumulated substantial reserves. Later, as benefits were raised and coverage of disability and health were added, both the tax and the ceiling on earnings were increased repeatedly. Beginning in 1973 the maximum taxable earnings level has been adjusted upward annually on the basis of increases in the consumer price index. In 1986 the payroll tax is expected to apply to the first $42,000 of earnings; and the tax rate will be 7.15 percent each on the employer and the employee (table A-9). The tax rate is scheduled to increase to 7.51 percent in 1988 and 7.65 percent in 1990.

The original act exempted agricultural and domestic labor, members of the professions, public employees, a few other classes of employees, and the self-employed. Coverage has been gradually expanded to include all employed people except federal civilian employees (who are covered by their own retirement system), self-employed persons who have self-employment income of less than $400 a year, domestic and farm workers earning less than specified amounts from a single employer, and state and local employees on an optional basis. Coverage of the self-employed began in 1951 at a rate one and one-half times the corresponding rate for employees (rounded to the nearest 0.1 percent beginning in 1962). The tax rate applicable to the earnings of the self-employed was fixed at lower levels—7.5 percent in 1971–72, 8.0 percent in 1973, 7.9 percent in

1974–77, 8.1 percent in 1978–80, 9.3 percent in 1981, and 9.35 percent in 1982–83. Beginning in 1984, the tax rate for the self-employed was raised to the combined tax paid by employers and employees, and a tax credit was allowed against the income tax to give the self-employed approximately the same offset provided to employers who deduct employee taxes in computing taxable income.

The Unemployment Insurance Tax

The unemployment insurance tax was originally imposed in 1936 on employers of eight or more persons at a rate of 1 percent of payrolls, with automatic increases to 2 percent in 1937 and 3 percent in 1938 and later years. The coverage was expanded to employers of four or more in 1956 and to employers of one or more in 1972. The tax rate was increased to 3.1 percent in 1961, raised temporarily to 3.5 percent in 1962 and 3.35 percent in 1963, restored to 3.1 percent in 1964–69, and raised to 3.2 percent in 1970–76 (except for 1973, when it was 3.28 percent), 3.4 percent in 1977–82, 3.5 percent in 1983–84, and 6.2 percent beginning in 1985. The 1985 tax includes a permanent tax of 6.0 percent and a temporary 0.2 percent that will remain in effect until all outstanding general revenue loans to the unemployment fund have been repaid. The tax was originally applicable to all wages and was limited to $3,000 of wages in 1939–71, $4,200 in 1972–77, $6,000 in 1978–82, and $7,000 beginning in 1983 (see table A-10).

The federal government allows a credit against its tax for amounts contributed to state unemployment insurance programs. The credit was originally set at 2.7 percent of covered wages and was increased to 5.4 percent beginning in 1985. The remainder of the federal tax (0.8 percent beginning in 1985 until loans to the trust fund are repaid and 0.6 percent thereafter) is used to pay the administrative costs of the state programs.

To use up the federal credit, state unemployment taxes will be levied at the standard rate of 5.4 percent beginning in 1985 (2.7 percent in prior years). In three states the tax is levied on employers and employees; in the others it is levied only on employers. In almost all states, employers are taxed according to an experience rating that may result in a larger or smaller tax than the standard rate. This device permits states to lower the tax rates on firms with stable employment and to increase it on those with unstable employment. However, the full credit is allowed against the federal tax where the tax rate has been reduced by a good experience rating. As a result of these provisions, tax rates differ greatly from one state to another as well as within a single state.

Railroad Taxes

Payroll tax rates have always been higher in the railroad industry than in other industries. The retirement tax for railroad employees dates back to 1937, when the rate was 2.75 percent each on employers and employees, and the maximum monthly wage subject to the tax was $300. Since 1937 the rates and wages subject to tax have been changed frequently, rising to 10.6 percent of wages up to $900 a month in the first nine months of 1973.

Beginning on October 1, 1973, the equal contribution scheme was abolished and a two-tier system was substituted. Tier I taxes are linked to the taxes paid for social security; Tier II taxes pay for the railroad retirement benefits, which are independent of social security. Railroad workers also pay the hospital insurance tax paid by workers covered under social security. The combined employer-employee taxes reached 27.15 percent of covered payrolls in 1983, of which 8.7 percent was paid by employees and the remaining 18.45 percent by employers. As in the case of social security, the maximum taxable earnings level has been automatically raised in accordance with increases in the consumer price index since 1973. The maximum taxable level for the Tier II taxes reached $2,225 a month in 1983 (table A-9).

The railroad unemployment insurance program is supported by a tax on wages of up to $400 per month per employee paid by the employers. Before 1948 the tax rate was 3 percent. It was reduced to 0.5–3 percent in 1948–59, the variation depending on the financial condition of the trust fund, and was raised to 1.5–3.75 percent on June 1, 1959, 1.5–4.0 percent from 1962 to 1975, and 0.5–8.0 percent beginning in 1976. The actual rates paid were 0.5 percent of payrolls in 1948–55, 4 percent in 1962–75, and 8 percent in 1981–83 (table A-10).

Estate and Gift Taxes

The 1916 estate tax was levied at rates ranging from 1 percent to 10 percent, with an exemption of $50,000. During World War I the rates ranged from 2 percent to 25 percent. In 1926 the top rate was reduced to 20 percent, and the exemption was increased to $100,000.

One of the major developments during the 1920s was the enactment of a credit for state death taxes against the federal tax. Some of the states requested that the federal government abandon the death tax field entirely, but the credit was enacted instead. It was first limited to 25 percent of the federal tax in 1924 and was then raised to 80 percent in 1926. The same credit (based on the 1926 rates) exists today, even though the federal tax has been increased (table A-11).

Substantial changes in rates and exemptions were made during the 1930s. The exemption was reduced to $50,000 in 1932 and to $40,000 in 1935, and then was raised to $60,000 in 1942, when a special $40,000 exclusion for life insurance (enacted in 1918) was repealed. In 1976 the exemption was converted to a tax credit, to be used for both estate and gift tax purposes; this tax credit started at the exemption equivalent of $120,667 in 1977 and rose to $175,625 in 1981. The 1981 act raised the credits to $62,800 in 1982, $79,300 in 1983, $96,300 in 1984, $121,800 in 1985, $155,800 in 1986, and $192,800 in 1987. These credits are equivalent to exemptions of $225,000, $275,000, $325,000, $400,000, $500,000, and $600,000, respectively.

The top rate was increased in several steps from 45 percent in 1932 to 77 percent in 1940. It was reduced to 70 percent in 1977, when the estate and gift taxes were unified and to 65 percent in 1982, 60 percent in 1983, 55 percent in 1984, and 50 percent in 1985 and later years (table A-12).

The gift tax was first levied for two years in 1924 and 1925 but was repealed on the ground that it was too complicated for the revenue it yielded. It was reenacted in 1932, when the estate tax rates were greatly increased, to limit avoidance of the estate and income taxes. The gift tax was unified with the estate tax beginning January 1, 1977.

Gift tax rates were originally set at 75 percent of estate tax rates and were raised to the full estate tax rates beginning in 1977. A lifetime gift tax exemption of $50,000 was adopted in 1932, when the present gift tax was enacted. This exemption was reduced to $40,000 in 1935 and to $30,000 in 1942; beginning in 1977, when the unified credit was made applicable to gifts and estates, the separate lifetime gift tax exemption was repealed. In addition to the lifetime exemption, taxpayers were allowed an annual exclusion of $5,000 for each donee under the 1932 act. This exclusion was reduced to $4,000 in 1938 and $3,000 in 1942, and increased to $10,000 in 1982 (table A-13).

Splitting estates and gifts between husbands and wives was allowed beginning in 1948. A marital deduction is allowed for bequests of noncommunity property to surviving spouses, up to one-half of the estate. Similarly, one-half of gifts of noncommunity property by one spouse to the other is not subject to gift tax. Gifts of noncommunity property to third persons are treated as though half were made by each spouse. In the case of community property, property acquired during marriage by a husband or wife (except property acquired by gift or inheritance) belongs equally to each spouse and is therefore automatically split for estate and gift tax purposes. In 1977 the marital deduction for bequests was liberalized to $250,000 or one-half the estate, whichever is higher; for gifts, the marital deduction was set at 100 percent of the first $100,000 and 50 percent for amounts above $200,000 (no deduction was allowed for amounts between $100,000 and $200,000). Beginning in 1982, a full deduction was allowed for all interspousal transfers under the unified estate and gift tax.

In addition to the conversion of the exemption to a credit and the unification of the estate and gift taxes, the Tax Reform Act of 1976 imposed a tax on "generation-skipping" transfers of trust property. This tax is intended to plug the generation-skipping loophole for transfers in trust under the former estate and gift taxes.

Table A-1. *History of Federal Individual Income Tax Exemptions and First and Top Bracket Rates*

Dollars unless otherwise specified

	Personal exemptions[a]			Tax rates[b]			
				First bracket		Top bracket	
Year	Single persons	Married couples	Depen- dents	Rate (percent)	Taxable income up to	Rate (percent)	Taxable income over
1913–15	3,000	4,000	. . .	1	20,000	7	500,000
1916	3,000	4,000	. . .	2	20,000	15	2,000,000
1917	1,000	2,000	200	2	2,000	67	2,000,000
1918	1,000	2,000	200	6	4,000	77	1,000,000
1919–20	1,000	2,000	200	4	4,000	73	1,000,000
1921	1,000	2,500[c]	400	4	4,000	73	1,000,000
1922	1,000	2,500[c]	400	4	4,000	56	200,000
1923	1,000	2,500[c]	400	3	4,000	56	200,000
1924	1,000	2,500	400	1.5[d]	4,000	46	500,000
1925–28	1,500	3,500	400	1⅛[d]	4,000	25	100,000
1929	1,500	3,500	400	⅜[d]	4,000	24	100,000
1930–31	1,500	3,500	400	1⅛[d]	4,000	25	100,000
1932–33	1,000	2,500	400	4	4,000	63	1,000,000
1934–35	1,000	2,500	400	4[e]	4,000	63	1,000,000
1936–39	1,000	2,500	400	4[e]	4,000	79	5,000,000
1940	800	2,000	400	4.4[e]	4,000	81.1	5,000,000
1941	750	1,500	400	10[e]	2,000	81	5,000,000
1942–43[f]	500	1,200	350	19[e]	2,000	88	200,000
1944–45[g]	500	1,000	500	23	2,000	94[h]	200,000
1946–47	500	1,000	500	19	2,000	86.45[h]	200,000
1948–49	600	1,200	600	16.6	4,000	82.13[h]	400,000
1950	600	1,200	600	17.4	4,000	91[h]	400,000
1951	600	1,200	600	20.4	4,000	91[h]	400,000
1952–53	600	1,200	600	22.2	4,000	92[h]	400,000
1954–63	600	1,200	600	20	4,000	91[h]	400,000
1964	600	1,200	600	16	1,000	77	400,000
1965–67	600	1,200	600	14	1,000	70	200,000
1968	600	1,200	600	14	1,000	75.25[i]	200,000
1969	600	1,200	600	14	1,000	77[i]	200,000

Table A-1 (continued)

Year	Personal exemptions[a]			Tax rates[b]			
				First bracket		Top bracket	
	Single persons	Married couples	Dependents	Rate (percent)	Taxable income up to	Rate (percent)	Taxable income over
1970	625	1,250	625	14	1,000	71.75[i,j]	200,000
1971	675	1,350	675	14	1,000	70[j,k]	200,000
1972–78	750[l]	1,500[l]	750[l]	14[m]	1,000	70[j,k]	200,000
1979–80	1,000	2,000	1,000	14[m]	2,100	70[j,k]	212,000
1981	1,000	2,000	1,000	13.825[m,n]	2,100	69.125[j,k,n]	212,000
1982	1,000	2,000	1,000	12[m]	2,100	50[j]	82,200
1983	1,000	2,000	1,000	12[m]	2,100	50[j]	106,000
1984 and after	1,000	2,000	1,000	12[m]	2,100	50[j]	159,000

Sources: Relevant public laws and summaries prepared by the Joint Committee on Taxation.

a. Since 1948 taxpayers who are blind or over sixty-five have been allowed additional exemptions.

b. Taxable income excludes zero-bracket amount beginning in 1977. Rates shown apply only to married persons filing joint returns beginning in 1948. For the relationship of other rates to these rates, see table A-4, note a. Beginning in 1922 lower rates applied to long-term capital gains. See text, pp. 109–14.

c. If net income exceeded $5,000, a married person's exemption was $2,000.

d. After earned-income credit equal to 25 percent of tax on earned income.

e. Before earned-income credit allowed as a deduction equal to 10 percent of earned net income.

f. Exclusive of Victory tax.

g. Exemptions shown were for surtax only. Normal tax exemption was $500 per tax return plus earned income of wife up to $500 on joint returns.

h. Subject to the following maximum effective rate limitations:

Year	Maximum effective rate	Year	Maximum effective rate
1944–45	90.0 percent	1951	87.2 percent
1946–47	85.5	1952–53	88.0
1948–49	77.0	1954–63	87.0
1950	87.0		

i. Includes surcharge of 7.5 percent in 1968, 10 percent in 1969, and 2.5 percent in 1970.

j. Does not include add-on minimum tax on preference items or alternative minimum tax.

k. Earned income was subject to maximum marginal rates of 60 percent in 1971 and 50 percent from 1972 through 1981.

l. In addition to the personal exemptions, a per capita tax credit of $30 was allowed for 1975, and $35 per capita or 2 percent of the first $9,000 of taxable income, whichever was higher, for 1976–78.

m. From 1975 through 1978 earned-income credit of 10 percent of earned income up to $4,000 (phased down to zero at $8,000) was allowed. Beginning in 1979, earned-income credit of 10 percent of earned income up to $5,000 allowed (phased down to zero between $6,000 and $10,000).

n. After tax credit of 1.25 percent against regular tax.

Table A-2. *Federal Individual Income Tax Rate Schedules, 1944–47*

Percent

Taxable income (dollars)	1944 act Calendar years 1944–45	1945 act Calendar years 1946–47
0–2,000	23	19.00
2,000–4,000	25	20.90
4,000–6,000	29	24.70
6,000–8,000	33	28.50
8,000–10,000	37	32.30
10,000–12,000	41	36.10
12,000–14,000	46	40.85
14,000–16,000	50	44.65
16,000–18,000	53	47.50
18,000–20,000	56	50.35
20,000–22,000	59	53.20
22,000–26,000	62	56.05
26,000–32,000	65	58.90
32,000–38,000	68	61.75
38,000–44,000	72	65.55
44,000–50,000	75	68.40
50,000–60,000	78	71.25
60,000–70,000	81	74.10
70,000–80,000	84	76.95
80,000–90,000	87	79.80
90,000–100,000	90	82.65
100,000–150,000	92	84.55
150,000–200,000	93	85.50
200,000 and over[a]	94	86.45

Sources: Relevant public laws and summaries prepared by the Joint Committee on Taxation.
a. Subject to the following maximum effective rate limitations: 90.0 percent for 1944–45 and 85.5 percent for 1946–47.

Table A-3. *Federal Individual Income Tax Rate Schedules, 1948–63*[a]
Percent

Taxable income (dollars)	1948 act Calendar years 1948–49	1950 act Calendar year 1950	1951 act Calendar year 1951	1951 act Calendar years 1952–53	1951 act Calendar years 1954–63
0–4,000	16.60	17.40	20.4	22.2	20
4,000–8,000	19.36	20.02	22.4	24.6	22
8,000–12,000	22.88	23.66	27.0	29.0	26
12,000–16,000	26.40	27.30	30.0	34.0	30
16,000–20,000	29.92	30.94	35.0	38.0	34
20,000–24,000	33.44	34.58	39.0	42.0	38
24,000–28,000	37.84	39.13	43.0	48.0	43
28,000–32,000	41.36	42.77	48.0	53.0	47
32,000–36,000	44.00	45.50	51.0	56.0	50
36,000–40,000	46.64	48.23	54.0	59.0	53
40,000–44,000	49.28	50.96	57.0	62.0	56
44,000–52,000	51.92	53.69	60.0	66.0	59
52,000–64,000	54.56	56.42	63.0	67.0	62
64,000–76,000	57.20	59.15	66.0	68.0	65
76,000–88,000	60.72	62.79	69.0	72.0	69
88,000–100,000	63.36	65.52	73.0	75.0	72
100,000–120,000	66.00	68.25	75.0	77.0	75
120,000–140,000	68.64	70.98	78.0	80.0	78
140,000–160,000	71.28	73.71	82.0	83.0	81
160,000–180,000	73.92	76.44	84.0	85.0	84
180,000–200,000	76.56	79.17	87.0	88.0	87
200,000–273,438.20	78.32	80.99 ⎫	89.0	90.0	89
273,438.20–300,000	80.3225	82.503 ⎭			
300,000–400,000	81.2250	83.43	90.0	91.0	90
400,000 and over[b]	82.1275	84.357	91.0	92.0	91

Sources: Relevant public laws and summaries prepared by the Joint Committee on Taxation.
a. Since 1948 married couples have been allowed to split their income for tax purposes. Rates shown are for married couples filing joint returns. Rate brackets for married persons filing separate returns are half the width of the joint return brackets. A separate rate schedule was adopted in 1952 for heads of households to give them approximately half the advantage of income splitting.
b. Subject to the following maximum effective rate limitations:

Year	Maximum effective rate
1948–49	77.0 percent
1950	87.0
1951	87.2
1952–53	88.0
1954–63	87.0

Table A-4. *Federal Individual Income Tax Rate Schedules, 1964–78*[a]

Percent

Taxable income (dollars)[b]	1964 act		1968 act		1969 act	
	Calendar year 1964	Calendar years 1965–67	Calendar year 1968[c]	Calendar year 1969[c]	Calendar year 1970[c,d]	Calendar years 1971–78[d,e,f]
0–1,000	16.0	14	14	14	14	14
1,000–2,000	16.5	15	15	15	15	15
2,000–3,000	17.5	16	17.2	17.6	16.4	16
3,000–4,000	18.0	17	18.275	18.7	17.425	17
4,000–8,000	20.0	19	20.425	20.9	19.475	19
8,000–12,000	23.5	22	23.650	24.2	22.55	22
12,000–16,000	27.0	25	26.875	27.5	25.625	25
16,000–20,000	30.5	28	30.1	30.8	28.7	28
20,000–24,000	34.0	32	34.4	35.2	32.8	32
24,000–28,000	37.5	36	38.7	39.6	36.9	36
28,000–32,000	41.0	39	41.925	42.9	39.975	39
32,000–36,000	44.5	42	45.15	46.2	43.05	42
36,000–40,000	47.5	45	48.375	49.5	46.125	45
40,000–44,000	50.5	48	51.6	52.8	49.2	48
44,000–52,000	53.5	50	53.75	55.0	51.25	50
52,000–64,000	56.0	53	56.975	58.3	54.325	53
64,000–76,000	58.5	55	59.125	60.5	56.375	55
76,000–88,000	61.0	58	62.35	63.8	59.45	58
88,000–100,000	63.5	60	64.5	66.0	61.5	60
100,000–120,000	66.0	62	66.65	68.2	63.55	62
120,000–140,000	68.5	64	68.8	70.4	65.6	64
140,000–160,000	71.0	66	70.95	72.6	67.65	66
160,000–180,000	73.5	68	73.1	74.8	69.7	68
180,000–200,000	75.0	69	74.175	75.9	70.725	69
200,000–400,000	76.5	70	75.25	77.0	71.75	70
400,000 and over	77.0	70	75.25	77.0	71.75	70

Sources: Relevant public laws and summaries prepared by the Joint Committee on Taxation.

a. Since 1948 married couples have been allowed to split their income for tax purposes. Rate brackets for married persons filing separate returns are half the width of the joint return brackets. A separate rate schedule was adopted in 1952 for heads of households to give them approximately half the advantage of income splitting. Under the 1969 act a separate schedule for single persons who are not heads of households was provided to limit the tax paid by single persons to no more than 20 percent more than the tax paid by married couples.

b. Excludes zero-bracket amount in 1977–78.

c. Includes surcharge of 7.5 percent in 1968, 10 percent in 1969, and 2.5 percent in 1970, beginning with the $2,000–$3,000 bracket. A partial surcharge exemption, based on a graduated scale, applied to this and the next higher bracket. The marginal rates in these brackets therefore varied slightly from those shown here.

d. Does not include minimum tax on preference items.

e. Earned income subject to maximum marginal rates of 60 percent in 1971 and 50 percent beginning in 1972.

f. Does not allow for 10 percent rebate of 1974 taxes (maximum of $200) or a refundable earned-income credit of 10 percent earned income up to $4,000 (phased down to zero at $8,000) beginning in 1975.

Table A-5. *Federal Individual Income Tax Rate Schedules,*
1979 and Later Years[a]
Percent

Taxable income (dollars)[b]	1978 act Calendar years 1979–80[c,d,e]	1981 act[c,e] Calendar year 1981[e,f]	1981 act[c,e] Calendar year 1982	1981 act[c,e] Calendar year 1983	1981 act[c,e] Calendar years 1984 and later
0–3,400	0	0	0	0	0
3,400–5,500	14	13.825	12	11	11
5,500–7,600	16	15.8	14	13	12
7,600–11,900	18	17.775	16	15	14
11,900–16,000	21	20.7375	19	17	16
16,000–20,200	24	23.7	22	19	18
20,200–24,600	28	27.65	25	23	22
24,600–29,900	32	31.6	29	26	25
29,900–35,200	37	36.5375	33	30	28
35,200–45,800	43	42.4625	39	35	33
45,800–60,000	49	48.3875	44	40	38
60,000–85,600	54	53.325	49	44	42
85,600–109,400	59	58.2625	50	48	45
109,400–162,400	64	63.2	50	50	49
162,400–215,400	68	67.15	50	50	50
215,400 and over	70	69.125	50	50	50

Sources: Relevant public laws and summaries prepared by the Joint Committee on Taxation.
a. These rate schedules apply only to married persons filing joint returns. For the relationship of other rates to these rates, see table A-4, note a.
b. Includes zero-bracket amount.
c. Does not include add-on minimum tax on preference items or alternative minimum tax.
d. Earned income subject to maximum marginal rate of 50 percent.
e. Does not allow for refundable earned-income credit of 10 percent of earned income up to $5,000 (phased down to zero between $6,000 and $10,000).
f. After tax credit of 1.25 percent against regular tax.

Table A-6. *History of Federal Corporation Income Tax Exemptions and Rates, 1909–83*

Year	Exemptions, brackets, or type of tax	Rate (percent)
1909–13	$5,000 exemption	1
1913–15	None after March 1, 1913	1
1916	None	2
1917	None	6
1918	$2,000 exemption	12
1919–21	$2,000 exemption	10
1922–24	$2,000 exemption	12.5
1925	$2,000 exemption	13
1926–27	$2,000 exemption	13.5
1928	$3,000 exemption	12
1929	$3,000 exemption	11
1930–31	$3,000 exemption	12
1932–35	None	13.75
1936–37	Range of graduated normal tax	
	First $2,000	8
	Over $40,000	15
	Range of graduated surtax	
	on undistributed profits	7–27
1938–39	First $25,000	12.5–16
	Over $25,000	19[a]
1940	First $25,000	14.85–18.7
	$25,000 to $31,964.30	38.3
	$31,964,30 to $38,565.89	36.9
	Over $38,565.89	24
1941	First $25,000	21–25
	$25,000 to $38,461.54	44
	Over $38,461.54	31
1942–45	First $25,000	25–29
	$25,000 to $50,000	53
	Over $50,000	40
1946–49	First $25,000	21–25
	$25,000 to $50,000	53
	Over $50,000	38
1950	First $25,000	23
	Over $25,000	42
1951	First $25,000	28.75
	Over $25,000	50.75
1952–63	First $25,000	30
	Over $25,000	52
1964	First $25,000	22
	Over $25,000	50

Table A-6 *(continued)*

Year	Exemptions, brackets, or type of tax	Rate (percent)
1965–67	First $25,000	22
	Over $25,000	48
1968–69[b]	First $25,000	24.2
	Over $25,000	52.8
1970[b]	First $25,000	22.55
	Over $25,000	49.2
1971–74	First $25,000	22
	Over $25,000	48
1975–78	First $25,000	20
	Next $25,000	22
	Over $50,000	48
1979–81	First $25,000	17
	$25,000 to $50,000	20
	$50,000 to $75,000	30
	$75,000 to $100,000	40
	Over $100,000	46
1982	First $25,000	16
	$25,000 to $50,000	19
	$50,000 to $75,000	30
	$75,000 to $100,000	40
	Over $100,000	46
1983	First $25,000	15
	$25,000 to $50,000	18
	$50,000 to $75,000	30
	$75,000 to $100,000	40
	Over $100,000	46

Sources: Relevant public laws and summaries prepared by the Joint Committee on Taxation.
a. Less adjustments: 14.025 percent of dividends received and 2.5 percent of dividends paid.
b. Includes surcharge of 10 percent in 1968 and 1969 and 2.5 percent in 1970.

310   FEDERAL TAX POLICY

Table A-7. *Marginal Rates of the Federal Corporation Income Tax,
1942–83*
Percent

Year	Under $5,000	$5,000– 20,000	$20,000– 25,000	$25,000– 50,000	$50,000– 75,000	$75,000– 100,000	Over $100,000
1942–45	25	27	29	53	40	40	40
1946–49	21	23	25	53	38	38	38
1950	23	23	23	42	42	42	42
1951	28.75	28.75	28.75	50.75	50.75	50.75	50.75
1952–63	30	30	30	52	52	52	52
1964	22	22	22	50	50	50	50
1965–67	22	22	22	48	48	48	48
1968–69[a]	24.2	24.2	24.2	52.8	52.8	52.8	52.8
1970[a]	22.55	22.55	22.55	49.2	49.2	49.2	49.2
1971–74	22	22	22	48	48	48	48
1975–78	20	20	20	22	48	48	48
1979–81	17	17	17	20	30	40	46
1982	16	16	16	19	30	40	46
1983	15	15	15	18	30	40	46

Sources: Relevant public laws and summaries prepared by the Joint Committee on Taxation.
a. Includes surcharge of 10 percent in 1968 and 1969 and 2.5 percent in 1970.

Table A-8. *Federal Excise Tax Rates on Selected Items as of December 31, Selected Years, 1913–83*

Dollars unless otherwise specified

Tax	1913	1919	1928	1932	1944	1952	1954	1963	1972	1983
Liquor taxes										
Distilled spirits (per proof or wine gallon)	1.10	2.20	1.10	1.10	9	10.50	10.50	10.50	10.50	10.50
Still wines (per wine gallon)										
Not over 14 percent alcohol	...	0.16	0.04	0.04	0.15	0.17	0.17	0.17	0.17	0.17
14 to 21 percent alcohol	...	0.40	0.10	0.10	0.60	0.67	0.67	0.67	0.67	0.67
21 to 24 percent alcohol	...	1	0.25	0.25	2	2.25	2.25	2.25	2.25	2.25
Beer (per barrel)	1	6	6	6	8	9	9	9	9	9[a]
Tobacco taxes										
Cigars, large (per thousand)	3	4–15	2–13.50	2–13.50	2.50–20	2.50–20	2.50–20	2.50–20	2.50–20	0.75–20
Cigarettes (per thousand, 3 pounds or less)	1.25	3	3	3	3.50	4	4	4	4	8
Tobacco and snuff (per pound)	0.08	0.18	0.18	0.18	0.18	0.10	0.10	0.10	...	...
Documentary, etc., stamp taxes										
Conveyances (per $500, or fraction thereof, if value is over $100)	...	0.50	...	0.50	0.55	0.55	0.55	0.55	...	...
Bond and stock issues (per $100, respectively)	...	0.05	0.05	0.10	0.11	0.11	0.11	0.11, 0.10	...	...
Playing cards (per package of not more than 54)	0.02	0.08	0.10	0.10	0.13	0.13	0.13	0.13	...	...
Manufacturers' excise taxes										
Lubricating oils (per gallon)	...	...	...	0.04	0.06	0.06	0.06	0.06	0.06	0.06
Matches, white phosphorus (per hundred)	0.02	0.02	0.02	0.02	0.02	0.02	0.02	0.02	0.02	...
Matches, in general (per thousand)	...	...	...	0.02	0.02	0.02	0.02	0.02	...	...
Gasoline (per gallon)	...	...	...	0.01	0.015	0.02	0.02	0.04	0.04	0.09
Electrical energy (percent of sale price)	...	...	...	3	3⅓	...	...	...	...	...
Tires (percent of sale price, 1919; per pound, 1932 and after)[b]	...	5	...	0.0225	0.05	0.05	0.05	0.10	0.10	0.0975

Table A-8 (continued)

Tax	1913	1919	1928	1932	1944	1952	1954	1963	1972	1983
Inner tubes (percent of sale price, 1919; per pound, 1932 and after)	...	5	...	0.04	0.09	0.09	0.09	0.10	0.10	0.10c
Tread rubber (per pound)	...	...	...	...	...	...	...	0.05	0.05	0.05c
Trucks (percent of sale price)	...	3	...	2	5	8	8	10	10	12d
Automobiles (percent of sale price)	...	5	...	3	7	10	10	10	...	...
Automobiles (based on mileage rating per gallon)										e
Truck accessories (percent of sale price)	...	5	...	2	5	8	8	8	8	12d
Automobile accessories (percent of sale price)	...	5	...	2	5	8	8	8	...	...
Radios and accessories (percent of sale price)	...	...	...	5	10	10	10	10	...	...
Refrigerators, household (percent of sale price)	...	...	...	5	10	10	5	5	...	...
Firearms, shells, cartridges, bows, arrows (percent of sale price)	...	10	...	10	11	11	11	11	11	11
Pistols and revolvers (percent of sale price)	...	10	10	10	11	11	10	10	10	10
Sporting goods other than fishing equipment (percent of sale price)	...	10	...	10	10	15	10	10	...	...
Fishing equipment (percent of sale price)	...	10	...	10	10	15	10	10	10	10
Musical instruments and phonographs (percent of sale price)	...	...	...	...	10	10	10	10	...	...
Records (percent of sale price)	...	5	...	5	10	10	10	10	...	...
Electric, gas, and oil appliances (percent of sale price)	...	5	...	...	10	10	5	5	...	...
Business and store machines (percent of sale price)	...	...	...	...	10	10	10	10	...	...

Item								
Cameras and photographic apparatus (percent of sale price)	⋯	10	10	25	20	10	10	⋯
Photographic film (percent of sale price)	⋯	5	⋯	15	20	10	10	⋯
Mixed flour (per barrel containing 99–196 pounds)	0.04	0.04	0.04					
Automatic slot vending machines (percent of sale price)		5						
Vending weighing machines (percent of sale price)		10	2					
Candy (percent of sale price)		5						
Coal, underground mines (per ton)								1.00
Coal, surface mines (per ton)								0.50
Retailers' excise taxes								
Jewelry (percent of sale price)		5	10[f]	20	20	10	10	
Furs (percent of sale price)		10[f]	10[f]	20	20	10	10	
Toilet preparations (per 25¢ or fraction, 1919; percent of sale price thereafter)		0.01	10[f]	20	20	10	10	
Luggage (percent of sale price)		10						
Gasoline used in noncommercial aviation (per gallon)							0.03	0.12[g]
Fuels other than gasoline used in noncommercial aviation (per gallon)							0.07	0.14[g]
Diesel (beginning 1951) and special motor fuels for highway vehicles or motorboats (per gallon)	0.01[f]	0.015[f]		0.02[f]	0.02	0.02	0.04	
Gasohol (per gallon)							0.04	0.09[h]
Inland waterway users' fuel (per gallon)							0.04	0.08

Table A-8 (continued)

Tax	1913	1919	1928	1932	1944	1952	1954	1963	1972	1983
Windfall profits tax										
Windfall profits on domestically produced crude oil (percent of windfall profit)[i]										
Tier one oil	…	…	…	…	…	…	…	…	…	70
Tier two oil	…	…	…	…	…	…	…	…	…	60
Tier three oil	…	…	…	…	…	…	…	…	…	30
Newly discovered oil	…	…	…	…	…	…	…	…	…	25[j]
Independent producer oil, tier one	…	…	…	…	…	…	…	…	…	50
Miscellaneous excise taxes										
Foreign insurance policies (percent of premium)										
Life insurance	…	3	3	3	1	1	1	1	1	1
Other insurance	…	3	3	3	4	4	4	4	4	4
General telephone service (percent of amount paid)	…	…	…	…	15	15	10	10	10	3[k]
Toll telephone service (percent of amount paid; before 1944, per message)	…	0.05–0.10	…	0.10–0.20	25	25	10	10	10	3[k]
Cable and radio messages, domestic (percent of amount paid; before 1944, per message)	…	0.10	…	0.10	25	15	10	10	10	…
Telegraph messages, domestic (percent of amount paid; 1919, per message)	…	0.10	…	5	25	15	10	10	…	…
Leased wires or teletypewriter and wire mileage service (percent of amount paid)	…	10	…	5	25	25	10	10	10[l]	3[k,l]
Wire and equipment service (percent of amount paid)	…	…	…	…	8	8	8	8	…	…

Transportation of oil by pipeline (percent of amount paid)	8	...	...	4	4.5	4.5	4.5	4.5
Bowling alleys, pool tables (per unit, per year)	10	...	...	...	20	20	20	20
Transportation of persons other than by air (percent of amount paid)	8	...	...	15	15	10	...	...
Transportation of persons, air (percent of amount paid)	...	...	...	15	15	10	8	8[g]
International flight (per person)	...	...	...	...	...	...	3	3[g]
Transportation of property (percent of amount paid)	3	...	...	3	3	3	3	...
Airfreight (percent of amount paid)	...	...	...	...	...	...	5	5[g]
Aircraft registration (annually, per civil aircraft)	...	...	...	...	...	...	25	...
Aircraft poundage fees, takeoff weight above 2,500 pounds								
Propeller-driven aircraft (per pound)	...	...	...	...	...	...	0.02	...
Turbine-powered aircraft (per pound)	...	...	...	...	...	...	0.035	...
Use tax on highway vehicles weighing over 26,000 pounds (per 1,000 lbs. per year)	...	...	...	...	...	3	3	3
Lease of safe deposit boxes (percent of amount collected)	...	10	20	20	10	10	...	...
Admissions (for every 10¢ or fraction, 1919–43 and 1954–63; 5¢ or major fraction, 1944–53)[m]	0.01	0.01	0.01	0.01	0.01	0.01	...	...
Leases of boxes or seats (percent of amount for which similar accommodations are sold)	10	10	20	20	10	10	...	...

Table A-8 (continued)

Tax	1913	1919	1928	1932	1944	1952	1954	1963	1972	1983
Cabarets, roof gardens, etc. (for every 10¢ or fraction of 20 percent of total charge, 1919–40; percent of amount paid, 1941–63)		0.015	0.015	0.015	20	20	20	10		
Wagers (percent of amount of wager)						10	10	10	10	0.25
Occupation of accepting wagers (per year)						50	50	50	50	50
Dues and initiation fees (percent of amount paid)		10		10	20	20	20	20		
Domestic oleomargarine (per pound)										
Uncolored	0.0025	0.0025	0.0025	0.0025	0.0025					
Colored	0.10	0.10	0.10	0.10	0.10					
Butter (per pound)										
Processed	0.0025	0.0025	0.0025	0.0025	0.0025	0.0025	0.0025	0.0025	0.0025	
Adulterated	0.10	0.10	0.10	0.10	0.10	0.10	0.10	0.10	0.10	
Filled cheese (per pound)										
Domestic	0.01	0.01	0.01	0.01	0.01	0.01	0.01	0.01	0.01	
Imported	0.08	0.08	0.08	0.08	0.08	0.08	0.08	0.08	0.08	
Use of boats (per foot, according to size, 1919; per boat, according to size or type, 1932; length, 1944)		1–4		10–200	5–200					
Coin-operated devices (per unit, per year)										
Amusement					10	10	10	10		
Gambling					100	250	250	250	250	
Narcotics										
Opium sold (per ounce)		0.01	0.01	0.01	0.01	0.01	0.01	0.01		
Opium for smoking (per pound)		300	300	300	300	300	300	300		
Importers of opium (per year)		24	24	24	24	24	24	24		
Marijuana (per ounce)[n]					1	1	1	1		
Marijuana, authorized users (per year)					2	2	2	2		

Firearms[o]

Transfers (per firearm)	200	200	200	200	200
	500	500	500	500	500
Occupational (per year)					
Interest equalization tax					
Stock (percent of actual value)	...	...	...	15	11.25
Bonds and loans with maturity of 1 year or longer (percent of actual value according to period remaining to maturity)	...	...	...	2.75–15	0.79–11.25
Deep seabed hard mineral removal (percent of imputed value of resource removed)	...	...	...	...	3.75
Petroleum (per barrel)	...	...	...	...	0.0079
Hazardous waste (per dry weight ton)	...	...	...	...	2.13

Sources: 1913–63, Tax Foundation, *Federal Non-Income Taxes: An Examination of Selected Revenue Sources* (New York, 1965), pp. 23–26, supplemented by data from U.S. Treasury Department, *Annual Report of the Secretary of the Treasury on the State of the Finances for the Fiscal Year Ended June 30, 1940,* pp. 484–511; *1950,* pp. 260–67; and *1962,* pp. 380–88, and relevant public laws; other years, relevant public laws enacted after 1963.

a. Tax is $7 per barrel on first 60,000 barrels for breweries producing less than 2 million barrels per year.

b. Rates shown apply to tires of type used on highway vehicles. Nonhighway tires have been taxed at various rates throughout the period, and taxes on such tires expired at the end of 1983.

c. No tax after December 31, 1983. Instead there is a graduated tax on highway tires weighing more than forty pounds.

d. Tax imposed on first retail sale of trucks, trailers, and truck accessories as of April 1, 1983.

e. Tax varies with mileage rating per gallon, up to $2,150 for a 1984 model car with a rating of less than 12.5. Tax increases for each car model year through 1986.

f. Tax levied at manufacturers' level.

g. No tax after December 31, 1987.

h. No tax after September 30, 1988.

i. Tax scheduled to expire over thirty-three-month period beginning January 1, 1988. Tier one oil refers to most oil in production before 1979. Tier two oil includes (1) stripper oil, that is, oil from any property from which the average daily per well production has been ten barrels or less for any consecutive twelve-month period after 1972, and (2) oil produced from a national petroleum reserve in which the United States has an economic interest. Tier three oil refers to heavy oil (oil having an API specific gravity of 16 degrees or less) and incremental tertiary oil, the amount produced from a property on which the producer uses a qualified tertiary method in excess of a statutory base level. Newly discovered oil is oil in production after 1978.

j. Rate is 22.5 percent in 1984, 20 percent in 1985, and 15 percent in 1986 and later years.

k. No tax after December 31, 1985.

l. Tax levied on teletypewriter service only.

m. Admission charges below specified amounts, which changed over the years, were usually exempt from the tax.

n. Tax applied to persons who had already paid required taxes on importers, users, or producers of marijuana. A tax of $100 per year applied to other persons selling marijuana.

o. Rates shown are maximum rates for manufacture and transfer of machine guns and most short-barreled firearms.

Table A-9. *History of Social Security and Railroad Retirement Tax Rates*

Year	Maximum taxable earnings[a] (dollars)	Tax rate (percent)		
		Employer	Employee	Self-employed
	Old age, survivors, disability, and health insurance			
1937–49	3,000	1.0	1.0	[b]
1950	3,000	1.5	1.5	[b]
1951–53	3,600	1.5	1.5	2.25
1954	3,600	2.0	2.0	3.0
1955–56	4,200	2.0	2.0	3.0
1957–58	4,200	2.25	2.25	3.375
1959	4,800	2.5	2.5	3.75
1960–61	4,800	3.0	3.0	4.5
1962	4,800	3.125	3.125	4.7
1963–65	4,800	3.625	3.625	5.4
1966	6,600	4.2	4.2	6.15
1967	6,600	4.4	4.4	6.4
1968	7,800	4.4	4.4	6.4
1969–70	7,800	4.8	4.8	6.9
1971	7,800	5.2	5.2	7.5
1972	9,000	5.2	5.2	7.5
1973	10,800	5.85	5.85	8.0
1974	13,200	5.85	5.85	7.9
1975	14,100	5.85	5.85	7.9
1976	15,300	5.85	5.85	7.9
1977	16,500	5.85	5.85	7.9
1978	17,700	6.05	6.05	8.1
1979	22,900	6.13	6.13	8.1
1980	25,900	6.13	6.13	8.1
1981	29,700	6.65	6.65	9.3
1982	32,400	6.70	6.70	9.35
1983	35,700	6.70	6.70	9.35
1984	37,800[c]	7.0	7.0	14.0
1985	[c]	7.05	7.05	14.10
1986–87	[c]	7.15	7.15	14.30
1988–89	[c]	7.51	7.51	15.02
1990 and later	[c]	7.65	7.65	15.30

Table A-9 (continued)

Year	Maximum taxable earnings[a] (dollars)	Tax rate (percent) Employer	Tax rate (percent) Employee	Self-employed
	Railroad retirement, survivors, disability, and health insurance			
1937–39	300	2.75	2.75	. . .
1940–42	300	3.00	3.00	. . .
1943–45	300	3.25	3.25	. . .
1946	300	3.50	3.50	. . .
1947–48	300	5.75	5.75	. . .
1949–51	300	6.00	6.00	. . .
1952–June 30, 1954	300	6.25	6.25	. . .
July 1, 1954–May 31, 1959	350	6.25	6.25	. . .
June 1, 1959–61	400	6.75	6.75	. . .
1962–Oct. 31, 1963	400	7.25	7.25	. . .
Nov. 1, 1963–64	450	7.25	7.25	. . .
1965–Sept. 30, 1965	450	8.125	8.125	. . .
Oct. 1, 1965–Dec. 31, 1965	450	7.125	7.125	. . .
1966	550	7.95	7.95	. . .
1967	550	8.65	8.65	. . .
1968	650	8.90	8.90	. . .
1969–70	650	9.55	9.55	. . .
1971	650	9.95	9.95	. . .
1972	750	9.95	9.95	. . .
1973–Sept. 30, 1973	900	10.60	10.60	. . .
Oct. 1, 1973–Dec. 31, 1973	900	15.35	5.85	. . .
1974	1,100	15.35	5.85	. . .
1975	1,175	15.35	5.85	. . .
1976	1,275	15.35	5.85	. . .
1977	1,375	15.35	5.85	. . .
1978	1,475	15.55	6.05	. . .
1979	1,575[d]	15.63	6.13	. . .
1980	1,700[d]	15.63	6.13	. . .
1981–Sept. 30, 1981	1,850[d]	16.15	6.65	. . .
Oct. 1, 1981–Dec. 31, 1981	1,850[d]	18.4	8.65	. . .
1982	2,025[d]	18.45	8.7	. . .
1983	2,225[d]	18.45	8.7	. . .
1984	[c]	19.45	9.45	. . .
1985	[c]	20.8	10.55	. . .
1986–89	[c]	21.9	11.4	. . .
1990 and after	[c]	22.3	11.9	. . .

Sources: Relevant public laws and summaries prepared by the Social Security Administration and the Railroad Retirement Board.

a. Maximum taxable wage is in dollars per year for OASDHI and in dollars per month for RRSDHI.

b. Not covered by the program until January 1, 1951.

c. Automatic adjustments apply to earnings bases for 1984 and later.

d. For 1979 and later years, figures shown are the tier II maximum taxable earnings. Tier I maximum taxable earnings are equal to the social security maximum taxable earnings. See text for details.

Table A-10. History of Unemployment Insurance Tax Rates

Year	Covered wages[a] (dollars)	Statutory range of rates[b] (percent)	Actual rate paid[c] (percent)
	Federal unemployment insurance[d]		
1936	All wages	...	1.0
1937	All wages	...	2.0
1938	All wages	...	3.0
1939–60	3,000	...	3.0
1961	3,000	...	3.1
1962	3,000	...	3.5
1963	3,000	...	3.35
1964–69	3,000	...	3.1
1970–71	3,000	...	3.2
1972	4,200	...	3.2
1973	4,200	...	3.28
1974–76	4,200	...	3.2
1977	4,200	...	3.4
1978–82	6,000	...	3.4
1983–84	7,000	...	3.5
1985 and later	7,000	...	6.2[e]
	Railroad unemployment insurance		
July 1, 1939–47	300	3.0	3.0
1948–June 30, 1954	300	0.5–3.0	0.5
July 1, 1954–Dec. 31, 1955	350	0.5–3.0	0.5
1956	350	0.5–3.0	1.5
1957	350	0.5–3.0	2.0
1958	350	0.5–3.0	2.5
Jan. 1, 1959–May 31, 1959	350	0.5–3.0	3.0
June 1, 1959–Dec. 31, 1961	400	1.5–3.75	3.75
1962–75	400	1.5–4.0	4.0
1976	400	0.5–8.0	5.5
1977	400	0.5–8.0	8.0
1978	400	0.5–8.0	8.0
1979	400	0.5–8.0	7.0
1980	400	0.5–8.0	5.5
1981–83	400	0.5–8.0	8.0
1984	400	0.5–8.0	8.0
1985 and later	400	0.5–8.0	...

Sources: Relevant public laws and summaries prepared by the Social Security Administration and the Railroad Retirement Board.

a. Covered wages are in dollars per year for federal unemployment insurance and dollars per month for railroad unemployment insurance.

b. For federal unemployment insurance, employers are taxed by the states on the basis of an experience rating determined by past unemployment records. For railroad unemployment insurance, the rate paid each year is determined by a sliding scale and is fixed annually in accordance with the balance in the railroad unemployment insurance account on September 30 of the preceding year.

c. For federal unemployment insurance, credit up to 90 percent of the tax is allowed for contributions paid into a state unemployment fund. Since 1961 credits up to 90 percent have been computed as if the tax rate were 3 percent. All employers are permitted to take the maximum credit allowed against the federal unemployment tax, even though they may actually pay a lower rate because of a good experience rating.

d. Applicable to employers of eight persons or more between 1936 and 1956, to employers of four or more from 1956 through 1971, and to employers of one or more in 1972 and later years.

e. The tax shown is composed of a permanent tax of 6.0 percent and a temporary tax of 0.2 percent. The latter will remain in effect until all outstanding revenue loans to the unemployment fund have been repaid.

Table A-11. *Federal Estate Tax Rates and Rates of the State Tax Credit since 1942*

Estates in thousands of dollars; rates in percent

	Basic schedule[a]				Schedule for computing state tax credit	
Taxable estate	1942–76	1977–81	1982 and later years[b]	Taxable estate	1942 and later years[c]
0–5	3	18	18	0–40	0.0
5–10	7	18	18	40–90	0.8
10–20	11	20	20	90–140	1.6
				140–240	2.4
20–30	14	22	22	240–440	3.2
30–40	18	22	22	440–640	4.0
40–50	22	24	24	640–840	4.8
50–60	25	24	24	840–1,040	5.6
60–80	28	26	26	1,040–1,540	6.4
80–100	28	28	28	1,540–2,040	7.2
100–150	30	30	30	2,040–2,540	8.0
150–250	30	32	32	2,540–3,040	8.8
250–500	32	34	34	3,040–3,540	9.6
500–750	35	37	37	3,540–4,040	10.4
750–1,000	37	39	39	4,040–5,040	11.2
1,000–1,250	39	41	41	5,040–6,040	12.0
1,250–1,500	42	43	43	6,040–7,040	12.8
1,500–2,000	45	45	45	7,040–8,040	13.6
2,000–2,500	49	49	49	8,040–9,040	14.4
2,500–3,000	53	53	50	9,040–10,040	15.2
3,000–3,500	56	57	50		
3,500–4,000	59	61	50	10,000 and over	16.0
4,000–4,500	63	65	50		
4,500–5,000	63	69	50		
5,000–6,000	67	70	50		
6,000–7,000	70	70	50		
7,000–8,000	73	70	50		
8,000–10,000	76	70	50		
10,000 and over	77	70	50		

Sources: Revenue Act of 1941; Tax Reform Act of 1976; Economic Recovery Tax Act of 1981.
a. Before credit for state taxes.
b. The maximum taxable estate is gradually reduced from $4.0 million in 1982 to $2.5 million in 1985. The maximum rate is similarly reduced from 65 percent in 1982 to 50 percent in 1985 and later years.
c. Eighty percent of rates in effect in 1926.

Table A-12. *History of Estate and Gift Tax Rates*

Revenue Act	Date of death	Tax rates (percent) Estates	Gifts	Bracket subject to Minimum rate (thousands of dollars)	Maximum rate (thousands of dollars)
1916	Sept. 9, 1916, to March 2, 1917	1.0–10.0	. . .	0–50	5,000 and over
1917[a]	March 3, 1917, to Oct. 3, 1917	1.5–15.0	. . .	0–50	5,000 and over
1917[b]	Oct. 4, 1917, to Feb. 23, 1919	2.0–25.0	. . .	0–50	10,000 and over
1918	Feb. 24, 1919, to Feb. 25, 1926	1.0–25.0	1.0–25.0[c]	0–50	10,000 and over
1926	Feb. 26, 1926, to June 5, 1932	1.0–20.0	. . .	0–50	10,000 and over
1932	June 6, 1932, to May 10, 1934	1.0–45.0	0.75–33.5	0–10	10,000 and over
1934	May 11, 1934, to July 29, 1935	1.0–60.0	0.75–45.0	0–10	10,000 and over
1935	July 30, 1935, to June 24, 1940	2.0–70.0	1.55–52.5	0–10	50,000 and over
1940	June 25, 1940, to Sept. 19, 1941	2.2–77.0[d]	1.65–57.75[d]	0–10	50,000 and over
1941	Sept. 20, 1941, to Dec. 31, 1976	3.0–77.0	2.25–57.75	0–5	10,000 and over
1976	Jan. 1, 1977, to Dec. 31, 1981	18.0–70.0[e,f]	18.0–70.0[e,f]	0–10	5,000 and over
1981	Jan. 1, 1982, to Dec. 31, 1982	18.0–65.0[e,f]	18.0–65.0[e,f]	0–10	4,000 and over
	Jan 1, 1983, to Dec. 31, 1983	18.0–60.0[e,f]	18.0–60.0[e,f]	0–10	3,500 and over
	Jan. 1, 1984, to Dec. 31, 1984	18.0–55.0[e,f]	18.0–55.0[e,f]	0–10	3,000 and over
	Jan. 1, 1985, and later years	18.0–50.0[e,f]	18.0–50.0[e,f]	0–10	2,500 and over

Sources: Relevant public laws and summaries prepared by the Joint Committee on Taxation.
a. Revenue Act of 1917.
b. War Revenue Act of 1917.
c. In effect June 2, 1924, to December 31, 1925.
d. Includes defense tax equal to 10 percent of tax liability.
e. Gift tax rates are the same as the estate tax rates.
f. Allowance for small estates provided by a tax credit (see table A-13, notes d and e).

Table A-13. *History of Estate and Gift Tax Exemptions and Exclusions*

Dollars

| Revenue Act | Estate tax | | Gift tax | |
	Specific exemption[a]	Insurance exclusion	Specific exemption[b]	Annual exclusion per donee
1916	50,000	. . .	[c]	[c]
1918	50,000	40,000	[c]	[c]
1924	50,000	40,000	50,000	500
1926	100,000	40,000	[c]	[c]
1932	50,000	40,000	50,000	5,000
1935	40,000	40,000	40,000	5,000
1938	40,000	40,000	40,000	4,000
1942	60,000	. . .	30,000	3,000
1976	175,625[d]	. . .	175,625[d]	3,000
1981	600,000[e]	. . .	600,000[e]	10,000

Sources: Relevant public laws and summaries prepared by the Joint Committee on Taxation.

a. Specific exemption granted to estates of nonresident citizens dying after May 11, 1934, on the same basis as resident decedents. No exemptions granted to estates of resident aliens until October 21, 1942, when a $2,000 exemption was made available.

b. Under the Revenue Act of 1924, exemption allowed each calendar year. Under the 1932 and later acts, specific exemption allowed only once.

c. No gift tax.

d. The Tax Reform Act of 1976 unified the estate and gift taxes and provided a unified tax credit in lieu of exemptions. The credit translates into the amount of exemption shown in the table. The credit increased from 1977 to 1981 as follows: 1977, $30,000; 1978, $34,000; 1979, $38,000; 1980, $42,500; 1981, $47,000. These credits are equivalent to the following amounts of exemptions, respectively: 1977, $120,667; 1978, $134,000; 1979, $147,333; 1980, $161,563; 1981, $175,625.

e. The Economic Recovery Tax Act of 1981 increases the amount of unified credit from 1982 to 1987 and later years as follows: 1982, $62,800; 1983, $79,300; 1984, $96,300; 1985, $121,800; 1986, $155,800; 1987 and later years, $192,800. The credits are equivalent to the following amounts of exemptions, respectively: 1982, $225,000; 1983, $275,000; 1984, $325,000; 1985, $400,000; 1986, $500,000; 1987 and later years, $600,000.

Tax Bases of the Major Federal Taxes

THE CONCEPTS of taxable income for both the individual and the corporation income taxes as defined by the internal revenue code differ substantially from the national income aggregates, which are widely used for purposes of economic analysis. This appendix derives the tax bases of the two income taxes and compares them with the official estimates of personal income and corporate profits incorporated in the national income accounts. It also presents the latest distributions by rate brackets of the tax bases of the income and estate and gift taxes.

The Individual Income Tax

Among the various tax concepts, *adjusted gross income* most nearly resembles personal income. Total personal income exceeds the aggregate of adjusted gross incomes reported on tax returns by a substantial amount each year. A large portion of the disparity can be explained by differences in definition. The individual income tax base is derived below in two steps: first, aggregate adjusted gross income of all people in the United States is estimated from personal income; second, personal exemptions and deductions are subtracted from adjusted gross income to obtain taxable income.

Relation between Personal Income and Adjusted Gross Income

Table B-1 summarizes the conceptual differences between personal income and adjusted gross income for calendar year 1981, the latest year for which such estimates are available. The differences are, first, items of income that are included in personal income but not in adjusted gross income (for example, transfer payments, practically all income in kind, tax-exempt interest), amounting to $663.9 billion; and second, income that is included in adjusted gross income but not in personal income (primarily the social security taxes paid by employers, taxable private pensions, and capital gains), amounting to $181.9 billion. When these differences are taken into account, the 1981 personal income of $2,435.0 billion corresponded to an adjusted gross income of $1,953.0 billion.

From 1947 to 1974, the difference between personal and adjusted gross income rose gradually as transfer payments increased. Since 1974 the difference has been between 18 and 20 percent of personal income (table B-2).

If all income recipients were required to file returns and everybody reported income accurately, the total adjusted income on tax returns would correspond closely to the amounts shown in table B-2. Since neither of these conditions holds, adjusted gross incomes reported on tax returns are lower than the aggregate for all recipients. As table B-3 indicates, this gap declined as a percentage of total adjusted gross income from 1947 to 1960; since 1960, the figure has varied between 7 and 9 percent.

In 1981 the gross difference between personal income and adjusted gross income reported on tax returns was $662.4 billion (see tables B-2 and B-3). Over 70 percent of this difference—or $482.0 billion—is explained by conceptual differences, and only $180.4 billion did not appear on tax returns. But this $180.4 billion cannot be regarded as a measure of underreporting. Included in this figure is the income received by people who were not required to file returns, the exact amount of which is unknown. Moreover, a large number of nontaxable people in such low-paid occupations as domestic service and farming do not bother to file even though the law requires them to do so. In view of the magnitudes involved, the portion of the total gap between personal income and adjusted gross income that remains unexplained is relatively small. If as much as two-thirds of the $180.4 billion was due to underreporting, the degree of underreporting was about 6 percent of estimated total adjusted gross income.

The Individual Income Tax Base

The steps in the derivation of the individual income tax base for the years 1947–81 are shown in table B-4. In 1981, $1,772.6 billion of adjusted gross income was reported on individual income tax returns. Nontaxable individuals reported $51.4 billion; those who were taxable reported

$1,721.2 billion. The personal exemptions of taxable individuals amounted to $188.2 billion, and their deductions amounted to $149.3 billion. Subtracting these two items from adjusted gross income leaves taxable income of $1,383.7 billion. To this must be added the small amount of taxable income—about $27.2 billion—of individuals whose tax liabilities were wiped out by tax credits. Thus, taxable income on all returns amounted to $1,410.9 billion. Since 1977 taxable income has included the zero-bracket amount (ZBA), which totaled $240.8 billion in 1981. Deducting the ZBA from taxable income leaves $1,170.1 billion as the amount of taxable income that was subject to positive rates in 1981.

Table B-5 compares the tax base with personal income since the end of World War II. From 39.7 percent of personal income in 1947, taxable income rose to 51.5 percent in 1969 and has remained between 47 and 50 percent since then.

Distribution of Taxable Individual Income

An estimated distribution of taxable income by rate brackets is shown for calendar year 1980 in table B-6. Only a small proportion of taxable income is subject to the very high rates. Of the total taxable income of $1,271.3 billion, $694.9 billion, or 54.7 percent, was subject to tax rates of less than 20 percent, and $57.8 billion, or 4.5 percent, was subject to rates of 50 percent or more.

The Corporation Income Tax

Table B-7 gives a detailed reconciliation for calendar year 1980 of three concepts of corporate profits: *profits before taxes* as defined in the national income accounts; *net profits* of all corporations as tabulated from the federal corporation income tax returns; and *taxable income* of corporations.

The major differences between the national income definition of profits before tax and net profits reported on tax returns are accounted for by differences in coverage and in definition of income. For example, profits before taxes include the income of government financial institutions and adjustments of the profits of insurance carriers and mutual financial intermediaries for national income purposes; on the other hand, they exclude dividends received from corporations and net capital gains (which are subject to a special reduced rate), include estimated profits resulting from audit, and do not allow for the deductions for depletion, state corporation income taxes, and adjustment for bad debts. In 1980 corporate profits under the national income definition were $234.6 billion, and net profits reported on tax returns amounted to $235.9 billion. As shown in table B-7, differences in coverage and in definition of the two profit concepts almost offset one another (amounting to + $12.2 billion and − $10.9 billion, respectively), leaving net profits on tax returns at $235.9 billion.

To arrive at taxable income, the losses of deficit corporations must be added back to reported net profits, and the nontaxable components of reported net profits must be eliminated. After these and other adjustments, corporate taxable income in 1981 was $246.6 billion, or $10.7 billion higher than reported net profits.

A comparison of the three income concepts for the years 1958–80 is given in table B-8. Of the total taxable income of $246.6 billion in 1980, $13.2 billion was taxed at the alternative tax rate of 28 percent on long-term capital gains and the remaining $233.4 billion was taxed at the regular rate, which ranged from 17 to 40 percent of profits below $100,000 and 46 percent of amounts above $100,000. Although data are not available from tax return tabulations, it is estimated that about 83 percent of corporate profits were taxed at the 46 percent rate in 1980.

Estate and Gift Taxes

In 1976, 201,000 estate tax returns were filed, of which 139,000 were taxable. The total wealth subject to tax amounted to $20.9 billion.

The decedents represented on the 1976 taxable estate tax returns were 7.65 percent of all decedents twenty or over in that year (table B-9). These returns showed gross estates of $40.6 billion; debts, mortgages, and policy loans against life insurance amounted to $2.0 billion, leaving *economic* estates of $38.6 billion. The $20.3 billion of taxable estates thus accounted for somewhat more than half the wealth left by decedents subject to estate tax (table B-10). Of the total taxable estates, 41.9 percent was subject to rates below 30 percent, 51.9 percent to rates between 30 percent and 50 percent, and 6.1 percent to rates of more than 50 percent (table B-11).

The latest data tabulated from gift tax returns are for gifts made in

1966, and the latest distribution of gifts by tax rate brackets is for 1963. Total gifts on taxable returns in 1966 amounted to $2.4 billion. After allowing for deductions and exclusions, $1.5 billion, or 61 percent, was taxable (table B-12). About 80 percent of the 1963 gift tax base was subject to rates below 30 percent; 15 percent to rates of 30 to 50 percent; and 5 percent to rates of 50 percent or more (table B-13).

Table B-1. *Derivation of Adjusted Gross Income from Personal Income, 1981*
Billions of dollars

Income and adjustment items	Amount
1. Personal income	2,435.0
2. Portion of personal income not included in adjusted gross income	663.9
a. Transfer payments (except taxable military pay and taxable government pensions)	297.2
b. Other labor income (except fees)	141.5
c. Imputed income	60.6
d. Investment income received by nonprofit institutions or retained by fiduciaries	24.4
e. Investment income retained by life insurance carriers and noninsured pension funds	55.3
f. Differences in accounting treatment	30.5
g. Other excluded or exempt income	54.4
3. Portion of adjusted gross income not included in personal income	181.9
a. Personal contributions for social insurance	104.6
b. Net gain from sale of assets	29.6
c. Taxable private pensions	35.6
d. Small business corporation income	−0.4
e. Other	12.6
4. Total adjustment for conceptual differences (line 2 minus line 3)	482.0
5. Estimated adjusted gross income of taxable and nontaxable individuals (line 1 minus line 4)	1,953.0

Source: U.S. Department of Commerce, Bureau of Economic Analysis. Figures are rounded.

Table B-2. *Personal Income and Total Adjusted Gross Income,*
1947–81

Billions of dollars unless otherwise specified

			Difference	
Year	Personal income	Total adjusted gross income	Amount	Percent of personal income
1947	190.1	172.7	17.4	9.1
1948	209.0	186.7	22.4	10.7
1949	206.4	184.0	22.4	10.9
1950	227.2	202.7	24.4	10.8
1951	254.9	229.2	25.7	10.1
1952	271.8	241.9	29.9	11.0
1953	287.7	256.7	31.0	10.8
1954	289.6	254.9	34.7	12.0
1955	310.3	275.0	35.3	11.4
1956	332.6	295.5	37.1	11.2
1957	351.0	308.1	43.0	12.2
1958	361.1	312.8	48.2	13.4
1959	384.4	336.2	48.2	12.5
1960	402.3	348.1	54.2	13.5
1961	417.8	360.6	57.2	13.7
1962	443.6	380.7	62.9	14.2
1963	466.2	400.8	65.4	14.0
1964	499.2	434.0	65.2	13.1
1965	540.7	467.3	73.3	13.6
1966	588.2	512.9	75.3	12.8
1967	630.0	546.2	83.8	13.3
1968	690.6	599.9	90.7	13.1
1969	754.7	652.7	102.0	13.5
1970	811.1	686.1	125.0	15.4
1971	868.4	730.5	137.9	15.9
1972	951.4	805.3	146.1	15.4
1973	1,065.2	901.4	163.8	15.4
1974	1,168.6	978.7	189.9	16.3
1975	1,265.0	1,019.6	245.3	19.4
1976	1,391.2	1,132.1	259.1	18.6
1977	1,540.4	1,253.4	287.0	18.6
1978	1,732.7	1,418.3	314.4	18.1
1979	1,951.2	1,598.1	353.1	18.1
1980	2,165.3	1,765.0	400.3	18.5
1981	2,435.0	1,953.0	482.0	19.8

Source: U.S. Department of Commerce, Bureau of Economic Analysis. Figures are rounded.

Table B-3. *Total Adjusted Gross Income and Adjusted Gross Income Reported on Tax Returns, 1947–81*
Billions of dollars unless otherwise specified

| | Adjusted gross income | | Difference | |
Year	Total U.S.	Reported on tax returns	Amount	Percent of total U.S.
1947	172.7	149.7	23.0	13.3
1948	186.7	163.6	23.2	12.4
1949	184.0	160.6	23.4	12.7
1950	202.7	179.1	23.6	11.6
1951	229.2	202.4	26.8	11.7
1952	241.9	215.3	26.6	11.0
1953	256.7	228.7	28.0	10.9
1954	254.9	229.2	25.7	10.1
1955	275.0	248.5	26.5	9.6
1956	295.5	267.8	27.7	9.4
1957	308.1	280.4	27.7	9.0
1958	312.8	281.2	31.6	10.1
1959	336.2	305.1	31.1	9.3
1960	348.1	315.5	32.6	9.4
1961	360.6	329.9	30.7	8.5
1962	380.7	348.7	32.0	8.4
1963	400.8	368.8	32.0	8.0
1964	434.0	396.7	37.3	8.6
1965	467.3	429.2	38.1	8.2
1966	512.9	468.5	44.4	8.7
1967	546.2	504.8	41.4	7.6
1968	599.9	554.4	45.5	7.6
1969	652.7	603.5	49.2	7.5
1970	686.1	631.7	54.4	7.9
1971	730.5	673.6	56.9	7.8
1972	805.3	746.0	59.3	7.4
1973	901.4	827.1	74.3	8.2
1974	978.7	905.5	73.2	7.5
1975	1,019.6	947.8	71.8	7.0
1976	1,132.1	1,053.9	78.2	6.9
1977	1,253.4	1,158.5	94.9	7.6
1978	1,418.3	1,302.4	115.9	8.2
1979	1,598.1	1,465.4	132.7	8.3
1980	1,765.0	1,613.7	151.3	8.6
1981	1,953.0	1,772.6	180.4	9.2

Source: Total adjusted gross income, from table B-2; adjusted gross income reported on tax returns, *Statistics of Income, Individual Income Tax Returns*. Figures are rounded.

Table B-4. Derivation of the Individual Income Tax Base, 1947–81

Billions of dollars

Year	Adjusted gross income — Amount reported on individual returns[a]	Deduct: amount reported on nontaxable returns[a]	Equals: amount reported on taxable returns[a]	Deduct: exemptions on taxable returns	Deduct: deductions on taxable returns	Equals: taxable income on taxable returns	Add: taxable income on nontaxable returns[b]	Equals: taxable income of individuals	Deduct: zero-bracket amount (ZBA)	Equals: taxable income of individuals excluding ZBA
1947	149.7	14.4	135.3	44.3	15.6	75.4	...	75.4	...	75.4
1948	163.6	21.5	142.1	50.9	16.4	74.8	...	74.8	...	74.8
1949	160.6	22.0	138.6	50.1	16.8	71.7	...	71.7	...	71.7
1950	179.1	20.6	158.5	55.2	19.0	84.3	...	84.3	...	84.3
1951	202.4	19.2	183.2	61.4	22.6	99.2	...	99.2	...	99.2
1952	215.3	18.7	196.6	64.5	24.9	107.2	...	107.2	...	107.2
1953	228.7	18.2	210.5	68.9	27.3	114.3	...	114.3	...	114.3
1954	229.2	19.5	209.7	67.0	27.5	115.2	0.1	115.3	...	115.3
1955	248.5	18.9	229.6	71.2	30.5	127.9	0.1	128.0	...	128.0
1956	267.8	18.2	249.6	74.6	33.6	141.4	0.1	141.5	...	141.5
1957	280.4	18.2	262.2	76.8	36.2	149.2	0.2	149.4	...	149.4
1958	281.2	19.0	262.2	75.8	37.2	149.2	0.2	149.3	...	149.3
1959	305.1	17.3	287.8	79.7	41.7	166.4	0.2	166.5	...	166.5
1960	315.5	18.3	297.2	81.2	44.5	171.5	0.2	171.6	...	171.6
1961	329.9	18.6	311.3	82.5	47.2	181.6	0.1	181.8	...	181.8
1962	348.7	18.1	330.6	85.1	50.5	195.0	0.4	195.3	...	195.3
1963	368.8	18.4	350.4	87.4	54.5	208.5	0.5	209.1	...	209.1
1964	396.7	20.7	376.0	88.3	58.4	229.3	0.6	229.9	...	229.9
1965	429.2	19.9	409.3	91.9	63.1	254.3	0.7	255.1	...	255.1
1966	468.5	18.3	450.2	96.2	68.3	285.7	0.8	286.3	...	286.3
1967	504.8	17.4	487.4	99.1	74.0	314.3	0.8	315.1	...	315.1
1968	554.4	16.1	538.3	102.6	83.7	352.0	0.8	352.8	...	352.8
1969	603.5	15.3	588.2	106.3	93.7	388.2	0.7	388.8	...	388.8
1970	631.7	21.4	610.3	107.0	102.6	400.9[c]	0.3	401.2	...	401.2
1971	673.6	22.4	651.3	115.6	122.4	413.4[c]	0.6	414.0	...	414.0
1972	746.0	28.6	717.4	128.2	142.8	446.7[c]	1.0	447.6	...	447.6
1973	827.1	27.4	799.7	132.4	156.9	510.6[c]	1.3	511.9	...	511.9
1974	905.5	25.1	880.4	136.8	171.5	572.4[c]	1.2	573.6	...	573.6
1975	947.8	49.5	898.3	123.8	184.4	590.4[c]	5.1	595.5	...	595.5
1976	1,053.9	49.5	1,004.4	128.0	207.5	669.4[c]	5.5	674.9	...	674.9
1977	1,158.5	60.8	1,097.7	125.0	66.9[d]	905.9[c]	33.1[e]	939.0[d]	205.2	733.8
1978	1,302.4	61.2	1,241.2	130.6	83.3[d]	1,027.3[c]	34.9[e]	1,062.2[d]	215.8	846.4
1979	1,465.4	63.1	1,402.3	178.5	96.4[d]	1,127.4	29.8[e]	1,157.2[d]	230.6	926.6
1980	1,613.7	57.6	1,556.1	183.5	120.6[d]	1,252.0	28.0[e]	1,280.0[d]	234.8	1,045.2
1981	1,772.6	51.4	1,721.2	188.2	149.3[d]	1,383.7	27.2[e]	1,410.9[d]	240.8	1,170.1

Source: *Statistics of Income, Individual Income Tax Returns.* Figures are rounded.
a. Adjusted gross income less deficit.
b. Taxable income of persons whose tax liability was completely offset by tax credits.
c. Taxable income for 1970–78 diverges from adjusted gross income minus exemptions and deductions because returns with minimum tax only are included in taxable returns, but for some of these returns, when exemptions and deductions are subtracted from adjusted gross income, the result is a negative number. Beginning in 1979, capital gains are excluded from the minimum tax base, reducing income on returns with minimum tax to small amounts.
d. Itemized deductions include only amounts above zero-bracket amount (that is, "excess itemized deductions"). Thus, zero-bracket amount is included in taxable income.
e. Increase in taxable income on nontaxable returns beginning in 1977 results from the inclusion of the zero-bracket amount in taxable income.

Table B-5. *Personal Income, Taxable Income, and Individual Income Tax, 1947–81*

Billions of dollars unless otherwise specified

Year	Personal income	Taxable income excluding zero bracket amount		Individual income tax		
		Amount	Percent of personal income	Amount	Percent of Personal income	Taxable income
1947	190.1	75.4	39.7	18.1	9.5	24.0
1948	209.0	74.8	35.8	15.4	7.4	20.6
1949	206.4	71.7	34.7	14.5	7.0	20.2
1950	227.2	84.3	37.1	18.4	8.1	21.8
1951	254.9	99.2	38.9	24.2	9.5	24.4
1952	271.8	107.2	39.4	27.8	10.2	25.9
1953	287.7	114.3	39.7	29.4	10.2	25.7
1954	289.6	115.3	39.8	26.7	9.2	23.2
1955	310.3	128.0	41.2	29.6	9.5	23.1
1956	332.6	141.5	42.5	32.7	9.8	23.1
1957	351.0	149.4	42.6	34.4	9.8	23.0
1958	361.1	149.3	41.3	34.3	9.5	23.0
1959	384.4	166.5	43.3	38.6	10.0	23.2
1960	402.3	171.6	42.6	39.5	9.8	23.0
1961	417.8	181.8	43.5	42.2	10.1	23.2
1962	443.6	195.3	44.0	44.9	10.1	23.0
1963	466.2	209.1	44.9	48.2	11.1	23.1
1964	499.2	229.9	46.1	47.2	9.5	20.5
1965	540.7	255.1	47.2	49.6	9.2	19.4
1966	588.2	286.3	48.7	56.1	9.5	19.6
1967	630.0	315.1	50.0	63.0	10.0	20.0
1968	690.6	352.8	51.1	76.7	10.4	21.7
1969	754.7	388.8	51.5	86.6	11.5	22.3
1970	811.1	401.2	49.5	83.9	10.3	20.9
1971	868.4	414.0	47.7	85.4	9.8	20.6
1972	951.4	447.6	47.0	93.6	9.8	20.9
1973	1,065.2	511.9	48.1	108.1	10.1	21.1
1974	1,168.6	573.6	49.1	123.5	10.6	21.5
1975	1,265.0	595.5	47.1	124.4	9.8	20.9
1976	1,391.2	674.9	48.5	140.8	10.1	20.9
1977	1,538.0	733.8	47.7	158.5	10.3	21.6
1978	1,721.8	846.4	49.2	188.2	10.9	22.2
1979	1,951.2	926.6	47.5	214.5	11.0	23.1
1980	2,165.3	1,045.2	48.3	250.3	11.6	24.0
1981	2,435.0	1,170.1	48.0	285.8	11.7	24.4

Sources: Tables B-2 and B-4; and *Statistics of Income, Individual Income Tax Returns.*

Table B-6. *Distribution of Taxable Income and Individual Income Tax, by Rate Bracket, 1980*
Amounts in billions of dollars

Rate (percent)	Amount Taxable income[a]	Tax[b]	Percentage distribution Taxable income	Tax
0	234.8	. . .	18.5	. . .
14	124.7	17.5	9.8	6.8
16	111.6	17.9	8.8	7.0
18	193.0	34.7	15.2	13.6
19	30.8	5.8	2.4	2.3
21	140.5	29.5	11.0	11.5
22	7.2	1.6	0.6	0.6
24	112.6	27.0	8.9	10.6
26	16.2	4.2	1.3	1.7
28	67.0	18.8	5.3	7.3
30	13.8	4.2	1.1	1.6
31	2.2	0.7	0.2	0.3
32	51.9	16.6	4.1	6.5
34	11.8	4.0	0.9	1.6
36	1.0	0.4	0.1	0.1
37	30.9	11.4	2.4	4.5
39	5.4	2.1	0.4	0.8
42	0.5	0.2	*	0.1
43	31.9	13.7	2.5	5.4
44	2.8	1.2	0.2	0.5
46	0.5	0.2	*	0.1
49	22.1	10.8	1.7	4.2
50[c]	24.0	12.0	1.9	4.7
54	9.1	4.9	0.7	1.9
55	1.7	0.9	0.1	0.4
59	4.0	2.4	0.3	0.9
63	1.4	0.9	0.1	0.3
64	4.4	2.8	0.3	1.1
68	2.8	1.9	0.2	0.7
70	10.4	7.3	0.8	2.8
Total	1,271.3	255.7	100.0	100.0

Source: *Statistics of Income, Individual Income Tax Returns*, 1980. Figures are rounded.
* Less than 0.05 percent.
a. Taxable income subject to regular rates.
b. Tax before credits.
c. Maximum rate on earned income.

Table B-7. *Reconciliation of Corporation Profits before Taxes,*
Net Profits Reported on Tax Returns, and Taxable Income, 1980
Billions of dollars

Income and adjustment items	Amount
Profits before taxes, national income definition[a]	234.6
Differences in coverage	
Income of Federal Reserve banks, federal home loan banks, and federal land banks	- 12.8
Adjustment for insurance carriers and mutual financial intermediaries	2.5
Corporate income from equities in foreign corporations and branches	52.4
Income received from equities in foreign corporations, net of corresponding outflows	- 29.9
Subtotal	12.2
Differences in definition	
Dividends received from domestic corporations	18.7
Net capital gains from sales of property	27.0
Costs of trading or issuing corporate securities	2.4
Depletion, drilling costs in excess of depreciation, and oil well bonus payments written off	- 16.3
State corporation income taxes	- 14.5
Bad debt adjustment	- 11.0
Income disclosed by audit	- 17.2
Subtotal	- 10.9
Equals: Net profits reported on tax returns, all corporations	235.9
Adjustments to compute taxable income	
Losses of corporations with no net income	55.0
Constructive taxable income from related foreign corporations	15.7
Wholly tax-exempt interest	- 12.6
Total special deductions[b]	- 8.4
Net operating loss deduction	- 9.4
Tax-deferred income of Domestic International Sales Corporations (DISCs)	- 9.9
Taxable income of Subchapter S corporations	- 2.5
Regulated investment company income	- 14.9
Other adjustments	- 2.3
Subtotal	10.7
Equals: Taxable income	246.6

Sources; U.S. Department of Commerce, Bureau of Economic Analysis; and *Statistics of Income, Corporation Income Tax Returns.* Figures are rounded.
a. Without inventory valuation and capital-consumption adjustment.
b. Intercorporate dividends, dividends paid on preferred stock of public utilities, and Western Hemisphere Trade Corporation deduction.

Table B-8. *Corporation Profits before Taxes, Net Profits,
and Taxable Income, 1958–80*

Billions of dollars

Year	Profits before taxes,[a] national income definition	Net profits reported on tax returns[b]	Taxable income
1958	41.9	39.2	39.3
1959	52.6	47.7	47.6
1960	49.8	44.5	47.2
1961	49.7	47.0	47.9
1962	55.0	50.8	51.7
1963	59.6	55.7	54.3
1964	66.5	63.1	60.4
1965	77.2	74.7	70.8
1966	83.0	81.3	77.1
1967	79.7	79.3	74.8
1968	88.5	87.5	81.4
1969	86.7	82.1	81.2
1970	75.4	68.0	72.4
1971	86.6	81.9	83.2
1972	100.6	96.8	95.1
1973	125.2	122.6	115.5
1974	136.7	148.2	144.0
1975	132.1	146.0	146.6
1976	166.3	186.6	183.5
1977	194.7	219.5	212.5
1978	229.1	247.4	239.6
1979	252.7	283.0	279.4
1980	234.6	235.9	246.6

Sources: Profits before taxes, U.S. Department of Commerce, Bureau of Economic Analysis. Reported net profits and taxable income, *Statistics of Income, Corporation Income Tax Returns.*

a. Without inventory valuation and capital-consumption adjustment.

b. Includes corporations with and without net income. Beginning in 1963, reported net profits are designated "receipts less deductions" in *Statistics of Income.*

Table B-9. *Number of Taxable Estate Tax Returns Filed as a Percentage of Deaths, Selected Years, 1939–76*

Year	Deaths (adults[a])	Taxable estate tax returns filed Number[b]	Taxable estate tax returns filed Percent of deaths
1939	1,204,080	12,720	1.06
1940	1,235,484	12,907	1.04
1941	1,215,627	13,336	1.10
1942	1,209,661	13,493	1.12
1943	1,275,400	12,726	1.00
1944	1,237,508	12,154	0.98
1945	1,238,360	13,869	1.12
1947	1,277,852	18,232	1.43
1948	1,284,535	19,742	1.54
1949	1,284,196	17,469	1.36
1950	1,303,171	17,411	1.34
1951	1,328,809	18,941	1.43
1954	1,331,498	24,997	1.88
1955	1,378,588	25,143	1.82
1957	1,475,320	32,131	2.18
1959	1,498,549	38,515	2.57
1961	1,548,061	45,439	2.94
1963	1,663,115	55,207	3.32
1966	1,727,240	67,404[c]	3.90
1970	1,796,940	93,424[c]	5.20
1973	1,867,689	120,761[c]	6.47
1976	1,819,107	139,115[c]	7.65

Sources: Deaths, U.S. Department of Health and Human Services, Division of Vital Statistics. Taxable estate returns, *Statistics of Income, Estate Tax Returns*.
a. Aged twenty and over.
b. Citizens and resident aliens.
c. Not strictly comparable with 1939–63 data. For 1966 and later years, the estate tax after credits was the basis for determining taxable returns. For prior years, the basis was the estate tax before credits.

Table B-10. *Number of Taxable Estate Tax Returns, Gross and Economic Estate, and Estate Tax before and after Credits, Selected Years, 1939–76*

Millions of dollars unless otherwise specified

Year[a]	Number of taxable returns	Gross estate on taxable returns	Economic estate[b] on taxable returns	Taxable estate[c]	Estate tax Before credits	Estate tax After credits
1939	12,720	2,564	2,390	1,538	330	277
1940	12,907	2,448	2,295	1,479	296	250
1941	13,336	2,578	2,410	1,561	346	292
1942	13,493	2,550	2,373	1,525	354	308
1943	12,726	2,452	2,284	1,397	398	362
1944	12,154	2,720	2,551	1,509	452	405
1945	13,869	3,246	3,081	1,900	596	531
1947	18,232	3,993	3,804	2,319	694	622
1948	19,742	4,445	4,224	2,585	799	715
1949	17,469	4,272	4,059	2,107	635	567
1950	17,411	4,126	3,919	1,917	534	484
1951	18,941	4,656	n.a.	2,189	644	577
1954	24,997	6,288	6,007	2,969	869	779
1955	25,143	6,387	6,109	2,991	872	778
1957	32,131	8,904	n.a.	4,342	1,353	1,177
1959	38,515	9,996	9,540	4,651	1,346	1,186
1961	45,439	12,733	12,213	6,014	1,847	1,619
1963	55,207	14,714	14,059	7,071	2,087	1,841
1966	67,404[d]	19,227[d]	17,974[d]	9,160	2,755	2,414
1970	93,424[d]	25,585[d]	22,140[d]	11,662	3,413	3,000
1973	120,761[d]	33,294[d]	29,066[d]	15,815	4,720	4,153
1976	139,115[d]	40,578[d]	38,590[d]	20,304	6,030	4,979

Sources: 1939–51, *Statistics of Income, Part I;* 1954–66, *Statistics of Income, Fiduciary, Gift, and Estate Tax Returns;* 1970–76, *Statistics of Income, Estate Tax Returns.* Data are for estate tax returns of citizens and resident aliens.

n.a. Not available.

a. Returns are classified by year in which they were filed.

b. Economic estate is gross estate reduced by the amount of debt (including mortgages and loans against life insurance policies).

c. Before 1953 "taxable estate" was labeled "net estate" in *Statistics of Income.*

d. Not strictly comparable with prior years. For 1966–73 estate tax after credits was the basis for determining taxable returns. For earlier years the basis was estate tax before credits.

Table B-11. *Distribution of Taxable Estates, by Rate Bracket, 1976*[a]

Estate tax rate (percent)	Amount (millions of dollars)		Percentage distribution	
	Taxable estate	Tax[b]	Taxable estate	Tax[b]
3	608	18	3.7	0.4
7	562	39	3.4	0.8
11	1,002	110	6.1	2.3
14	864	121	5.3	2.6
18	751	135	4.6	2.9
22	660	145	4.0	3.1
25	587	147	3.6	3.1
28	1,825	511	11.2	10.8
30	3,431	1,029	21.0	21.8
32	2,164	693	13.3	14.7
35	993	348	6.1	7.4
37	584	216	3.6	4.6
39	392	153	2.4	3.2
42	280	118	1.7	2.5
45	376	169	2.3	3.6
49	242	119	1.5	2.5
53	171	91	1.0	1.9
56	130	73	0.8	1.5
59	98	58	0.6	1.2
63	139	88	0.9	1.9
67	98	66	0.6	1.4
70	66	46	0.4	1.0
73	53	39	0.3	0.8
76	69	53	0.4	1.1
77	181	139	1.1	2.9
Total	16,328	4,722	100.0	100.0

Source: *Statistics of Income—1976, Estate Tax Returns*, table 15. Figures are rounded.

a. For decedents who died in 1976 or prior years. Excludes $4,576 million of taxable estates and $1,449 million of tax on returns of decedents who died in 1977 and were classified in the 1976 *Statistics of Income;* such returns were subject to a different rate schedule enacted under the Tax Reform Act of 1976.

b. Tax before credits.

Table B-12. *Number of Taxable Gift Tax Returns, Total Gifts,*
Taxable Gifts, and Gift Tax, Selected Years, 1939–66
Millions of dollars

Year[a]	Number of taxable returns	Total gifts on taxable returns	Taxable gifts (current year)	Gift tax (current year)
1939	3,929	220	132	19
1940	4,930	347	226	34
1941	8,940	714	484	70
1942	4,380	222	121	25
1943	4,656	209	124	30
1944	4,979	276	148	38
1945	5,540	289	170	37
1946	6,808	426	265	62
1947	6,822	439	257	64
1948	6,559	391	209	45
1949	6,114	340	178	36
1950	8,366	596	338	78
1951	8,360	516	304	67
1953	8,464	489	258	56
1957	14,736	923	518	113
1959	15,793	928	478	105
1961	17,936	1,219	657	158
1963	20,598	1,402	790	183
1966	29,547	2,373	1,455	413

Sources: 1939–53, *Statistics of Income, Part I;* 1957–66, *Statistics of Income, Fiduciary, Gift, and Estate Tax Returns.*

a. Returns are classified by year in which they were filed. Data after 1966 are not published.

Table B-13. *Distribution of Taxable Gifts, by Rate Bracket, 1963*[a]

	Amount (thousands of dollars)		Percentage distribution	
Rate (percent)	Taxable gifts	Tax	Taxable gifts	Tax
2¼	39,386	887	5.0	0.5
5¼	31,671	1,664	4.0	0.9
8¼	50,371	4,155	6.4	2.3
10½	38,513	4,044	4.9	2.2
13½	31,136	4,203	3.9	2.3
16½	26,129	4,311	3.3	2.4
18¾	22,415	4,203	2.8	2.3
21	65,366	13,727	8.3	7.5
22½	122,698	27,607	15.5	15.1
24	91,880	22,051	11.6	12.0
26¼	51,861	13,614	6.6	7.4
27¾	33,964	9,425	4.3	5.1
29¼	25,701	7,518	3.3	4.1
31½	22,590	7,116	2.9	3.9
33¾	32,195	10,866	4.1	5.9
36¾	19,780	7,269	2.5	4.0
39¾	15,015	5,968	1.9	3.3
42	10,072	4,230	1.3	2.3
44¼	6,641	2,939	0.8	1.6
47¼	14,671	6,932	1.9	3.8
50¼	11,510	5,784	1.5	3.2
52½	8,479	4,452	1.1	2.4
54¾	4,703	2,575	0.6	1.4
57	2,939	1,675	0.4	0.9
57¾	10,623	6,135	1.3	3.3
Total	790,311	183,351	100.0	100.0

Source: *Statistics of Income, Fiduciary, Gift, and Estate Tax Returns, 1962.* Figures are rounded.
a. The year 1963 is the latest for which a distribution of taxable gifts by rate brackets is available.

Tax Expenditures

THE TERM *tax expenditures* is often applied to the special provisions of the income tax laws that reduce the tax liability of those who make payments or receive incomes in certain designated forms. Many of these tax subsidies are the equivalent of direct federal expenditures. But direct expenditures are shown in the budget as outlays, whereas tax subsidies are reflected in lower income tax receipts. The term *tax expenditures* emphasizes the similarity between tax subsidies and direct outlays. The Congressional Budget Act of 1974 requires a listing of tax expenditures in each budget and directs all congressional committees to identify any changes made in them by new legislation.

The 1974 act defines tax expenditures as "revenue losses attributable to provisions of the federal tax laws which allow a special exclusion, exemption, or deduction from gross income or which provide a special credit, a preferential rate of tax, or a deferral of tax liability." A tax expenditure, then, is a result of any deviation from the normal tax structure. The law does not define the normal tax structure, but it is generally regarded as being as close to economic income as practical measurement permits. (Thus capital gains are included in full, but imputed incomes such as rental values of owned homes are not because they are difficult to measure.) The normal individual income tax structure includes the personal exemption, the standard deduction, and the rate schedules.

The Reagan administration made thirteen modifications of the reference standard for calculating tax expenditures, none of which have been accepted by the Congressional Budget Office and the Joint Taxation Committee. The chief modifications are to omit from the tax expenditure budget the accelerated cost recovery system enacted under the Economic Recovery Tax Act of 1981, the graduated rates of the corporation income tax, and the deduction for two-earner couples. The tables in this appendix follow the reference standard of the CBO and the Joint Taxation Committee.

341

Tax expenditures are now estimated as outlay equivalents rather than as revenue reductions. These estimates measure tax expenditures as the outlays that would be required to provide an equal after-tax income to taxpayers. Since taxpayers would have to pay taxes on the higher income derived from the usual budget outlays, the outlay equivalents for many tax expenditures are higher than the revenue losses. The federal deficit is not changed by the methodology, because both outlays and receipts are raised by the amount of the outlay equivalent.

Tax expenditures in fiscal 1982 are estimated at $337.2 billion. If they were replaced by direct expenditures of the same value to taxpayers, both outlays and receipts would be raised by this amount; thus outlays in 1982 would have been $1,065.6 billion instead of the $728.4 billion reported in the budget, and receipts would have been $955.0 billion, so that the deficit would have remained at $110.6 billion (table C-1). (Total tax expenditures are the sum of the revenue effects of the individual items, each computed separately and assuming no other changes in the tax laws. They probably understate the total revenue effects because individuals would be pushed into higher brackets if all or a group of tax expenditures were removed simultaneously.)

The major tax expenditures are (1) personal deductions under the individual income tax (for state and local income, sales, and property taxes, charitable contributions, medical expenses, and interest paid); (2) exclusions from taxable income (state and local government bond interest, employee benefits, and transfer payments such as social security, unemployment compensation, and welfare); (3) preferential treatment of long-term capital gains; and (4) tax credits and accelerated depreciation for investment. A list of the major tax expenditures is given in table C-2.

Publication of estimates of tax expenditures in the budget encourages the administration and the Congress to take them into account in budget decisions. Tax expenditures constitute about 46 percent of budget outlays (see table C-3), and in recent years they have grown faster than outlays. For some budget functions, tax expenditures (for example, aid for housing and to state and local governments) exceed direct outlays. The distributional effects of tax expenditures are often quite different from those of direct expenditures. For example, the deductibility of mortgage interest is of little benefit to the poor, whereas outlays for rent subsidies do help them.

There is a continual tug-of-war between proponents of tax credits and budget and tax experts who resist the proliferation of special tax provisions because they complicate the tax laws and are frequently less efficient than direct expenditures. Congressional appropriations committees prefer direct outlays, and the tax committees prefer tax credits. The budget committees, recognizing both the similarities of and the differences between the two approaches, try to focus the attention of Congress on the merits of alternative approaches rather than on the choice of the committee that originates the legislation. Only when it is understood and accepted that a vote for a tax expenditure is in many ways the same as a vote for a direct expenditure can the budget process be said to work.

Table C-1. *Effect of Tax Expenditures on the Federal Budget, Fiscal Year 1982*
Billions of dollars

Item	Outlays	Receipts	Deficit
Official budget	728.4	617.8	− 110.6
Tax expenditures	337.2	337.2	. . .
Revised total	1,065.6	955.0	− 110.6

Sources: *Special Analyses, Budget of the United States Government, Fiscal Year 1984*, pp. A-13, G-26–28; and *Tax Expenditures: Budget Control Options and Five-Year Budget Projections for Fiscal Years 1983–1987* (Congressional Budget Office, 1982), p. 20.

Table C-2. *Tax Expenditures, by Function, Fiscal Years 1982–84*[a]

Millions of dollars

Item	1982	1983	1984
National defense			
Exclusion of benefits and allowances to armed forces personnel	2,890	2,780	2,820
Exclusion of military disability pensions	165	165	160
International affairs			
Exclusion of income earned abroad by U.S. citizens	1,850	2,155	2,165
Deferral of income of domestic international sales corporations	2,870	2,565	2,000
Deferral of income of controlled foreign corporations	520	560	605
General science, space, and technology			
Expensing of research and development expenditures	115	−1,160	−1,070
Credit for increasing research activities	640	1,060	1,180
Suspension of regulations relating to allocation under section 861 of research and experimental procedures	100	220	110
Energy			
Expensing of exploration and development costs			
Oil and gas	3,285	1,830	1,710
Other fuels	45	45	50
Excess of percentage over cost depletion			
Oil and gas	3,065	2,545	2,295
Other fuels	600	730	790
Capital gains treatment of royalties on coal	310	275	295
Exclusion of interest on state and local government industrial development bonds for certain energy facilities	5	15	20
Residential energy credits			
Supply incentives	390	515	690
Conservation incentives	435	400	390
Alternative, conservation and new technology credits			
Supply incentives	250	240	255
Conservation incentives	290	155	100
Alternative fuel production credit	20	45	70
Alcohol fuel credit[b]	5	5	5
Energy credit for intercity buses	10	15	15
Natural resources and environment			
Expensing of exploration and development costs, nonfuel minerals	85	90	100
Excess of percentage over cost depletion, nonfuel minerals	595	640	690
Exclusion of interest on state and local government pollution control bonds	870	1,020	1,150
Exclusion of payments in aid of construction of water, sewage, gas, and electric utilities	30	40	75
Tax incentives for preservation of historic structures	245	320	385
Capital gains treatment of iron ore	40	40	40
Capital gains treatment of certain timber income	565	730	910
Investment credit and seven-year amortization for reforestation expenditures	20	30	40

Table C-2 *(continued)*

Item	1982	1983	1984
Agriculture			
Expensing of certain capital outlays	550	570	590
Capital gains treatment of certain income	775	725	745
Deductibility of patronage dividends and certain other items of cooperatives	1,010	1,040	1,075
Exclusion of certain agricultural cost-sharing payments	105	90	80
Commerce and housing credit			
Dividend and interest exclusion	1,530	615	605
Exclusion of interest on state and local industrial development bonds	1,795	2,250	2,625
Exemption of credit union income	225	245	270
Excess bad debt reserves of financial institutions	660	680	1,090
Exclusion of interest on life insurance savings	6,625	6,780	7,310
Deductibility of interest on consumer credit	10,900	10,710	10,530
Deductibility of mortgage interest on owner-occupied homes	23,495	25,255	28,335
Deductibility of property tax on owner-occupied homes	8,405	8,810	9,645
Exclusion of interest on state and local housing bonds for owner-occupied housing	955	1,185	1,315
Depreciation on rental housing in excess of straight line	565	705	820
Depreciation on buildings other than rental housing in excess of straight line	300	400	465
Capital gains (other than agriculture, timber, iron ore, and coal)	26,590	22,865	23,465
Deferral of capital gains on home sales	2,090	2,225	2,515
Exclusion of capital gains on home sales for persons aged 55 and over	710	765	865
Carryover basis of capital gains at death	3,120	3,330	3,685
Investment credit, other than for ESOPs, rehabilitation of structures, energy property, and reforestation expenditures	19,255	17,170	18,325
Safe harbor leasing rules	2,880	3,270	3,035
Accelerated depreciation on equipment other than leased property	7,300	12,400	18,620
Amortization of start-up costs	125	195	290
Exclusion of interest on certain savings certificates	1,970	840	105
Reinvestment of dividends in public utility stock	400	590	670
Reduced rates on first $100,000 of corporate income	12,230	13,195	14,935
Transportation			
Deferral of tax on shipping companies	25	35	40
Exclusion of interest on state and local government bonds for mass transit	*	5	15
Community and regional development			
Five-year amortization for housing rehabilitation	45	60	70
Investment credit for rehabilitation of structures (other than historic)	295	360	460

Table C-2 *(continued)*

Item	1982	1983	1984
Education, training, employment, and social services			
Exclusion of interest on state and local student loan bonds	115	175	240
Parental personal exemption for students aged 19 or over	1,065	985	945
Exclusion of scholarship and fellowship income	465	415	375
Exclusion of employee meals and lodging (other than military)	730	755	805
Employer educational assistance	55	55	15
Exclusion of contributions to prepaid legal services plans	20	25	25
Investment credit for ESOPs	2,455	2,220	2,405
Deduction for two-earner married couples	1,005	5,685	10,040
Deductibility of charitable contributions (education)	830	770	805
Deductibility of charitable contributions other than education and health	7,550	7,085	7,170
Credit for child and dependent care expenses	1,830	2,110	2,430
Exclusion of employer-provided child care	. . .	10	30
Credit for employment of AFDC recipients and public assistance recipients under work incentive programs	30	. . .	. . .
General jobs credit	115	35	5
Targeted jobs credit	360	495	705
Health			
Exclusion of employer contributions for medical insurance premiums and medical care	22,555	25,412	28,980
Deductibility of medical expenses	3,970	2,950	2,635
Exclusion of interest on state and local hospital bonds	730	925	1,115
Deductibility of charitable contributions (health)	1,240	1,155	1,185
Tax credit for orphan drug research	. . .	15	25
Income security			
Exclusion of social security benefits			
Disability insurance benefits	1,770	1,675	1,660
OASI benefits for retired workers	14,940	15,765	16,800
Benefits for dependents and survivors	3,735	3,765	3,890
Exclusion of railroad retirement system benefits	790	780	725
Exclusion of workmen's compensation benefits	1,735	1,875	2,105
Exclusion of special benefits for disabled coal miners	185	170	165
Exclusion of untaxed unemployment insurance benefits	2,615	3,330	2,940
Exclusion of disability pay	190	170	150
Exclusion of public assistance benefits	445	430	430
Net exclusion of pension contributions and earnings			
Employer plans	65,805	70,005	78,780
Plans for self-employed and others	5,150	5,875	6,480
Exclusion of other employee benefits			
Premiums on group term life insurance	2,890	2,910	3,095
Premiums on accident and disability insurance	165	160	160
Income of trusts to finance supplementary unemployment benefits	10	5	5
Additional exemption for the blind	35	35	35
Additional exemption for the elderly	2,385	2,360	2,420
Tax credit for the elderly	135	135	135
Deductibility of casualty losses	1,295	705	520

Table C-2 (continued)

Item	1982	1983	1984
Earned-income credit[c]	460	390	340
Exclusion of interest on state and local bonds for rental			
housing	425	580	770
Deduction for motor carrier operating rights	115	115	115
Deduction for certain adoption expenses	15	15	15
Veterans' benefits and services			
Exclusion of veterans' disability compensation	1,860	1,815	1,835
Exclusion of veterans' pensions	330	305	295
Exclusion of GI bill benefits	175	150	125
General government			
Credits and deductions for political contributions	185	195	295
General-purpose fiscal assistance			
Exclusion of interest on general-purpose state and local debt	7,215	8,335	9,430
Deductibility of nonbusiness state and local taxes other than			
on owner-occupied homes	19,085	20,000	21,755
Tax credit for corporations receiving income from doing			
business in U.S. possessions	2,365	2,150	1,830
Interest			
Deferral of interest on savings bonds	315	450	500

Sources: *Special Analyses, Fiscal 1984*, pp. G-26–28; and *Tax Expenditures*, p. 20. All estimates have been rounded to the nearest $5 million.

* Less than $5 million.

a. Outlay equivalent estimates.

b. In addition, the exemption from the excise tax for alcohol fuels results in a reduction of excise tax receipts of $55 million in 1982, $80 million in 1983, and $90 million in 1984.

c. The figures in the table indicate the tax subsidies provided by the earned-income tax credit. The effect on outlays is $1,280 million for 1982, $1,205 million for 1983, and $1,125 million for 1984.

Table C-3. *Federal Outlays and Tax Expenditures, by Function, Fiscal Year 1982*

Billions of dollars unless otherwise indicated

		Tax expenditures	
Budget function	Outlays	Amount[a]	Percent of outlays
National defense	187.4	3.1	1.7
International affairs	10.0	5.2	52.0
General science, space, and technology	7.1	0.9	12.7
Energy	4.7	8.7	185.1
Natural resources and the environment	12.9	2.5	19.4
Agriculture	14.9	2.4	16.1
Commerce and housing credit	3.9	132.1	3,387.2
Transportation	20.6	. . .	. . .
Community and regional development	7.2	0.3	4.2
Education, training, employment, and social services	26.3	16.6	63.1
Health	74.0	28.5	38.5
Income security	248.3	105.3	42.4
Veterans' benefits and services	24.0	2.4	10.0
Administration of justice	4.7	. . .	. . .
Net interest	84.7	0.3	0.4
General government	4.7	0.2	4.3
General-purpose fiscal assistance to state and local government	6.4	28.7	448.4
Subtotal	741.9	337.2	45.5
Undistributed offsetting receipts	−13.2	. . .	. . .
Total	728.4	337.2	46.3

Sources: *Special Analyses. Fiscal 1984*, pp. A-7, G-26–28; and *Tax Expenditures*, pp. 20, 51–60. Figures are rounded.

a. Outlay equivalent estimates. Amount obtained by addition of individual items in each category.

Statistical Tables

Table D-1. *Federal Receipts, Expenditures, and Surpluses or Deficits, under the Official and National Income Accounts Budget Concepts, Fiscal Years 1955–82*

Billions of dollars

	Official (unified) federal budget[a]			National income accounts budget[a]		
Fiscal year	Receipts	Expenditures	Surplus (+) or deficit (−)	Receipts	Expenditures	Surplus (+) or deficit (−)
1955	65.5	68.5	−3.0	67.4	67.2	+0.2
1956	74.5	70.5	+4.1	76.3	70.0	+6.3
1957	80.0	76.7	+3.2	81.0	76.0	+5.0
1958	79.6	82.6	−2.9	78.1	82.8	−4.7
1959	79.2	92.1	−12.9	85.4	91.2	−5.8
1960	92.5	92.2	+0.3	94.8	91.3	+3.5
1961	94.4	97.8	−3.4	95.0	98.1	−3.1
1962	99.7	106.8	−7.1	104.0	106.2	−2.2
1963	106.6	111.3	−4.8	110.0	111.7	−1.7
1964	112.7	118.6	−5.9	115.6	117.2	−1.6
1965	116.8	118.4	−1.6	120.0	118.5	+1.5
1966	130.9	134.7	−3.8	132.7	132.7	0.0
1967	148.9	157.6	−8.7	146.0	154.9	−8.9
1968	152.0	178.1	−25.1	160.0	172.2	−12.2
1969	186.9	183.6	+3.2	190.1	184.7	+5.4
1970	192.8	195.7	−2.8	194.9	195.6	−0.7
1971	187.1	210.2	−23.0	192.5	212.7	−20.2
1972	207.3	230.7	−23.4	213.5	232.9	−19.4
1973	230.8	245.6	−14.8	240.7	255.7	−14.9
1974	263.2	267.9	−4.7	271.6	278.2	−6.6
1975	279.1	324.2	−45.2	283.4	328.8	−45.4
1976	298.1	364.5	−66.4	314.9	370.7	−55.8
1977	355.6	400.5	−44.9	365.9	411.2	−45.3
1978	399.6	448.4	−48.8	414.3	450.4	−36.1
1979	463.3	491.0	−27.7	480.8	495.6	−14.8
1980	517.1	576.7	−59.6	525.7	577.1	−51.4
1981	599.3	657.2	−57.9	612.4	667.9	−55.5
1982	617.8	728.4	−110.6	621.5	740.4	−118.9

Sources: *The Budget of the United States Government*, various years. Figures are rounded.
a. For an explanation of the differences between the two budget concepts, see p. 17.

Table D-2. *High-Employment Receipts, Expenditures, and Surpluses or Deficits, under the National Income Accounts Budget Concept, 1955–82*[a]

Billions of dollars

Year	Receipts	Expenditures	Surplus (+) or deficit (−)
1955	73.1	67.9	+5.2
1956	79.8	71.9	+7.9
1957	85.6	79.5	+6.1
1958	86.8	86.8	0
1959	95.3	89.9	+5.4
1960	104.0	92.0	+12.1
1961	107.1	100.0	+7.1
1962	112.3	109.3	+3.0
1963	120.5	113.0	+7.4
1964	118.6	117.5	+1.1
1965	124.5	123.7	+0.9
1966	138.4	144.0	−5.6
1967	149.0	164.1	−15.1
1968	170.2	181.2	−11.0
1969	194.3	189.4	+4.9
1970	199.7	204.3	−4.6
1971	206.7	218.0	−11.3
1972	230.0	242.1	−12.1
1973	254.1	263.5	−9.3
1974	298.7	298.6	+0.1
1975	317.5	346.0	−28.4
1976	357.1	373.6	−16.6
1977	392.3	412.7	−20.4
1978	440.6	456.5	−15.9
1979	504.9	506.9	−1.9
1980	576.8	593.9	−17.1
1981	678.5	674.0	+4.5
1982	705.3	735.1	−29.8
Alternative estimates[b]			
1980	562.9	597.5	−34.6
1981	661.7	678.5	−16.8
1982	686.0	741.0	−55.0

Source: U.S. Department of Commerce, Bureau of Economic Analysis. Figures are rounded.

a. Assumes that the high-employment unemployment rate increased from 4.0 percent in 1955 to 5.1 percent in 1975 and that the potential GNP grew between 3.3 and 3.9 percent in 1955–73, 3 percent in 1974–78, and 2.9 percent beginning in 1979. For details, see Frank de Leeuw and others, "The High-Employment Budget: New Estimates, 1955–80," *Survey of Current Business*, vol. 60 (November 1980), pp. 13–43; and Frank de Leeuw and Thomas M. Holloway, "The High-Employment Budget: Revised Estimates and Automatic Inflation Effects," ibid., vol. 62 (April 1982), pp. 21–33.

b. Assumes high-employment unemployment rate of 6 percent.

Table D-3. *Relation of Federal, State, and Local Government Receipts to Gross National Product, 1955–82*[a]

National income accounts basis

| | Gross national product (billions | Receipts of federal, state, and local governments | | | | | |
| | | Amount (billions of dollars) | | | Percent of gross national product | | |
Year	of dollars)	Total	Federal	State and local[b]	Total	Federal	State and local[b]
1955	399.3	101.1	72.6	28.5	25.3	18.2	7.1
1956	420.7	109.6	78.0	31.7	26.1	18.5	7.5
1957	442.8	116.2	81.9	34.3	26.2	18.5	7.7
1958	448.9	115.0	78.7	36.3	25.6	17.5	8.1
1959	486.5	129.4	89.8	39.6	26.6	18.5	8.1
1960	506.0	139.5	96.1	43.4	27.6	19.0	8.6
1961	523.3	144.8	98.1	46.8	27.7	18.7	8.9
1962	563.8	156.7	106.2	50.5	27.8	18.8	9.0
1963	594.7	168.5	114.4	54.1	28.3	19.2	9.1
1964	635.7	174.0	114.9	59.1	27.4	18.1	9.3
1965	688.1	188.3	124.3	64.0	27.4	18.1	9.3
1966	753.0	212.3	141.8	70.4	28.2	18.8	9.4
1967	796.3	228.2	150.5	77.7	28.7	18.9	9.8
1968	868.5	263.4	174.7	88.7	30.3	20.1	10.2
1969	935.5	296.3	197.0	99.3	31.7	21.1	10.6
1970	982.4	302.6	192.1	110.5	30.8	19.5	11.2
1971	1,063.4	322.2	198.6	123.6	30.3	18.7	11.6
1972	1,171.1	367.4	227.5	139.9	31.4	19.4	11.9
1973	1,306.6	411.2	258.3	152.9	31.5	19.8	11.7
1974	1,413.2	454.6	288.2	166.4	32.2	20.4	11.8
1975	1,516.3	466.4	286.5	179.9	30.8	18.9	11.9
1976	1,718.0	538.3	331.8	206.7	31.3	19.3	12.0
1977	1,918.3	605.4	375.2	230.2	31.6	19.6	12.0
1978	2,163.9	682.0	431.6	250.4	31.5	19.9	11.6
1979	2,417.8	765.1	493.6	271.5	31.6	20.4	11.2
1980	2,631.7	838.3	540.9	297.4	31.9	20.6	11.3
1981	2,954.1	957.2	627.0	330.2	32.4	21.2	11.2
1982	3,073.0	972.6	617.4	355.2	31.6	20.1	11.6

Source: U.S. Department of Commerce, Bureau of Economic Analysis. Figures are rounded.

a. The receipts in this table are on the national income accounts basis of the Department of Commerce and therefore differ from the official unified budget receipts as defined in the budget message. In this table, receipts of trust funds and taxes other than corporation taxes are on a cash basis, but, unlike the unified budget, corporation taxes are on an accrual basis.

b. State and local receipts have been adjusted to exclude federal grants-in-aid.

Table D-4. *Federal Budget Receipts, by Source, Fiscal Years 1955–82*[a]

Fiscal year	Total				Taxes			
		Indi-vidual	Corpo-ration	Excise	Estate and gift	Em-ploy-ment[b]	Cus-toms	Other receipts[c]
				Amount (millions of dollars)				
1955	65,469	28,747	17,861	9,131	924	7,866	585	355
1956	74,547	32,188	20,880	9,929	1,161	9,323	682	384
1957	79,990	35,620	21,167	10,534	1,365	9,997	735	572
1958	79,636	34,724	20,072	10,638	1,393	11,239	782	786
1959	79,249	36,776	17,309	10,578	1,333	11,722	925	605
1960	92,492	40,741	21,494	11,676	1,606	14,684	1,105	1,187
1961	94,389	41,338	20,954	11,860	1,896	16,438	982	919
1962	99,676	45,571	20,523	12,534	2,016	17,046	1,142	843
1963	106,560	47,588	21,579	13,194	2,167	19,804	1,205	1,022
1964	112,662	48,697	23,493	13,731	2,394	22,012	1,252	1,085
1965	116,833	48,792	25,461	14,570	2,716	22,258	1,442	1,594
1966	130,856	55,446	30,073	13,062	3,066	25,567	1,767	1,876
1967	148,906	61,526	33,971	13,719	2,978	32,703	1,901	2,107
1968	152,973	68,726	28,665	14,079	3,051	33,923	2,038	2,491
1969	186,882	87,249	36,678	15,222	3,491	39,015	2,319	2,909
1970	192,807	90,412	32,829	15,705	3,644	44,362	2,430	3,424
1971	187,139	86,230	26,785	16,614	3,735	47,325	2,591	3,858
1972	207,309	94,737	32,166	15,477	5,436	52,574	3,287	3,632
1973	230,799	103,246	36,153	16,260	4,917	63,115	3,188	3,920
1974	263,224	118,952	38,620	16,844	5,035	75,071	3,334	5,368
1975	279,090	122,386	40,621	16,551	4,611	84,534	3,676	6,712
1976	298,060	131,603	41,409	16,963	5,216	90,769	4,074	8,027
1977	355,559	157,626	54,892	17,548	7,327	106,485	5,150	6,531
1978	399,561	180,988	59,952	18,376	5,285	120,967	6,573	7,419
1979	463,302	217,841	65,677	18,745	5,411	138,939	7,439	9,252
1980	517,112	244,069	64,600	24,329	6,389	157,803	7,174	12,748
1981	599,272	285,917	61,137	40,839	6,787	182,720	8,083	13,790
1982	617,766	297,744	49,207	36,311	7,991	201,498	8,854	16,162

Table D-4 *(continued)*

Fiscal year	Total	Indi-vidual	Corpo-ration	Excise	Estate and gift	Em-ploy-ment[b]	Cus-toms	Other receipts[c]
				Percent of total				
1955	100	43.9	27.3	13.9	1.4	12.0	0.9	0.5
1956	100	43.2	28.0	13.3	1.6	12.5	0.9	0.5
1957	100	44.5	26.5	13.2	1.7	12.5	0.9	0.7
1958	100	43.6	25.2	13.4	1.7	14.1	1.0	1.0
1959	100	46.4	21.8	13.3	1.7	14.8	1.2	0.8
1960	100	44.0	23.2	12.6	1.7	15.9	1.2	1.3
1961	100	43.8	22.2	12.6	2.0	17.4	1.0	1.0
1962	100	45.7	20.6	12.6	2.0	17.1	1.1	0.8
1963	100	44.7	20.3	12.4	2.0	18.6	1.1	1.0
1964	100	43.2	20.9	12.2	2.1	19.5	1.1	1.0
1965	100	41.8	21.8	12.5	2.3	19.1	1.2	1.4
1966	100	42.4	23.0	10.0	2.3	19.5	1.4	1.4
1967	100	41.3	22.8	9.2	2.0	22.0	1.3	1.4
1968	100	44.9	18.7	9.2	2.0	22.2	1.3	1.6
1969	100	46.7	19.6	8.1	1.9	20.9	1.2	1.6
1970	100	46.9	17.0	8.1	1.9	23.0	1.3	1.8
1971	100	46.1	14.3	8.9	2.0	25.3	1.4	2.1
1972	100	45.7	15.5	7.5	2.6	25.4	1.6	1.8
1973	100	44.7	15.7	7.0	2.1	27.3	1.4	1.7
1974	100	45.2	14.7	6.4	1.9	28.5	1.3	2.0
1975	100	43.9	14.6	5.9	1.7	30.3	1.3	2.4
1976	100	44.2	13.9	5.7	1.7	30.5	1.4	2.7
1977	100	44.3	15.4	4.9	2.1	29.9	1.4	1.8
1978	100	45.3	15.0	4.6	1.3	30.3	1.6	1.9
1979	100	47.0	14.2	4.0	1.2	30.0	1.6	2.0
1980	100	47.2	12.5	4.7	1.0	30.5	1.4	2.5
1981	100	47.7	10.2	6.8	1.1	30.5	1.3	2.3
1982	100	48.2	8.0	5.9	1.3	32.6	1.4	2.6

Source: Office of Management and Budget. Figures are rounded.

a. Receipts in this table are on the official unified budget basis and are net after refunds.

b. Includes payroll taxes for social security and unemployment insurance, employee contributions for federal retirement, and contributions for supplementary medical insurance.

c. Includes deposits of earnings by Federal Reserve banks and miscellaneous receipts.

Table D-5. Tax Revenues as a Percentage of Gross Domestic Product and Distribution of Tax Revenues, by Source, Selected Countries, 1981[a]

Tax source	United States	Canada	Japan	Australia	Austria	Belgium	Denmark	France	Germany	Italy	Netherlands	Norway	Sweden	Switzerland	United Kingdom
	Percent of gross domestic product														
Individual income	11.8	11.8	6.6	14.4	10.1	15.8	23.7	5.7	10.8	8.9	11.2	12.8	20.5	10.8	11.0
Corporate income	2.7	4.0	5.5	3.5	1.4	2.5	1.3	2.2	1.9	3.0	3.2	7.8	1.5	1.8	3.5
Payroll	8.3	4.0	8.1	1.6	16.1	14.0	1.0	19.3	13.3	12.1	18.2	10.1	16.6	9.3	7.5
Goods and services[c]	5.5	12.1	4.4	9.5	13.8	12.2	17.0	14.2	10.4	8.3	11.2	17.0	12.3	6.1	10.6
Property	2.7	2.9	2.1	2.4	1.1	0.5	2.1	1.3	0.9	1.3	1.5	0.8	0.3	2.0	4.6
Inheritances and gifts	0.3	*	0.2	0.1	0.1	0.4	0.2	0.3	0.1	0.1	0.2	*	0.1	0.2	0.2
Total	31.3	34.8	26.9	31.5	42.6	45.4	45.3	43.0	37.4	33.7	45.5	48.5	51.3	30.2	37.4
	Distribution by source														
Individual income	37.7	33.9	24.5	45.7	23.7	34.8	52.3	13.3	28.9	26.4	24.6	26.4	40.0	35.8	29.4
Corporate income	8.6	11.5	20.4	11.1	3.3	5.5	2.9	5.1	5.1	8.9	7.0	16.1	2.9	6.0	9.4
Payroll	26.5	11.5	30.1	5.1	37.8	30.8	2.2	44.9	35.6	35.9	40.0	20.8	32.4	30.8	20.1
Goods and services[b]	17.6	34.8	16.4	30.2	32.4	26.9	37.5	33.0	27.8	24.6	24.6	35.1	24.0	20.2	28.3
Property	8.6	8.3	7.8	7.6	2.6	1.1	4.6	3.0	2.4	3.9	3.3	1.6	0.6	6.6	12.3
Inheritances and gifts	1.0	*	0.7	0.3	0.2	0.9	0.4	0.7	0.3	0.3	0.4	*	0.2	0.7	0.5
Total	100.0	100.0	100.0	100.0	100.0	100.0	100.0	100.0	100.0	100.0	100.0	100.0	100.0	100.0	100.0

Source: Organisation for Economic Co-operation and Development, *Revenue Statistics of OECD Member Countries, 1965–82* (Paris: OECD, 1983). Figures are rounded.
* Less than 0.05 percent.
a. Includes national and local taxes.
b. Includes sales, value-added, and excise taxes, taxes on imports and exports, taxes on transfers of property and securities, other transaction taxes paid by enterprises, and miscellaneous other taxes.

Table D-6. Standard and Itemized Deductions, Taxable and Nontaxable Federal Individual Income Tax Returns, 1944–81

Year	Total number of returns (millions)	Standard deduction[a] Number[b] (millions)	Standard deduction[a] Amount (billions of dollars)	Itemized deductions Number[b] (millions)	Itemized deductions Amount (billions of dollars)	Total deductions Amount (billions of dollars)	Total deductions Percent of adjusted gross income
1944	47.1	38.7	8.0	8.4	4.8	12.8	11.0
1945	49.9	41.5	8.1	8.5	5.5	13.6	11.3
1946	52.8	44.1	8.9	8.8	6.3	15.2	11.3
1947	55.1	44.7	9.8	10.4	7.8	17.6	11.8
1948	52.1	43.2	11.5	8.8	7.9	19.4	11.9
1949	51.8	42.1	11.1	9.7	8.8	19.9	12.4
1950	53.1	42.7	12.0	10.3	9.9	21.9	12.2
1951	55.4	43.9	13.3	11.6	11.9	25.2	12.5
1952	56.5	43.7	13.7	12.8	13.6	27.3	12.7
1953	57.8	43.4	14.2	14.4	15.6	29.8	13.0
1954	56.7	41.0	13.3	15.7	17.4	30.7	13.4
1955	58.3	41.4	13.6	16.9	20.0	33.6	13.5
1956	59.2	40.7	13.8	18.5	22.6	36.4	13.6
1957	59.8	39.7	13.8	20.2	25.7	39.5	14.1
1958	59.1	38.3	13.2	20.8	27.5	40.7	14.5
1959	60.3	37.8	13.4	22.5	32.0	45.4	14.9
1960	61.0	36.9	13.1	24.1	35.3	48.4	15.3
1961	61.5	36.2	12.9	25.3	38.4	51.3	15.6
1962	62.7	36.3	13.1	26.5	41.7	54.8	15.7
1963	63.9	35.8	13.1	28.2	46.1	59.2	16.1
1964	65.4	38.5	20.2	26.9	46.8	67.0	16.9
1965	67.6	39.7	20.6	27.9	50.7	71.4	16.6
1966	70.2	41.6	21.8	28.6	54.6	76.4	16.3
1967	71.7	41.9	22.1	29.8	59.6	81.7	16.2
1968	73.7	41.7	22.1	32.0	69.2	91.3	16.4
1969	75.8	40.9	21.6	34.9	80.2	101.8	16.8
1970	74.3	38.8	32.4	35.4	88.2	120.5	19.0
1971	74.6	43.9	48.1	30.7	91.9	139.9	20.7
1972	77.6	50.6	69.8	27.0	96.7	166.4	22.2
1973	80.7	52.6	73.6	28.0	107.0	180.6	21.8
1974	83.3	53.8	76.1	29.6	119.4	195.5	21.6
1975	82.2	56.1	100.9	26.1	122.3	223.2	23.5
1976	84.7	58.7	113.8	26.0	133.9	247.6	23.5
1977	86.6	63.7	137.7	22.9	138.5	276.2	23.8
1978	89.8	64.0	139.8	25.8	164.4	304.2	23.4
1979	92.7	66.2	148.8	26.5	184.2	333.0	22.7
1980	93.9	65.0	146.0	29.0	218.0	364.0	22.6
1981	95.4	63.8	144.7	31.6	256.4	401.2	22.6

Source: *Statistics of Income, Individual Income Tax Returns.* Amount of standard deduction for 1944–57 estimated by author on the basis of the distribution of the number of tax returns by income classes and marital status in *Statistics of Income*, and for 1958–81 obtained directly from *Statistics of Income*. Figures are rounded.

a. Zero-bracket amount for 1977 and later years.

b. Returns with standard deduction, 1955–81, include a small number with no adjusted gross income and no deductions. For 1944–54, returns with no adjusted gross income are included in the number of returns with itemized deductions.

Table D-7. *Federal Individual Tax Liabilities, Prepayments, and Final Balances of Tax Due and Overpayments, 1944–81*
Billions of dollars

	Tax liabilities			Prepayments		Final balances	
Year	Total	Income tax	Self-employ-ment tax	With-holding[a]	Declara-tion pay-ments[b]	Tax due	Over-pay-ments
1944	16.2	16.2	...	9.6	5.5	2.4	1.4
1945	17.1	17.1	...	10.5	6.0	2.4	1.8
1946	16.1	16.1	...	9.2	6.0	2.7	1.9
1947	18.1	18.1	...	11.2	5.8	3.0	2.0
1948	15.4	15.4	...	10.6	5.3	2.2	2.7
1949	14.5	14.5	...	9.6	4.7	2.1	2.0
1950	18.4	18.4	...	11.8	5.6	3.1	2.1
1951	24.4	24.2	0.2	16.6	6.6	3.7	2.5
1952	28.0	27.8	0.2	20.3	7.1	3.6	2.9
1953	29.7	29.4	0.2	22.6	7.0	3.4	3.3
1954	27.0	26.7	0.3	20.5	7.2	3.0	3.7
1955	30.1	29.6	0.5	22.7	7.2	3.8	3.6
1956	33.3	32.7	0.5	25.2	7.9	4.1	4.0
1957	35.0	34.4	0.6	27.4	8.2	3.9	4.5
1958	34.9	34.3	0.6	27.6	8.0	4.1	4.8
1959	39.3	38.6	0.7	30.8	8.6	5.1	5.1
1960	40.3	39.5	0.8	32.7	8.6	4.7	5.7
1961	43.1	42.2	0.8	34.4	9.0	5.7	6.0
1962	45.8	44.9	0.9	37.4	9.3	5.6	6.6
1963	49.2	48.2	1.0	40.2	9.7	6.3	6.9
1964	48.2	47.2	1.0	36.9	10.1	7.1	5.9
1965	50.6	49.6	1.1	39.3	10.7	7.5	6.8
1966	57.6	56.1	1.5	46.9	11.8	7.6	8.6
1967	64.5	63.0	1.6	53.1	13.1	8.4	10.2
1968	78.4	76.7	1.7	62.9	16.0	10.6	11.0
1969	88.5	86.6	1.9	75.2	17.5	10.5	14.6
1970	85.8	83.9	1.8	76.1	16.7	8.7	15.7
1971	87.5	85.4	2.0	75.9	17.5	9.5	15.4
1972	95.9	93.6	2.3	91.2	18.4	9.9	23.5
1973	111.2	108.2	3.0	103.6	19.6	12.8	24.9
1974	127.0	123.7	3.3	117.9	21.4	14.8	27.1
1975	127.9	124.6	3.4	118.8	23.4	14.2	28.5
1976	145.7	141.9	3.8	132.5	26.1	17.5	30.4
1977	164.0	159.9	4.1	147.8	29.1	20.0	32.8
1978	193.2	188.5	4.7	170.5	32.3	25.0	34.6
1979	220.1	214.7	5.4	200.0	37.1	27.4	44.4
1980	256.3	250.6	5.7	229.4	42.1	32.8	48.1
1981	291.1	284.4	6.7	261.0	50.6	34.9	55.4

Source: *Statistics of Income, Individual Income Tax Returns.* Figures are rounded.
a. Includes excess social security taxes withheld.
b. Includes payments with requests for extension of filing time, credit for gasoline, fuel, and oil, and other tax payments or credits.

Table D-8. *Number of Federal Individual Income Tax Returns,*
by Type of Final Settlement, 1944–81
Millions

Year	Total number of returns	Returns with		No over-payments or balances due
		Tax due	Overpayments	
1944	47.1	22.6	22.9	1.6
1945	49.9	14.5	33.5	1.9
1946	52.8	13.6	34.4	4.8
1947	55.1	15.3	33.0	6.7
1948	52.1	8.1	38.4	5.6
1949	51.8	13.8	30.2	7.9
1950	53.1	14.3	32.0	6.8
1951	55.4	18.6	31.0	5.8
1952	56.5	19.3	32.1	5.1
1953	57.8	19.0	32.7	6.2
1954	56.7	16.6	35.2	5.0
1955	58.3	18.7	35.4	4.2
1956	59.2	19.4	36.1	3.7
1957	59.8	18.6	37.6	3.6
1958	59.1	18.1	37.4	3.6
1959	60.3	19.1	38.4	2.8
1960	61.0	18.1	39.4	3.5
1961	61.5	18.6	40.0	2.9
1962	62.7	18.7	40.9	3.1
1963	63.9	19.3	41.4	3.3
1964	65.4	22.5	39.3	3.5
1965	67.6	20.0	44.3	3.2
1966	70.2	17.8	49.4	3.0
1967	71.7	17.5	51.2	3.0
1968	73.7	20.3	50.6	2.8
1969	75.8	17.9	54.9	3.0
1970	74.3	16.5	55.3	2.5
1971	74.6	17.0	55.3	2.4
1972	77.6	11.9	63.3	2.3
1973	80.7	14.2	64.2	2.2
1974	83.3	15.4	65.8	2.1
1975	82.2	15.8	63.8	2.6
1976	84.7	16.9	65.0	2.8
1977	86.6	17.8	66.0	2.8
1978	89.8	21.6	65.5	2.7
1979	92.7	18.8	71.4	2.4
1980	93.9	21.8	69.9	2.3
1981	95.4	23.0	70.0	2.4

Source: *Statistics of Income, Individual Income Tax Returns.* Figures are rounded.

Table D-9. *Distribution of Federal Individual Income Tax Returns and Tax Liabilities, 1960, 1970, and 1981*

Adjusted gross income class (dollars)	Returns		Tax liabilities[a]	
	Number (thousands)	Percent of total	Amount (millions of dollars)	Percent of total
1960				
Under 5,000[b]	35,443	58.1	6,274	15.9
5,000–10,000	20,266	33.2	15,362	38.9
10,000–25,000	4,751	7.8	9,844	24.9
25,000–50,000	441	0.7	3,598	9.1
50,000–100,000	101	0.2	2,273	5.8
100,000–200,000	19	*	1,001	2.5
200,000–500,000	5	*	607	1.5
500,000–1,000,000	1	*	226	0.6
1,000,000 and over	c	*	281	0.7
Total	66,028	100.0	39,464	100.0
1970				
Under 5,000[b]	28,308	38.1	3,625	4.3
5,000–10,000	22,303	30.0	16,659	19.9
10,000–25,000	21,554	29.0	40,503	48.3
25,000–50,000	1,686	2.3	10,756	12.8
50,000–100,000	351	0.5	6,631	7.9
100,000–200,000	62	0.1	2,986	3.6
200,000–500,000	13	*	1,508	1.8
500,000–1,000,000	2	*	511	0.6
1,000,000 and over	1	*	609	0.7
Total	74,280	100.0	83,787	100.0
1981				
Under 5,000[b]	18,726	19.7	553	0.2
5,000–10,000	17,651	18.5	7,392	2.6
10,000–25,000	34,308	36.0	66,631	23.6
25,000–50,000	20,593	21.6	114,904	40.7
50,000–100,000	3,443	3.6	50,675	18.0
100,000–200,000	517	0.5	21,142	7.5
200,000–500,000	118	0.1	12,380	4.4
500,000–1,000,000	15	*	3,945	1.4
1,000,000 and over	5	*	4,679	1.7
Total	95,396	100.0	282,302	100.0

Source: *Statistics of Income, Individual Income Tax Returns.* Figures are rounded.
* Less than 0.05 percent.
a. Income tax after credits.
b. Includes returns with no adjusted gross income.
c. Fewer than 500 returns.

Table D-10. Tax Saving for Single Persons, Heads of Households, and Married Couples Filing Joint Returns under Income Splitting and Associated Provisions, by Taxable Income, 1984 Rates

Dollars

Taxable income	Basic (married, separate returns)	Tax liability			Tax saving over basic tax			Tax saving as percent of basic tax		
		Single	Head of house-hold	Married, joint return[a]	Single	Head of house-hold	Married, joint return[a]	Single	Head of house-hold	Married, joint return[a]
2,000	33	0	0	0	33	33	33	100.0	100.0	100.0
5,000	409	325	303	176	84	106	233	20.5	25.9	57.0
10,000	1,230	1,075	1,012	819	155	218	411	12.6	17.7	33.4
15,000	2,409	2,001	1,894	1,581	408	515	828	16.9	21.4	34.4
20,000	3,929	3,205	2,966	2,461	724	963	1,468	18.4	24.5	37.4
25,000	5,684	4,565	4,226	3,565	1,119	1,458	2,119	19.7	25.7	37.3
30,000	7,584	6,113	5,674	4,818	1,471	1,910	2,766	19.4	25.2	36.5
40,000	11,784	9,749	9,051	7,858	2,035	2,733	3,926	17.3	23.2	33.3
50,000	16,200	13,889	12,922	11,368	2,311	3,278	4,832	14.3	20.2	29.8
60,000	20,912	18,371	17,122	15,168	2,541	3,790	5,744	12.2	18.1	27.5
70,000	25,812	23,171	21,604	19,368	2,641	4,208	6,444	10.2	16.3	25.0
80,000	30,715	27,971	26,104	23,568	2,744	4,611	7,147	8.9	15.0	23.3
90,000	35,700	32,935	30,850	27,900	2,765	4,850	7,800	7.7	13.6	21.8
100,000	40,700	37,935	35,650	32,400	2,765	5,050	8,300	6.8	12.4	20.4
150,000	65,700	62,935	60,484	56,524	2,765	5,216	9,176	4.2	7.9	14.0
200,000	90,700	87,935	85,484	81,400	2,765	5,216	9,300	3.0	5.8	10.3
500,000	240,700	237,935	235,484	231,400	2,765	5,216	9,300	1.1	2.2	3.9
1,000,000	490,700	487,935	485,484	481,400	2,765	5,216	9,300	0.6	1.1	1.9

Source: Economic Recovery Tax Act of 1981.
a. Assumes one earner in couple.

Table D-11. *Influence of Various Provisions on Effective Rates of Federal Individual Income Tax, 1985*
Percent

				Reduction due to				
Total income class[a]	Nominal tax rate[b]	Personal exemptions	Deductions	Transfer payments	Capital gains, etc.[c]	Income splitting[d]	Tax credits[e]	Actual tax rate
0–3,000	11.6	7.3	4.3	. . .	*	. . .	1.0	−1.0
3,000–5,000	12.6	4.7	6.7	0.4	*	. . .	1.3	−0.5
5,000–7,000	13.6	4.1	5.6	1.0	0.2	. . .	1.5	1.2
7,000–10,000	14.8	3.5	4.8	1.5	0.1	0.1	1.4	3.4
10,000–15,000	17.3	3.5	4.8	2.3	0.2	0.4	0.7	5.4
15,000–20,000	20.3	4.0	5.0	3.0	0.3	1.0	0.2	6.8
20,000–25,000	23.2	4.0	5.7	3.1	0.5	1.7	0.2	8.0
25,000–35,000	26.9	4.0	7.0	2.8	0.7	3.0	0.2	9.2
35,000–50,000	31.2	3.5	8.4	1.7	1.6	4.8	0.2	11.0
50,000–75,000	35.4	2.8	9.1	1.8	1.5	5.9	0.4	13.9
75,000–100,000	39.5	2.0	9.5	1.6	2.5	5.9	0.9	17.1
100,000–150,000	42.2	1.5	9.4	1.4	3.4	5.4	1.3	19.8
150,000–200,000	44.3	1.1	9.0	1.2	4.2	4.3	1.6	22.9
200,000–500,000	46.1	0.7	8.6	1.0	6.0	2.5	1.7	25.6
500,000–1,000,000	47.8	0.3	8.6	0.6	9.8	0.7	1.7	26.1
1,000,000 and over	48.7	0.1	8.0	0.3	16.4	*	1.1	22.9
Total	30.1	3.3	7.6	2.1	1.5	3.6	0.5	11.5

Source: Brookings 1980 tax file projected to 1985. Figures are rounded.
* 0.05 percent or less.
a. Total income is the sum of adjusted gross income, excluded sick pay, dividends and capital gains, and other tax preferences, social security benefits in excess of employee contributions, unemployment compensation, employer-provided health insurance, employer-provided life insurance, veterans' benefits, workmen's compensation, life insurance interest, and state and local bond interest.
b. Rate schedule for married persons filing separate returns applied to total income.
c. Includes effect of capital gains exclusion, individual retirement and Keogh accounts, and other tax preferences.
d. Includes tax advantage of income splitting for married couples filing joint returns, special rate schedules for single persons and heads of households, and 10 percent deduction (up to $30,000 of earned income) for two-earner couples.
e. Credits for earned income, child care, investment outlays, and foreign taxes.

Table D-12. *Itemized Deductions as a Percentage of Adjusted Gross Income, by Adjusted Gross Income Class, Taxable Federal Individual Income Tax Returns, 1981*

Adjusted gross income class (dollars)	Total	Contributions	Interest	Taxes	Medical and dental	Other
Under 5,000	96.8	6.1	39.0	17.8	18.5	15.4
5,000–10,000	63.2	6.3	22.2	11.2	18.2	5.3
10,000–15,000	42.3	4.5	17.3	9.1	8.0	3.3
15,000–20,000	31.6	3.4	13.9	7.8	4.0	2.5
20,000–25,000	26.7	2.7	12.1	7.6	2.2	2.1
25,000–30,000	23.8	2.3	10.8	7.2	1.6	1.8
30,000–50,000	21.5	2.3	9.4	7.2	1.0	1.6
50,000–100,000	21.3	2.7	8.8	7.5	0.7	1.5
100,000–200,000	21.8	3.6	8.4	7.6	0.5	1.7
200,000–500,000	22.2	5.1	7.6	7.4	0.3	1.8
500,000–1,000,000	25.0	7.5	7.8	7.4	0.2	2.1
1,000,000 and over	27.1	9.7	7.7	7.5	*	2.1
All taxable returns	24.1	2.9	10.2	7.5	1.7	1.8

Source: *Statistics of Income—1981, Individual Income Tax Returns*, table 2.1. Figures are rounded.
* Less than 0.05.

Table D-13. *Estimated Revenue from Capital Gains and Income Taxation, 1954–81*

Billions of dollars unless otherwise specified

	Individuals			Corporations			Individuals and corporations		
		Estimated tax on capital gains and losses		Total income and	Estimated tax on capital gains and losses		Total income and	Estimated tax on capital gains and losses	
Year	Total income taxes	Amount	Percent of total tax	excess profits taxes	Amount	Percent of total tax	excess profits taxes	Amount	Percent of total tax
1954	26.7	0.9	3.4	16.1	0.5	3.1	42.8	1.4	3.3
1955	29.6	1.4	4.7	20.8	0.5	2.4	50.4	1.9	3.8
1956	32.7	1.3	4.0	20.4	0.5	2.5	53.1	1.8	3.4
1957	34.4	1.0	2.9	19.5	0.4	2.1	53.9	1.4	2.6
1958	34.3	1.2	3.5	17.7	0.6	3.4	52.0	1.8	3.5
1959	38.6	1.8	4.7	21.3	0.4	1.9	59.9	2.2	3.7
1960	39.5	1.5	3.8	20.6	0.5	2.4	60.1	2.0	3.3
1961	42.2	2.3	5.5	20.7	0.7	3.4	62.9	3.0	4.8
1962	44.9	1.7	3.8	21.5	0.5	2.3	66.4	2.2	3.3
1963	48.2	1.9	3.9	23.3	0.6	2.6	71.5	2.5	3.5
1964	47.2	2.3	4.9	24.3	0.6	2.5	71.5	2.9	4.1
1965	49.5	2.8	5.7	27.3	0.6	2.2	76.8	3.4	4.4
1966	56.1	2.7	4.8	30.0	0.8	2.7	86.1	3.5	4.1
1967	62.9	3.9	6.2	28.1	0.9	3.2	91.0	4.8	5.3
1968	76.6	5.7	7.4	33.6	1.0	3.0	110.2	6.7	6.1
1969	86.6	4.9	5.7	33.4	1.1	3.3	120.0	6.0	5.0
1970	83.9	2.7	3.2	27.8	0.8	2.9	111.7	3.5	3.1
1971	85.4	4.0	4.7	30.2	1.1	3.6	115.6	5.1	4.4
1972	93.6	5.4	5.8	33.5	1.5	4.5	127.1	6.9	5.4
1973	108.1	5.0	4.6	39.1	1.7	4.3	147.2	6.7	4.6
1974	123.6	3.7	3.0	41.1	1.6	3.9	164.7	5.3	3.2
1975	124.5	4.0	3.2	39.7	1.3	3.3	164.2	5.3	3.2
1976	141.8	6.1	4.3	49.8	1.8	3.6	191.6	7.9	4.1
1977	159.8	7.3	4.6	56.7	2.2	3.9	216.5	9.5	4.4
1978	188.2	8.4	4.5	64.3	3.0	4.7	252.5	11.4	4.5
1979	214.5	10.8	5.0	65.8	3.8	5.8	280.3	14.6	5.2
1980	250.3	11.5	4.6	62.9	3.7	5.9	313.2	15.2	4.9
1981	284.1	11.1	3.9	n.a.	n.a.	n.a.	n.a.	n.a.	n.a.

Source: U.S. Treasury Department, Office of Tax Analysis.
n.a. Not available.

Table D-14. *Built-in Flexibility and Elasticity of the Federal Individual Income Tax, 1954–81*

	Built-in flexibility[a]			Elasticity[b]		
Year	Taxable income with respect to adjusted personal income[c]	Tax liabilities with respect to taxable income[d]	Tax liabilities with respect to adjusted personal income[c,d]	Taxable income with respect to adjusted personal income[c]	Tax liabilities with respect to taxable income[d]	Tax liabilities with respect to adjusted personal income[c,d]
1954	0.6090	0.2314	0.1409	1.4325	1.0035	1.4375
1955	0.6166	0.2315	1.1427	1.4132	1.0035	1.4182
1956	0.6209	0.2316	0.1438	1.4026	1.0035	1.4075
1957	0.6234	0.2316	0.1444	1.3967	1.0035	1.4017
1958	0.6296	0.2316	0.1458	1.3824	1.0035	1.3872
1959	0.6378	0.2317	0.1478	1.3642	1.0035	1.3691
1960	0.6391	0.2317	0.1481	1.3614	1.0035	1.3662
1961	0.6461	0.2318	0.1498	1.3466	1.0035	1.3514
1962	0.6487	0.2318	0.1504	1.3415	1.0035	1.3462
1963	0.6533	0.2319	0.1515	1.3323	1.0035	1.3370
1964	0.6679	0.2371	0.1584	1.3049	1.1532	1.5048
1965	0.6754	0.2267	0.1532	1.2916	1.1708	1.5123
1966	0.6814	0.2308	0.1572	1.2815	1.1767	1.5079
1967	0.6883	0.2368	0.1630	1.2703	1.1854	1.5058
1968	0.6969	0.2619	0.1825	1.2568	1.2060	1.5157
1969	0.7009	0.2704	0.1895	1.2508	1.2118	1.5157
1970	0.6965	0.2565	0.1787	1.2573	1.2128	1.5248
1971	0.6912	0.2515	0.1739	1.2656	2.1065	1.5269
1972	0.6848	0.2565	0.1756	1.2757	1.2119	1.5461
1973	0.6922	0.2630	0.1820	1.2639	1.2188	1.5406
1974	0.6962	0.2647	0.1843	1.2577	1.2189	1.5331
1975	0.6983	0.2713	0.1894	1.2546	1.2267	1.5390
1976	0.7047	0.2799	0.1973	1.2450	1.2343	1.5367
1977	0.7040	0.2944	0.2073	1.2460	1.2447	1.5510
1978	0.7120	0.3039	0.2164	1.2344	1.2507	1.5438
1979	0.6988	0.2978	0.2081	1.2537	1.2634	1.5838
1980	0.7073	0.3090	0.2186	1.2412	1.2700	1.5764
1981	0.7163	0.3209	0.2298	1.2285	1.2752	1.5666

Source: Congressional Budget Office.

a. Built-in flexibility is the ratio of the absolute increase (decrease) in tax liabilities to the absolute increase (decrease) in adjusted personal income.

b. Elasticity is the ratio of the percentage change in tax liabilities to the percentage change in adjusted personal income.

c. Adjusted personal income is personal income less transfer payments and other labor income plus personal contributions for social insurance and government employee retirement benefits.

d. Tax liabilities include surcharge for 1968–70 and are before tax credits.

Table D-15. *Relation of Total Corporate Profits and Total Corporate Taxes to Profits and Taxes on Domestic Operations, 1946–82*

Billions of dollars

| | Corporate profits before tax | | | | | | | | | Corporate tax | | | |
| | | Additions | | | Subtractions | | | | | | Subtractions | | |
Year	Total[a]	Liberalized depreciation allowances[b]	Dividends allocated to noninsured pension plans[c]	Net gains from sales of property[d]	Taxable foreign income	State income taxes	Federal Reserve Board earnings	Subchapter S income	Domestic profits before tax	Total[a]	Federal Reserve payments to Treasury	Surcharge and excess profits tax	Tax on domestic profits
1946	24.8	−0.9	0.0	1.0	0.7	0.5	0.1	...	23.6	8.6	0.0	0.3	8.3
1947	31.8	−0.4	0.0	0.7	1.0	0.6	0.1	...	30.4	10.7	0.1	...	10.6
1948	35.6	0.2	0.0	0.6	1.3	0.7	0.2	...	34.2	11.8	0.2	...	11.6
1949	29.2	−0.2	0.0	0.5	1.1	0.6	0.3	...	27.5	9.6	0.2	...	9.4
1950	42.9	−0.3	0.0	0.8	1.3	0.8	0.2	...	41.1	17.2	0.2	1.4	15.6
1951	44.5	0.1	0.1	0.9	1.7	0.9	0.3	...	42.7	21.7	0.3	2.5	18.9
1952	39.6	0.2	0.1	1.1	1.9	0.8	0.4	...	37.9	18.6	0.3	1.6	16.7
1953	41.7	0.7	0.1	1.1	1.8	0.8	0.4	...	40.6	19.5	0.3	1.6	17.6
1954	38.7	1.2	0.1	1.5	2.0	0.8	0.4	...	38.3	16.9	0.3	...	16.6
1955	49.2	2.4	0.2	1.2	2.4	1.0	0.3	...	49.3	21.1	0.3	...	20.8
1956	49.6	2.5	0.2	1.2	2.8	1.0	0.5	...	49.2	20.9	0.4	...	20.5
1957	48.1	2.9	0.2	1.2	3.1	1.0	0.7	...	47.6	20.4	0.5	...	19.9
1958	41.9	2.8	0.3	2.6	2.5	1.0	0.6	0.1	43.4	18.0	0.5	...	17.5
1959	52.6	3.2	0.3	1.2	2.7	1.2	0.8	0.4	52.2	22.5	0.9	...	21.6

Year													
1960	49.8	3.5	0.4	2.1	3.0	1.2	1.0	0.4	50.2	21.4	0.9	...	20.5
1961	49.7	3.5	0.5	3.2	3.2	1.3	0.8	0.6	51.0	21.5	0.7	...	20.8
1962	55.0	6.1	0.6	2.8	3.6	1.5	0.9	0.7	57.8	22.5	0.8	...	21.7
1963	59.6	6.6	0.7	2.9	3.9	1.7	1.0	0.8	62.4	24.6	0.9	...	23.7
1964	66.5	7.1	0.8	2.9	4.2	1.8	1.2	1.0	69.1	26.1	1.6	...	24.5
1965	77.2	7.9	1.0	3.7	4.5	2.0	1.5	1.4	80.4	28.9	1.3	...	27.6
1966	83.0	8.7	1.1	3.6	4.2	2.2	1.8	1.7	86.5	31.4	1.6	...	29.8
1967	79.7	9.4	1.2	4.7	4.4	2.5	2.1	1.9	84.1	30.0	1.9	0.1	28.0
1968	88.5	10.5	1.4	5.1	5.2	3.1	2.6	1.9	92.7	36.1	2.5	3.4	30.2
1969	86.7	12.0	1.6	5.8	6.1	3.4	3.2	2.2	91.2	36.1	3.0	3.4	29.7
1970	75.4	12.2	1.7	4.7	6.5	3.5	3.6	1.9	78.5	30.6	3.5	0.8	26.3
1971	86.6	13.0	1.9	6.2	7.1	4.1	3.4	2.2	90.9	33.5	3.4	...	30.1
1972	100.6	16.3	2.2	7.7	8.6	5.0	3.5	2.9	106.8	36.6	3.2	...	33.4
1973	125.6	17.5	2.3	8.7	13.7	5.8	4.7	3.7	126.2	43.3	4.3	...	39.0
1974	136.7	19.9	2.6	7.5	16.3	6.5	6.1	3.5	134.3	45.6	5.6	...	40.0
1975	132.1	22.0	2.5	8.5	13.0	7.1	5.5	3.2	136.3	43.6	5.4	...	38.2
1976	166.3	22.8	2.8	9.6	14.3	9.3	6.2	3.7	168.0	54.6	5.9	...	48.7
1977	194.7	29.6	3.3	13.0	15.1	11.1	6.6	4.8	203.0	61.6	5.9	...	55.7
1978	229.1	35.1	3.9	14.9	19.7	11.9	8.4	5.3	237.7	71.3	7.0	...	64.3
1979	252.7	41.6	4.6	19.5	30.6	13.4	10.4	8.6	255.4	74.2	9.3	...	64.9
1980	234.6	51.0	5.4	23.5	29.9	14.5	12.8	2.5	254.8	70.3	11.7	...	58.6
1981	229.0	67.2	6.2	15.0e	23.7	15.3	14.5e	2.0	261.9	67.5	14.0e	...	53.5
1982	174.2	83.2	6.8	25.0e	21.8	12.7	15.4e	1.0	238.3	46.5	15.2e	...	31.3

Sources: U.S. Department of Commerce, Bureau of Economic Analysis; Internal Revenue Service.

a. As reported in the national income and product accounts.
b. Depreciation allowances in excess of straight-line depreciation over the useful lives of corporate assets.
c. Included in the household sector for purposes of national income accounting.
d. Not included in profits for purposes of national income accounting.
e. Author's estimates based on incomplete data.

Table D-16. *Schedule of Transition to the Current Payment System for Corporations*

Percentage of tax liability due in each installment

	Income year				Following year				
Income year	April	June	September	December	March	June	September	December	Total
1949	...	...	...	...	25	25	25	25	100
1950	...	...	...	...	30	30	20	20	100
1951	...	...	...	...	35	35	15	15	100
1952	...	...	...	...	40	40	10	10	100
1953	...	...	...	...	45	45	5	5	100
1954	...	...	...	...	50	50	...	...	100
1955[a]	...	...	5	5	45	45	...	...	100
1956[a]	...	...	10	10	40	40	...	...	100
1957[a]	...	...	15	15	35	35	...	...	100
1958[a]	...	...	20	20	30	30	...	...	100
1959[a]	...	...	25	25	25	25	...	...	100
1960[a]	...	...	25	25	25	25	...	...	100
1961[a]	...	...	25	25	25	25	...	...	100
1962[a]	...	...	25	25	25	25	...	...	100
1963[a]	...	...	25	25	25	25	...	...	100
1964[a]	1	1	25	25	24	24	...	...	100
1965[a]	4	4	25	25	21	21	...	...	100
1966[a]	12	12	25	25	13	13	...	...	100
1967[a] and later years[b]	25	25	25	25	...	...	...	...	100

Sources: Relevant public laws and summaries prepared by the Joint Committee on Taxation.

a. Applicable only to tax liability in excess of $100,000. The first $100,000 of a corporation's tax liability was paid in equal installments in March and June of the following year.

b. Beginning in 1968, the $100,000 exclusion was reduced to $5,500. A transitional exemption was provided for 1968–71 (80 percent in 1968, 60 percent in 1969, 40 percent in 1970, and 20 percent in 1971). A second transitional period began in 1972 that put corporations on a completely current basis in 1977.

Table D-17. *Selected Ratios Relating to the Corporate Sector,*
1929–82

Year	National income originating in corporate business as percent of income originating in business	Gross domestic corporate product as percent of gross business domestic product	Gross corporate saving as percent of gross national product	Property income as percent of gross corporate product less indirect taxes[a]	Dividends as percent of domestic corporate cash flow, nonfinancial corporations[b]
1929	57.9	56.1	7.3	31.6	35.9
1930	57.7	56.8	5.5	29.2	55.6
1931	55.1	53.5	2.4	23.7	79.2
1932	52.4	51.7	−0.2	18.5	104.3
1933	52.7	52.5	0.0	17.9	40.0
1934	57.0	56.3	3.1	24.5	34.8
1935	55.7	56.0	4.4	26.8	32.0
1936	59.0	56.8	4.0	28.3	43.6
1937	59.1	58.1	4.8	27.3	40.0
1938	57.2	56.0	5.3	26.0	31.7
1939	58.8	57.1	5.5	27.0	31.1
1940	60.9	59.1	6.8	30.3	28.7
1941	62.1	60.6	6.1	32.5	24.8
1942	61.8	61.3	6.2	32.8	22.8
1943	62.7	62.4	6.0	31.9	23.1
1944	62.2	60.4	5.8	30.8	25.3
1945	58.9	57.2	4.8	28.5	28.7
1946	56.1	56.4	4.6	25.0	20.0
1947	60.2	59.2	6.1	27.2	17.7
1948	60.9	60.7	8.1	29.9	17.2
1949	61.3	60.3	8.4	29.6	19.2
1950	62.8	61.5	7.0	31.3	19.7
1951	63.5	61.7	6.8	30.9	19.1
1952	63.4	61.9	7.0	28.7	19.6
1953	64.6	62.8	6.6	27.5	19.7
1954	64.0	62.2	7.3	27.8	19.7
1955	65.9	64.1	8.1	30.0	19.8
1956	66.2	65.1	7.8	28.2	19.2
1957	66.2	65.0	7.8	27.7	19.4
1958	64.5	63.4	7.4	27.2	20.4
1959	66.6	65.4	8.2	28.7	19.6
1960	67.0	66.1	7.8	27.3	21.5
1961	67.0	66.1	7.7	27.4	21.6
1962	68.1	66.9	8.3	28.1	22.6
1963	68.8	67.5	8.4	28.5	23.6
1964	69.4	68.3	8.7	28.8	23.1

Table D-17 (*continued*)

Year	National income originating in corporate business as percent of income originating in business	Gross domestic corporate product as percent of gross business domestic product	Gross corporate saving as percent of gross national product	Property income as percent of gross corporate product less indirect taxes[a]	Dividends as percent of domestic corporate cash flow, nonfinancial corporations[b]
1965	70.1	69.1	9.2	29.7	23.3
1966	70.9	69.6	9.0	29.3	23.2
1967	71.3	69.9	8.7	28.3	23.8
1968	72.3	70.8	8.2	27.9	24.5
1969	72.8	71.6	7.6	26.3	24.1
1970	72.7	71.3	6.9	24.5	23.2
1971	73.2	71.2	7.7	25.5	19.5
1972	73.7	71.8	8.0	25.7	19.5
1973	73.2	71.6	7.8	24.9	17.4
1974	73.7	71.7	6.7	23.6	14.8
1975	74.2	72.0	8.3	26.1	15.1
1976	75.2	72.8	8.5	26.4	15.0
1977	75.9	73.4	9.1	27.1	14.3
1978	76.0	73.7	9.2	27.1	14.8
1979	75.6	73.4	8.8	25.8	13.9
1980	76.1	73.5	8.0	25.0	13.5
1981	76.1	73.9	8.4	26.3	16.1
1982	75.4	73.1	8.4	25.0	18.5

Source: U.S. Department of Commerce, Bureau of Economic Analysis.
a. Property income includes corporate profits before taxes after capital-consumption and inventory valuation adjustments, and net interest.
b. Cash flow is net corporate profits after taxes before capital-consumption and inventory valuation adjustments plus corporate capital-consumption allowance.

Table D-18. *Rates of Return before and after Federal Income Tax, Manufacturing Corporations, 1927–41, 1948–61, and 1964–80*

Percent

| | Rate of return | | | | | General |
| | On equity capital[a] | | On total capital[b] | | Debt- | corporation |
Year	Before tax	After tax[c]	Before tax	After tax[c]	capital ratio[d]	income tax rate
1927	7.5	6.5	7.6	6.7	15.1	13.50
1928	9.1	8.0	9.0	8.0	15.6	12.00
1929	9.9	8.8	9.6	8.7	14.9	11.00
1930	2.1	1.5	2.9	2.4	15.3	12.00
1931	−1.6	−2.0	−0.4	−0.6	15.4	12.00
1932	−3.9	−4.2	−2.3	−2.5	15.5	13.75
1933	0.5	0.0	1.3	0.9	15.5	13.75
1934	2.4	1.8	2.8	2.3	13.7	13.75
1935	4.8	3.9	4.9	4.1	14.9	13.75
1936	9.5	8.0	8.8	7.5	14.2	15.00
1937	9.2	7.6	8.6	7.3	15.4	15.00
1938	3.9	3.0	3.9	3.2	15.4	19.00
1939	8.5	7.0	7.9	6.6	14.9	19.00
1940	12.2	8.7	11.1	8.1	14.4	24.00
1941	22.3	11.7	19.6	10.6	14.9	31.00
1948	22.4	14.0	19.5	12.4	15.7	38.00
1949	16.4	10.1	14.5	9.2	14.7	38.00
1950	25.4	14.3	22.2	12.8	14.8	42.00
1951	24.5	10.9	21.2	9.8	17.3	50.75
1952	18.9	8.3	16.2	7.5	19.2	52.00
1953	19.1	8.5	16.2	7.6	19.1	52.00
1954	15.6	7.9	13.4	7.2	18.9	52.00
1955	20.6	10.8	17.6	9.5	18.2	52.00
1956	18.2	9.6	15.5	8.5	20.0	52.00
1957	15.9	7.8	13.6	7.2	20.5	52.00
1958	12.2	6.4	10.7	6.1	20.4	52.00
1959	15.8	8.4	13.6	7.7	20.4	52.00
1960	13.4	7.0	11.7	6.6	20.6	52.00
1961	13.0	7.0	11.4	6.6	20.6	52.00

Table D-18 (continued)

Year	Rate of return					General corporation income tax rate
	On equity capital[a]		On total capital[b]		Debt-capital ratio[d]	
	Before tax	After tax[c]	Before tax	After tax[c]		
1964	16.3	8.9	14.1	8.3	22.3	50.00
1965	18.8	10.6	15.8	9.5	23.9	48.00
1966	19.5	11.2	16.1	9.9	26.6	48.00
1967	16.5	9.4	13.7	8.5	27.7	48.00
1968	16.8	8.8	13.8	8.1	29.9	52.80
1969	14.4	7.2	12.3	7.3	32.1	52.80
1970	10.5	5.0	9.7	6.1	34.5	49.20
1971	12.2	6.2	10.6	6.6	34.3	48.00
1972	14.3	8.0	12.0	7.8	33.8	48.00
1973	17.4	11.7	14.6	10.8	34.5	48.00
1974	18.3	12.8	15.5	11.9	35.7	48.00
1975	16.0	11.1	13.6	10.5	35.7	48.00
1976	19.4	13.2	15.6	11.6	35.3	48.00
1977	20.6	14.3	16.4	12.2	33.0	48.00
1978	21.2	14.8	17.4	13.2	33.7	48.00
1979	21.6	15.8	18.1	14.3	34.6	46.00
1980	18.0	13.4	16.6	13.6	36.5	46.00

Sources: 1935–38, Marian Krzyaniak and Richard A. Musgrave, *The Shifting of the Corporation Income Tax* (Johns Hopkins University Press, 1963), p. 73; other years, *Statistics of Income, Corporation Income Tax Returns.*
a. Equity capital is average of book value of stock and undistributed surplus at the beginning and end of the year.
b. Profits plus interest paid as percentage of average equity capital plus debt capital at the beginning and end of the year.
c. For 1927–49, 1952, and 1957, no allowances have been made for the foreign tax credit. The rates of return are therefore slightly understated, probably by 0.3 percentage point or less.
d. End of year.

Table D-19. Sources and Uses of Funds, Nonfarm Nonfinancial Corporate Business, 1960, 1965, 1970, 1975, 1980

Item	Amount (billions of dollars)					Percentage distribution				
	1960	1965	1970	1975	1980	1960	1965	1970	1975	1980
Source of funds										
Internal	34.7	56.1	58.9	119.7	197.5	72.7	61.8	56.6	76.3	59.2
Domestic undistributed profits	8.8	20.0	8.1	34.0	57.1	18.4	22.0	7.8	21.7	17.1
Capital-consumption and inventory valuation adjustments	-2.0	1.7	-3.5	-21.2	-59.7	-4.2	1.9	-3.4	-13.5	-17.9
Depreciation allowances	26.8	32.6	52.7	93.8	169.8	56.2	35.9	50.6	59.8	50.9
Foreign branch profits	1.1	1.8	1.6	13.0[a]	30.3[a]	2.3	2.0	1.5	8.3	9.1
External	12.0	20.4	40.5	30.7	95.7	25.2	22.5	38.9	19.6	28.7
Net new equity issues	1.4	0.0	5.7	9.9	12.9	2.9	0.0	5.5	6.3	3.9
Debt instruments[b]	10.6	20.4	34.8	20.8	82.8	22.2	22.5	33.4	13.3	24.8
Foreign direct investment in United States	n.a.	n.a.	n.a.	2.6	13.7	...	...	...	1.7	4.1
Other[c]	1.0	14.3	4.7	3.9	26.9	2.1	15.7	4.5	2.5	8.1
Sources, total	47.7	90.8	104.1	156.9	333.8	100.0	100.0	100.0	100.0	100.0
Use of funds										
Capital expenditures	38.0	61.9	80.0	109.7	220.5	93.4	75.4	83.7	72.7	69.4
Plant and equipment	33.8	51.6	73.3	116.3	218.4	83.0	62.9	76.7	77.1	68.7
Residential structures	1.5	2.9	3.0	1.4	1.5	3.7	3.5	3.1	0.9	0.5
Change in business inventories	2.7	7.3	3.4	-9.3	-4.4	6.6	8.9	3.6	-6.2	-1.4
Mining rights from U.S. government	0.0	0.0	0.3	1.3	5.0	0.0	0.0	0.3	0.9	1.6
Net increase in financial assets	2.7	20.2	15.6	41.2	97.4	6.6	24.6	16.3	27.3	30.6
Liquid assets	-4.1	2.6	2.3	19.8	15.8	-10.1	3.2	2.4	13.1	5.0
Consumer credit	0.3	1.0	0.9	0.7	0.4	0.7	1.2	0.9	0.5	0.1
Trade credit	4.2	13.2	8.1	5.8	47.6	10.3	16.1	8.5	3.8	15.0
Other financial assets[d]	2.3	3.4	4.2	14.9	33.7	5.7	4.1	4.4	9.9	10.6
Uses, total	40.7	82.1	95.6	150.9	317.9	100.0	100.0	100.0	100.0	100.0
Discrepancy (sources less uses)	7.0	8.7	8.5	6.0	15.9	...	...	...	...	...

Source: Board of Governors of the Federal Reserve System. Figures are rounded.
n.a. Not available.
a. Sum of earnings received from abroad and earnings retained abroad.
b. Includes mortgages, bank loans, commercial paper, acceptances, financial company loans, and U.S. government loans.
c. Includes trade debt, profit tax liability, and miscellaneous liabilities.
d. Includes foreign direct investment, insurance receivables, equity in sponsored agencies, and other.

Table D-20. *Assets of Selected Federal Trust Funds, Fiscal Years 1937–82*

Billions of dollars

Year[a]	Old age and survivors insurance	Disability insurance	Hospital insurance	Supple- mentary medical insurance	Unem- ployment insurance	Railroad retirement
1937	0.3	. . .	. . .	. . .	0.3	*
1938	0.8	. . .	. . .	. . .	0.9	0.1
1939	1.2	. . .	. . .	. . .	1.3	0.1
1940	1.7	. . .	. . .	. . .	1.7	0.1
1941	2.4	. . .	. . .	. . .	2.3	0.1
1942	3.2	. . .	. . .	. . .	3.2	0.1
1943	4.3	. . .	. . .	. . .	4.4	0.2
1944	5.4	. . .	. . .	. . .	5.9	0.3
1945	6.6	. . .	. . .	. . .	7.3	0.5
1946	7.6	. . .	. . .	. . .	7.4	0.7
1947	8.8	. . .	. . .	. . .	7.9	0.8
1948	10.0	. . .	. . .	. . .	8.3	1.4
1949	11.3	. . .	. . .	. . .	8.2	1.8
1950	12.9	. . .	. . .	. . .	7.4	2.2
1951	14.7	. . .	. . .	. . .	8.1	2.5
1952	16.6	. . .	. . .	. . .	8.7	2.9
1953	18.4	. . .	. . .	. . .	9.2	3.2
1954	20.0	. . .	. . .	. . .	9.0	3.4
1955	21.1	. . .	. . .	. . .	8.5	3.5
1956	22.6	. . .	. . .	. . .	8.8	3.7
1957	23.0	0.3	. . .	. . .	9.1	3.7
1958	22.8	1.1	. . .	. . .	7.8	3.7
1959	21.5	1.7	. . .	. . .	6.7	3.6
1960	20.8	2.2	. . .	. . .	6.7	3.9
1961	20.9	2.5	. . .	. . .	5.8	3.8
1962	19.7	2.5	. . .	. . .	5.8	3.8
1963	19.0	2.4	. . .	. . .	6.3	3.8
1964	19.7	2.3	. . .	. . .	6.9	3.9
1965	20.2	2.0	. . .	. . .	7.9	4.0
1966	19.9	1.7	0.9	. . .	9.3	4.2
1967	23.5	2.0	1.3	0.5	10.6	4.5
1968	25.5	2.6	1.4	0.3	11.6	4.6
1969	28.2	3.7	2.0	0.4	12.7	4.7

Table D-20 (continued)

Year[a]	Old age and survivors insurance	Disability insurance	Hospital insurance	Supplementary medical insurance	Unemployment insurance	Railroad retirement
1970	32.6	5.1	2.7	0.1	13.1	4.9
1971	34.3	6.4	3.1	0.3	11.3	4.9
1972	36.4	7.4	2.9	0.5	9.8	4.8
1973	36.4	7.9	4.4	0.7	11.1	4.6
1974	37.9	8.3	7.9	1.3	12.4	4.6
1975	40.0	8.2	9.9	1.4	7.2	4.3
1976	38.0	6.9	10.8	1.2	5.7	4.1
1977	35.4	4.2	11.1	2.3	6.5	3.2
1978	31.0	4.4	11.8	4.0	10.4	3.1
1979	27.8	5.6	13.4	5.0	15.1	3.1
1980	24.6	7.7	14.9	4.5	14.9	2.7
1981	23.8	3.4	18.1	3.8	14.4	2.0
1982	12.5	6.8	20.8	5.8	10.2	1.5

Sources: *Treasury Bulletin* (August 1944, 1952, 1961, 1970, and November 1982).
* Less than $50 million.
a. As of June 30 from 1937 to 1976, and as of September 30 from 1977 to 1982.

Table D-21. *Number of Estate Tax Returns, Value of Estates, and Amount of Tax, by Size of Gross Estate, 1976*[a]

Millions of dollars unless otherwise specified

Size of gross estate (dollars)	Number of returns	Gross estate	Estate tax before state tax credit[b]	State death tax credit	Estate tax after credit
60,000–100,000	58,968	4,702	34	*	34
100,000–150,000	51,983	6,417	170	3	168
150,000–200,000	30,243	5,217	275	8	267
200,000–300,000	27,781	6,727	574	24	549
300,000–500,000	17,907	6,791	844	52	792
500,000–1,000,000	9,341	6,345	1,042	87	955
1,000,000–2,000,000[c]	3,108[c]	4,334	815	91	724
2,000,000–3,000,000	681	1,644	382	50	331
3,000,000–5,000,000	432	1,634	409	59	350
5,000,000–10,000,000	213	1,435	399	64	336
10,000,000 and over	90	2,956	587	113	474
Total	200,747	48,202	5,531	552	4,979

Source: *Statistics of Income—1976, Estate Tax Returns*, table 1. Figures are rounded.

* $500,000 or less.

a. Returns are classified by the year in which they were filed. Includes taxable and nontaxable returns.

b. Estate tax after credit for federal gift taxes, foreign death taxes, estate tax on prior transfers, and unified credit, but before state death taxes.

c. The $1,000,000–$2,000,000 gross estate class contains data for 104 nontaxable returns of $1,000,000 and over for which a more detailed breakdown by size of gross estate is not available. The gross estate for the 104 returns was $285 million.

Table D-22. *Number of Gift Tax Returns, and Amounts of Gifts and Gift Tax, by Size of Total Gifts before Splitting, 1966*[a]

Millions of dollars unless otherwise specified

Size of total gifts before splitting (dollars)	Number of returns	Total gifts[b]	Taxable gifts			Gift tax, current year
			Current year	Prior years	All years	
Taxable returns	29,547	2,373	1,455	2,949	4,404	413
No total gifts before splitting[c]	4,615	. . .	198	287	485	47
Under 10,000	3,199	19	21	171	192	4
10,000–20,000	3,897	57	45	264	309	15
20,000–30,000	2,970	73	27	157	184	3
30,000–40,000	2,870	100	34	134	168	5
40,000–50,000	2,394	106	34	100	134	4
50,000–100,000	5,613	393	147	304	451	20
100,000–500,000	3,462	638	365	649	1,014	79
500,000–1,000,000	291	202	126	227	353	34
1,000,000–2,000,000	144	198	120	173	293	36
2,000,000–3,000,000	40	95	51	89	140	18
3,000,000–5,000,000	25	98	48	64	112	18
5,000,000–10,000,000	16	103	50	28	78	20
10,000,000 and over	10	292	189	301	490	109
Nontaxable returns	83,249	1,589	. . .	1,026[d]	1,026[d]	. . .
Total, all returns	112,796	3,962	1,455	3,975	5,430	413

Source: *Statistics of Income, Fiduciary, Gift, and Estate Tax Returns, 1965*, pp. 41, 50–51. Figures are rounded.
a. Returns are classified by the year in which they were filed. Data after 1966 are not published.
b. Total gifts are before splitting provision for gifts by and between husband and wife.
c. Taxed on spouse's gifts, under gift splitting provisions.
d. Returns were nontaxable for current year gifts but taxable for prior year gifts.

Table D-23. *General Expenditure of State and Local Governments, by Major Function, Fiscal Years 1971, 1978, and 1981*

Millions of dollars unless otherwise specified

Function	Amount 1971	Amount 1978	Amount 1981	Increase 1971–81 Amount	Increase 1971–81 Percentage distribution of increase	Increase 1971–81 Percentage increase	Increase 1978–81 Amount	Increase 1978–81 Percentage distribution of increase	Increase 1978–81 Percentage increase
			Total state and local government expenditure						
Total general expenditure[a]	150,674	295,510	405,576	254,902	100.0	169.2	110,066	100.0	37.2
Education	59,413	110,758	145,784	86,371	33.9	145.4	35,026	31.8	31.6
Highways	18,095	24,609	34,603	16,508	6.5	91.2	9,994	9.1	40.6
Public welfare	18,226	37,679	52,248	34,022	13.3	186.7	14,569	13.2	38.7
Health and hospitals	11,205	24,951	36,101	24,896	9.8	222.2	11,150	10.1	44.7
Police and fire	7,531	16,108	21,283	13,752	5.4	182.6	5,175	4.7	32.1
Natural resources	3,082	4,225	6,175	3,093	1.2	100.4	1,950	1.8	46.2
Sewerage and other sanitation	4,087	9,869	14,898	10,811	4.2	264.5	5,029	4.6	51.0
Housing and urban renewal	2,554	3,699	7,086	4,532	1.8	177.4	3,387	3.1	91.6
General control and financial administration	5,298	12,293	16,771	11,473	4.5	216.6	4,478	4.1	36.4
Interest on debt	5,089	11,983	17,131	12,042	4.7	236.6	5,148	4.7	43.0
Other	16,094	39,336	53,496	37,402	14.7	232.4	14,160	12.9	36.0

State government expenditure

Total general expenditure[a,b]	56,478	112,515	160,474	103,996	100.0	184.1	47,959	100.0	42.6
Education	15,800	29,577	39,664	23,864	22.9	151.0	10,087	21.0	34.1
Highways	12,304	14,658	20,688	8,384	8.1	68.1	6,030	12.6	41.1
Public welfare	10,518	25,729	38,580	28,062	27.0	266.8	12,851	26.8	49.9
Health and hospitals	5,400	12,319	18,028	12,628	12.1	233.9	5,709	11.9	46.3
Police	797	1,683	2,270	1,473	1.4	184.8	587	1.2	34.9
Natural resources	2,484	3,241	4,725	2,241	2.2	90.2	1,484	3.1	45.8
Sewerage	0	300	345	345	0.3	...	45	0.1	15.0
Housing and urban renewal	32	165	402	370	0.4	1,156.3	237	0.5	143.6
General control and financial administration	1,950	4,700	6,563	4,613	4.4	236.6	1,863	3.9	39.6
Interest on debt	1,761	5,268	7,844	6,083	5.8	345.4	2,576	5.4	48.9
Other	5,432	14,875	21,365	15,933	15.3	293.3	6,490	13.5	43.6

Local government expenditure

Total general expenditure[a,b]	94,196	182,995	245,102	150,906	100.0	160.2	62,107	100.0	33.9
Education	43,613	81,181	106,121	62,508	41.4	143.3	24,940	40.2	30.7
Highways	5,792	9,951	13,915	8,123	5.4	140.2	3,964	6.4	39.8
Public welfare	7,708	11,950	13,667	5,959	3.9	77.3	1,717	2.8	14.4
Health and hospitals	5,806	12,632	18,073	12,267	8.1	211.3	5,441	8.8	43.1
Police and fire	6,733	14,425	19,013	12,280	8.1	182.4	4,588	7.4	31.8
Natural resources	597	984	1,451	854	0.6	143.0	467	0.8	47.5
Sewerage and other sanitation	4,087	9,569	14,553	10,466	6.9	256.1	4,984	8.0	52.1
Housing and urban renewal	2,522	3,534	6,684	4,162	2.8	165.0	3,150	5.1	89.1
General control and financial administration	3,349	7,595	10,208	6,859	4.5	204.8	2,613	4.2	34.4
Interest on debt	3,328	6,715	9,288	5,960	3.9	179.1	2,573	4.1	38.3
Other	10,661	24,459	32,129	21,468	14.2	201.4	7,670	12.3	31.4

Sources: Bureau of the Census, *Governmental Finances in 1970–71*, p. 23; *Governmental Finances in 1977–78*, p. 32; *Governmental Finances in 1980–81*, p. 32. Figures are rounded.
a. Excludes insurance trust, utility, and liquor store expenditures. Includes federal grants-in-aid.
b. Grants-in-aid are shown according to final spending level.

Table D-24. *General Revenue of State and Local Governments, by Source, Fiscal Years 1971, 1978, and 1981*
Millions of dollars unless otherwise specified

	Amount			Increase 1971–81			Increase 1978–81		
Source	1971	1978	1981	Amount	Percentage distribution of total increase	Percentage distribution of revenue from own sources	Amount	Percentage distribution of total increase	Percentage distribution of revenue from own sources
				Total state and local government revenue					
General revenue[a]	144,927	315,960	423,404	278,477	100.0	...	107,444	100.0	...
Revenue from federal government[b]	26,146	69,592	90,294	64,148	23.0	...	20,702	19.3	...
General revenue from own sources	118,782	246,368	333,109	214,327	77.0	100.0	86,741	80.7	100.0
Taxes	94,975	193,642	244,514	149,539	53.7	69.8	50,872	47.3	58.6
Property	37,852	66,422	74,969	37,117	13.3	17.3	8,547	8.0	9.9
Sales and gross receipts	33,233	67,596	85,971	52,738	18.9	24.6	18,375	17.1	21.2
Individual income	11,900	33,176	46,426	34,526	12.4	16.1	13,250	12.3	15.3
Corporation income	3,424	10,738	14,143	10,719	3.8	5.0	3,405	3.2	3.9
Other	8,567	15,709	23,004	14,437	5.2	6.7	7,295	6.8	8.4
Charges and miscellaneous	23,807	52,726	88,595	64,788	23.3	30.2	35,869	33.4	41.4

			State government revenue						
General revenue^c	85,099	189,099	258,159	173,060	100.0	. . .	69,060	100.0	. . .
Revenue from federal government^b	22,754	50,200	67,868	45,114	26.1	. . .	17,668	25.6	. . .
Revenue from local governments	1,054	3,261	2,918	1,864	1.1	. . .	−343	−0.5	. . .
General revenue from own sources	61,290	135,638	187,373	126,083	72.9	100.0	51,735	74.9	100.0
Taxes	51,541	113,261	149,738	98,197	56.7	77.9	36,477	52.8	70.5
Property	1,126	2,364	2,949	1,823	1.1	1.4	585	0.8	1.1
Sales and gross receipts	29,570	58,270	72,751	43,181	25.0	34.2	14,481	21.0	28.0
Individual income	10,153	29,105	40,895	30,742	17.8	24.4	11,790	17.1	22.8
Corporation income	3,424	10,738	14,143	10,719	6.2	8.5	3,405	4.9	6.6
Other	7,268	12,784	18,999	11,731	6.8	9.3	6,215	9.0	12.0
Charges and miscellaneous	9,749	22,377	37,636	27,887	16.1	22.1	15,259	22.1	29.5
			Local government revenue						
General revenue^d	91,964	194,783	257,179	165,215	100.0	. . .	62,396	100.0	. . .
Revenue from federal government^b	3,391	19,393	22,427	19,036	11.5	. . .	3,034	4.9	. . .
Revenue from state governments	31,081	64,661	89,017	57,936	35.1	. . .	24,356	39.0	. . .
General revenue from own sources	57,491	110,730	145,736	88,245	53.4	100.0	35,006	56.1	100.0
Taxes	43,434	80,381	94,776	51,342	31.1	58.2	14,395	23.1	41.1
Property	36,726	64,058	72,020	35,294	21.4	40.0	7,962	12.8	22.7
Sales and gross receipts	3,662	9,326	13,220	9,558	5.8	10.8	3,894	6.2	11.1
Individual income	1,747	4,071	5,531	3,784	2.3	4.3	1,460	2.3	4.2
Other	1,298	2,925	4,005	2,707	1.6	3.1	1,080	1.7	3.1
Charges and miscellaneous	14,058	30,349	50,960	36,902	22.3	41.8	20,611	33.0	58.9

Sources: Same as table D-23 (pp. 20, 17, and 17, respectively, of the sources). Figures are rounded.
a. Excludes insurance trust, liquor store, and utility revenues. Total state and local general revenue does not equal the sum of state general revenue and local general revenue because duplicative transactions between state and local governments are excluded.
b. Includes grants-in-aid, shared taxes, payments for services performed on a reimbursement or cost-sharing basis, and payments in lieu of taxes. Excludes loans and commodities or other aids in kind.
c. Excludes insurance trust and liquor store revenues.
d. Excludes insurance trust, liquor store, and utility revenues.

Table D-25. *State and Local Government Debt, Fiscal Years*
1959–81

End of fiscal year	Debt outstanding	
	Amount (millions of dollars)	*Index (1959 = 100)*
1959	64,110	100.0
1960	69,955	109.1
1961	75,023	117.0
1962	81,278	126.8
1963	85,056	132.7
1964	92,222	143.8
1965	99,512	155.2
1966	107,051	167.0
1967	113,659	177.3
1968	121,158	189.0
1969	133,548	208.3
1970	143,570	223.9
1971	158,827	247.7
1972	174,502	272.2
1973	188,485	294.0
1974	206,616	322.3
1975	221,224	345.1
1976	240,086	375.5
1977	257,532	401.7
1978	280,433	437.4
1979[a]	304,104	474.3
1980	336,603	525.0
1981	363,892	567.6

Sources: *Governmental Finances*, annual issues.
a. Figures for 1979 and later years are adjusted to exclude refunding transactions no longer carried in state and local records.

Table D-26. *Major Tax Sources Used by the States, January 1, 1984*

Tax	States using tax
Sales	Forty-five states and the District of Columbia; exceptions are Alaska, Delaware, Montana, New Hampshire, Oregon
Individual income	Forty states and the District of Columbia; exceptions are Alaska, Connecticut, Florida, Nevada, New Hampshire, South Dakota, Tennessee, Texas, Washington, Wyoming
Corporation income	Forty-five states and the District of Columbia; exceptions are Nevada, South Dakota, Texas, Washington, Wyoming
Estate and inheritance tax[a]	Forty-nine states and the District of Columbia; exception is Nevada
Gift tax[b]	Delaware, Louisiana, New York, North Carolina, Oregon, Rhode Island, South Carolina, Tennessee, Wisconsin
Motor fuel	All fifty states and the District of Columbia
Cigarette	All fifty states and the District of Columbia
Alcoholic beverage	All fifty states and the District of Columbia

Source: Advisory Commission on Intergovernmental Relations.
a. Ten states levy a tax that picks up only the equivalent of the credit for state death taxes under the federal estate tax.
b. The Oregon gift tax will be phased out by January 1, 1987.

Table D-27. *Marginal Burden of State Individual and Corporation Income Taxes before and after Allowing for Federal and State Deductibility, January 1, 1984*[a]

Percent

	Individual income tax			Corporation income tax	
		Marginal burden of state tax in			Marginal burden of state tax in highest federal tax bracket
State	Range of state's nominal rates	Lowest federal tax bracket	Highest federal tax bracket	State's highest nominal rate	
Alabama[b]	2.0–5.0	1.6	1.3	5.0	1.5
Alaska	. . .	. . .	. . .	9.4	5.1
Arizona[b]	2.0–8.0	1.6	2.1	10.5	3.2
Arkansas	1.0–7.0	0.9	3.5	6.0	3.2
California	1.0–11.0	0.9	5.5	9.6	5.2
Colorado[b]	2.5–8.0	2.0	2.1	5.0	2.7[c]
Connecticut[d]	. . .	. . .	. . .	10.0	2.8
Delaware[e]	1.4–13.5	1.2	6.8	8.7	4.7
Florida	. . .	. . .	. . .	5.0	2.7
Georgia	1.0–6.0	0.9	3.0	6.0	3.2
Hawaii[d]	2.25–11.0	1.7	2.6	6.435	1.8
Idaho	2.0–7.5	1.8	3.8	7.7	4.2
Illinois	3.0	2.7	1.5	6.5	3.5
Indiana	3.0	2.7	1.5	7.0	3.8
Iowa[b]	0.5–13.0	0.4	3.5	12.0	3.7
Kansas[f]	2.0–9.0	1.8	4.5	4.5	2.4
Kentucky[b]	2.0–6.0	1.6	1.5	6.0	3.2[c]
Louisiana[b]	2.0–6.0	1.6	1.5	8.0	2.4
Maine	1.0–10.0	0.9	5.0	6.93	3.7
Maryland	2.0–5.0	1.8	2.5	7.0	3.8
Massachusetts	5.375	4.8	2.7	8.33	4.5
Michigan	6.1	5.4	3.1	2.35	1.3
Minnesota[b]	1.76–17.6	1.4	4.8	12.0	6.5[c]
Mississippi	3.0–5.0	2.7	2.5	5.0	2.7
Missouri[b]	1.5–6.0	1.2	1.5	5.0	1.5
Montana[b]	2.0–11.0	1.6	2.9	6.75	3.6[c]
Nebraska[d]	2.2–10.0[g]	1.7	2.4	6.3	1.8
New Hampshire	. . .	. . .	. . .	8.0	4.3
New Jersey	2.0–3.5	1.8	1.8	9.0	4.9
New Mexico[d]	0.7–7.8	0.6	1.9	7.2	2.0

Table D-27 (*continued*)

State	Individual income tax			Corporation income tax	
		Marginal burden of state tax in			Marginal burden of state tax in highest federal tax bracket
	Range of state's nominal rates	Lowest federal tax bracket	Highest federal tax bracket	State's highest nominal rate	
New York	2.0–14.0	1.8	7.0	10.0	5.4
North Carolina	3.0–7.0	2.7	3.5	6.0	3.2
North Dakota[b]	2.0–9.0	1.6	2.4	10.5	3.2
Ohio	0.95–9.5	0.8	4.8	4.8645	2.6
Oklahoma	0.5–6.0[h]	0.4	3.0	4.0	3.2[d]
Oregon[i]	4.0–10.0	3.6	5.0	7.5	4.1
Pennsylvania	2.2	2.0	1.1	10.5	5.7
Rhode Island	2.86–13.0[j]	2.5	6.5	9.0	4.9
South Carolina[k]	2.0–7.0	1.8	3.5	6.0	3.2
Tennessee[d]	. . .	. . .	. . .	6.0	1.7
Utah[b]	2.75–7.75	2.2	2.0	4.65	2.5[c]
Vermont[d]	2.75–12.5[l]	2.1	2.9	7.5	2.1
Virginia	2.0–5.75	1.8	2.9	6.0	3.2
West Virginia	2.1–14.56	1.9	7.3	8.05	4.3
Wisconsin	3.4–10.0	3.0	5.0	7.9	4.3
District of Columbia	2.0–11.0	1.8	5.5	9.9	5.3

Source: Advisory Commission on Intergovernmental Relations.
a. State individual and corporate income taxes are fully deductible against the federal tax.
b. Federal tax deductible against state tax.
c. Federal tax not deductible against state corporation income tax.
d. State tax deductible against state tax.
e. Deduction for federal tax limited to $300 for single returns ($600 for joint returns).
f. Deduction limited to the greater of $5,000 or the product of the federal tax liability and the ratio of Kansas adjusted gross income to federal adjusted gross income.
g. State tax is 20 percent of federal liabilities.
h. Taxpayers may elect to deduct federal income tax against state taxes, in which case the range of nominal rates is 0.5–17.0.
i. Deduction for federal tax limited to $7,000, less the amount of any refund of federal taxes previously accrued for which a tax benefit was received.
j. State tax is 26 percent of federal liabilities.
k. Deduction for federal tax limited to $500 for single returns ($1,000 for joint returns).
l. State tax is 24 percent of federal liabilities.

Bibliographical Notes

Chapter 1. Introduction

Among standard textbooks in public finance devoting considerable space to taxation are the following: James M. Buchanan and Marilyn R. Flowers, *The Public Finances: An Introductory Textbook,* 5th ed. (Irwin, 1980); John F. Due and Ann F. Friedlaender, *Government Finance: Economics of the Public Sector,* 7th ed. (Irwin, 1981); Richard Goode, *Government Finance in Developing Countries* (Brookings Institution, 1984); and Richard A. Musgrave and Peggy B. Musgrave, *Public Finance in Theory and Practice,* 4th ed. (McGraw-Hill, 1984).

The most authoritative advanced books are by Richard A. Musgrave, *The Theory of Public Finance* (McGraw-Hill, 1959); Carl S. Shoup, *Public Finance* (Aldine, 1969); Alan S. Blinder and others, *The Economics of Public Finance* (Brookings, 1974); Arnold C. Harberger, *Taxation and Welfare* (Little, Brown, 1974); Anthony B. Atkinson and Joseph E. Stiglitz, *Lectures on Public Economics* (McGraw-Hill, 1980); Henry J. Aaron and Joseph A. Pechman, eds., *How Taxes Affect Economic Behavior* (Brookings, 1981); and Richard W. Tresch, *Public Finance: A Normative Theory* (Business Publications, 1981).

Outstanding articles in the history of taxation are reprinted in Richard A. Musgrave and Alan T. Peacock, eds., *Classics in the Theory of Public Finance* (Macmillan, 1958); and in Richard A. Musgrave and Carl S. Shoup, eds., *Readings in the Economics of Taxation* (Irwin, 1959).

The articles on "Taxation" in the *International Encyclopedia of the Social Sciences* (Macmillan and Free Press, 1968), vol. 15, give a general overview of the objectives of taxation and analyses of the major taxes now in use in the United States and other countries. Reviews of the literature on the incidence and economic effects of taxation are provided by Peter Mieszkowski, "Tax Incidence Theory: The Effects of Taxes on the Distribution of Income," *Journal of Economic Literature* 7 (December 1969); and by George F. Break, "The Incidence and Economic Effects of Taxation," in *The Economics of Public Finance* (cited above).

For competent analyses of the requirements of a modern tax system, see the Canadian *Report of the Royal Commission on Taxation* (Carter Commission), 6 vols., and the accompanying *Studies of the Royal Commission on Taxation,* 30 vols. (Ottawa: Queen's Printer, 1966 and 1967); *The Structure and Reform of Direct Taxation,* report of a committee chaired by Professor J. E. Meade for the Institute for Fiscal Studies (London: Allen and Unwin, 1978); and the Irish *First Report of the Commission on Taxation, Direct Taxation* (Dublin: Government Publications Sales Office, 1982).

Methods used to estimate the incidence of federal, state, and local taxes by income classes in 1966 are described in detail by Joseph A. Pechman and Benjamin A. Okner, *Who Bears the Tax Burden?* (Brookings, 1974); estimates for 1970 are given by Benjamin A. Okner, "Total U.S. Taxes and their Effects on the Distribution of Family Income in 1966 and 1970," in Henry J. Aaron and Michael J. Boskin, eds., *The Economics of Taxation* (Brookings, 1980).

The ratios of taxes to gross domestic product in various countries are provided annually by the Organization for Economic Cooperation and Development. The latest data are given in *Revenue Statistics of OECD Member Countries, 1965–82* (Paris: OECD, 1983).

Chapter 2. Taxes and Economic Policy

Methods of assessing the economic impact of the government budget are evaluated by Joergen Lotz, "Techniques of Measuring the Effects of Fiscal Policy," in Organization for Economic Cooperation and Development, *OECD Economic Outlook, Occasional Studies* (Paris: OECD, July 1971). Wilfred Lewis, Jr., in *Federal Fiscal Policy in the Postwar Recessions* (Brookings, 1962), measures the quantitative impact of the automatic stabilizers and discretionary actions taken during the recessions and recoveries after World War II.

The various budget concepts in use by the federal government and a proposed revision of the budget, which was later adopted as the official unified budget, are discussed in *Report of the President's Commission on Budget Concepts* and *Staff Papers and Other Materials Reviewed by the President's Commission* (Government Printing Office, 1967).

The concept of the high-employment surplus and the role of tax policy in economic decisions are lucidly presented in *Economic Report of the President, January 1962.* The concept is integrated into the analysis of saving and investment in *Economic Report of the President, January 1966.* For an able defense of the high-employment budget and an analysis of the problems of interpretation during inflationary periods, see Arthur M. Okun and Nancy H. Teeters, "The Full Employment Surplus Revisited," *Brookings Papers on Economic Activity, 1:1970.* For an exchange of views on the merits of the high-employment budget, see William Fellner, "The High-Employment Budget and Potential Outlook," and Frank de Leeuw and Thomas M. Holloway, "A Response," *Survey of Current Business* 62 (November 1982).

The budget policy of the Committee for Economic Development was first presented in *Taxes and the Budget: A Program for Prosperity in a Free Economy,* A Statement on National Policy by the Research and Policy Committee (CED, 1947).

Much has been written about fiscal policy and its impact on economic growth and stability. For a sample of the literature, see Paul A. Samuelson, "Principles and Rules in Modern Fiscal Policy: A Neo-Classical Reformulation," in *Money, Trade, and Economic Growth: In Honor of John Henry Williams* (Macmillan, 1951); *Foreign Tax Policies and Economic Growth,* A Conference Report of the National Bureau of Economic Research and the Brookings Institution (Columbia University Press, 1966); and Alan S. Blinder and Robert M. Solow, "Analytical Foundations of Fiscal Policy," in *The Economics of Public Finance* (cited above for chapter 1). The implications of the rational expectations theory for fiscal and monetary policies are developed in Robert E. Lucas, Jr., *Studies in Business Cycle Theory* (MIT Press, 1981); and David K. H. Begg, *The Rational Expectations Revolution in Macroeconomics* (Johns Hopkins University Press, 1982). For a critique of the theory, see James Tobin, *Asset Accumulation and Economic Activity: Reflections on Contemporary Macroeconomic Theory* (University of Chicago Press, 1980).

The issues raised by wage-price or incomes policies to help reconcile high employment with price stability are presented in George P. Shultz and Robert Z. Aliber, eds., *Guidelines, Informal Controls, and the*

Market Place (University of Chicago Press, 1966); and John Sheahan, *The Wage-Price Guideposts* (Brookings, 1967). Tax-based incomes policies are evaluated in Arthur M. Okun and George L. Perry, eds., *Curing Chronic Inflation* (Brookings, 1978). Wage-price policy in European countries is reviewed and appraised in Robert J. Flanagan, David W. Soskice, and Lloyd Ulman, *Unionism, Economic Stabilization, and Incomes Policies: European Experience* (Brookings, 1983).

For a discussion of national debt policy, see Marshall A. Robinson, *The National Debt Ceiling* (Brookings, 1959). Different views on the "burden" of the national debt are summarized in James M. Ferguson, ed., *Public Debt and Future Generations* (University of North Carolina Press, 1964). For the rational expectations view of government debt, see R. J. Barro, "Are Government Bonds Net Wealth?" *Journal of Political Economy* 82 (1974).

Methods of evaluating government expenditures are discussed critically in Charles L. Schultze, *The Politics and Economics of Public Spending* (Brookings, 1968); Peter O. Steiner, "Public Expenditure Budgeting," in *The Economics of Public Finance* (cited above for chapter 1); and Edward M. Gramlich, *Benefit-Cost Analysis of Government Programs* (Prentice-Hall, 1981). The annual volumes *Setting National Priorities* published by the Brookings Institution provide an analysis of the choices in the federal budget.

The pros and cons of the balanced-budget amendment are discussed in Congressional Budget Office, *Balancing the Federal Budget and Limiting Federal Spending: Constitutional and Statutory Approaches* (GPO, 1982); and Alvin Rabushka and Pauline Ryan, *The Tax Revolt* (Hoover Institution, 1982).

Chapter 3. The Tax Legislative Process

The standard work on the tax legislative process is Roy Blough, *The Federal Taxing Process* (Prentice-Hall, 1952). In addition to the discussion of legislative procedures, this book examines in detail the interest and pressure groups involved in tax legislation and also reviews considerations relating to the level and distribution of taxes. The political crosscurrents that influence the tax decisionmaking process are analyzed in John F. Manley, *The Politics of Finance: The House Committee on Ways and Means* (Little, Brown, 1970); Lawrence C. Pierce, *The Politics of Fiscal Policy Formation* (Goodyear, 1971); and Thomas J. Reese, *The Politics of Taxation* (Quorum Books, 1980).

The reader will obtain some insight into the intricacies of the legislative process by reviewing the tax messages, hearings, and reports by the House Ways and Means Committee and the Senate Finance Committee relating to any one of the major tax bills listed in table 3-1.

The congressional method of conducting responsible and thorough reviews of federal tax issues is best illustrated by the 1955 and 1972–74 inquiries of the Joint Economic Committee and the 1959 and 1975 inquiries of the House Ways and Means Committee. In each case, a set of papers by leading experts was first published, and hearings or discussions on these papers were later held to permit the committee members to interrogate the experts. See the following publications: Joint Committee on the Economic Report, *Federal Tax Policy for Economic Growth and Stability,* 84:1 (GPO, 1955 and 1956), 2 vols. (Papers and Hearings); House Ways and Means Committee, *Tax Revision Compendium,* Compendium of Papers on Broadening the Tax Base (GPO, 1959), 3 vols., and *Income Tax Revision,* Panel Discussions, 86:1 (GPO, 1960); Joint Economic Committee, *The Economics of Federal Subsidy Programs,* 92:2 (GPO, 1972) and 93:1 and 2 (GPO, 1973 and 1974), 9 vols. (Papers and Hearings); House Ways and Means Committee, *Tax Reform (Invited Panelists),* Panel Discussions, and *Tax Reform (Administration and Public Witnesses),* Public Hearings, 5 vols. 94:1 (GPO, 1975).

Federal excise taxes are evaluated in a series of papers by some of the nation's leading experts in House Ways and Means Committee, *Excise Tax Compendium* (GPO, 1964); panel discussions on June 15 and 16, 1964, were published in *Federal Excise Tax Structure,* 88:2 (GPO, 1964), part 2; and subsequent hearings were published in parts 3–6. These papers and hearings were influential in the preparation of the Excise Tax Reduction Act of 1965.

The impact of the congressional budget process on tax legislation is discussed in Allan Schick, *Congress and Money: Budgeting, Spending and Taxing* (Urban Institute, 1980).

Chapter 4. The Individual Income Tax

The most authoritative treatise on this tax by an economist is Richard Goode, *The Individual Income Tax,* rev. ed. (Brookings, 1976), and by a lawyer, Boris I. Bittker, *Federal Taxation of Income, Estates, and Gifts,* 4 vols. (Warren, Gorham, and Lamont, 1981). A scholarly analysis of the arguments for and against progressivity will be found in Walter J. Blum and Harry Kalven, Jr., *The Uneasy Case for Progressive Taxation* (University of Chicago Press, 1953); a review of the issues is given in Charles O. Galvin and Boris I. Bittker, *The Income Tax: How Progressive Should It Be?* (American Enterprise Institute for Public Policy Research, 1969). The reader may also wish to consult the following classics: Henry C. Simons, *Personal Income Taxation* (University of Chicago Press, 1938); and William Vickrey, *Agenda for Progressive Taxation* (Ronald Press, 1947).

The general reader interested in income tax reform may refer to Louis Eisenstein, *The Ideologies of Taxation* (Ronald Press, 1961); George F. Break and Joseph A. Pechman, *Federal Tax Reform: The Impossible Dream?* (Brookings, 1975); Robert M. Brandon, Jonathan Rowe, and Thomas H. Stanton, *Tax Politics* (Pantheon, 1976); Michael J. Boskin, ed., *Federal Tax Reform: Myths and Realities* (Institute for Contemporary Studies, 1978); Joseph A. Pechman, ''Tax Policies for the 1980s,'' in Joseph A. Pechman and N. J. Simler, eds., *Economics in the Public Service* (Norton, 1982); and Congressional Budget Office, *Revising the Individual Income Tax* (GPO, 1983).

The views of supply-side economists on the effects of tax policy on economic incentives are given in David G. Raboy, *Supply Side Economics* (Institute for Research on the Economics of Taxation and Heritage Foundation, 1982). For an appraisal of these views, see *The Supply-Side Effects of Economic Policy* (St. Louis: Center for the Study of American Business, Washington University, 1981); and Richard H. Fink, ed., *Supply-Side Economics: A Critical Appraisal* (Alethia Books, University Publications of America, 1982). Quantitative estimates of the effects of taxation on labor supply, saving, and investment are given in *How Taxes Affect Economic Behavior* (cited above for chapter 1).

For a summary of econometric analyses of the relation between wages and work effort, see Glen G. Cain and Harold W. Watts, eds., *Income Maintenance and Labor Supply: Econometric Studies* (Rand McNally for Markham, 1973). A new econometric approach to estimating the effect of taxes on work effort is provided by Jerry A. Hausman, ''Labor Supply,'' in *How Taxes Affect Economic Behavior* (cited above).

Estimates of the built-in flexibility of the individual income tax are given by Joseph A. Pechman, ''Responsiveness of the Federal Individual

Income Tax to Changes in Income," *Brookings Papers on Economic Activity, 2:1973,* and "Anatomy of the U.S. Individual Income Tax," in Sijbren Cnossen, ed., *Comparative Tax Studies,* Essays in Honor of Richard Goode (North-Holland, 1983).

The usefulness of the concept of a comprehensive income tax is discussed in detail by Boris I. Bittker, Charles O. Galvin, Richard A. Musgrave, and Joseph A. Pechman in *A Comprehensive Income Tax Base? A Debate* (Federal Tax Press, 1968); and Joseph A. Pechman, ed., *Comprehensive Income Taxation* (Brookings, 1977). Methods of simplifying the individual income tax base are analyzed in Charles H. Gustafson, ed., *Federal Income Tax Simplification* (American Law Institute, 1979). Measures of the percentage of capital income subject to individual income tax are provided by Eugene Steuerle, "Is Income from Capital Subject to Individual Income Tax?" *Public Finance Quarterly* 10 (July 1982). A comprehensive income tax is compared with a comprehensive consumption expenditure tax in U.S. Treasury Department, *Blueprints for Tax Reform* (GPO, 1977). Estimates of the rate reductions that would be possible with a comprehensive income tax base, including a flat tax, are provided by Joseph A. Pechman and Benjamin A. Okner, "Individual Income Tax Erosion by Income Classes," in *The Economics of Federal Subsidy Programs* (cited above for chapter 3), pt. 1 (Brookings Reprint 230); and by Joseph A. Pechman and John Karl Scholz, "Comprehensive Income Taxation and Rate Reduction," *Tax Notes,* October 11, 1982 (Brookings Reprint 390). For an ingenious flat-tax proposal, which is billed as an income tax but is actually based on the concept of the consumption expenditure tax, see Robert E. Hall and Alvin Rabushka, *Low Tax, Simple Tax, Flat Tax* (McGraw-Hill, 1983).

The major structural features of the individual income tax are discussed in detail in the following sources: Lawrence H. Seltzer, *The Nature and Tax Treatment of Capital Gains and Losses* (National Bureau of Economic Research, 1951); C. Harry Kahn, *Personal Deductions in the Federal Income Tax* (Princeton University Press for the NBER, 1960); Martin David, *Alternative Approaches to Capital Gains Taxation* (Brookings, 1968); Arnold C. Harberger and Martin J. Bailey, eds., *The Taxation of Income from Capital* (Brookings, 1969); William D. Andrews, "Personal Deductions in an Ideal Income Tax," *Harvard Law Review* 86 (December 1972); Eugene Steuerle, Richard McHugh, and Emil Sunley, "Who Benefits from Income Averaging?" *National Tax*

Journal 31 (March 1978); George G. Kaufman, *Efficiency in the Municipal Bond Market: The Use of Tax Exempt Financing for "Private" Purposes* (Jai Press, 1981); and Rudolph G. Penner, *Taxing the Family* (American Enterprise Institute, 1983).

Estimates of the incentive effects of the charitable deduction are provided by Charles T. Clotfelter and C. Eugene Steuerle, "Charitable Contributions," in *How Taxes Affect Economic Behavior* (cited above for chapter 1). For an analysis of the effects of taxes on work incentives, see C. V. Brown, *Taxation and the Incentive to Work* (Oxford University Press, 1980). Estimates of the effects of tax rates on the realization of capital gains are provided by Martin Feldstein, Joel Slemrod, and Shlomo Yitzhaki, "The Effects of Taxation on the Selling of Stocks and the Realization of Capital Gains," *Quarterly Journal of Economics* 94 (June 1980); and by Joseph J. Minarik, "Capital Gains," in *How Taxes Affect Economic Behavior* (cited above for chapter 1). For analyses of the effects of the tax system on saving and investment, see Martin J. Bailey, "Progressivity and Investment Yields Under Income Taxation," *Journal of Political Economy* 82 (November–December 1974); George M. Von Furstenberg, ed., *The Government and Capital Formation* (Ballinger, 1980), and *Capital Efficiency and Growth* (Ballinger, 1980); *Public Policy and Capital Formation*, A Study by the Federal Reserve System (Board of Governors, 1981); Barry P. Bosworth, "Capital Formation and Economic Policy," *Brookings Papers on Economic Activity, 2:1982;* and Martin Feldstein, *Capital Taxation* (Harvard University Press, 1983).

Negative income taxation in the form suggested in the text was first discussed by Milton Friedman in *Capitalism and Freedom* (University of Chicago Press, 1962). The philosophy and mechanics of negative taxation are analyzed in detail in Christopher Green, *Negative Taxes and the Poverty Problem* (Brookings, 1967); and James Tobin, Joseph A. Pechman, and Peter M. Mieszkowski, "Is A Negative Income Tax Practical?" *Yale Law Review* 77 (November 1967). The negative income tax proposed by President Nixon—called the Family Assistance Plan— is described in detail in Senate Finance Committee, *H.R. 16311, The Family Assistance Act of 1970*, Revised and Resubmitted to the Senate Committee on Finance by the Administration, 91:2 (GPO, 1970). President Carter's plan—called the Program for Better Jobs and Income—is analyzed in Congressional Budget Office, *The Administration's Welfare Reform Proposal: An Analysis of the Program for Better Jobs and*

Income (GPO, 1978). The labor supply results of social experiments in negative income taxation are summarized and evaluated in Joseph A. Pechman and P. Michael Timpane, eds., *Work Incentives and Income Guarantees: The New Jersey Negative Income Tax Experiment* (Brookings, 1975); John L. Palmer and Joseph A. Pechman, eds., *Welfare in Rural Areas: The North Carolina–Iowa Income Maintenance Experiment* (Brookings, 1978); and Philip K. Rohns and Richard W. West, *Labor Supply Response to the Seattle and Denver Income Maintenance Experiments* (SRI International, 1981).

For analyses of the effects of inflation on the personal income tax, see Henry J. Aaron, ed., *Inflation and the Income Tax* (Brookings, 1976); Vito Tanzi, *Inflation and the Personal Income Tax: An International Perspective* (Cambridge University Press, 1980); and Martin Feldstein, *Inflation, Tax Rules, and Capital Formation* (University of Chicago Press, 1983). For methods of adjusting the personal income tax to inflation, see *Inflation Accounting,* Report of the Inflation Accounting Committee, F. E. P. Sandelands, Chairman (London: Her Majesty's Stationery Office, 1975); Organization for Economic Cooperation and Development, *The Adjustment of Personal Income Tax Systems for Inflation* (Paris: OECD, 1976); and Congressional Budget Office, *Indexing Taxes for Inflation* (GPO, September 1980).

Chapter 5. The Corporation Income Tax

Richard Goode's classic, *The Corporation Income Tax* (Wiley, 1951), provides a thorough analysis and appraisal of the role of the corporation income tax. A discussion of the merits of this tax in comparison with other taxes is given in a symposium volume of the Tax Institute of America, *Alternatives to Present Federal Taxes* (Tax Institute, 1964). For a more recent evaluation of the corporate tax, see J. Gregory Ballentine, *Equity, Efficiency and the U.S. Corporation Income Tax* (American Enterprise Institute, 1980).

For differing viewpoints on the incidence of the corporation income tax, see Arnold C. Harberger, "The Incidence of the Corporation Income Tax," *Journal of Political Economy* 70 (June 1962); Marian Krzyzaniak and Richard A. Musgrave, *The Shifting of the Corporation Income Tax* (Johns Hopkins University Press, 1963); Marian Krzyzaniak, ed., *Effects of Corporation Income Tax* (Wayne State University Press, 1966);

Robert J. Gordon, "The Incidence of the Corporation Income Tax in U.S. Manufacturing, 1925–62," *American Economic Review* 57 (September 1967); Peter Mieszkowski, "Tax Incidence Theory: The Effects of Taxes on the Distribution of Income" (cited above for chapter 1); Martin Feldstein, "Tax Incidence in a Growing Economy with Variable Factor Supply," *Quarterly Journal of Economics* 88 (November 1974); John B. Shoven and John Whalley, "A General Equilibrium Calculation of the Effects of Differential Taxation of Income from Capital in the U.S.," *Journal of Public Economics* 1 (November 1972); and Joseph E. Stiglitz, "The Corporation Tax," *Journal of Public Economics* 5 (April–May 1976).

The problems of integrating the corporation and individual income taxes are analyzed by Charles E. McLure, Jr., *Must Corporate Income Be Taxed Twice?* (Brookings, 1979); and Alan J. Auerbach, "Tax Integration and the New View of the Corporate Tax: A 1980 Perspective," National Tax Association and Tax Institute of America, *Proceedings of the Seventy-Fourth Annual Conference on Taxation* (1981). Estimates of the resource allocation effects of integration are presented by Don Fullerton, A. Thomas King, John B. Shoven, and John Whalley, "Corporate Tax Integration in the United States: A General Equilibrium Approach," *American Economic Review* 71 (September 1981).

The influence of federal taxation on corporate financial policy is appraised by Mervyn A. King, *Public Policy and the Corporation* (London: Chapman and Hall, 1977); and Roger H. Gordon and Burton Malkiel, "Corporate Finance," in *How Taxes Affect Economic Behavior* (cited above for chapter 1). John A. Brittain, in *Corporate Dividend Policy* (Brookings, 1966), measures the impact of the income taxes on the dividend payout policy of corporations.

The basic articles on the incentive effects of capital-consumption allowances are by E. Cary Brown, "Business-Income Taxation and Investment Incentives," in Lloyd A. Metzler and others, *Income, Employment and Public Policy: Essays in Honor of Alvin H. Hansen* (Norton, 1948); and Paul A. Samuelson, "Tax Deductibility of Economic Depreciation to Insure Invariant Valuations," *Journal of Political Economy* 72 (December 1964). Measures of the impact of investment tax incentives are provided in Gary Fromm, ed., *Tax Incentives and Capital Spending* (Brookings, 1971). For a survey of the literature on the factors influencing investment behavior, see Dale W. Jorgenson, "Econometric Studies of Investment Behavior: A Survey," *Journal of Economic*

Literature 9 (December 1971). Methods of achieving tax neutrality of investment incentives are explained by Melvin White and Ann White, "Tax Neutrality of Instantaneous versus Economic Depreciation," in Richard M. Bird and John G. Head, eds., *Modern Fiscal Issues: Essays in Honor of Carl S. Shoup* (University of Toronto Press, 1972); David Bradford, "Tax Neutrality and the Investment Tax Credit" and Arnold C. Harberger, "Tax Neutrality in Investment Incentives," in Henry J. Aaron and Michael J. Boskin, eds., *The Economics of Taxation* (Brookings, 1980); and Charles R. Hulten, ed., *Depreciation, Inflation, and the Taxation of Income from Capital* (Urban Institute, 1981). Estimates of effective tax rates on capital income in various countries are provided by Mervyn A. King and Dan Fullerton, eds., in *The Taxation of Income from Capital: A Comparative Study of the U.S., U.K., Sweden, and West Germany* (University of Chicago Press, 1984). For a series of theoretical and empirical analyses of the effect of taxation on capital formation, saving, and portfolio behavior, see Martin Feldstein, *Capital Taxation* (cited above for chapter 4).

Other structural features of the corporation income tax are discussed in Gerard M. Brannon, ed., *Studies in Energy Tax Policy* (Ballinger, 1975); *Essays in International Taxation: 1976* (U.S. Treasury Department, 1976); Joint Committee on Taxation, *Analysis of Safe-Harbor Leasing* (GPO, 1982); and Henry J. Aaron, *The Peculiar Problem of Taxing Life Insurance Companies* (Brookings, 1983). The effect of the corporation income tax on export prices is analyzed by Robert Z. Aliber and Herbert Stein in "The Price of U.S. Exports and the Mix of U.S. Direct and Indirect Taxes," *American Economic Review* 54 (September 1964). A report of the National Bureau of Economic Research and the Brookings Institution, *The Role of Direct and Indirect Taxes in the Federal Revenue System* (Princeton University Press, 1964), discusses the effect of various taxes on the balance of payments under a system of federal exchange rates.

Inflation accounting for business income is analyzed in detail in *Inflation Accounting,* Report of the Inflation Accounting Committee, Cmnd. 6225 (London: HMSO, 1975); William Fellner, Kenneth W. Clarkson, and John H. Moore, *Correcting Taxes for Inflation* (American Enterprise Institute, 1975); and Henry J. Aaron, ed., *Inflation and the Income Tax* (cited above for chapter 4). Estimates of business profits adjusted for inflation are given by John B. Shoven and Jeremy I. Bulow, "Inflation Accounting and Nonfinancial Corporate Profits: Financial

Assets and Liabilities," *Brookings Papers on Economic Activity, 1:1976.* For a proposal to prevent erosion of depreciation allowances by inflation, see Alan J. Auerbach and Dale W. Jorgenson, "Inflation-Proof Depreciation of Assets," *Harvard Business Review* 58 (September–October, 1980).

Chapter 6. Consumption Taxes

There are numerous books on the major consumption taxes. John F. Due, in *Sales Taxation* (University of Illinois Press, 1957), discusses the role of consumption taxes in the tax structure and evaluates the different forms and features of sales and value-added taxes, taking the experience of various countries into account. The value-added tax is explored by the Advisory Commission on Intergovernmental Relations, *The Value-Added Tax and Alternative Sources of Revenue* (GPO, 1973). The experience with the value-added tax is appraised by Henry J. Aaron, ed., *The Value-Added Tax: Lessons from Europe* (Brookings, 1981). The most recent evaluation of broad-based and selective consumption taxes is given by John F. Due ("Retail Sales Tax: The United States Experience"), Dieter Pohmer ("Value Added Tax after Ten Years: The European Experience"), and Carl S. Shoup ("Current Trends in Excise Taxation") in Sijbren Cnossen, ed., *Comparative Tax Studies* (cited above for chapter 4).

The use of taxation to control pollution is explained by Allen V. Kneese and Charles L. Schultze, *Pollution, Prices and Public Policy* (Brookings, 1975). The economic effects of taxes on energy are analyzed in *Energy Taxation: An Analysis of Selected Taxes* (National Academy of Sciences, 1980).

A brilliant defense of, and plea for, the adoption of a graduated consumption expenditure tax may be found in Nicholas Kaldor, *An Expenditure Tax* (London: Allen and Unwin, 1955). The administrative and compliance problems of an expenditure tax are examined in Advisory Commission on Intergovernmental Relations, *The Expenditure Tax: Concept, Administration and Possible Applications* (GPO, 1974). Another influential defense of the expenditure tax is by William D. Andrews, "A Consumption-Type or Cash Flow Personal Income Tax," *Harvard Law Review* 87 (April 1974). For a critique of this view and a rebuttal, see Alvin C. Warren, Jr., "Fairness and a Consumption-Type or Cash

Flow Personal Income Tax," and William D. Andrews, "A Reply to Professor Warren," both in *Harvard Law Review* 88 (March 1975). For additional analyses of income and expenditure taxes, see Alvin Warren, "Would a Consumption Tax Be Fairer Than an Income Tax?" *Yale Law Journal* 89 (May 1980); and Joseph A. Pechman, ed., *What Should Be Taxed: Income or Expenditure?* (Brookings, 1980). A model of the design of a graduated expenditure tax is given in *Blueprints for Tax Reform*, and a design of a flat-rate expenditure tax is given in Hall and Rabushka, *Low Tax, Simple Tax, Flat Tax* (both cited above for chapter 4). A committee of experts in the United Kingdom recommended the replacement of the income tax by an expenditure tax in its report, *The Structure and Reform of Direct Taxation* (cited above for chapter 1). For a defense of the expenditure tax addressed to the general reader, see J. A. Kay and M. A. King, *The British Tax System* (Oxford University Press, 1978).

The relative merits of income and consumption taxes are examined in detail in *The Role of Direct and Indirect Taxes in the Federal Revenue System* (cited above for chapter 5); and Richard A. Musgrave, ed., *Broad-Based Taxes: New Options and Sources* (Johns Hopkins University Press, 1973). For an evaluation of the federal excise tax structure, see the *Excise Tax Compendium* (cited above for chapter 3). A discussion of excise taxes used in various countries is given by Sijbren Cnossen in *Excise Systems: A Global Study of the Selective Taxation of Goods and Services* (Johns Hopkins University Press, 1977).

Chapter 7. Payroll Taxes

The literature on payroll taxes is an outgrowth of discussions and analyses of the major issues in social security. One of the earliest analyses of payroll taxation is contained in Seymour E. Harris, *Economics of Social Security* (McGraw-Hill, 1941); part 2 of this volume is devoted to the incidence of payroll taxes. For a comprehensive analysis, see Joseph A. Pechman, Henry J. Aaron, and Michael K. Taussig, *Social Security: Perspectives for Reform* (Brookings, 1968), chap. 8. For an analysis of the economic and distributional effects of payroll taxes, see John A. Brittain, *The Payroll Tax for Social Security* (Brookings, 1972). The history of how social security developed is ably reviewed by Martha Derthick, *Policymaking for Social Security* (Brookings, 1979). The impact of social security on saving and labor supply is appraised in George M. Von Furstenberg, ed., *Social Security Versus Private Saving* (Ballinger, 1979); and Henry J. Aaron, *Economic Effects of Social Security* (Brookings, 1982).

Issues in social security policy are discussed by Alicia H. Munnell, *The Future of Social Security* (Brookings, 1977); and Robert M. Ball, *Social Security, Today and Tomorrow* (Columbia University Press, 1978). Questions of financing are discussed in the quadrennial reports of the Advisory Councils on Social Security, and in the *Report of the National Commission on Social Security Reform* (GPO, 1983). The report of the 1979 Advisory Council, *Social Security Financing and Benefits* (GPO, 1979) discusses the major issues in social security yet to be resolved.

A survey of social security systems in other countries is provided in Social Security Administration, Office of Policy, *Social Security Programs Throughout the World, 1981*, Research Report 58 (GPO, 1981).

Chapter 8. Estate and Gift Taxes

Although it is out of date now as a statement of current law, the classic account of the development of the federal estate and gift taxes in this country is still Randolph E. Paul, *Federal Estate and Gift Taxation,* 2 vols. (Little, Brown, 1942), and *1946 Supplement* (Little, Brown, 1946). A later historical review and analysis of these taxes is Louis Eisenstein, "The Rise and Decline of the Estate Tax," in *Federal Tax Policy for Economic Growth and Stability* (cited above for chapter 3 and reprinted with minor changes in *Tax Law Review* 11 [March 1956]). The most recent volumes on wealth taxation are Alan A. Tait, *The Taxation of Personal Wealth* (University of Illinois Press, 1967); C. T. Sandford, *Taxing Personal Wealth* (London: Allen and Unwin, 1971); C. T. Sandford, J. R. M. Wallis, and D. J. Ironside, *An Annual Wealth Tax* (London: Heinemann, 1975); and Edward C. Halbach, Jr., ed., *Death, Taxes and Family Property* (West, 1977).

Robert J. Lampman provided estimates of the size distribution of wealth in the United States in *The Share of Top Wealth-Holders in National Wealth, 1922–56* (Princeton University for the National Bureau of Economic Research, 1962), based largely on data from federal estate tax returns. His estimates have been updated by James D. Smith and

Stephen D. Franklin, "The Concentration of Personal Wealth, 1922–1969," *American Economic Review* 64 (May 1974). Estimates of the distribution of wealth are prepared periodically on the basis of estate tax returns by the Internal Revenue Service, most recently in *Statistics of Income—1972, Personal Wealth Estimated from Estate Tax Returns* (GPO, 1976).

The first estimates of the amount of gift and trust transfers were made on the basis of 1945 estate tax returns and prior gift tax returns of the same decedents. These estimates were presented by Secretary of the Treasury John W. Snyder in Exhibit 5 of his statement before the House Ways and Means Committee on February 3, 1950, and published in vol. 1 of the Hearings, *Revenue Revision of 1950*, 81:2 (GPO, 1950), pp. 75–89. More recent data on gift and trust transfers and a thorough analysis of the major structural problems in estate and gift taxation may be found in Carl S. Shoup, *Federal Estate and Gift Taxes* (Brookings, 1966). The use of trusts and the methods of taxing them under the transfer taxes are explored in detail in Gerald R. Jantscher, *Trusts and Estate Taxation* (Brookings, 1967). The incentive effect of the full deduction for bequests to charitable organizations is estimated by Michael J. Boskin, "Estate Taxation and Charitable Bequests," *Journal of Public Economics* 5 (January–February 1976).

Proposals for reforming the estate and gift taxes are analyzed by Jerome Kurtz and Stanley S. Surrey, "Reform of Death and Gift Taxes: The 1969 Treasury Proposals, the Criticisms, and a Rebuttal," *Columbia Law Review* 70 (December 1970); and David Westfall, "Revitalizing the Federal Estate and Gift Taxes," *Harvard Law Review* 83 (March 1970). The defects of the present U.S. estate and gift tax are explained by George Cooper, *A Voluntary Tax? New Perspectives on Sophisticated Estate Tax Avoidance* (Brookings, 1979).

A thorough analysis of the tax issues relating to private philanthropy is provided in *Research Papers Sponsored by the Commission on Private Philanthropy and Public Needs*, 5 vols. (Treasury Department, 1977).

The recommendations of the American Law Institute estate and gift tax project are contained in *Federal Estate and Gift Taxation: Recommendations Adopted by the American Law Institute and Reporters' Studies* (American Law Institute, 1969). The proposals of the Carter Commission in Canada appear in vol. 3, chap. 17, and vol. 4, chap. 21, of the *Report of the Royal Commission on Taxation* (cited above for chapter 1). A model accessions tax was worked out in detail under the direction of the American Law Institute estate and gift tax project and appears in the project cited above. A briefer discussion is contained in William D. Andrews, "The Accessions Tax Proposal," *Tax Law Review* 22 (May 1967). An analysis of this type of tax is given by C. T. Sandford, J. R. M. Willis, and D. J. Ironside, *An Accessions Tax* (London: Institute for Fiscal Studies, 1973).

Chapter 9. State and Local Taxes

The best general sources on the state and local tax structure and the major issues in this area are Dick Netzer, "State-Local Finance and Intergovernmental Fiscal Relations," in Blinder and others, *Economics of Public Finance* (cited above for chapter 1); Advisory Commission on Intergovernmental Relations, *Tax Capacity of the Fifty States: Methodology and Estimates* (GPO, 1982), "Tax Capacity of the Fifty States, Supplement: 1980 Estimates" (1982), and *Significant Features of Fiscal Federalism, 1981–82 Edition* (GPO, 1983); and James A. Maxwell and J. Richard Aronson, *Financing State and Local Governments,* 3d ed. (Brookings, 1977).

There is a large literature on the property tax. Jens P. Jensen, *Property Taxation in the United States* (University of Chicago Press, 1931), evaluates this tax from the vantage point of the late 1920s and early 1930s; Dick Netzer, *Economics of the Property Tax* (Brookings, 1966), analyzes the economic impact of the tax and its role in the U.S. tax system in the mid-1960s; and A. R. Prest, *The Taxation of Urban Land* (Manchester University Press, 1981), and C. Lowell Harriss, ed., *The Property Tax and Local Finance* (Academy of Political Science, 1983), review and evaluate recent developments in property taxation in the United Kingdom and the United States, respectively. The new view that the property tax is a tax on capital is explained by Henry J. Aaron, *Who Pays the Property Tax?* (Brookings, 1975). The movement to limit the level and growth of the property tax is reviewed and evaluated by Helen F. Ladd and T. Nicholaus Tideman, eds., *Tax and Expenditure Limitations* (Urban Institute, 1981).

Recent developments in property tax administration are summarized in ACIR, *The Property Tax in a Changing Environment* (GPO, 1974). The "circuit breaker" idea is explained in ACIR, *Property Tax Circuit-Breakers: Current Status and Policy Issues* (GPO, 1975). For a critique of circuit breakers, see Henry J. Aaron, "What Do Circuit-Breaker Laws Accomplish?" in George E. Peterson, ed., *Property Tax Reform* (John C. Lincoln Institute and Urban Institute, 1973) (Brookings Reprint 277).

Problems of land value taxation are discussed in *Building the American City*, Report of the National Commission on Urban Problems, House Document 91-34 (GPO, 1969), part 4, chap. 6. The value of real estate in the United States is estimated by Allen D. Manvel, "Trends in the Value of Real Estate and Land, 1956 to 1966," in *Three Land Research Studies*, prepared for the National Commission on Urban Problems, Research Report 12 (GPO, 1968).

Federal, state, and local fiscal relations may be studied by referring to Richard A. Musgrave, ed., *Essays in Fiscal Federalism* (Brookings, 1965); Wallace E. Oates, *Fiscal Federalism* (Harcourt Brace Jovanovich, 1972); George F. Break, *Financing Government in a Federal System* (Brookings, 1980); R. J. Bennett, *The Geography of Public Finance* (Methuen, 1980); and ACIR, *The Federal Role in the Federal System, The Dynamics of Growth*, 11 vols. (GPO, 1980–83).

The early literature on revenue sharing is summarized in *Revenue Sharing and Its Alternatives: What Future for Fiscal Federalism?* Hearings before the Subcommittee on Fiscal Policy of the Joint Economic Committee, 90:1 (GPO, 1967). For an evaluation of the revenue-sharing plan adopted by the federal government during the first two years of the plan's operation, see Richard P. Nathan, Allen D. Manvel, Susannah E. Calkins, and associates, *Monitoring Revenue Sharing* (Brookings, 1975). The National Science Foundation supported a large number of studies of general revenue sharing, which are summarized in *General Revenue Sharing: Research Utilization Project*, National Science Foundation, Research Applied to National Needs, 5 vols. (GPO, 1975). See also Robert P. Inman and others, *Financing the New Federalism: Revenue Sharing, Conditional Grants, and Taxation* (Johns Hopkins University Press for Resources for the Future, 1975).

For more specific aspects of intergovernmental tax relations, see ACIR, *Coordination of State and Federal Inheritance, Estate, and Gift Taxes* (GPO, 1961), *Federal-State Coordination of Personal Income Taxes* (GPO, 1965), and *State Taxation of Multinational Corporations* (GPO, 1983); and *State Taxation of Interstate Commerce*, Report of the Special Subcommittee on State Taxation of Interstate Commerce of the House Committee on the Judiciary, vols. 1 and 2, House Report 1480,

88:2 (GPO, 1964), and vols. 3 and 4, House Reports 565 and 952, 89:1 (GPO, 1975).

Numerous official state and city tax commission reports provide excellent sources of information on and analyses of state and local tax problems. Some examples are *Report of the Connecticut State Revenue Task Force,* Submitted to the Governor and General Assembly (State of Connecticut, 1971), and *Papers,* Prepared for the Connecticut State Revenue Task Force, 6 vols. (1970); *Financing an Urban Government,* Final Report of the District of Columbia Tax Revision Commission (Department of Economics, University of the District of Columbia, 1978); Harvey E. Brazer, ed., *Michigan's Fiscal and Economic Structure* (University of Michigan Press, 1982); and James A. Papke, ed., *Indiana's Revenue Structure, Major Components and Issues* (Purdue University, 1983).

Appendix A. Historical Summary of the Major Federal Taxes

Edwin R. A. Seligman, in "Income Tax," *Encyclopedia of the Social Sciences* (Macmillan, 1932), vol. 7, traces income taxation in Europe and the United States up to the early 1930s. The reader may also wish to refer to the history of the development of progressivity in the British income tax in F. Shehab, *Progressive Taxation* (Oxford University Press, 1953). For histories of taxation in this country, see Sidney Ratner, *Taxation and Democracy in America* (Wiley, 1942); and Randolph Paul, *Taxation in the United States* (Little, Brown, 1954). Lewis H. Kimmel analyzes the changes in American attitudes toward government taxing, spending, and borrowing in *Federal Budget and Fiscal Policy, 1789–1958* (Brookings, 1959). Herbert Stein traces the changes in attitudes toward federal budget deficits by government officials, economists, and businessmen in *The Fiscal Revolution in America* (University of Chicago Press, 1969).

The *Annual Reports of the Secretary of the Treasury on the State of the Finances* summarize the major features of tax legislation enacted each year in a section titled "Taxation Developments." Comprehensive summaries of tax rates are provided for 1913–40 in the 1940 report; for 1940–50 in the 1950 report; for 1950–62 in the 1962 report; and for later years see the tables in this appendix. Detailed explanations of the various revenue acts have been prepared by the Joint Taxation Committee, beginning with the *General Explanation of the Tax Reform Act of 1969*.

Appendix B. Tax Bases of the Major Federal Taxes

Basic data on the individual and corporation income taxes are provided in the annual statistical volumes published by the Internal Revenue Service, entitled *Statistics of Income: Individual Income Tax Returns* and *Statistics of Income: Corporation Income Tax Returns*. Data on the estate tax and estimates of wealth are provided in *Statistics of Income: Estate Returns* and *Statistics of Income: Personal Wealth Estimates from Estate Tax Returns*, which are published every four years.

For analyses of the individual income tax base, see Eugene Steuerle and Michael Hartzmark, "Individual Income Taxation, 1947–79," *National Tax Journal* 34 (June 1981); and Joseph A. Pechman, "Anatomy of the Individual Income Tax," *Comparative Tax Studies* (cited above for chapter 4). Estimates of underreporting are given by the Internal Revenue Service, *Estimates of Income Unreported on Individual Income Tax Returns* (U.S. Treasury Department, 1979), and *Income Tax Compliance Research: Estimates for 1973–81* (U.S. Treasury Department, 1983).

Appendix C. Tax Expenditures

A detailed exposition of the rationale of tax expenditures is provided by Stanley S. Surrey, *Pathways to Tax Reform: The Concept of Tax Expenditures* (Harvard University Press, 1973); and Paul R. McDaniel and Stanley S. Surrey, "Tax Expenditures: How to Identify Them, How to Control Them," *Tax Notes* (May 24, 1982).

Official estimates of tax expenditures are given annually in *Special Analyses, Budget of the United States Government*, and in annual reports by the Congressional Budget Office and the Joint Taxation Committee. The latest CBO report is *Tax Expenditures: Budget Control Options and Five-Year Projections for Fiscal Years 1983–87* (GPO, 1982). The latest Joint Taxation Committee Report is *Estimates of Federal Tax Expenditures for Fiscal Years 1983–1988* (GPO, 1983).

Index

403